The
Heart & Soul
of
Business

To Les,
my fellow colleague in teaching
for Nations University at Rustov-on-Don
and my respected friend
Best wishes to you, Peggy,
and your entire family.

Sincerely,
Perry

Aug. 11, 1998

The Heart & Soul of Business

of

A CHRISTIAN PERSPECTIVE

Perry C. Cotham

PROVIDENCE HOUSE PUBLISHERS
Franklin, Tennessee

Printed in the United States of America

02   01   00   99   98   5   4   3   2   1

Library of Congress Catalog Card Number:98-66609

ISBN: 1-57736-105-9

Cover design by Gary Bozeman

Unless otherwise noted, all scripture quotations are taken from the HOLY BIBLE, NEW INTERNATIONAL VERSION. Copyright © 1973, 1978, 1984 International Bible Society. Used by permission of Zondervan Bible Publishers.

Several paragraphs of the book were taken directly from the author's work, *Harsh Realities/Agonizing Choices* (College Press, 1996) and have been used by permission.

PROVIDENCE HOUSE PUBLISHERS
238 Seaboard Lane • Franklin, Tennessee 37067
800-321-5692

In Loving Memory
of a Life Lived Well

Teresa Overby Cotham

(1914–1998)

When I was a high school senior, most of my relatives were gently, yet clearly pointing me toward becoming a pulpit minister in the church as had been my dad, one grandfather, and one uncle.

"Son, you don't have to be a preacher if you don't feel you have that calling," my mother had counseled me. "You might make a good businessman. And if you go into business, I just ask you to become the best Christian businessman that you can possibly be."

I entered the ministry and higher education, but that counsel was never forgotten.

In the last stages of preparing this volume, my mother departed this life for a better world.

Contents

How To Succeed in Business Without Really Losing Your Soul

OK. I'LL CONFESS UP FRONT THAT MY PREFACE TITLE IS INTENDED primarily to get your attention. It is, actually, a slight variation of the title of a 1952 book by Sheperd Mead, which was turned into a musical first opening on Broadway in 1961 by the same name, *How To Succeed in Business without Really Trying*. The award-winning musical traces J. Pierrepont Finch's step-by-step, back-stabbing way up the corporate ladder. This clear-eyed, wily window washer at the giant World Wide Wicket Company (where "nobody knows exactly what anyone else is doing") climbs from the mailroom to the boardroom by following the instructions of a handy, dandy guidebook entitled (you guessed it!), *How to Succeed in Business without Really Trying*. Along the way he gets the female, gets the money, and nearly gets the boot! The musical comedy skewers such aspects of big business as nepotism, old-school ties, the coffee break, the office party, the sycophantic yes-men, the executive washroom (where Finch serenades his image in the mirror with the worshipful "I Believe in You"), and the boardroom presentation.

The realities of our lives surely seem much more serious than the concerns of J. Pierrepont Finch since we, as Christian men and women, are using our God-given gifts and talents in the work world. Work consumes the largest percentage of our waking hours in life. Employment is a major contributor to our well-being and happiness, on and off the job. In a pluralistic society, business is the one place where different cultural values and personal values are compelled to coexist and cooperate. We toil in all kinds of situations, make highly ethical choices with both major and minor consequences, face intense pressures and expectations, and interact with all kinds of people. At times we desperately need concrete direction. Of course, we are familiar with some lofty religious ideals, such as Christianity's Golden Rule (Matt. 7:12), but such injunctions, although inspiring, do not translate easily into precise policy and procedure. And usually we need loyal support for our moral principles and warm encouragement for our efforts to do the right thing.

Newspapers and news magazines inform us of investigations of wrongdoing in all kinds of businesses. Whether it is the fraud of a major health-care system to bilk Medicare or a major cigarette producer's treatment of tobacco which lowers tar but enhances the addictiveness of nicotine in order to "hook" young smokers, we may suspect that the corporate sordidness that gets exposed is only the tip of the proverbial iceberg. Rather than allowing the Jekyll and Hyde managers we encounter in the business world—those moral schizophrenics who tightly compartmentalize their moral principles and their corporate policies—to breed cynicism about corporate business life, we are better served by sober reflection on the nature of business in our society and the ways biblical faith can be applied in practical ways to business and professional realities. To that end, this work is designed to

1. give readers an introduction to basic issues in business ethics;
2. root business and professional ethics solidly in biblical theology;
3. discuss some practical issues in the workplace which have moral dimensions; and
4. raise provocative questions for group discussion and personal thought. Along the way, it is hoped that readers will be truly challenged to think for themselves about tough issues—even when they cannot find clear answers!

Several realities have driven this project, one of which is most sobering: a man or woman in business and professional life may expect to make a number of mistakes, but no mistake is quite as damaging to one's career and reputation, or quite as difficult to forgive and forget for that matter, as an ethical wrongdoing. A major unethical and/or illegal act in the business and professional world certainly does not represent a deficiency in technical training, but reveals a serious deficiency in moral character and moral judgment.

All of the discussion to follow is based on two important propositions. The first is that Holy Scripture is relevant to our lives. Though the Bible is not a handbook on business ethics, God has communicated to us through his Word, and mainly through the life and teaching of his Son, the moral principles by which he expects us to order our lives. Second, God has given us the power of choice. Ethical behavior at work is a choice. Unethical behavior is no accident. Human behavior is caused. And all behavior has an explanation if we can find it.

Of course, not being completely certain about what's right and wrong is more commonplace than many of us like to think, and in moments of uncertainty it's always easy to follow the path of least resistance, whatever that might be. Still, we can choose the good and the right. Likewise, unethical behavior is no accident—it is a *choice*, even though many business people may slide into unethical behavior rather than make one quantum leap from good to bad.

This work was originally intended to provoke college students and other thoughtful adults to think about the moral choices they make at work. Any belief that a course or class in business and professional ethics can dramatically change people's ethical behavior seems naive. An effective course in business ethics should convey a body of information, lead students to think about options, and present reasons why one's behavior in the workplace should or should not change. However, when it comes to making a positive change, only an individual with conviction can *pull it off*. No person can rely on someone to make personal change. If any of us wants our work environment to be more ethical, then an improved moral climate starts with us. Hopefully, this work will point Christian workers and professionals in the right direction.

The first ten chapters of the book are intended to be discussions of basic foundations and concepts. The remaining chapters are intended to discuss the moral dimensions of some practical issues in the workplace. Throughout, I have attempted to downplay pure ethical theory and to highlight practical concerns. Of course, no clear line can be drawn between the foundations and the practical applications. For this reason, I have painted the landscape of business and professional ethics with a broad brush.

The reader will find that a comprehensive look at business ethics will draw from several disciplines: moral philosophy, theology, law, history, psychology, and interpersonal relations.

The case studies cited herein are real incidents in the workplace that I know of personally, although the names attached to the stories to personalize the moral dilemmas are sometimes arbitrarily chosen; a written permission was solicited from friends whose actual names are connected with a case study. At times the material may seem more academic than light reading, especially in the first ten chapters. Regardless, I have attempted to present all material in an informal, readable style, and at times I will invite the reader to smile with me as points are made.

Certainly it would be useful to include detailed discussions of the ethical issues faced by various professionals. Such an endeavor might well entail the production of a volume of several thousand pages. Alternatively, I offer the reader an appendix with several sets of "Ten Commandments." I have identified the contributors of these special decalogues of professional ethics, all cherished friends of mine, mostly, in my home congregation. I encouraged them to write with a sense of humor and obviously some of them did just that. The appendices also include other lighter material readers should find helpful and interesting. Some material of substance is included in the question and discussion section at the end of chapters; some material (e.g., the topics of "political correctness at work" or "blowing the whistle") was arbitrarily placed in certain chapters that could have been easily placed elsewhere.

Acknowledgments

STUDENTS IN MY BUSINESS AND PROFESSIONAL ETHICS CLASSES AT David Lipscomb University in Nashville, Tennessee, have stirred my interest and sharpened my thinking on this subject. I'm grateful to Dr. Michael Moss, chairman of the department of Bible, for the opportunity to teach these classes, and to Professor Mac Lynn for both encouragement and opportunities.

A number of dear friends and associates at Fourth Avenue Church, Franklin, Tennessee, especially in a Sunday school class that I have led on this subject, have shared stories and experiences which have influenced this work.

Robert C. Brannon, a long-time friend and retired distinguished audit partner with the Nashville office of Peat Marwick, Mitchell and Company, was gracious enough to appear as a guest in one of my classes and to offer for my perusal a notebook filled with articles and other brief materials on business and professional ethics. Readers will easily pick up on my close affiliation with my religious and academic ties.

Special thanks go also to my Fourth Avenue Church secretaries Janet Lambert and Karen Osborne for clerical assistance on this project. And finally, special acknowledgment and gratitude are also expressed to Andrew B. Miller, president of Providence House Publishers, for his support of this project, and to his highly capable and congenial staff, including especially Mary Bray Wheeler, Holly Jones, Debbie Sims, Marilyn Friedlander, Elaine Kernea Wilson, Michael Epps Utley, and Gary Bozeman for their counsel and technical expertise.

The
Heart & Soul
of
Business

Chapter 1

The Character of Business

You can't eat for eight hours a day nor drink for eight hours a day nor make love for eight hours a day—all you can do for eight hours is work. Which is the reason why man makes himself and everybody else so miserable and unhappy.

William Faulkner

Early to bed, and early to rise, makes a man healthy, wealthy, and wise.

Then plow deep, while sluggards sleep, And you shall have corn to sell and to keep.

Benjamin Franklin

The business of America is business.

Calvin Coolidge

The business of America is not business. It never was. The business of America is individual liberty, with the law enforcing an even-handed justice among equal persons. When the law provides a free field and no favor—which was the original implication of laissez faire—the economic order is the free market.

Edmund A. Opitz

I like my job and am good at it, but it sure grinds me down sometimes, and the

last thing I need to take home is a headache.

TV commercial for Anacin

Work is still the complicated and crucial core of most lives, the occupation melded inseparably to the identity; Freud said that the successful psyche is one capable of love and of work. Work is the most thorough and profound organizing principle in American life. If mobility has weakened old blood ties, our co-workers often form our new family, our tribe, our social world; we become almost citizens of our companies, living under the protection of salaries, pensions and health insurance. . . . all work expresses the laborer in a deeper sense: all life must be worked at, protected, planted, replanted, fashioned, cooked for, coaxed, diapered, formed, sustained. Work is the way that we tend the world, the way that people connect. It is the most vigorous, vivid sign of life—in individuals and in civilizations.

Lance Morrow

Hard work fascinates me—I could sit and watch it for hours.

Bumper sticker on an old *clunker*

3

WE CAN ONLY IMAGINE THE WORLD'S FIRST WORKERS (OF COURSE, it helps to have seen some old Hollywood flicks such as *Planet of the Apes*)—unkempt men and women wearing animal skins, laboring either inside or outside the cave, holding sharp pieces of metal or stone, attempting to prepare prey for supper or to manufacture something worthwhile (maybe invent the wheel?)! Perhaps the biggest ethical decision a prehistoric man made was whether to kill his neighbor for trying to steal his supper or his prized tool.

What a different work world in which we live! In today's demanding business world of intricate communications systems, new computers and other electronic technologies, diverse workforce, global expansion, corporate downsizings, and increased government regulations, people at every level of a business organization must make decisions quickly and perform at optimum levels of accuracy, efficiency, and success. If their business organization's basic policies are not rooted in sound values, such as integrity, justice, trust, and respect for others, these workers are exposed to ethical vulnerabilities that may lead to harmful, unfair, and even illegal activities.

Where do today's millions upon millions of managers and other workers turn for guidance amidst a maze of ethical challenges and complexities on issues and problems that threaten the health of their organizations? What resources can be tapped for ethical guidance in today's highly competitive business environment? Does any ancient book, especially the Bible, have any relevance for managers and laborers today? Are there any moral absolutes for corporate America? Is there a big ethical picture for big business? Or, on the other hand, must we proceed by making each ethical dilemma in business an ad hoc decision, thus contending that a moral position in one industry or market may prove disastrous in another?

Such questions are but a few of the major issues to be raised here and in subsequent chapters. In some instances, we may have to be satisfied only by asking the question—answers always come faster and sweat-free in textbooks but arrive after much soul-searching and agony in board rooms, offices, and shop floors. As we begin our quest for some answers, we will draw from perspectives in theology, history, narrative, ethical theory, and, hopefully, ordinary good sense gained from real-life experience. We begin with some fundamentals.

ETHICS

The word "ethics" comes from the Greek word "ethos," meaning character or custom. Both words have taken on a variety of connotations.

Ethics is moral philosophy: the philosophical study of moral values. Applied ethics focuses on practical concerns, such as business ethics or medical ethics. In another sense, ethics refers to the particular moral outlook of a group or individual. We speak of "the Protestant work ethic" or of "the ethics of Abraham Lincoln" or "the ethic of rural America." The word "ethical" has positive connotation, such as when we declare that Jimmy Carter was an ethical president of this nation.

We use the word "**ethos**" to refer to the distinguishing disposition, character, or attitude of a specific people, culture, or group, as in "the business ethos" or "the American ethos."

Business ethics is the study of what constitutes right and wrong, or good and bad human conduct in a business context. It is not a separate·moral standard from basic ethics, but a discipline that applies ethical standards—the "shoulds" and "oughtness"— to the unique problems of business. Professional ethics is a particular facet of the broader subject of business ethics. **Professional ethics** is the application of standards of ethical conduct and moral evaluation to the unique issues and challenges of contemporary professional life.

Business ethics is now a well-established academic subject. Most colleges and universities offer courses in business ethics and textbooks abound in this subject. Some cynics scoff at the idea of business ethics, saying that the concept is as much an oxymoron as "jumbo shrimp," "government compassion," "friendly fire," or "bureaucratic efficiency."

BUSINESS

The major difficulty in talking about business ethics is, perhaps, that "business organizations," "business," and "business men and women" are such broad, all-encompassing terms. An **organization** is any group of people working together to achieve a common purpose, whether to offer a product or service primarily for profit or to serve the common good. Nearly all people who work outside the home might consider themselves to be employees or business people of some kind.

Business organizations have been around throughout nearly all of history. Shareholder organizations were known in Europe by 1700, but there has been an increasing complexity and influence of corporations during the recent past by their growth in size and number. All of our lives are impacted by business organizations. At the outset, let's identify three main forms of business: sole proprietorships, partnerships, and corporations:

1. In a **sole proprietorship,** the owner is the business. We tend to think of sole proprietors as individuals who own small businesses, say, wall-papering firms and appliance-repair shops, but this need not be so. For example, individuals can own large import-export businesses. In sole proprietorships, the owner's personal estate is liable for his/her business debts.

2. **Partnerships** arise from agreements between two or more individuals to organize and conduct a business. Two types of partnerships are usually distinguished. First, there are ordinary partnerships in which, roughly, all partners co-own the business, have joint control of its operations and the right to share in its profits, and maintain joint liability for all debts and contracts of the partnership. Second, in limited partnerships at least one general partner has all the rights of partners in ordinary partnerships, and there is at least one limited partner, who

contributes capital and has a right to share in the profits, but not to manage or control the business.

3. By contrast, **corporations** come into existence by an act of state and, typically, have perpetual existence. They can be owned by a single person or have thousands of shareholders. A central characteristic of corporations is that the liability of their owners is limited to their investments. Their personal estates are usually not liable for the corporation's debt. Limited liability raises questions as to the moral status and obligations assumed by corporations.

In this volume we are also concerned about private and public non-profit organizations which exist to provide vital goods and services to segments of the general public. A state or federal department, for example, operates much like other businesses, though its accountability is broad-based. Churches may sponsor an institution which provides social services. Most charities and volunteer organizations are operated on a non-profit basis. Schools, colleges, and universities provide many opportunities for professionals and other workers to serve the general public. Ethical conduct is just as important in these organizations as it is in "for-profit" businesses.

MORAL VALUES

Moral values and **moral standards** are concerned with behavior that has serious consequence on other people. Whether one wears shorts and tee shirt or a suit and tie to a dinner party may be a matter of etiquette, but it is hardly a matter of serious consequence to other people. A public speaker may "murder the king's English" with slang and double negatives, but the standards that are violated are hardly moral standards. Moral standards are distinguishable from other standards by

1. profoundly injuring or benefiting oneself and other people;
2. taking priority over other standards, including self-interest; and
3. being sound only by the adequacy of reasons that support or justify them.

Etiquette refers to any special code of behavior or courtesy. Rules of etiquette are generally non-moral assertions: don't eat with your fingers, turn your head away from others when you cough or sneeze, say "please" when requesting a favor and "thank you" when receiving the favor, etc. There are countless rules of etiquette. Etiquette is always changing with the times and means of communication and transacting business. Consider, however, two points:

1. Scrupulous observance of rules of etiquette does not make one moral.
2. Violations of etiquette may have some moral implications. Consider the male boss who refers to female subordinates as "chick," "babe," or "honey."

LAW AND MORALITY

The relationship between law and morality is complex and at times inconsistent. To speak of law generally may fail to distinguish between kinds of law: **constitutional law** (law rooted in a nation's basic constitution which, in this nation, is the supreme law of the land); **statutory law** (laws passed by duly authorized legislative bodies);

common law (laws applied in the English-speaking world before there were statutes); and **administrative regulations** (rules established by official boards and agencies to regulate behavior within agencies and organizations).

In theory, law codifies customs, ideals, beliefs, and a society's moral values. Sometimes laws remain "on the books" long after they have lost popular support and respect: such laws become disregarded. Laws usually reflect the change that a society makes about what is right and wrong. Some laws become relaxed, such as the 1996 vote in California to permit use of marijuana by certain medical patients, and some laws become more strict, such as laws against sexual harassment.

Law is not the all-sufficient guide to establish moral standards that should guide an individual, a profession, an organization, or a society. Law simply cannot cover the variety of individual or group conduct. The purpose of criminal and civil law is to uphold minimal or "common core" morality. Law is intended to render illegal the most egregious affront to a society's moral standards and thus provides a "bottom floor" of moral conduct.

Conformity with law is not sufficient for moral conduct any more than conformity with etiquette or religious ritual is. By the same token, nonconformity with law is not necessarily immorality, for the law that a person disobeys may be an unjust law. Martin Luther King Jr. was adamant about disobeying the unjust racial segregation laws of the 1950s and 1960s in the United States.

PROFESSIONAL CODES OF CONDUCT

Contemporary codes have historic precedents, rare as they may be. The Code of Hammurabi is dated around 3500 B.C. and the Hippocratic Oath was formulated around 350 B.C., dealing with legal-commercial and medical ethics respectively. Thus, contemporary codes may be viewed as products of a long evolution and accumulation of the ethical wisdom of the centuries. There are two kinds of codes: one is an organizational conduct code which is intended to guide employees in a business organization, and the other is a code which is produced by professional organizations to forward standards expected of their members regardless of employment arrangement. Professions and corporations generally use "codes by committee," thus reflecting the practical wisdom of several professionals or business executives, while as late as the nineteenth century leaders would produce codes as sole authors (e.g., Florence Nightingale's nursing code and other classical codes were written by one practitioner.)

Professional codes of ethics lie somewhere between etiquette and law. These professional codes contain rules which govern the conduct of members of a given profession. The trend toward developing such codes began in earnest in the late 1970s, and it is now routine for companies to place such codes of ethics in employee handbooks, operating manuals, and other materials. Some of the professional codes read like the Ten Commandments with numerous "Thou shalt nots," while others are more positive in tone. Professional codes cover a wide range of topics, most typically conflicts of interest, gifts to corporate personnel, unauthorized payments, sexual harassment, rights of privacy, affirmative action, and relations with customers and competitors.

Generally, the members of the professions have committed (perhaps in a signed statement) to follow the professional code. Violation of the professional code is not a criminal offense, but may result in something as light as disapproval of one's professional peers or as severe as loss of one's license to practice that profession. Sometimes codes are largely unwritten and exist as part of the common understanding among colleagues of a profession. The sobering reality is that there appears to be no significant correlation between the establishment of codes of ethics and ethical or unethical behavior. Codes work when there is genuine commitment by employees to them and strict enforcement of the rules.

By nature, professional codes of ethics are neither a complete nor a completely reliable guide to one's moral obligations. Sometimes the rules are so vague and general that they render little moral direction in concrete situations. Furthermore, not all of the rules are moral in nature. In most professions there is a need to continually update the code to cover the complex moral dilemmas posed by new knowledge, new technology, and new social attitudes.

Professionals should take the professional codes of conduct seriously, but have the responsibility of critically assessing the rules for themselves. Keep in mind that by joining a profession one is committing to respect and follow the code of ethics formulated and tested earlier by others in that profession.

WHAT DOES "BUSINESS ETHICS" MEAN?
(A LOOK AT SEVEN REALITIES)

Is there anything unique about business ethics? What does "business ethics" mean? Peter Drucker has suggested a view that many Christian ethicists accept. In essence, although the term suggests some ethical standard applies to business people that is more rigorous than the standard applied to everyone else, the same ethical rules and standards that apply outside of business should also define business ethics (in other words, business ethics is nothing more than basic ethical principles applied to business and professional life).

True enough, the same personal ethical principles that guide family, friendship, and other social relationships must be applied to our business and professional life. On the other hand, special problems and issues arise in business that do not arise outside the business setting. Consider these realities:

1. **Many business and professional people act as though a clear line can be drawn between personal ethics and business ethics.** They seem to leave their personal ethics at home and, once they arrive at work, are willing to engage in a variety of behaviors in their business role that would be unthinkable in their personal lives. In essence, business has an ethic of its own, and it is not the same ethic you practice at home, at church, in the civic club, or in personal relationships.

2. **Personal ethics are unable to answer adequately issues concerning a corporation's social responsibilities.** A broader, more comprehensive ethic is clearly needed. "Just apply your personal ethics on your job" may be unrealistic, oversimplified advice to any business or professional person.

3. **The individual employee assumes a role that is quite different from any role played outside the workplace.** That role is usually a highly interdependent role with other individuals. Any strategically significant ethical action an employee might take will not only impact him/her, but possibly many others as well. How many dishonest acts or cover-ups have taken place by generally honest workers who did not want to cause trouble for others or let the unit or company down?
4. **Business ethics are imprecise and situational, at least in many cases.** What is ethical is what people are led to believe is ethical. Humans interpret reality in whatever ways insure their survival; workers interpret reality in whatever ways insure their job or career survival. What's ethical in corporate business life may depend on the identity of the competitors and the constituents.
5. **The workplace can be a pressurized environment where employees must produce results, avoid mistakes, reduce errors, and placate the boss—pressures one does not encounter in other social environments.**
6. **There is a wide spectrum of ethical business behavior.** Some business executives say that there are situations in which there is no ethically correct answer. Often, one must choose a resolution or course of action which seems highly ethical for one constituent and not for another. (We'll explore this notion in chapter 10.)
7. **Business executives have a general reluctance to discuss moral issues.** Most likely, professionals in various service fields are less reluctant and more adept at discussing moral dimensions of their career, as compared with business executives. A mention in the corporate boardroom of a possible ethical violation may evoke feelings of discomfort among those present. Reluctance to discuss moral concerns in big business may be called "moral muteness." Some managers consider it disruptive to bring up moral issues at work, believing such mention will initiate rounds of finger-pointing, distracting judgment, and recrimination. And some managers associate ethics with rigid rules and intrusive regulations.

These seven realities make many Christians uncomfortable. There is the temptation to throw up our hands in resignation and declare, "It's a jungle out there!" Those who accept "the jungle" view of the business world see the work environment as a wild, untamable, and cut-throat place where only the toughest and shrewdest survive. Alas, the "dog-eat-dog" business world is no place for Jesus-following lambs, some say. For in the U.S. corporate life, a number of unpublished worldly instructions and beatitudes seem to be the standard of practice, such as: "Do unto others before they do unto you" or "Blessed are the rich, who make all their dreams a reality" or "Blessed are the bold and daring, whose self-confidence will take them far," or "Blessed are the powerful, who have control over others and events," or, perhaps the most popular, "Don't get mad—get even!"

In this book we will pursue a more optimistic view of business executives, professionals, and salaried workers. As we dispense with pure pessimism, however, we must not jettison reality—the modern workplace is a moral minefield. Officials, managers, and professionals must find their way through a moral maze dotted with dilemmas or quandaries that present tough choices within organizations be they in the public, private, or nonprofit sector. And we conclude, perhaps reluctantly, that the presence of high personal standards of morality alone may be insufficient to guide today's business and professional people through that maze of ethical issues and dilemmas of pressurized, business organizational life.

ASSUMPTIONS UNDERGIRDING BUSINESS ETHICS

Sound ethical decision-making in today's competitive business environment requires tough, incisive thinking. There must be careful thought given to four critical dimensions of corporate action:
1. goals;
2. methods;
3. motives; and
4. consequences.

Verne E. Henderson, in *What's Ethical in Business*, offers five basic assumptions to undergird ethical decision-making in business:
1. **Business ethics is a process.** Ethics is an on-going process of clarifying what constitutes the newest and best definition of society's welfare and mandating the behavior to secure it. Henderson's point: what's ethical is always changing/evolving. The emphasis should be on process. How the problem is resolved ranks a higher priority than what the answer is. Process is the essence of ethics in several professions. (In medicine, for example, a surgeon is not merely jesting who says, "The operation was a success but the patient died.")
2. **Human behavior is caused.** This is not some profound philosophical insight. It's a practical acknowledgment that people have reasons for doing what they do; human behavior does not occur randomly. If we are to evaluate the ethical behavior of others, it is both fair and realistic to inquire into the motivation behind the behavior (all the while knowing we will not reach infallible answers). To examine motives is to look at the deepest and most personal aspects of human and corporate behavior. Motives involve the personal values and leadership styles of key decision-makers. Motives are seldom out in the open. They are not easy to read like mission statements. And, all too often, they are the hidden agenda driving the ethical decisions of everyone in the workplace.
3. **Actions have consequences.** Toss a pebble into a tranquil pond of water and concentric waves move out from the point of entry. In today's business world that pond is neither small nor tranquil, but moral (or immoral) action creates a rippling of waves moving in all directions. Some of the consequences are obvious; others remain below the surface of public gaze. Moral actions always have consequences, whether seen or unseen, and they should be taken into account before decision-making.
4. **What's perceived as ethical depends on the viewpoint of the constituent.** In a complex corporate moral situation there may be many

people impacted by a decision that must be made. The group of people impacted may be called stakeholders, or they may be called constituents: people to whom business leaders feel responsible. And the eye of each stakeholder or constituent perceives what is ethical from a different personal perspective. Business leaders who take ethical decision-making seriously face a formidable task in reconciling the diverse perceptions of the many people impacted by a decision.

5. **The need for good ethics rests on our mutual vulnerability**. All of us know what it is like to be vulnerable. We are at the mercy of someone else, or at the mercy of some organization (or impersonal computer) that is "out there." The situation of vulnerability needs to be avoided at all costs, but that is probably impossible in every case. All of us have scars from losing in vital situations because of personal vulnerability. Because people are vulnerable there must be business ethics. As it is, business and technology are already impersonal and automated enough; the sheer size of a corporation can be intimidating to many.

WHO'S RESPONSIBLE FOR BUSINESS ETHICS?

For centuries, work was much simpler. Except for a few teachers and nurses, women worked in and around the home. Farmers possessed a mental list of all the chores and knew a schedule for the biggest assignments which harmonized with the seasons and climate. At first, factory workers knew the precise boundaries of their job assignments. Individual artisans crafted and sold their own products. Each farmer was responsible for his own acreage and answered to himself and his God for the bounty of harvest. Other workers usually answered to a single supervisor.

Those days are mostly past, of course. Our age is one of multinational corporations and multileveled institutions. The sense of responsibility for both quality of workmanship or service and for corporate ethics is diffused throughout the corporation. Imagine a scenario in which an automobile accident seriously injures the driver and several passengers; let's say the one-car accident was caused by either faulty design or shoddy workmanship on the car. Is there corporate liability and responsibility? Most of us would say yes. But was the automobile design at fault? And who directed the design team? Who approved the design? Or did one worker fail to do his/her job on the assembly line? If there was worker failure, did the immediate supervisor share responsibility? Is a work team involved? And what about the plant manager? Did pressure from government regulations play any part?

The old work ethic would declare that the individual is responsible for work ethics. The new work ethic would contend that ethical responsibility is shared. And this is just one manifestation of the highly complex world in which we live—the more widespread the problem, the more diffused the responsibility. Who or what, for example, is responsible for violent crime in this nation? Is it the general lawlessness and lack of respect for authority by the criminal element? Is the breakdown of the family a factor? Is it poverty in the inner city? The inefficiency of our criminal justice system? Availability of weapons? What about realistic portrayals of violence as the answer to human conflict in the entertainment media? Not knowing how to approach crime best, or other major issues such as welfare or environmentalism stems from our collective confusion about who's responsible for what consequences.

The Industrial Revolution essentially redesigned work and responsibility. A chain of command, much like military hierarchy, became prominent. Most workers attempted to limit personal responsibility and personal liability. In the late 1960s, the 1970s, and early 1980s, younger industrial workers found routine assembly line work held little satisfaction for them, and the subsequent work ethic that emerged was one of limited ethical responsibility. If the job did not require the full range of workers' skills and capabilities, and if they saw workers laid off as though they were not essential to company success, it was only natural that they question their own importance to the production process. An influx of Japanese-manufactured products awakened labor and management alike to a greater sense of shared responsibility for quality and ethics.

To our question: Who is responsible for ethics in today's business world? An idealistic answer would be "everyone, from the highest boss all the way down to the lowest-paid employee." And, of course, that's true. But that answer doesn't always translate into precise answers in concrete situations. Shared responsibility introduces several degrees of uncertainty for both supervisors and subordinates. It would be easy to say, "If everybody's responsible, then nobody's responsible." Furthermore, in today's highly competitive work world, there are many extenuating circumstances which arise unexpectedly and impinge upon the outcome of a process. It's so easy to blame a disastrous development on some external factor.

A better answer to the question: It all depends on the corporate culture of the individual company. In one company there may be heavy delegation of responsibility with much flexibility. In another company there may be rigid lines of authority and very little delegation. Encouragingly, many corporations, large ones especially, have demonstrated a courageous willingness and ability to assume responsibility for all their workers.

The next declaration may be the most important one in this volume: Though the nature and structure of modern corporate organizations allow virtually everyone to share moral accountability for an action, *responsibility for high ethical standards must begin at the very top of the business organization. The person at the top is the role model for everyone else in the organization.* Managers do more than simply set the tone at the top—they manage, monitor, and improve the firm's ethical performance on a continuing basis. Ethical managers also create incentives which advance highly ethical business practices without sacrificing the organization's economic performance.

Let's imagine a highly unethical chief-executive officer. He/she hardly hides his/her ethical transgressions, makes no pretense of resolving business issues according to any ethical values, and has little regard for truthfulness in business transactions. Now what kind of impact will this management style have on all employees under this CEO? All too many of them may say, "Well, I could handle these matters fairly and honestly, but ethics are not important to our CEO, so why should they be important to me? It doesn't pay to be honest anyway!"

On the other hand, a CEO widely known for the highest ethical standards of conducting business affairs should inspire the majority of people in the same organization to say, "It's clear that our top boss means business when he/she talks about high standards of business ethics, because he/she not only talks a good ethical game but models high standards. It's clear that I had better perform as ethically as I can if I want to remain at home in this organization."

IS THERE SUCH A CATEGORY AS "CHRISTIAN BUSINESS ETHICS"?

An assumption made here is that readers are Christians in business or professional life or at work in some business or production environment (we'll make this category broad enough to include students). As Christians, wouldn't it be a reassuring experience to turn to a book in the Bible entitled "Business and Professional Ethics," perhaps including a separate "Ten Commandments for All Workers of the World"?

The question raised in the subheading above is not frivolous. As we shall consider in the next chapter, the managers and employees of ancient times functioned in a culture and society almost unrecognizable in modern America. Despite the glory and wealth of King Solomon, Israel's entire gross national product under his reign was no doubt less than the net worth of Ford Motor Company or General Motors Corporation.

Many of us have heard countless sermons and lessons extolling Jesus not only as Savior but as our ultimate role model for all of life; thus we are instructed, when facing a moral dilemma, to ask, "What would Jesus do?" Supposedly, by asking the question of what Jesus would do, we are pointed toward the one right answer.

The question is a good one. What would Jesus actually do if he learned through confidential sources that his corporation would lay off a certain group of employees within six months? Would he forewarn the unsuspecting workers? If Jesus were CEO of a major corporation, would he downsize operations and workforce in order to realize greater salary for himself and higher profits for shareholders? Would he seek to advertise his company's products even though they were not necessities? Would Jesus ever fire an incompetent employee? If so, how would he proceed to do it? If Jesus were supervisor of a work unit, how strict would he write performance evaluations? Would occasional personal use of company equipment such as computers and copiers by his coworkers trouble Jesus? Would he go to the company's wine-and-cheese party at open house? What would Jesus say to a song director who was making unauthorized photocopies of hymns for his congregation? To a preacher who was taking sermon illustrations of another preacher and passing them off as his own experiences?

Can Christianity be translated into everyday activities? Is there any way to relate Sunday to Monday? Enough questions. There could be many more. Let's begin with a basic premise that will color everything that follows: *For the Christian, the biblical ethic has relevance to all life, including business life.* To address business and professional life, much like addressing any other dimension of contemporary life, we must begin with foundational principles and move toward practical applications. Most of us can concur on fundamental principles—it's the practical applications which spark debate.

While acknowledging the value of the Judeo-Christian perspective on business ethics, be aware of two fallacies or pitfalls in moral reasoning. One fallacy is the belief that uttering simple admonitions to "always tell the truth," "always treat people with respect," "always read your Bible," or "always live and act ethically" will equip people to enter the complex business environment. If life in corporate America were that simple!

The other fallacy attempts to find a concrete moral rule in Scripture, or any other moral philosophy for that matter, to fit every conceivable ethical situation. Scripture could be used as a business rule book much the way attorneys use the voluminous legal code! Most ethical dilemmas involve the clash of competing values, the balancing of self-interest with moral commitments, and/or the consideration of obligations to third parties. Finding the right thing to do in a business or professional dilemma can become an intense struggle; mustering the courage to do the right thing can become a greater struggle.

Be wary of those who consider themselves experts in ethics. Solutions to problems in professional and corporate ethics depend on the savvy, wisdom, moral values and sound judgment of all parties involved. Yes, there are moral rules, but there is no exact science of making sound, moral decisions. Look for the big ethical picture, all the while acknowledging that the moral prescription appropriate in one situation, market, shop, or industry may be inappropriate, even unworkable, in another.

A final pitfall for Christian business people to avoid is the temptation to moralize one's ethical prescriptions and judgment as the precise will of God. A strong dose of Christian humility will prevent us from transforming our personal opinions and private judgments into the omniscient, absolute will of God. A little humility will go a long way in keeping lines of communication open in moral discussion.

THE CORPORATE WORK ETHIC

A work ethic defines what employers and employees may do. It clarifies what they may expect of each other. It is a dynamic process, not a static tradition. The work ethic includes the ethical standards of a business organization. Each business organization develops, consciously or unconsciously, a work ethic. These habits and expectations compose a corporate culture, a subject we'll discuss later.

Unethical behavior does not "just happen." There is always an explanation, though managers may need to look hard or even seek outside counsel to find a full explanation. Conscientious managers will seek the major and minor motivations for unethical employee behavior. Then they can act to remove those incentives and temptations to unethical deeds in the workplace.

We conclude with a modern parable. There was a dangerous curve in a road just outside a small town. All too often cars driving a little too fast failed to make the curve and plunged over the cliff. The town's council decided to do something about this dangerous situation. They placed an ambulance at the bottom of the cliff. Obviously, a well-supported guardrail with warning signs and reflectors would have been a better solution to the town's problem, preventing the accident from occurring in the first place. The point is made: All too often Americans use the ambulance rather than the guard rail and reflectors when it comes to important matters—personal health is one and corporate ethics is another.

In the midst of testing liver function, testing for HIV, getting annual chest x-rays, and checking cholesterol, it is no wonder the medical profession is increasingly encouraging Americans to pay more attention to the prevention of disease rather than diagnosis and treatment. Likewise, in the business world, the best focus would aim at prevention of unethical practices.

A good work ethic does more than simply recognize and deal strictly with unethical conduct—it acts to prevent or at least forestall unethical behavior. Managers may not be able to pinpoint all the subtle influences and incentives for unethical acts; they may not be able to change either the workers or the causes which motivate them. Starting with the CEO and moving to all levels of management, managers can prescribe preventive measures for the health of an organization that are as efficient as physicians prescribing preventative measures for the physical and mental health of an individual.

In a pluralistic society, the sizable workplace, especially in a large urban setting, may be the place where different subcultures and value systems are compelled to compromise and cooperate to achieve a goal. What unites these workers? One cohesive force is obviously the product or service they produce. Perhaps the only other cohesive force is the corporate work ethic. Consider that the measure of a company code of ethics is just and fair punishment *after* the unethical deed; the strength of a strong work ethic is prevention of unethical deeds *before* they are seriously considered.

A strong work ethic has relevance to every business decision and every business action. The wise business manager knows that every action can have ethical consequences. The consequences may be direct, where some constituent's welfare is deeply impacted, or it may be indirect and subtle, where the impact is on the morale and moral climate of the organization. Clearly, the ethical challenge is greater for managers assuming this expanded view of business ethics than for those with traditional views. In the long run, however, the rewards and satisfactions for companies taking the ethical high road are far greater than the payoff for those who aim for short-term advantage with "business as usual."

THE GOAL OF ETHICAL BUSINESS LIFE

Traditionally, business ethics has been attached to business and professional life as a necessary appendage. The business organization was expected to pass muster on certain ethical concerns and avoid dramatic scandal. If a company could pull a "fast one" and get away with it, it was more likely to be jested about rather than regretted.

The healthier concept of business ethics to which we have just referred is one which is far more comprehensive in nature. Ethics has a pervasive relevance in all business and professional decisions. Ethical behavior should be like breathing—automatic! When business and professional people are rooted in a personal ethical philosophy and are determined to allow moral principles to guide their lives, moral considerations become so imbedded in every decision and action that they become commonplace and taken for granted.

What a wonderful commitment when business executives, professionals, and all employees have made a standing decision always to act ethically, according to whatever moral insight they possess, in every challenge and dilemma at work!

QUESTIONS FOR GROUP DISCUSSION
AND PERSONAL REFLECTION

1. Do you think that morality must be based on religion, either in the sense that without religion people would have no incentive to be moral or in the sense that only religion can provide us guidance? Is all morality based on the commands of God?

2. All normal adults have a personal system of moral standards and moral values. We have been influenced by our parents, our teachers, our peers, what we experience, and how we entertain ourselves. What are the major influences in your own moral standards and moral values? List these in the order of the greatest impact on your moral values.

3. "Passive experience" is an oxymoron, a contradiction in terms. Anyone we call "experienced" has reflected on and learned from life's experiences. Practical wisdom includes the ability to draw lessons from seemingly disconnected events and the most ordinary experiences; for example, learning to cope with one's mother-in-law might be excellent training for coping with one's boss. What are some experiences which have shaped your moral beliefs and values?

4. Do you consider any matter of etiquette to be a moral issue? What about the illustration given earlier in this chapter? Is what a supervisor calls his employees a moral issue?

5. Is there such a thing as "business ethics"? Are there people in the world who care about such ethics?

6. Are business ethics and professional ethics nothing more than good personal ethics that are applied in the work world?

7. Is the term "business" limited to those activities that are designed or intended to make money (or a profit)? What about non-profit organizations—do business ethics apply? Should the church (or a local congregation) be operated like a business?

8. Is there any value for a profession in having a code of ethics? Do you feel that most codes of ethics are disregarded?

9. Do you think there is a true relationship between observance of business ethics and profit margin? There seems to be evidence that ethical practices are linked with rising profits. Does this mean that ethical acts create profit? Or that competition and economic hard times lead to unethical behaviors? That organizations which are doing well can afford to behave in an ethical fashion? Could companies act ethically because they fear negative publicity and enforcement agencies?

10. We have all felt the pangs of conscience at times. That is a good sign because it means that we have reflected on and developed a set of moral principles. But what exactly is a conscience?

11. "Follow your conscience" and "You should never go against your conscience." These statements constitute advice we have all heard. Is this advice helpful? Could it be dangerous advice?

12. Do you think that high-principled moral living is inconsistent with tending to self-interest? Is not following our moral principles always in our best interest? Does moral behavior always pay off in strictly selfish terms?

13. **Ethical egoism** is the theory that the morality of an act is determined by one's long range self-interest. If a person's actions serves his/her long-term best personal interest, the act is moral. Under this system, a person covers one's backside, to say it nicely. The individual looks for something positive and good in making moral choices and/or intends to prevent something negative and bad. Thus, morality of an action might depend on whether it brings a promotion or salary increase or that it avoids a lawsuit or reprimand.

    Ethical egoism is used in Scripture. God's people were motivated to obey God's commands so that they might receive a reward and avoid punishment. Moses set forth covenant blessings and curses (Deut. 27-30). Jesus warned of hell fire.

    Does Scripture condemn self-interest? Should self-interest be balanced with concern for other moral values? If everyone pursues a narrow vision of self-interest, how could intense conflicts be resolved without appealing to other moral systems?

14. **Ethical relativism** is the doctrine that there is no absolute right or wrong in morality and that everything is relative to the individual, the organization, or the culture. What is right in one place may be wrong in another place. There is great diversity in human values and numerous moral codes point adherents in different directions. Is there such a thing as absolute moral truth? Given that business practices and concerns vary from culture to culture, are there moral standards in business ethics that you would consider to be absolute?

15. **Utilitarianism** is the moral doctrine that we should always act to produce the greatest possible balance of good effects over bad effects for everyone affected by our action. By this doctrine, what would make a business decision moral? The answer: a decision which produces the most good for the most amount of people and the least harm for the least amount of people. "Good" would be understood as benefit, happiness, or pleasure. Jeremy Bentham and John Stuart Mill were the first to develop the theory in detail.

    Every big business decision, and many small ones for that matter, impact several important constituents or stakeholders (see chapter 10). A decision that is good for one constituent may not be for other constituents. Would not utilitarianism be the most logical, most equitable, method of resolving business dilemmas?

    Before answering "yes," consider if utilitarianism is really workable. Can business decision-makers really know what will maximize good for most people? Can those calculations always be made accurately? Could there be some deeds that are always wrong, even if they do produce good for a lot of people?

16. Many people, often from a moral or ethical point of view, exclaim: "There ought to be a law!" These same people, observing some other practice of which they are more tolerant, may exclaim: "Well, you can't legislate morality!" Are people inconsistent? Can we have it both ways? Can we or can we not, as a society, legislate morality?

17. Is it correct to assume that "business ethics" has not always been this important, or that the emphasis on it is new?

18. Do you agree with the statement about the two pitfalls for Christian business people to avoid—one as uttering of simplistic, dogmatic generalizations and the other being the search for a concrete, absolute moral rule for every business situation?

19. Cite some instances in which you felt vulnerable to some business corporation because of your personal limitations or the impersonal nature of a company's handling of your complaint or concerns. What could have been done to render the situation easier to handle?

20. Although there is no complete list of adequate criteria for moral judgments, could you produce three standards that moral judgments should reach in order for them to be strong moral arguments or reasons? For example, might one say that moral decisions and judgments should be based on facts that are known? That they should be sensible or logical? That they square with sound moral principles? Are there others you would add?

21. Let's be practical: Can business ethics really be taught? Do you think a man or woman who does not know right from wrong prior to getting his or her M.B.A. is likely to learn the distinction by taking some required course in business ethics? Don't ethical values develop over a lifetime and aren't people resistant to changing their ethical values?

Chapter 2

"Six Days Shalt Thou Labor"
Theological and Historical Perspectives on Work

His work will be shown for what it is, because the Day will bring it to light. It will be revealed with fire, and the fire will test the quality of each man's work.

1 Cor. 3:13

In the strongest sense of a "calling," work constitutes a practical ideal of activity and character that makes a person's work morally inseparable from his or her life . . . activity has meaning in itself, not just the output or profit that results from it. . . . A calling links a person to a larger community, a whole in which the calling is a contribution to the good of all. . . . When the trajectory of a career flattens out, and it becomes clear that one will not, after all, make it to the top, then making it loses its meaning—as opposed to continuing in a calling and practicing law, carpentry, or scholarship as best one can, even if one cannot be the best.

Robert Bellah

Bowed by the weight of centuries he leans Upon his hoe and gazes on the ground The emptiness of ages in his face And on his back the burden of the world.

Edwin Markham

THERE CAN BE NO DOUBT: WORK IS THE DEFINING PRINCIPLE IN most adults' existence and identity. Our work occupies a third of our day, perhaps half or more of our waking hours. Whenever we meet someone for the first time, the next question after "Your name is . . . ?" is most likely to be "And what do you do?"

Work is a vivid sign that there is life in us. Work expresses our character and our personality. While generations past labored with sweat and soreness for the purpose of being able "to eat," work for current generations has acquired new meanings and significance. Most of us do not work simply for the basic necessities of food, clothing, and shelter—indeed we can accomplish that in a few hours a week—but we work for fulfillment, for the good life for ourselves, for the good life for our mates and children.

There are approximately 110 million Americans working in the U.S. labor force today. These men and women are working at approximately 25,000 different full-time occupations. But what does it mean to work? Do you think of God as a worker? Does

Holy Scripture offer any perspective on work, career, and vocation? How have various generations felt about work? And how have they interpreted certain Scriptures on work? We'll move toward answering some of these questions in this chapter and in the one to follow, and hopefully we can proceed from the philosophical, theological, and historical dimensions of work to practical applications in our own lives.

In a general sense, work is any form of producing something of value, whether or not one is compensated for it. Seeking to define work from a Christian perspective, John Stott proposes this definition: "Work is the expenditure of energy (manual or mental or both) in the service of others, which brings fulfillment to the worker, benefit to the community, and glory to God." It's unlikely, of course, that the vast majority of the world's workers would think of their toil in light of such grandiose purposes. There is certainly a distinction between "work" and "employment." Although all employment is work (we must not be paid for doing nothing), not all work is employment (i.e., we can work without being paid for it). What discourages many people is not the lack of employment, but the lack of meaningful work which challenges their creative energies and physical skills. To employ people to do mindless, meaningless tasks brings pay without significance; to work creatively but voluntarily brings significance without pay. Most of us do not have the liberty of almost unlimited free time to work creatively and voluntarily.

The distinction between work and play, on the other hand, is not always easy to distinguish. Those who truly enjoy their work are truly blessed; such enjoyment is a form of play. Some of us are fortunate enough to apply to our work a sense of creativity and imagination similar to the most enjoyable and rewarding games and pastimes of our childhood and leisure time. Others who earn income from occupations that seem more like "play"—such as professional performing arts, recording stars, and professional athletes—may work so hard to stay competitive in their respective fields that the sense of fun and play has been long gone. Purposeful work means "getting something done," whether it is work that seems like drudgery or work that seems like play.

We often declare that we "have to work for a living" and conclude, grudgingly on many Monday mornings, that work is one of the necessities of life to "keep body and soul together." There is always the fantasy of being rich from birth and "not having to work one day in a lifetime" and that such an existence would be paradise. Such daydreaming misses the place of work in our lives, our happiness, and our character development. There is nothing intrinsic to work that *makes* it unpleasant. Perhaps much of the unpleasantness of work that people experience is caused by their attitude about work as something they must but do not want to do. If our jobs can be infused with creativity, imagination, and a positive attitude, perhaps the sense of playfulness can replace the sense of dull routine.

THE CONCEPT OF WORK—ANTIQUITY
THROUGH THE MIDDLE AGES

The concept of work is taught in the first narrative of Holy Scripture. Arduous work, not work per se, was the punishment leveled by God for the sin of Adam, the prototype for the entire human family. Unfortunately, the notion that work is a curse upon the human family is mistakenly accepted in popular culture as an idea that is rooted in biblical theology (see Gen. 3:17–19 for the statement of the actual curse).

The geographical setting for the biblical treatment of vocation is far away and long ago. Work life in the Garden of Eden and in generations afterward was carried on in a primitive rural setting, a simple agricultural economy, bleak and grim, where men eked out of dry soil an existence at the level of bare subsistence. God called the human family to cultivate the earth and exercise dominion over all life forms. Generations later, the exalted view of work was encoded into the Decalogue: "Six days you shall labor and do all your work . . . You shall not steal. . . . You shall not covet . . . " (Exod. 20:8-11, 15, 17).

Civilization did not develop on this earth where the living was easy. Culture and civilization developed where people were challenged, where they had to work together to bring food out of the ground and care for flocks. Consequently, the Bible is filled with stories about peasant workers—their toils, their troubles, their needs, their anxieties, and their triumphs. Thus, one reads about prayers for harvest, prayers for rain, prayers for nets filled with fish.

The Bible depicts the God of the Judeo-Christian tradition as a deity who works, in contrast to the deities of ancient Near Eastern cultures who were depicted as asleep while human slaves toiled. While humans obviously need rest before and after their labors, the Psalmist declares the providential care of Yahweh: ". . . he who watches over you will not slumber; indeed, he who watches over Israel will neither slumber nor sleep. . . . The Lord will keep you from all harm—he will watch over your life" (Ps. 121:3, 7). Jesus declared: "My Father is always at his work to this very day, and I, too, am working" (John 5:17). Numerous scriptures depict God entering into a partnership with men and women in the vital work of creation, preservation, redemption or recreation, and Christians are challenged to see their work in light of God's work (e.g., Gen. 1:28; 2:15) and as an expression of devoting our entire bodies and minds to God (Rom. 12:1-2). "Serve wholeheartedly ["Render service with enthusiasm" NRSV], as if you were serving the Lord," the apostle Paul admonished, "because you know that the Lord will reward everyone for whatever good he does, whether he is slave or free" (Eph. 6:7).

Trading existed in the Middle East as far back as the Sumerian civilization, which flourished almost three thousand years before Christ. Weapons, jewels, household goods, and slaves were offered for barter. In ancient Greece, Aristotle, the most influential philosopher and writer of antiquity, theorized about the rules of trade and the nature of "distributive justice." He made a distinction between ordinary household trading, which he called *oecinomicus* (from which we get "economics") and trading with the idea of making a profit, which he called *chrematiske*. In ancient civilizations the principle that those who produce the wealth should keep it was not known. Instead, the wealth would go to military generals and powerful statesmen, to religious leaders, and to others who do not "produce" anything at all; in essence, those who toiled were rarely the ones who reaped.

Somewhere and at some time in ancient history, men concluded that the exchange of one's possessions and energy for someone else's possessions and energy required some mutually agreed upon medium of exchange. Little wonder, then, money was invented. It was probably invented early in the history of societies when intelligent, practical-minded men sat around and sought answers to the question, "What objects have common value to all of us around here, but do not weigh too much to carry around?" Among the answers in various societies: shells, stones, ivory, furs, and even tobacco. Precious metals such as gold and silver were the most common mediums of exchange throughout nearly all of civilized history.

As gold and silver were recognized for their scarcity and beauty, and thus their value, certain amounts of these metals were placed in government-minted coins; eventually, these coins were engraved. Much later, paper currency was printed to represent a certain amount of gold or silver. Early on, money assumed a value of its own, not for what it was, but for what it represented. People have given money nicknames, measured people's worth by it, saved it, loaned it, hoarded it, banked it, invested it, gambled it, borrowed it, stolen it, counterfeited it, and, most of all, spent it. The love of this "stuff," Paul warns us, that is the root of all kinds of evil (1 Tim. 6:10). (A quote from an anonymous wise-cracker comes to mind: "Money is the root of all evil, and everyone needs roots.")

In the New Testament there are stories of men who were scribes, rabbis, tax collectors, tentmakers, teachers, statesmen, and military leaders, as well as farmers and fishermen. In many ways, Christianity has always been the religion of the working classes. The people of Jesus' day were astonished that an apprentice carpenter could become such an authoritative teacher ("Is not this the carpenter . . . ?"). The apostle Paul, a tentmaker as well as a missionary, summed up the ancient world's philosophy of work concisely: work or starve (2 Thess. 3:10). In another epistle this tentmaker-missionary comments that not many high and noble by the world's standards answer the summons to Christian faith (1 Cor. 1:26–27). Interestingly, next to none of the leading New Testament figures earned their living in a church job.

In the Middle Ages the ancient prejudice against business affairs became more deeply rooted because of the religious ideology which supported it. The real calling of life is the salvation of souls and business was but a temporary matter and even a danger, compared to personal salvation. Medieval thinkers considered work to be a disagreeable necessity: We must work in order to eat and we must eat in order to sustain the body, but the body will soon pass away. The medieval monastics believed that what moderns call "ambition" to be avarice and what moderns call "business sense" to be greed. Trade was permissible, of course, but an attempt to reap profits was considered usury. Spiritual callings were considered the noblest professions of all, and wealth was suspect for "it is easier for a camel to pass through the eye of a needle, than it is for a rich man to get into the Kingdom of Heaven."

In centuries past the church's doctrine about usury was widely acknowledged. Usury has been defined two ways. In biblical usage usury was the lending of money with an interest charge for its use. Subsequent generations "cut some slack" on usury and defined it as an unconscionable or exorbitant rate of interest in excess of the legal rate. The ancient Hebrew law forbade charging interest in loans to fellow Israelites (Exod. 22:25; Deut. 23:19–20; Lev. 25:35–38), but this legislation reflects an era when most loans were personal, charitable loans to friends and not commercial loans for starting a new camel hair coat factory or purchasing a new, fully equipped chariot. Some of these ancient loans were intended to help a poor person or an Israelite brother hit hard by an emergency situation. Throughout the Old Testament, Yahweh's concern for the poor and needy was clearly stated in many ways, including prohibitions against exploitation of the less fortunate. Regrettably, the church of past generations often failed to grasp the true principle of these laws and made an unworkable, legalistic application of them in business situations.

A REFORMATION PERSPECTIVE ON WORK

The distinction made in the Middle Ages between "sacred" callings and "secular" callings came under serious critique by the Protestant reformers. Martin Luther gave considerable thought to the concept of vocation. He made a distinction between the kingdom of heaven and the kingdom of earth. To the heavenly kingdom belongs one's relationship with God, based on faith, and to the earthly kingdom belongs our relationship to our neighbor, which is to be based on love. Careers and vocations are located within the kingdom of earth. All people must find their stations in life. A station may or may not be a position of paid employment; for example, marriage is a station as well as is being a parent. Being a baker, a cobbler, a shoemaker, or a farmer were among the various ways to assume a station.

Martin Luther's exposition of justification by faith implied that such faith is bestowed by God's grace regardless of one's merit or station, whether one wears a clerical robe and collar or overalls and flannel shirt. Grace comes to anyone, not just to "sacred" workers, just as God's announcement of the Incarnation was announced first to shepherds in the fields rather than to priests and scribes in the temple. Any common needful work becomes the occasion for the fulfillment of one's calling to God and, according to Luther and Calvin, all callings were "sacred" callings. The call to love one's neighbor goes out to all, but what this call requires specifically is discovered in the stations occupied by godly men and women. All honorable callings represent specific and concrete opportunities of loving and serving our neighbors.

John Calvin contended that one need not enter a monastery to serve God, for the entire world is God's monastery. Through pursuit of vocations across the wide array of stations in life the hungry are fed, the sick are healed, the naked are clothed, the vulnerable are protected, and the fallen are lifted up. Indeed, by working we are actually participating in God's continuing providence for the human race.

To cite an example: a preacher might eloquently admonish his congregation to pray for the good health and safety of all fellow citizens; the preacher has exercised his gift. The Christian who is a shoemaker believes in producing quality shoes at a fair market price; he has exercised his gift. When people wear the shoes their feet are protected from snow and cold, from rainy surfaces as well as dangerous objects on walking surfaces. Therefore, the shoemaker and clothing makers no less than the preacher are cooperating with one another and with God, at least in some small way, to answer the prayers of the congregation for comfort, good health, and safety. To follow Christ it is not necessary to abandon one's earthly station; indeed, the station provides the arena in which the Christian life is lived in the context of daily work.

THE PROTESTANT WORK ETHIC
AND THE GOSPEL OF WORK

The Industrial Revolution was undergirded by the Protestant work ethic, an ideology which attempted a marriage between capitalism and Protestant doctrine. The "ethos" or spirit of capitalism was expressed in the virtues of initiative, individualism, hard work, thrift, self-discipline, accumulation, and investment. Such beliefs and values were characteristic of middle-class entrepreneurs and had been forwarded to the early industrial period as duties by such popular philosophers as Benjamin Franklin.

The gospel of work, calling for strenuous effort, frugality, shrewdness, and rugged individualism, soon became the gospel of wealth, adopted in the nineteenth century by a Scotch Presbyterian named Andrew Carnegie, who felt it his vocation to make money hand-over-fist to the glory of God. A popular slogan of wealthy business leaders at the turn of the twentieth century was "Make all you can, can all you make, give away all you can." With the latter part of the slogan, many capitalists were convinced that the good ends of philanthropy would justify whatever hard bargains and ruthlessness were required as means of getting money.

In modern times the industrial and technological revolutions of Western Europe, the United States, and Japan have overturned the mode of work by substituting machines for the hand, the factory for the farm, the sprawling urban complex for the village and small town. Products of every conceivable usage are produced in mass quantities. Productivity has increased enormously, especially after widespread acceptance of Frederick Taylor's system of "scientific management." Taylor advocated breaking jobs down into their smallest separate steps and adjusting machines to replace people for many of the steps. Neither intelligence nor heart and soul were really necessary to succeed in most manufacturing jobs.

The downside of this revolution was that life became more compartmentalized than ever before; work was something that happened away from home and separated from the rest of life. Much work was boring, mindless routine, and personal skills and pride of workmanship seemed less important. One's work gave less sense of identity. A great deal of work was done by the many, often in unsafe working conditions, for the financial benefit reaped by the few. There emerged an increasing alienation of production workers from any sense of meaning or value in their occupations, and often there was even alienation from management and coworkers.

The modern labor movement was rooted in the courageous attempts of workers to defend themselves against very low wages, unsafe working conditions, and unfair labor practices. By the 1950s, a decade of relative prosperity, over one-third of U.S. workers were members of labor unions. Management theorists such as Eldon Mayo, Chris Argyris, and Frederick Herzberg determined what motivated people and what demoralized them; although, at times the information was used more for worker control rather than work enrichment.

In recent years the philosophies of "Total Quality" and participative management have affected systems of work and styles of interaction on the job. The goal of creative management has been to return a sense of meaning and value to one's work by job enrichment, as well as to empower workers with greater self-determination of what happens in the workplace and how much they are paid to perform there. The decline in union membership may be interpreted as evidence that management is now much more sensitive and responsive to worker issues and needs.

RECAPTURING A BIBLICAL SENSE OF VOCATION

Is it possible to recapture a biblical sense of the vocation? Regrettably, the word "vocation" or calling has come to mean no more than a way of describing how a man or woman earns a living, what one does when he/she is not on vacation. We often speak of "choosing a vocation," though such a phrase is foreign to biblical language.

The word "vocation" is the latinized form of the Teutonic-English word "calling." "To call" has two principal meanings:
1. to give a name to something or somebody; and
2. to summon.

Both of these usages appear in the Bible (cf. 1 John 3:1; Isa. 43:1 and 49:1–3; Hos. 11:1). The apostle Paul employs both senses of the word when he writes, for example, of "the prize of the high calling of God in Christ Jesus" (Phil. 3:14), or of the peace of God "to which you were called in one body" (Col. 3:15). To the Ephesians the same writer admonished that Christians "walk worthy of the calling" in which they were called (4:1).

In view of the many scriptures on calling, does this mean that God calls us to some special vocation such as plumbing, farming, teaching, selling, or engineering? Few would contend that their present employment is the only job they are capable of handling or the only job in which they could find fulfillment and contentment. Fewer still would contend that they entered their present vocation through a sudden and vividly clear revelation from God who told them what work field to enter and that they had an instant impulse to answer and obey. Even a good many who settle in Christian ministry will admit they tried other professional careers first and eventually entered pulpit ministry with much uncertainty and skepticism.

The vocation to which Christians are called is much more general, more encompassing, and more noble than the calling to any specific form of employment, such as mechanics, law, medicine, carpentry, and so forth. In the New Testament, the primary, if not exclusive, meaning of "vocation" *(klesis)* pertains simply but profoundly to the call of the gospel. God calls us through his Word to be his children, his friends, to enjoy fellowship with Jesus Christ (1 Cor. 1:9), to abandon darkness for the light (1 Pet. 2:9), to live holy lives (1 Pet. 1:15; 1 Cor. 1:2), to be saints (Rom. 1:7), to use whatever gifts God has given us to administer his grace in its various forms (1 Pet. 4:10; Romans 12:4-21), and to seek to bring others into this realm of fellowship through a witness in the world of words and deeds. Once we have been able to accept this higher calling, our specific employment in a community is merely a means of furthering in the best way we can the goals of the higher commitment. Paul was employed as a tentmaker, but his higher vocation or calling was to the faithful dissemination of the good news.

Once our general calling is understood, we may appropriately speak of particular callings—roles and occupations to which not all Christians are called. With respect to roles and occupations in the church, Paul recognizes diversity in "gifts" of the Spirit—serving as a prophet, a teacher, an administrator, and so forth (1 Cor. 12:28–31).

From a strictly secular viewpoint, the particular callings we enter are the result of the accidental nature of our genetics, identities, and interests. We find ourselves thrown into professions and careers for no apparent purpose or reason other than the fickle finger of fate. From a Christian perspective, life looks different. Who we are is not a result of cosmic fate, but is the consequence of God's intended purpose in our lives. If I suddenly am bestowed millions of dollars, either through inheriting a family fortune or by having been given the winning lottery ticket, then is this good fortune an incredible bit of luck? No. A Christian would see this happy turn of events as God's will for the direction of the remainder of my life—a life that can be invested to maximum benefit of my church, my family, and others for whom I learn to care deeply.

A SPECIAL EXERCISE

Consider the following scriptures which contain the word "work" or at least allude to labor. Two requests:

1. State your understanding of the original meaning of these scriptures in their context of biblical narrative and doctrine.
2. Then state the impact and application, if any, of each of these scriptures for our contemporary lives.

> **Gen. 2:15**—The Lord God took the man and put him in the Garden of Eden to *work* it and take care of it.
>
> **Gen. 4:12**—When you *work* the ground, it will no longer yield its crops for you. You will be a restless wanderer on the earth.
>
> **Exod. 1:14**—They made their lives bitter with hard labor in brick and mortar and with all kinds of *work* in the fields; in all their hard labor the Egyptians used them ruthlessly.
>
> **Exod. 20:9**—Six days you shall labor and do all your *work*.
>
> **Exod. 20:10**—But the seventh day is a Sabbath to the Lord your God. On it you shall not do any *work*, neither you, nor your son or daughter, nor your manservant or maidservant, nor your animals, nor the alien within your gates.

Prov. 12:11—He who *works* his land will have abundant food, but he who chases fantasies lacks judgment.

Prov. 12:14—From the fruit of his lips a man is filled with good things as surely as the *work* of his hands rewards him.

Prov. 14:23—All hard *work* brings a profit, but mere talk leads only to poverty.

Prov. 16:26—The laborer's appetite *works* for him, his hunger drives him on.

Prov. 18:9—One who is slack in his *work* is brother to one who destroys.

Prov. 21:25—The sluggard's craving will be the death of him, because his hands refuse to *work*.

Prov. 22:29—Do you see a man skilled in his *work*? He will serve before kings; he will not serve before obscure men.

Prov. 24:27—Finish your outdoor *work* and get your fields ready; after that, build your house.

Prov 31:13—She selects wool and flax and *works* with eager hands.

Eccles. 2:17—So I hated life, because the *work* that is done under the sun was grievous to me. All of it is meaningless, a chasing after the wind.

Eccles. 2:24—A man can do nothing better than to eat and drink and find satisfaction in his *work*. This too, I see, is from the hand of God.

Eccles. 3:22—So I saw that there is nothing better for a man than to enjoy his *work*, because that is his lot. For who can bring him to see what will happen after him?

Eccles. 8:15—So I commend the enjoyment of life, because nothing is better for a man under the sun than to eat and drink and be glad. Then joy will accompany him in his *work* all the days of the life God has given him under the sun.

Acts 20:33—I have not coveted anyone's silver or gold or clothing.

Acts 20:34—You yourselves know that these hands of mine have supplied my own needs and the needs of my companions.

Acts 20:35—In everything I did, I showed you that by this kind of hard *work* we must help the weak, remembering the words the Lord Jesus himself said: "It is more blessed to give than to receive."

Eph. 4:28—He who has been stealing must steal no longer, but must *work*, doing something useful with his own hands, that he may have something to share with those in need.

Col. 3:17—And whatever you do, whether in word or deed, do it all in the name of the Lord Jesus, giving thanks to God the Father through him.

Col. 3:22—Slaves, obey your earthly masters in everything; and do it, not only when their eye is on you and to win their favor, but with sincerity of heart and reverence for the Lord.

Col. 3:23—Whatever you do, *work* at it with all your heart, as *working* for the Lord, not for men.

Col. 3:24—Since you know that you will receive an inheritance from the Lord as a reward. It is the Lord Christ you are serving.

1 Thess. 4:11—Make it your ambition to lead a quiet life, and to mind your own business and to *work* with your hands, just as we told you.

2 Thess. 3:8—Nor did we eat anyone's food without paying for it. On the contrary, we *worked* night and day, laboring and toiling so that we would not be a burden to any of you.

2 Thess. 3:9—We did this, not because we do not have the right to such help, but in order to make ourselves a model for you to follow.

2 Thess. 3:10—For even when we were with you, we gave you this rule: "If a man will not *work*, he shall not eat."

2 Thess. 3:11—We hear that some among you are idle. They are not busy; they are busybodies.

2 Thess. 3:12—Such people we command and urge in the Lord Jesus Christ to settle down and earn the bread they eat.

QUESTIONS FOR GROUP DISCUSSION AND PERSONAL REFLECTION

1. How do you define "work"? Originally, was work given by God for the sin of Adam and Eve? Is work a curse upon the human family?

2. Do you think that work has intrinsic value? That is, is there something valuable in work that is worth doing for its own sake?

3. Can a Christian make a distinction between a "sacred" and a "secular" calling? Is it possible to serve God in all careers and vocations?

4. Do our jobs and careers define us more than anything else about our lives? How would the apostle Paul have answered the question, "What do you do?"

5. Does God command us to "work hard"? (See Eccles. 9:10; Col. 3:17, 23.) Is it our moral responsibility to work hard? Do Christian employees need supervision? Would Christian workers need to be told when to start working? Would they need little pep talks to keep their morale high? And what does it mean to work "as for the Lord"?

6. How do you understand the Protestant work ethic? Do you think it has relevance for our times?

7. Do you think the work ethic of previous generations is now dead? While our fathers and grandfathers and great grandfathers concentrated energy upon plow and drill press and pressure gauge and tort, do not younger workers ask questions about the point of knocking themselves out for corporate bosses who live in another city and state? Do today's workers care about the quality of their product or service?

8. Read Colossians 3:1-2. Paul urges us to focus on the "things above" and not the "things on the earth." Is it possible to hold a "secular" job and still seek the heavenly agenda? The issue here is spirituality, the capacity to know, experience, and respond to God. Common sense tells us that we cannot all resign our "secular" jobs and enter salaried Christian ministry. Then, how is it possible to bring spirituality into "secular" work?

9. Do you know people who seem to spend more time and more creative energy in getting out of work rather than simply working?

10. "We work for fulfillment, for the good life for ourselves, for the good life for our mates and children." In the 1996 presidential campaign, Robert Dole often stated that many Americans feel like they are also working for the government. This was a statement about high taxes. Do you feel that average citizens (i.e., non-government workers) also work for the government?

11. That employees have obligations of loyalty to their employers is largely assumed without question within the business community. The major concern of top managers is how to retain and strengthen the bonds of loyalty. People have different conceptions of loyalty, but ideally it includes willing devotion and is freely given. While obedience can be demanded, loyalty cannot. To be loyal is to serve a cause; it is ongoing and sustained.

    a. Is anything worthy of loyalty in this idealistic sense?

    b. How do you define loyalty to your present employer? Is loyalty mainly about discharging your obligations and responsibilities conscientiously or does it demand feelings or pride and affection?

    c. Is there anything your current employer could do to strengthen your sense of loyalty and dedication to the firm and to your job?

    d. What do you see as the moral limits to loyalty?

12. Jesus told a parable about a landowner who went out early in the morning to hire transient labor to work his vineyard (Matt. 20:1–16). In Palestine, the work day was not eight hours, but from sunrise until sunset. People spent most of their daylight hours working, and there were many workers who lived day to day at the mercy of chance employment. Workers who were not hired early in the day lingered in the marketplace, perhaps with tools in hand, hoping to be hired for the balance of the day. At the end of each day, each worker expected to be paid according to his contribution.

    The landowner in the story Jesus told paid each group a full day's wages. This evoked a grievance from those who had worked throughout the entire day. The employer then defends his treatment of the full-day employees by citing his original oral contract:"Friend, I am doing you no wrong; did you not agree with me for a denarius? Take what is yours and go your way, but I wish to give to this last man the same as to you" (Matt. 13–14).

    What lessons should be learned from this story? Is this a story about employment practices and contracts? Is this a story about God's grace? Is there anything about employer or employee rights that we can learn from this story? Was the landowner fair? Regardless, if the employer continued the practice he would soon find that no worker would report to his acreage during the first hours of the day; most would report in the late afternoon.

    Have you ever signed a contract to perform in a certain job or position at a set wage, only later to experience another person hired for a similar position at better wages? How did you feel? What should a Christian do if he/she believes that personal wages are not simply low, but unfair? Have you ever heard a Christian say, "I know I'm being overpaid for this job"?

13. Jesus told another parable which is even more perplexing, the parable of "The Dishonest Steward" or, as labeled by the New International Version translators, the

parable of "The Shrewd Manager" (Luke 16:1–13). To paraphrase the story, a wealthy man owns a business enterprise. He summons his middle manager and acts on an accusation of poor stewardship of resources. The manager is faced, rightly or wrongly, with losing his job; he knows that dismissal is certain. The manager realizes his plight. "I am not strong enough to dig and I'm ashamed to beg," he concedes (Luke 16:3). He thus hatches a plan calculated to win clients away from his immediate boss. Since his employer's books were still under his control, he tampers with the financial records of client indebtedness, reducing greatly the amount owed to his employer. This manager thus owes the gratitude of the various debtors, who in turn could be relied on to help him build a new business. Thus the manager's security is ensured by his shrewdness. And also by his crass dishonesty, one might add. Nonetheless, the master praises his manager for his shrewdness.

Hardly a well-known parable, right? The application Jesus made also seems puzzling: "I tell you, use worldly wealth to gain friends for yourselves, so that when it is gone, you will be welcomed into eternal dwellings" (Luke 16:9).

Do you think Jesus is defending dishonesty in business accounting? Surely not. Typically, each of Jesus' parables contain one major point. In this case, could Jesus be urging his listeners to seize opportunities in this life which will bring dividends in the future? What do you make of this story?

14. Read Proverbs 6:6–8. What could a lazy person learn by observing the ants?

15. How do Christian employees work diligently and faithfully for employers and coworkers who do not deserve or appreciate their best efforts?

16. We have usually focused on what an employee owes an employer. Specifically, what does an employer owe to a worker? (We'll revisit this issue in chapter 10.)

17. Employees desire their employer to be loyal to them. No one wants dismissal without just cause. Does an employee have a lifelong moral obligation to remain available to a good employer?

18. Do you believe that permanent job security with full benefits is a basic right of all Americans?

19. Do you think a preacher really works—at least like everybody else? Does the average preacher do an honest day's work in his life? As the old saying goes, he is "six days invisible and one day incomprehensible."

20. How many sermons have you heard concerning work? Have you heard much teaching in the church about work or how to apply your Christian faith in the workplace? If your answer is no, how do you explain the lack of spiritual aid and direction for the worker and professional? Do you think that preachers and evangelists are the best people to consult for spiritual training and counsel in business?

21. Do you think that animals work? Consider the following statement by Pope John Paul II: "Work is one of the characteristics that distinguish man from the rest of the creatures, whose activity for sustaining their lives cannot be called work" (from encyclical on "Human Work").

22. In Scripture, work has meaning. But can work be placed in true perspective apart from an understanding of biblical doctrine about the Sabbath? What was the purpose of the Sabbath? (You might want to consult a Bible resource book on this one.)

23. What do you think it is like to experience long-term unemployment? Is unemployment a tragedy, even if one did not need the income from a job?

24. Does the Bible teach the concept of "merit"? Did not Paul apply the principle of merit in a negative way by denying welfare to those who refuse to work?

25. Do you agree with the author that it is difficult to draw a distinction between work and play?

26. Do you agree with the statement in this chapter: "From a Christian perspective, life looks different. Who we are is not a result of cosmic fate, but is the consequence of God's intended purpose in our lives."?

   (See questions at the conclusion of the next chapter for more thought and discussion about biblical teaching on work and calling and in chapter 4 for discussion of work and wealth.)

Chapter 3

Answering a Calling
Choosing a Vocation

If God shows you a way in which you may lawfully get more than in another way (without wrong to your soul or to any other), if you refuse this, and choose the less gainful way, you cross one of the ends of your calling, and you refuse to be God's steward, and to accept His gifts and use them for Him when He requireth it: you may labour to be rich for God, though not for the flesh and sin.

Richard Baxter,
19th Century American Preacher

The highest reward for man's toil is not what he gets for it, but what he becomes by it.

John Ruskin

The more I want to get something done, the less I call it work.

Richard Bach

Our age is characterized by non-meaning. All psycho-sociologists agree ultimately that the work we do is marked by this fault. It makes no sense. It has no obvious value of its own. We have on the one side the dividing up of tasks, monotony, and the production of articles of no evident utility, while on the other side we find a break with matter, then with the machine, then a break between the function of thought and that of execution, the growth of an enormous labor organization and bureaucracy, a mass of paper work, often with no recognizable content, for every conceivable function, and finally the wastage of giving complex and highly advanced training to men who are then entrusted with jobs far below their competence. These things, and many others, contribute to the fact that work has no meaning in modern society.

Jacques Ellul

Without productivity, a business fails. Without productivity, an employee or owner becomes dissatisfied. Productivity results from genuine interest. . . . You'll be productive if you love what you are doing. For example, if you work in a chocolate chip cookie factory and love chocolate chip cookies, you will communicate that love to the owner, your coworkers, and the customers. You'll all have fun producing a product you love personally. This applies to any product or service. Did you ever wonder why people who are financially independent continue to work when they really don't have to? The answer is that they're having fun.

Nancy Anderson

Enjoyment, in human life, isn't a fluke. It's part of God's plan. God wants us to eat; therefore God designs us so that eating is enjoyable. God wants us to sleep; therefore God designs us so that sleeping is enjoyable. God wants us to procreate, love, and make love; therefore God designs us so that sex is enjoyable, and love even more so. God gives us unique (or at least unusual) skills and talents; therefore God designs us so that, when we use them, they are enjoyable.

Richard Bolles

Do you see a man skilled in his work? He will serve before kings; he will not serve before obscure men.

Prov. 22:29

From what we get, we make a living; what we give, however, makes a life.

Arthur Ashe

Each of us has her or his own gifts and limitations. Each also has infinite value and a unique place to fill. God's grace to us is the chance to do the best we can with this uneven experience called life.

Rubel Shelly

The really crucial decision comes, not when a person decides to be a foreign missionary rather than a farmer; the really crucial decision comes when a man decides that he will live his whole life in holy obedience; whether that leads to farming or banking or evangelistic work in Africa is then wholly secondary. The major decision has already been made.

Richard Chewning

Each one should retain the place in life that the Lord assigned to him and to which God has called him.

1 Cor. 7:17

MANY READERS MAY BE COLLEGE STUDENTS. YOU WILL BE addressed directly in this chapter. Most of you have gone to some college or university in order to prepare for a career.

There may be some exceptions: a person looking for a lifetime mate; a person attending school for the sheer joy of learning (sometimes true for older students); a person attending college because parents sent him/her with hopes and expectations that maturity might happen; a person spending time waiting for real life to happen.

By the time you have gone to college, most likely you have already held one or more jobs, part-time employment at least. Perhaps you have waited tables at O'Charley's, checked out customers at Kroger, operated a lawn service in your neighborhood, delivered newspapers, or held one of an almost unlimited number of low-paying service jobs. Often those jobs lead to worthwhile opportunities for job training and advancement. Just as often, however, those jobs are tolerated for short periods of time in order to earn money toward some goal (for example, to pay college tuition or to pay for a new car) or to earn some spending money. Some summer jobs are tolerable, no matter what fancy job title one holds, only by the fact that they will last only three months.

Is it fair to say that going to college or training and vocational school is largely an attempt to avoid being saddled for life with one of those low-paying, uninteresting, and unpleasant jobs? It's all right to admit those jobs often do not challenge our minds or skills. They can be boring routines. They do not command instant respect from an admiring world. We want good jobs. We talk about developing "marketable skills" for jobs far better than minimum-wage opportunities.

Perhaps in the performance of less than satisfying work, we may pause and reflect on the nature of work itself and its proper place in our lives. All of us develop some philosophy about work, whether we do it unconsciously or through careful thought and evaluation. Along the way we must answer certain questions for ourselves: What is the purpose of work? Is it simply to earn money on which to live and purchase consumer goods and nothing else? Is all work a good thing so that we should be grateful for just any job? Should work be fun? Should our jobs be something we would do for no salary if we were independently wealthy? Or is work essentially a curse upon the human experience? And what should people do if they cannot find the job they seem best suited for? How much of your self-concept and your self-esteem should be connected with your job? How would you spend your time if you did not have to work?

Such questions are weighty. A look at history provides several different answers to some of these questions. Historically, many people have tried to avoid work. They knew it was arduous and swallows up a lot of time. Because work was viewed in such a negative light, those who held power and wealth in the great ancient empires arranged an economic system wherein other people, namely slaves, would be compelled to do work for them. The ancient Egyptians enslaved the Hebrews, as all Bible students know. The ancient Greeks despised work as a necessary evil, and the unemployed were considered fortunate indeed. The Greeks believed that ordinary citizens worked in order to eat and ate in order to work until their bodies wore down and they disintegrated into dust. Both the Roman and Greek societies accepted a singular answer to the drudgery and loss of time to work: slavery. If a Roman or Greek was wealthy or powerful enough to own slaves, he could dictate that they perform all necessary tasks, thus freeing him to pursue honor and nobility by doing great things. Even a philosopher as great and learned as Aristotle believed that in the natural order of the universe, some people were naturally developed (or "underdeveloped," as the case may be) to be slaves.

As Americans we know that slavery took a mighty hold on our own southern soil during the colonial and early national periods of our history. Slaveholders were buttressed by negative views and stereotypes of Africans as members of an inferior "mud sill" class. So entwined with southern culture and folkways was the image of Africans picking cotton beneath the hot sun that a civil war was necessary to dismantle the slavery system. With the coming of the industrial revolution, a system of "wage slavery" developed in the factories, coal fields, and rail yards of the northern states. Out of the frustration and alienation felt by American workers who toiled long hours for low wages in order to make the Carnegies, the Rockefellers, the Vanderbilts, and a few others incredibly wealthy was born the American labor movement.

There's nothing noble about slaveholding, of course. Few slaveholders and other exploiters of labor ever became known as great men. If they ever became admired, however, it was not because they found inhumane ways of avoiding work but because they achieved something else worthwhile in life or gave away millions of dollars to charitable causes.

There's another view of work. It, too, has historic roots, but is positive and optimistic in nature: work is a positive experience which expresses our character and personality. As we noted in the last chapter, work is any form of expending energy for the purpose of producing something of value, regardless of whether one is compensated for it. Not all work is compensated, either at all or adequately—alas, there are starving artists in all civilized societies. Work gives people a sense of identity; historically, many surnames were assumed by men on the basis of their occupations: carpenter, hunter, mason, workman, cook, taylor, driver, and so forth. Because significant work produces something of value, it is not simply a means of livelihood—it is also a major force in shaping the inner life of the worker and impacting his/her significant relationships.

We may further break down this positive view of work into two driving forces which energize a person's work:

1. Work is done for the pursuit of personal success, usually measured financially. A man or woman thus becomes hard-working, highly competitive, relentless, and ready to sacrifice in order to advance a career. Climbing the corporate ladder will lead to greater salaries and benefits, as well as the admiration of peers, all along the way.

2. Work is foremost service to one's neighbor to build a better community, to make a better world. The English Calvinists who founded Massachusetts Bay Colony placed an emphasis on work as a form of mutual service and vocation. Discovering what a community needs and then working to meet those needs, consistent with one's skills and training, will lead one to find ultimate gratification in life. What a man or woman achieves in the world of work and humanitarian service becomes the legacy of that person bequeathed to future generations.

Let's return to the practical questions: How do you select a profession? What career is best for you? How can you know when God is calling you to a specific vocation? How do you make responsible career choices? Responsible career choice involves identifying your talents and abilities and pinpointing the location of a place wherein those talents and abilities can be exercised in the service of humanity.

Most of all, you want a career or job which connects in some meaningful way with your inner life, your deepest convictions, and your core values. Admittedly, that may be an idealistic expectation, but it is worth striving for—too many people feel trapped in artificial, mechanical, near mindless jobs which provide no worthy challenge and utilize only the smallest part of their greatest gifts and best skills. Borrowing jingles from advertising for the army, most of us would like to "be all that you can be" and be invited to accept "not just a job, but an adventure."

We all know how a career counselor or an employment agency might approach career selection. These advisers would focus on questions pertaining to the discovery of your talents, skills, and interests. Then they would point you toward job opportunities and career possibilities where your talents and skills can best be utilized. The Christian concept of work and calling as a place and a way of employing your gifts in service to others leads one to consider other factors.

How do you know what God might be calling you to do? As we attempt to answer this questions, keep in mind our discussion in the previous chapter on recapturing a biblical sense of vocation. Most of all, God calls you to be a Christian. But does God really care in what job you live out your discipleship or in what community?

At the outset, please keep this counsel in mind: Do not feel you need to seek special signs, miracles, and wonders. You may feel that God addresses you through natural phenomena such as a starry night, a colorful rainbow, a bright sunset over the blue ocean, or billowy clouds, but even still, do not expect to be called through a burning bush as was Moses or be given a "whale" of an ocean ride if you resist God as was Jonah. Instead, you will need to be attentive, introspective, and reflective to all the character and personal traits that define you.

Here are some briefly stated practical suggestions:

1. **Identify the gifts, talents, and abilities that God has given you.** Of course, those gifts and attributes will probably not be unique. If along with your intelligence you have manual dexterity, your interests might point you to becoming a dentist, a surgeon, or an electrician. The *absence* of certain gifts and attributes will mean that certain doors are closed to you.

2. **Consider the most driving and lively interests you have developed.** What subjects do you enjoy best? What do you enjoy reading and hearing about? How do you best enjoy spending your leisure time?

3. **Weigh heavily any special concern or passion on behalf of others that God has given you.** Is there a special concern you have for a certain group such as handicapped citizens, special-needs children, poor people, public school children, sick people, and on and on we could go? Of course, exclude any special concern for self, a concern of all normal people. A special concern for others may be viewed as the leading of the Spirit in calling you to special ministry.

   Do not be reluctant to pursue your strongest interests and passions, for any person who can fill a vocation with interest and passion is blessed indeed! In what vocation can you best develop enthusiasm? Literally, enthusiasm means "God within us" or "inspired by God." In previous generations, Christians were taught that enthusiasm meant God was working in people's hearts, attracting them to a vocation or calling.

4. **Consider the direction your academic and technical training has pointed you.** What have been your chosen major and minor fields? What opportunities have opened because of this specialization? In what subject have been the courses that you have enjoyed most? To what careers would this subject point?

5. **Consider the doors of service opportunity that are open to you.** In what jobs and assignments have you been invited to use your gifts and talents? Who is seeking and valuing your services?

6. **Consider what encouragement, counsel, and other reinforcement you have received.** In what roles have you received the greatest compliments and encouragement? Consider advice from a wise author: "Plans fail for lack of counsel, but with many advisers they succeed" (Prov. 15:22, RSV).

7. **Consider the roles and jobs which have given you the greatest sense of satisfaction and gratification.** When did you complete a task feeling really "good inside"? When have you worked at a project that was more important than the remuneration you received?

8. **Consider that the Spirit of God may be leading you into a calling that is not the one for which you are best qualified.** God may call people to do what they at first feel greatly reluctant and even opposed to doing. There are several biblical narratives about servants who resisted God's calling because they felt unwilling or inadequate for the assignment. Moses resisted God's request to make demands about his people before Pharaoh because of a speech and confidence problem. Jonah resisted the Lord because he had no regard for the Ninevahites. The apostle Paul felt he was an unimpressive, nervous public speaker.

Your first career choice is important, but it's hardly ever irretrievably critical. Most well-educated professionals will make major career changes two or three times in their lifetime. If you are able to admit making a mistake in a career choice, you will be a more purposeful and wise person as a result of the experience.

Finally, remember this most important principle: All honorable work can be an opportunity for accomplishing God's plan for this world. And in all kinds of work you can witness to others something of God's marvelous grace and glory. All of us as Christians have received gifts from the Holy Spirit (see 1 Cor. 12, Rom. 12, and 1 Pet. 4:10–11 for some instruction), but do not assume that the local congregation is the sole outlet for discovering and using those gifts. The New Testament does not strait jacket the use of spiritual gifts, and Christians are salt and light in all relationships and all places. The gift of teaching skill can be used in a labor-management conference as well as in a Sunday school classroom.

No honorable work—"honorable" defined as work which accomplishes some amount of good in the world—should be despised as useless before God. An occupation which may be considered insignificant in the eyes of society may be nonetheless important. For example, the man who is a garbage collector, or the man who washes dishes at Shoney's, or the man who cleans septic tanks, or the woman who changes diapers and empties bed pans at the nursing home— all these hard-working, perhaps underpaid, workers perform a far more valuable role in our community than the highly salaried advertising executive who uses his creative gifts to design commercials promoting products for the strictly adult entertainment industry, tobacco companies, distilleries, and breweries! Yes, that statement is a little judgmental, but so be it!

9. **Consider the truth that God's master plan and timing may differ from your own.** Be prepared for setbacks, failures, even firing. In tough times God may lead you to discover your highest fulfillment in calling and career. Be patient but not complacent. Develop the wisdom or seek the counsel to know when you've reached a real roadblock to your dreams and plans and when you're merely encountering an obstacle.

10. **Pray that God's Spirit will lead you in all career and business decisions.** Fervently pray that God will guide you in your major decisions about your work. As a Christian you may pray with confidence that God will answer those prayers. After you have prayed for something, work to make it happen! There is no reason to believe that God will honor prayers that are offered without a willingness on your part to be an instrument in answering those prayers. Pray that God will teach you something valuable from every major business and career experience.

MAKING A CAREER CHANGE?

Many people stay in careers chosen early in life. Some of these people later regret having "stuck it out" in a career that brought less satisfaction than expected when it was chosen. It seems unrealistic to stick with an unsatisfactory career decision made at the unripe age of twenty. More and more American business and professional people are open to career changes at mid-life than ever before.

Consider the following concerns if you have been contemplating a job or career change:

1. Have you achieved enough in your current career? Have you known what it is like to be successful and effective in your current job or career so that you can make an informed decision? Perhaps only by achieving full potential at a job are we fully informed about the values and satisfaction level of that job.

2. Is your frustration about your current job or career a temporary, situational experience or is it deep-seated? All careers have their "slow periods" and frustrating moments that seem to last too long. If your dissatisfaction is deeply rooted, if you feel disillusionment and despair, perhaps it's truly time to consider a change in career direction.

3. Can you distinguish personality issues from job issues? Internal unhappiness and emotional struggles are often blamed on a job, career, or marriage. People sometimes think that a change in external circumstances can make them happy and fulfilled. A chronic complainer, cynic, or pessimist will retain those traits in any relationship. To such a person, no job or career will be good enough. If you are

unhappy on the job or in any major relationship, take a close look at the man or woman in the mirror!

4. Can you serve God more effectively in another career? The dedicated Christian may find dissatisfaction with a job or career that provides little opportunity to impact the hearts and lives of other people. What a noble decision to leave a more lucrative job or career and pursue another because of enhanced opportunities for spiritual growth and servant leadership!

In conclusion, the counsel of an ancient sage to his son seems appropriate in your own venture into the real world:

> Trust in the Lord with all your heart and lean not on your own understanding; in all your ways acknowledge him, and he will make your paths straight. Do not be wise in your own eyes, fear the Lord and shun evil. This will bring health to your body and nourishment to your bones. (Prov. 3:5–8)

QUESTIONS FOR GROUP DISCUSSION
AND PERSONAL REFLECTION

1. What was your first salaried job away from home? What did you earn? What did you learn from that job that you have carried to other jobs?

2. One could argue theologically that God plans everything (e.g., Leaves and snowflakes are unique. God gave special missions to Abraham, Moses, David, John the Baptist, Jesus [cf., John 17:4], Saul, and others). How specific is our calling from God? Does God call all men and women to do something in this world or does he call only select individuals? Is God's calling general, such as a call to accept his grace and live and think as his Son demonstrated, or is the call specific, such as a call to be a physician, an attorney, a teacher, or a clerk? If God calls us to specific vocations, how can we know his call?

3. Do you think that God values our work even when it has no eternal value? Do we not often ask about the career choices of ourselves and others: "Will the work last?" "Does what you are achieving 'really count' for eternity? Will this work be to "the glory of God"?

4. In Philippians, Paul takes stock of his life. Facing the prospect of execution, he had to wrestle with what mattered most in his life. His conclusion: Christ (Phil. 1:21). With his readers he rehearsed his achievements—the ones that mattered eternally and the ones which mattered only temporarily (Phil. 3:7–14). In light of Paul's inspired reflections of his life, consider these important questions in your own life and thinking: (a) How do you define success in life? (b) What have you sacrificed in order to reach that success? (c) How have your priorities and loyalties changed over time? (d) In what ways are God and his purposes being served by the life you are pursuing?

5. Can we assume that those careers which promise the highest pay are at the same time those careers that best serve our neighbor?

6. Of all the characters in the Bible, which one would you propose as having the most interesting career? We might exclude Jesus from consideration, since his role as God's divine

Son was unique and his death accomplished what no other person's death could accomplish. One might consider Moses, the great emancipator and lawgiver of the Old Testament era. Moses actually pursued three careers during three distinct periods of his life. First, having been raised in Pharaoh's palace, he worked as an Egyptian administrator; that career ended when he fled for his life after killing an Egyptian who was abusing a Hebrew brother. Moses' second career was much more stress free—he was a shepherd in western Arabia. In this secure routine he must have done much reflection on his heritage, but seemed content to raise his family and die peacefully away from his national ties. And then, after forty years, Moses was called to return to Egypt in a totally different role— emancipator of his people. His new career was one of political leader, negotiator, reformer, and lawgiver. His greatest challenge was in the third trimester of his life.

Moses "led three lives." Were these three careers of Moses totally unrelated? Can you think of a New Testament character who had a career just as challenging and fascinating as Moses?

Most people face challenge and crisis earlier in life rather than in years nearest retirement. Do you know people who, like Moses, faced their greatest career challenges later in life?

7. What do you think are the toughest jobs in our society? What are the easiest jobs?

8. Do you feel that there are some salaried jobs which are "beneath your dignity"? Apart from jobs which are illegal (e.g., operating gambling establishment where prohibited by law) or immoral (e.g., pimping for prostitution), what are some jobs you would not do under any circumstances?

9. Do you know people who seem to spend more time and more creative energy in getting out of work rather than simply working?

10. Are there some jobs which are insignificant? What about jobs which manufacture, distribute, and/or sell products which are frivolous, trivial, or possibly dangerous when used in excess?

11. Do you feel challenged by your current job? Does it utilize all of your skills? Does your work offer intrinsic rewards or do you find yourself just waiting for the weekend?

12. Have you ever been unemployed? What was the impact of unemployment on you financially? emotionally?

13. Do you see the massive welfare rolls of modern America as indication that large numbers of people are attempting to avoid work?

14. Can fun and play ever become a livelihood? What about professional athletes? actors? musicians? Should you seek a job that is "fun"?

15. The academy award-winning movie of the mid-1980s, *Chariots of Fire,* touches on the theme of vocation through the story of the 1924 Olympics. Track star and missionary Eric Liddell made the tough decision to delay his missionary trip until after the Olympics, offering this inspiring explanation: "I believe that God made me for a purpose, for China. But he also made me fast and when I run I feel his pleasure."

Have you ever felt "God's pleasure" when you have pursued a task or an assignment well or when you have achieved something important? When do you think God takes pleasure in your work?

16. Is retirement something you look forward to or do you consider retirement a form of death?

17. Is there any spiritual significance to choosing a big company over a small one?

18. Many corporations and public agencies prepare mission statements which declare what they are "about." Decisions and policies which get made are first examined in light of that mission statement. Try writing a mission statement for your life. You may feel that it is too early in your life to write such a statement. However, a philosophy of life is not something we arrive at once and for all in the first year of adult life. The development of a philosophy of life and a sense of mission continues for as long as we live. As long as we remain curious, as long as we study God's word, as long as we remain reflective on our life experiences and open to new learning, we can revise and rebuild our conceptions of the world. Our work can have a particular meaning for us when we are adolescent, another meaning during adulthood, and still another meaning as we reach old age.

Write a mission statement for this point in your life. This mission statement can be only one sentence or it could be a brief paragraph. Focus on (a) the principles and values on which you base your life; (b) what you hope to be (character); (c) what you hope to achieve (contributions and accomplishments). Your personal mission statement will reflect your uniqueness at this point in your life.

Chapter 4

How Shall We Live?
Some Thoughts on Christianity and Lifestyle

What about greed? Is that a virtue? No. Capitalism is wicked because it fosters greed, materialism, consumerism . . . Are material things evil in themselves? Oh, no. We should be sensitive to material pleasures, but "small is beautiful." We should desire and get and use just what we naturally and truly need, not what the ad-men tell us and sell us. If we all practiced Thoreau's or Buddha's detachment from greed, our present economy would soon collapse. Well then, let it. Let us make a new one, where only natural needs are satisfied. A noneconomist economy, where people make and use what they truly need. Material things are our servants, not our masters; our horses, not our riders . . . It's a good world, but we should treat it as a work of art, raw material for beauty, not conquest.

Peter Kreeft

As a society becomes increasingly affluent, wants are increasingly created by the process by which they are satisfied. This may operate passively. Increase in consumption . . . act by suggestion or emulation to create wants. Or producers may proceed actively to create wants through advertising and salesmanship. Wants thus come to depend on output.

John Kenneth Galbraith

In an Age of Hunger most Christians (regardless of theological labels) will be severely tempted to succumb to the liberal heresy of following current cultural and societal values rather than biblical truth. Society will offer demoniacally convincing justification for enjoying our affluence and forgetting about a billion hungry neighbors. But if the Christ of Scripture is our Lord, then we will refuse to be squeezed into the mold of our affluent, sinful culture. In an Age of Hunger Christians of necessity must be radical nonconformists. But nonconformity is painful. Only if we are thoroughly grounded in the scriptural view of possession, wealth and poverty will we be capable of living an obedient lifestyle.

Ronald J. Sider

AMERICA IS BECOMING A HOUSE DIVIDED! A STRIKING STATEMENT, to be sure. When that observation was first made by an American, the observer was Abraham Lincoln and his strong moral concern was the practice of slavery within our national boundaries.

Today the statement is made about the income gap between rich and poor Americans. The ties that bind—military service or even watching network TV—are receding into the past. In metropolitan areas throughout the United States, residential patterns are formalizing the drift. The sense of community is being lost.

This is a drama without villains. Most people seek only a better life for themselves. Most families seek the best living conditions attainable.

What have been the results of individual choices? In 1950 there were fewer than one million individuals nationwide with annual incomes, in today's dollars, of one-hundred thousand dollars or more. Today, there are almost six million. For millions of others there is the nitty gritty reality of poverty. Many attempt to flee the large cities in order to find a higher standard of living and safer lifestyle in the suburbs.

Economists conclude that the gap between rich and poor is greater in the United States than any other nation with the possible exception of Russia. Only Great Britain and Sweden have seen as much growth as the United States in overall inequality since 1980. Making comparisons between nations is difficult due to differences in what is left after taxes and how much quality of life is impacted by government services.

Quite obviously, there is a wide disparity between the United States' wealth and the dire poverty of other parts of the world, especially in "third world" or "underdeveloped" nations. American citizens constitute approximately 6 percent of the world's population but consume 30 percent of the world's energy. As the fourth largest nation in the population, the average American consumes more of the earth's resources than an average citizen of any of the other "big ten" nations with more than one-hundred million people. The more goods we produce, the more energy we burn, the more agricultural products we grow, the more pollution we create. The use of the automobile alone in the United States is a major factor in consumerist disparity with other nations of the world.

One does not need the insight of a brilliant philosopher to find prime evidence of materialist values in our society, especially including even the Christian church. One need only note the magnificence of the houses in which we live and the houses in which we worship. For that matter, visit the parking lot on a Sunday morning of your nearest suburban church. Quite possibly, one might find a number of late-model cars bearing the name Lincoln, Cadillac, BMW, Mercedes, or Lexus—perhaps even more luxury cars than Chevy Metros, Toyota Tercels, and Honda Civics. Truth is, these luxury cars, with worth within the thirty-five thousand to sixty-five thousand dollar range, cost in excess of the annual salary of many members of the same church and certainly in excess of multiple millions of people around the world.

"By any objective criterion, the 6 percent of the world's people who live in the United States are an incredibly rich aristocracy living among a vast, hungry proletariat," writes Ron Sider in his stirring volume *Rich Christians in an Age of Hunger.* "Surely one of the most astounding things, therefore, about this affluent minority is that we honestly think we barely have enough to survive in modest comfort." The real question is: How much economic growth with ever more production and consumption among developed nations can the world accommodate? Is greed our biggest "gross national product"? Are radical measures called for to reduce dramatically the American standard of living?

THE ROLE OF ADVERTISING

And what about the role of advertising in the American society? Is not the pervasive advertising we hear and see on our air waves, through cable lines, in print media, and, seemingly in every public place (including restroom walls) the constant and seductive tool of America's own brand of hedonism and materialism? Luxuries are renamed necessities by advertising.

It is estimated that the average American teenager has heard or watched 350,000 advertisements by the time he/she leaves high school and that more money is spent on advertising than on all our public institutions of higher education. Advertising for new homes convinces us that our adequate residences are shabby cottages by comparison. Advertising for new automobiles convinces us that we are "behind times" with a model that is four or five years old. Advertising and other hype let us know when our computers and other electronic equipment need to be updated.

The most devastating role of advertising in affluent societies is its obvious message that material possessions and personal products will bring us happiness and fulfillment in life. The right automobile will bring us the thrill of speed and the satisfaction of comfort. The right toothpaste and deodorant will bring us security in tense situations. The right diamond will bring us love. The right grooming and perfuming products will enhance our sex appeal. Choosing the right gifts to give at Christmas or on other special occasions will bring us respect. The latest machines and gadgets evoke the envy of our neighbors, and on and on. This basic message—that our deepest needs and longings can be met by goods and services—is inextricably bound to society's commitment to a growth economy and ever-rising standard of living. (More about advertising from another perspective is in chapter 10.)

BIBLICAL RESOURCES FOR A SIMPLER, MORE COMPASSIONATE LIFESTYLE

In both the Old and New Testaments the issues of wealth, poverty, and economic justice are central. God made abundantly clear his charges for his special people as to their attitude toward wealth and their attitude toward fellow citizens with major human needs. There is more Scripture in the Bible on money and possessions than on heaven and hell. Our money and our material possessions are not simply private matters—they raise deeply spiritual issues at the core of human experience and our attitude and practice regarding them reveal more about one's spiritual life than any other barometer.

Year of the Jubilee

In the covenant relationship Yahweh established with the Israelites, there was deep concern about the misuse of power and wealth in the oppression and exploitation of the poor and needy. Yahweh wanted his people to know that the earth and its resources were his and they were but stewards of these resources. To cite one example, the Year of the Jubilee was one of the most radical notions in all divine history (Lev. 25). Each fifty years, Yahweh commanded, all land was to return to the original owners—without compensation! In an agricultural society, land was capital. Some people must relinquish their capital because of poor health, hardship, misfortune, or physical handicap, yet such disadvantages were not to create greater poverty. Every half century this divine law would equalize land ownership and redistribute the wealth. Let's not raise the knotty issue of the practical ways in which this command was carried out (yes, a lot can happen in fifty years), but simply acknowledge the premise underlying the law of Jubilee: Yahweh owns everything and the land cannot be sold permanently because Yahweh owns it.

The Sabbatical Year

The Sabbatical Year provides another illustration of divine passion for social and economic justice. Every seven years the land was to lie fallow (Exod. 23:10–11; Lev. 25:2–7), and in that seventh year the poor were free to gather whatever vegetation grows spontaneously in the fields and vineyards. Hebrew slaves were scheduled to receive their freedom in the Sabbatical Year (Deut. 15:12–18). Some of the Hebrews were so poverty stricken that they sold themselves into slavery, but this yoke, Yahweh decreed, would not be permanent. Every seven years all debts were to be cancelled, and Yahweh warned against withholding a loan to a poor man because it was the sixth year and a late loan constituted a high risk of loss (Deut. 15:9–10). In all its provisions, the Sabbatical Year warred against any widening gap between the rich and the poor in ancient Hebrew society, as well as provided compassion to the less fortunate.

Tithe

The Israelites were commanded to donate one-tenth of all farm produce, whether animal, grain, or wine, to be set aside as a tithe. Out of this tithe the sojourner, the stranger, the orphan, and the widow were to be fed and housed (Deut. 14:28–29; 26:12–15; and other passages). The law of gleaning was established for preventing abject poverty from engrossing fellow Israelites. Surely all Bible students know the heart-tugging story of the poor widow Ruth, how she and her mother-in-law were able to survive on gleaning, and how she caught the observant eye of her new man (Boaz) while in the field gleaning.

In the New Testament, the teaching on money, wealth, and earthly possessions is intensified. Jesus easily drew his oral messages from the warnings of the prophets about the dangers and distortions of personal wealth and the neglect of the poor. Jesus taught that the love of mammon (money) is completely incompatible with discipleship within the kingdom of God; he did not say "You *should* not serve God and mammon," but "You *cannot* serve God and mammon" (Matt. 6:24). He once issued a warning: "Woe to you that are rich" (Luke 6:24). He warned listeners in his audience not to lay up treasures for themselves on earth amidst corrosive elements, but to "lay up treasures in heaven" (Matt. 6:19–21), and he urged his closest disciples to renounce all their earthly possessions (Luke 14:33). He told the story of a wealthy farmer whose life was abruptly ended by divine intervention because he mistakenly believed he could provide for spiritual needs by hoarding his bounty and seeking early, hedonistic retirement (Luke 12:13–21). He invited a rich, young man to sell his goods and give to the poor and join a community of loving discipleship (Matt. 19:16–24). Jesus' apostles shared a common purse (John 12:6), and Judas administered the common fund, buying provisions or giving to the poor at Jesus' direction (John 13:29).

Do you know the most sobering aspect of these radical teachings? Might it be that Jesus declared this doctrine to men and women living in a simple, agrarian society? Now what would Jesus say to prosperous Americans—people with their savings accounts, investment portfolios, multiple vehicles for transportation and leisure, modern appliances for better living in the most affluent nation of all human history— fleshing out their discipleship on the verge of the twenty-first century? How would Jesus live if he had come to modern America rather than to ancient Palestine? Would he drive a BMW 535i? Would he lease a condominium along the beach? Would he wear a Hart Shaffner Marx suit? Would he get his hair styled by a professional stylist? Would he take a European vacation? Would he grill steaks? Would he own a computer? Would he surf the net? Would he eat at fancy restaurants? Would he drink socially? Would he purchase a membership in the country club, perhaps also buying golf lessons from a pro? Would he fly to New York to see a Broadway show? Would Jesus subscribe to a cable service? On and on we could go. Most likely, some of these questions make us highly uncomfortable.

The new community that Jesus established reaffirmed the teaching of the prophets and Jesus in terms of sharing and compassion. The economic sharing of the first church in Jerusalem was widespread, with the disciples being "of one heart and soul" and not laying claim to personal possessions but having "everything in common" (Acts 4:32). When any brother or sister was in need, the early disciples shared; physical needs in the early community of believers was eliminated (Acts 4:34–35). This example of total economic sharing has presented a major enigma to Restorationist churches who claim their major mission is to restore in tact the simple faith and practice of the New Testament Christians. One mitigating consideration is that the earliest church did not demand absolute economic equality nor did it abolish private property (see Acts 5:4); sharing was voluntary, not mandatory.

The New Testament provides other examples of a depth level of sharing and caring which impacted early Christian economic life. The Jerusalem church responded to a financial need experienced by Hellenist (Greek-speaking Jews) widows by appointing an ad hoc committee to disburse funds for this needy minority group (Acts 6). By mid-century the early Christians in Judea faced financial difficulty, the main causes being famine and food scarcity. The apostle Paul devoted a great deal of time to raising money for the Jewish Christians' survival during days of famine. In his plea to Gentile churches to aid Jewish believers, he expanded the concept of intrachurch assistance (within one local congregation) into interchurch fellowship (sharing) among several of the scattered congregations of disciples. The collection that Paul campaigned for (mentioned in 1 Cor.16:1–4) became the major subject for some of the most powerful writing in the New Testament on stewardship (see 2 Cor. 7–9). Paul even risked his own life while traveling amidst the Gentile churches to gather the collection, but he believed the contribution of Gentile funds for Jewish Christians was not simply a matter of meeting human need—it was a symbol of the fellowship *(koinonia)* that Christ has with all believers and that one ethnic group of Christians shares with another ethnic group of Christians. Put simply, koinonia with Christ inevitably includes koinonia with all members of the body of Christ.

What relevance does all this instruction and these examples have for Christians living in the United States today? Surely we can conclude that being a Christian transforms our relationships socially, but does not conversion also transform attitudes toward our material possessions and our economic relationships? How does such transformation impact our practices of caring and sharing in concrete ways? Surely we need not slavishly and legalistically imitate every detail of the practice of the primitive church in that hot, dry agrarian society into which our Lord came. At the other extreme, surely we must not totally discount the radical nature of Jesus' bold declarations about wealth and poverty or his powerful example of renouncing worldly values and his caring about others; nor can we ignore the earliest disciples' implementing what both the Old Testament prophets and Jesus commanded.

Is there a "happy medium" between these extremes? And what is the relevance of biblical doctrine and narrative on the issues of money, wealth, and stewardship? Finding answers is tough enough. Having the grit and determination to implement needed changes in our attitudes and actions is the greater challenge.

QUESTIONS FOR GROUP DISCUSSION AND PERSONAL REFLECTION

1. Does the Bible sanction or condemn private property? Did Jesus consider ownership of property and money to be legitimate?
2. Does Scripture inform us on what our attitude toward private property should be? Consult Ps. 24:1; 50:12; Deut. 26:10; Exod. 19:5; Job 41:11. What might we learn from Yahweh's command for a the Year of the Jubilee (Lev. 25:23; Deut. 10:14)?
3. What did Jesus instruct his followers about their attitude toward material possessions? Consult Luke 12:22–31; 2 Cor. 9:8–11.
4. What is mammon (Matt. 6:24)? Does it make sense that we cannot serve God and mammon?
5. The usage of the word "covetousness" (pleonexia) occurs nineteen times in the New Testament. What is covetousness and what is so wrong with it?
6. When we speak of lifestyle and social advantages, it might be helpful to distinguish between personal sins and institutional or structural evil. The latter is sometimes called "systemic evil." Christians sometimes restrict the study of ethics to personal sins, such as sexual immorality or deliberate falsehood. Should Christian moral thought include

consideration of structural evil? Provide illustrations of institutional evil. How does it relate to understanding a Christian critique of a society's lifestyle?

7. Income inequality means some people make a lot more money than other people. Is there something morally wrong or politically inexpedient with that?

8. Throughout all history there have been poor people and there have been wealthy people. Jesus declared that there would always be poor people around. The Bible tells stories of wealthy people such as Abraham and Solomon, to name two, as well as about poor people. Should Christians give the slightest concern about who is rich and who is poor in this nation?

9. Define "rich" and define "poor." Are there objective standards for these definitions?

10. Do you think that income inequality is affected by the breakdown of the family or a change in family size?

11. Income inequality measures only income. Given that people have many more conveniences than people of earlier generations, is just measuring income still valid?

12. Don't the advantages of the American lifestyle outweigh the disadvantages? Isn't it important to keep the American economy healthy and its people employed by economic growth and the increase in the gross national product? Is there any moral purpose or advantage in living through another economic depression? Does economic depression create great character traits?

13. Americans should feel blessed by God to live in such a land of material wealth and prosperity, but should they feel guilty that others are not so fortunate? And what if Americans have far more cars per capita than any other nation? The operation of millions and millions of cars in this country is costly, to be sure, but the cost in terms of oil, manufacturing, highway construction, deaths on the highway and so forth is only one side of the coin. How about the advantages of speed and comfort in private transportation? What about all the jobs that the manufacture, sales, and maintenance of these automobiles provide for millions of fellow Americans? What about all the pleasure and hobbies associated with automobiles?

14. Many Christians seem to exhibit a schizophrenic attitude toward money and wealth. There is no doubt that money is necessary as a medium of exchange in meeting personal and family needs; one could not live in this society without having at least some cash. On the other hand, there are numerous Scriptures warning godly people about money, mammon, and wealth. We are taught about the relative ease of the camel passing through the proverbial needle's eye compared to the immense difficulty of the wealthy person's passage into the heavenly portals (Luke 18:25). We are admonished to give to the poor.

    Jesus, standing in the succession of the prophets who emphasized the danger of wealthy people exploiting the poor, offered clear indictment of greed, acquisitiveness, and putting one's trust in material rather than spiritual goods (cf., Matt. 6:24; Luke 12:15–21). As noted in the text of this chapter, Jesus was forthright on the perils of riches (Matt. 19:23). Yet this does not mean he thought lightly of the material foundations of life, evidenced by a model prayer which included the petition to the Father "Give us this day our daily bread."

Preachers admonish us to give sacrificially. With pain, no less. Furthermore, we know the rich farmer and the rich man at whose doorstep sat poor ole Lazarus will not be faring well come judgment time. Is God biased toward the poor? Some theologians have said "yes." Many Christians face guilt when they reconcile their push for more profits and a higher standard of living with the old teaching that this earth is not their home and that they are supposed to lay up their treasures in heaven where moth and rust do not corrupt. And rare indeed are the Christians who pay any serious attention to Jesus' instruction to demonstrate a bias toward the poor and indigent when planning dinner invitations (Luke 14:12–14; see Heb. 13:1–3).

How do we resolve all of this? Consider the following questions, some of which touch on themes already discussed in this chapter:

    a. Is money inherently evil? If not, is money inherently powerful over the lives of people who begin to accumulate it?

    b. Is it immoral to be extremely wealthy? May Christians accumulate much wealth and material holdings?

    c. Can money become an idol and then assume sinister control over people who make it an idol?

    d. At what point does one draw a line between a reasonable lifestyle or reasonable comfort and security on the one hand and morally unjustifiable affluence and luxury on the other hand?

    e. Is it possible for individual Christians to meet human obligations (e.g., supporting worthy causes or caring for aged parents) without having certain financial resources?

    f. How literally should we take Jesus' instruction in Luke 6:30 about giving to everyone who begs something from us? If we give away virtually everything that we have and own to help care for the poor and indigent, will God take care of us?

    g. What kind of financial lifestyle is appropriate for Christians in the United States?

    h. How much may a person exploit tax loopholes, class advantage, and good connections (e.g., insider information) to accumulate wealth and property?

15. Connecting the above questions is a statement made by author and professor Ron Sider in a Nashville lecture appearance, February 1998: "If you're not helping the poor, then you're defying Jesus just as surely as you would be by commiting adultery. . . . I want people to know two things: Caring for the poor is not optional for followers of Jesus. And individual Christians are not powerless in the face of world hunger" (*Tennessean,* 22 Feb. 1998). Do you agree with Professor Sider?

16. What do you think of the "lifeboat ethic," which contends that rich nations of the world are lifeboats that will survive only if they refuse to waste their limited resources on the hungry masses swimming in surrounding waters and begging to get in the lifeboat. Furthermore, since poor countries "irresponsibly" permit unchecked population growth among their peoples, affluent nations should not send food or other aid to the poor nations during a time of famine or other crisis. Increased aid in the way of food and medicine only postpones the day of reckoning and increases the number of people who will die of starvation.

What do you think of this logic? Does sending food and medicine simply enable these nations to proliferate in population, thus increasing the burden in the lifeboat for the next generation? Can the "lifeboat ethic" be harmonized with the Christian ethic that calls for compassion and mercy? Can poor countries cut population growth rapidly? Is the affluence of wealthy nations any factor in the poverty of other nations?

17. Isn't advertising criticized a little unfairly in this chapter? After all, are there not ads which appeal to the best character traits in people? Aren't many ads so harmlessly entertaining? Besides, advertisements provide consumer education to people who need to know what products and services are available. Don't most people pretty much ignore ads that provide no consumer education or have no entertainment value? The worst abuses of advertising can be controlled by watchdog agencies, publications such as *Consumer Reports,* and, as a last resort, our civil courts. Advertising enables business people and manufacturers to present their products and services to the public. Is there any valid reason to believe that advertising contributes to the loss of community or to a moral decline in this nation?

18. Do you believe that capitalism is compatible with the ideals and values of Christianity? Doesn't capitalism give a predominant place to greed, selfishness, and other non-Christian values? Does it not encourage overconsumption, as fueled by advertising? Does it not increase poverty and the misery of the poor? Hasn't the fruit of capitalism in the United States been slavery, exploitation of child labor, dehumanizingly long hours and unsafe working conditions, low wages, periodic times of recession with much unemployment, shoddy and dangerous products, and exploitation of natural resources? Have these evils existed and, if so, what system or what party is responsible for their presence? Would socialism or communism be more compassionate?

19. Capitalism gets a bad rap in the previous question. To balance the scales, cite what you believe are the positive merits to a capitalist economy.

20. Bill Moyers, a native Texas Baptist, broadcaster, and former aid to President Lyndon Johnson, visited Nashville, Tennessee, in November 1996 to promote a new television series on Genesis. While in Nashville, Moyers suggested that a deep contradiction existed at the heart of America—deeply religious, deeply secular—drives the national spiritual style.

"The richer and more materialistic we get, the more we perhaps realize that the promises of capitalism exact a price on family and community, and many go to church to overcome that tendentiousness in our lives," Moyers declared.

Do you agree with Moyers's assessment of the American society—that we are both highly religious and highly secular? Does materialism exact a price on our family and community life?

21. What about the American cultural values that we teach by the salaries we give? Is it fair that a dedicated school teacher with a master's degree be paid $27,500 per school year and an uneducated, profane "rap artist" receives several hundred thousand dollars for a few recordings and live performances? Should a Cecil Fielder be paid seven to eight million dollars for being a designated hitter in the New York Yankees baseball line-up for one year, or an emotionally erratic outfielder named Albert Belle be paid fifty-five million

dollars by the Chicago White Sox for six years, and the pulpit minister of a large congregation receive fifty thousand dollars per year for his services? Should Michael Jordan be paid thirty million a year to play basketball for the Chicago Bulls (not to mention millions more for endorsements for Nike and other corporations) and an eligibility counselor for human services only receive twenty-five thousand a year? What actually is fair? Who determines how different professions and occupations get reimbursed?

22. Does Jesus actually teach that it is difficult for a wealthy person to go to heaven (see Matt. 19:24)? Does this teaching make sense to you? Don't you know many wealthy people who are quite generous?

23. Are poor people automatically closer to God and God's will? Is there a special place in God's heart for poor people?

24. Is there a mandate in Scripture for the redistribution of wealth and real estate? What about the Year of Jubilee (see Lev. 25:14–17)? Could not Christians engage in a limited form of income redistribution by giving generously to those in need?

25. There are commandments against coveting and loving the world (Exod. 20:17; 1 John 2:15–16). One Christian author has written: "A poor person who turns to government to seize the possessions of his richer neighbors, no less than a wealthy man who devotes his life to making money in the marketplace, has fallen in love with the world." Do you agree?

26. Would you favor a legal "cap" or "ceiling" on how much a person could earn in one year's time? If, for example, one placed that ceiling at one million dollars, could one contend that a debt-free man had any need to earn more than a million dollars in one year?

27. Mohandas K. Gandhi, the spiritual and political leader of India's freedom struggle, warned against what he called "the seven deadly sins." They were "politics without principle, wealth without work, commerce without morality, pleasure without conscience, education without character, science without humanity, and worship without sacrifice." Clearly, Gandhi's maxims speak to the heart of any moral and political crisis which may exist in the United States today. How many sins have our corporations and other business organizations and their executives committed in the names of "bottom line" and business expediency?

28. The abuse of the consumerist ethic has led to a rising number of individuals declaring bankruptcy. Under federal bankruptcy laws, debtors can seek a wipeout of their debt or get help in meeting creditors' demands by filing with the courts, which appoint a trustee to arrange payments.

    Several states were headed for records based on latest estimates of bankruptcy filings nationwide. Through the twelve months ending in September 1997, more than 1.37 million bankruptcy cases were filed nationwide, up 23 percent from the year earlier (*Nashville Banner,* 2 Jan. 1998). Officials say the high rate of filings is being driven by easy access to and misuse of credit cards, typical perceptions about bankruptcy, and social factors such as divorces and high medical costs. Chapter 7 bankruptcies are easier to file because no repayment plan is required and debtors often can get full relief from their debt because of an inability to pay (chapter 13 involves a repayment plan).

Do you think that most cases of heavy personal and family indebtedness is because people desire to maintain a lifestyle which they truly cannot afford? Is the credit-card system a blessing or a curse in American cultural life? Do you think it is morally proper to declare a person free from repayment of debts he/she does not seem to be able to manage?

29. Consider charitable giving or contributions to a local church. Is not some of the most genuine generosity often displayed by those who have the least to give? Consider the poor widow that Jesus praised for having given two of the least valuable coins to the temple treasury (Mark. 12:41f). Or consider the example of the impoverished Macedonian Christians, praised by the apostle Paul for having given spontaneously and generously to the collection on behalf of Judean Christians impacted by famine (2 Cor. 8:1–5). How does one account for this paradox of generosity from poor people? Are Jesus and Paul teaching that there is a difference between the quality of a gift and the quantity of a gift?

30. In response to biblical teaching, some have proposed that American Christians live as simply as possible. Scaling down a lifestyle might mean different things to different people and would be dependent on the cost of living in the region in which one lives. Rae and Wong, in *Beyond Integrity* (p. 224), report one proposal: a family sets a goal of living on approximately twenty thousand dollars per year and give the remainder of income away to the church and charitable causes.

Would this proposal be workable? Would it enable you to walk more faithfully with Christ? What would you have to give up to do it? Would you be willing to do it?

Chapter 5

Is American Business Ethical?
Yes and No!

Don't look to corporate America for moral leadership. Too many chief executives share the ethics of a welfare cheat. The welfare cheat breaks the law to chisel the government. Well, many a CEO twists company rules to raise his pay—and bilk the company. Welfare cheats probably need the money and grasp their wrongdoing. The CEOs don't need the money and are oblivious to their wrongdoing. Who's more honest?

Robert J. Samuelson

A business cannot be ethical or unethical. Only people are ethical or unethical. Therefore, a business's practices reflect the ethics of the people who manage it.

William J. Ransom

Managing only for profit is like playing tennis with your eye on the scoreboard and not on the ball . . . Nice guys may appear to finish last, but usually they're running in a different race.

Kenneth Blanchard and
Norman Vincent Peale

LET'S CONSIDER THE DEBATE OVER THE ETHICS OF AMERICAN business as currently practiced.

PROPOSITION ONE: AMERICAN BUSINESS IS ETHICAL!

The Image of the Unethical Businessman Is Based on Stereotypes

Businessmen have always had bad press in this country. Business is usually depicted as shady dealings between two dishonest, conniving parties. Think of any movies that have dealt with business, movies such as "Wall Street," "The Pelican Brief," "Barbarians at the Gate," or "Working Girl," to name only four. Don't these movies always depict at least some major roles in the plot development as nonprincipled, manipulative business operators?

The businessman has rarely been treated with accuracy and fairness in television or movies, two media which exert strong influence on the popular mind. How many movies or programs have you seen that depicted business persons as loving, caring individuals who are devoted to their family and their church? Or who become moral heroes? Or who donate large sums to charity or to worthwhile civic projects? Or who pursue cultural and educational goals as well as profit margins? Or who would choose fidelity to a mate rather than a secret rendezvous with a lover?

The reason for this unfairness, in part at least, is that the drama and fiction written for production is the product of artists who have little experience in the workaday business world. The lifestyle and values of artists in general places them at odds with business people who make deals and work for profits. How can we expect them to entertain a fair and positive view toward business life?

There is a Long-standing but Unfair Bias against Businessmen

The stereotypes of businessmen that people see in the entertainment media are merely symptomatic of a much deeper bias against business professionals. Such a bias is rooted in great historical documents.

The Greek philosophers believed that the truly happy life came in terms of one's intellect, especially dialectic with eager students and quiet contemplation. Jesus himself seemed to view wealthy people with great suspicion, telling one to sell all his possessions and give to the poor and follow him and then warning all his disciples about the immense difficulty of a rich man entering heaven. In general, the Bible seems to oppose the loaning of money for the price of fair interest. And Karl Marx, whose political and economic doctrines fueled a communist revolution, contended that under capitalism, the workers are exploited by unscrupulous bosses and factory owners who reap obscene profits by the sweat of others' brows. Students of American history know about the Rockefellers, the Vanderbilts, the Carnegies, the Mellons, and other wealthy industrialists who became obscenely rich under a laissez-faire system.

True enough, business organizations are concerned with profit. And true enough again, business corporations can seem to be impersonal because they exist separately from the people associated with them. However, one cannot feature a world that operates smoothly without business people and business corporations. We cannot all be islands with no connection to anyone else or any group. Furthermore, while a corporation is not something that can be seen or touched, it does have prescribed rights and legal obligations within the community it serves. Like you or me, a business organization may enter into contracts and may sue or be sued in courts of law. Both individuals and organizations are subject to the laws of the land. If business affairs, capitalization, and all normal transactions that go with the business world are evils, then they are surely necessary evils.

Business People Need No More Regulation than Any Other Profession

If you examine the ledger of sins of which business people are guilty you will discover that, alas, these are the same sins that are committed by people in all other walks of life. There's a theological reason for this—the Bible tells us that every man and woman is a sinner. All of us break either the letter or the spirit of some of the Ten Commandments. Folks who run corporations, own businesses, and invest money have no more monopoly on sin than do folks who teach school, practice law or medicine, or repair automobiles. And, quite possibly, a thoroughly dishonest man could last longer in preaching and teaching than he could in managing a business.

We need to stop thinking of the quest for profit as evil. Profit in the form of money is the lifeblood of our capitalist system. Sure, there are businessmen who seem to have an insatiable appetite for more and more money, but all of us have economic self-interests. There are people outside the field of business who have an insatiable appetite for power or for control of others or sex or food. What's worse?

The Free-market System Ultimately Brings a Sense of Justice and Fairness to All Business People

Most of us understand how the free-market system works. Each of us is free to provide a service or manufacture a product and offer it to the public at a price the producer deems to be fair. Then, each producer will be judged by his/her peers. Our goods and services will be evaluated by consumers who will meet our price if they feel that, given all the other factors (their need, their ability to pay, the nature of competing goods and services, etc.), our offerings make a "good buy." This is the ultimate judgment on the value of the fruit of our labor.

Is not the general public at times uninformed, biased, ignorant on certain subjects, and easily swayed by advertising? The answer is yes. But that's the way the system works for all business people. Do we have a product or service that other people need or want? If the answer is yes, these consumers will reward us handsomely and render us successful as a business person. If the answer is no, it matters not that we have labored long and hard over a product that we dearly adore. The customer renders a verdict. The playing field is level. The rules of the game are fair. The customer calls the shots.

Consider how the free-market system keeps business people on their toes. Free competition, said Adam Smith in his classic *Wealth of Nations* (1776), is the regulator that keeps a society from degenerating into a mob of ruthless profiteers. When all individuals have equal access to raw material and markets, all of us are free to pursue our own interests. As we pursue our own interests, however, we run smack into others similarly motivated. If any of us allow blind self-interest to run unrestrained, we will quickly find ourselves beaten out by a competitor who, let's say, builds a better mouse trap, charges less, or provides a better service. Free competition and the open market are the best regulators of individual economic activity.

Corporations Realize That Responsibility Goes Hand-in-hand with Power and That They Owe Something Back to Society

Corporations now realize that they do not exist in a vacuum. They exist in a society and they cannot be oblivious to the ills of society. Corporate leaders know that society faces an array of social problems. There are major changes in the workforce. There are increasing number of married couples where both spouses work, for example. The stresses of double-income marriages and raising a family certainly impact a business; therefore, many companies are providing assistance in child care. Also, the American economy is experiencing a shift from manufacturing to service industries; therefore, some companies have provided for counsel and re-training of employees for new jobs.

The largest American corporations have become multinational in operation, and they take in more money than governments of most countries have to spend. These corporations are beginning to realize they owe something in return to a society that gives them the freedom to function.

Business Corporations Know That Social Responsibility Is in Their Best Interests; Therefore They Are Increasingly Becoming More Socially Responsible

Corporations and their shareholders now realize that they have common interests with the remainder of society. They know that we're all in this thing together. Some critics of business have contended that business people don't care about poverty, but, truth is, they know if poverty increases consumers will not have the revenue to purchase goods and services. Businesses and corporations have to be as concerned about crime as the rest of us. Corporate leaders know that if they don't treat their employees or the consumers fairly, they risk labor organization and strife, consumer boycott, and additional governmental regulations and red tape. No business wants any more of that.

PROPOSITION TWO: AMERICAN BUSINESS IS NOT ETHICAL!

The Number of Business Scandals Seems To Be Rising

There seems to have been an eruption of questionable and sometimes downright criminal behavior throughout corporate America. Sure, all statistics are suspect, but consider the factors that put pressure on today's business people and their employees: plant closings and downsizings, corporate mergers, rise of both domestic and foreign competition, the number of young graduates entering the workforce each year, dwindling natural resources which drive costs upward, and the increase in the cost of living, to cite only a few factors.

The result of these changes in society and the economy: the fear of losing status and/or jobs. Therefore, why not juggle the sales reports to make a better impression? Why not misrepresent product claims to gain more sales? Why not cut corners in laboratory testing? Why not abuse a competitor? Why not falsify an internal audit? After all, time is of the essence. And if you don't look out for "number one," nobody else will.

The Interest in Business Ethics Does Not Guarantee an Enhanced Moral Responsibility in the World of Business

True enough, there are increasing numbers of business schools offering courses in business ethics and there are companies which have ethics programs and ethical guidelines in place. However, there have been major scandals at corporations which had substantial ethics programs in place for several years. Whether or not ethical programs are in place, all the newly learned ethical guidelines can be shelved when an employee is convinced that he/she must be perceived as a top performer or be laid off. Nobody knows how many high-level managers are intentionally dismissing ethical guidelines when considering questionable acts simply because those actions are paying financial dividends.

Much Recent Corporate Restructuring and Business Decisions Have Been Accomplished with Little Regard for Consequences on People

Corporate leaders who have been desperate for greater profits have made decisions which have displaced workers and adversely affected families. Many job reductions have been necessary, the result of poor business management, but at least some top managers have axed employees to pump up short-term profits or impress investors. Companies which expect a high measure of loyalty from their employees may be loathe to extend any measure of loyalty to their employees.

Corporations have turned to exploit emerging markets overseas, often dispatching a management team into a foreign business culture where bribery, game-playing, disregard for patents, and sloppy accounting are a way of business life. We all have heard of automobile manufacturers who decided it was cheaper to risk the lives of innocent motorists and their passengers than to redesign their vehicles. How many companies would really care about the toxic wastes and pollution they create if the government did not keep a close eye on them?

Corporation Shareholders Believe That Corporate Social Responsibility Is Both Unfair and Economically Irresponsible

Why do people buy stock in the first place? To improve the environment? To solve social problems? To end pollution? Of course not! People invest with a company because they believe it will bring the best return on their money. If investors and shareholders wanted to right the ills of society or improve the environment they could more directly address these concerns by contributing huge sums to such organizations as United Fund, Green Peace, or Habitat for Humanity.

Many investors are ordinary working people who buy stocks to prepare for their retirement years or to have a nest egg to handle some unexpected financial setback. To contend that corporate leaders should chip away at the legitimate earnings of ordinary citizens, all in the name of social progress, is grossly unfair to them.

Furthermore, corporate social responsibility is bad economics. A corporation is like an individual; each has the right to pursue, within the confines of the law, private economic interests without the burden of social responsibility. A social agency should do what it does best, namely help people, and a corporation should do what it does best, namely provide goods and services to profit its management, employees, and investors.

Corporate Leaders Do Not Know How a Socially Responsible Corporation Should Act

How can American business be more ethical when it does not know how to be socially responsible? A business is not a church. It is not a school. It is not an institute for the study of social problems. It is simply an organization attempting to make a profit.

Even if a corporation could identify all the social woes of the society in which it conducted operations, how would it know what to do about those ills? Even social scientists and environmentalists cannot agree among themselves. What standards must be met for a "decent living"? What standards must be met for clean air and clean water? How much noise pollution is "too much"? Should the dam project be spared or the tiny snail darter fish? How endangered must spotted owls become before northern forest lands are sealed off from loggers? What standards must be met for product safety? Obviously, people's lives must not be endangered, but how safe is "safe enough"? Who's right? The Sierra Club or the Business Roundtable?

The burden of these matters is too great for American business leaders. Rightly or wrongly, they will be deferred to market forces or to government bureaucracies.

QUESTIONS FOR GROUP DISCUSSION
AND PERSONAL REFLECTION

1. The image of the U.S. business person is that of an unethical person. Are business people basically unethical? If not, on what is such an image based? If so, why are business people more unethical than other kinds of workers and professionals?
2. Is there a book or a movie that you have read or seen which depicts American business persons fairly and realistically? Consider "Wall Street," "Disclosure," "Working Girl," "It's a Wonderful Life," and others.
3. Yes, we've had mass layoffs ever since big business was invented. We've had greedy CEOs and anxious workers. It once was thought shameful to lay off workers en masse. In the 1980s and 1990s, the more people a company fires, the more Wall Street seems to love it. Obviously, some company downsizings had to occur for the corporation to survive.
   Question: Can corporate downsizing become a moral issue? If so, when does that happen?
4. In a 1996 *Newsweek* cover story, the salaries of some of the U.S. top CEOs were reported, along with the number of employees laid off within the companies. Robert Allen, CEO at AT&T, earned $3,362,000 in one year and also laid off forty thousand workers. Walter Shipley, CEO at Chemical/Chase Manhattan, earned $2,496,154 and laid off twelve thousand employees. Charles Lee, the GTE chief, earned $2,004,115 and laid off seventeen thousand workers. More modestly, Ronald Allen, CEO at Delta Airlines, earned $475,000 and laid off fifteen thousand employees. Several other examples were cited.
   The world is changing, of course. And no matter how big and how rich a company is, it must adapt or die. In many companies, payrolls became bloated. To recoup losses,

employees are offered up as "human sacrifices" to the god of Wall Street. Stock prices rise. The ingenuity of CEOs is highly commended. They are then rewarded with fat raises.

Question: Is there any moral inconsistency between large CEO annual salaries and the same CEO laying off thousands of employees? Do these stories provide examples of American greed or of American capitalism at its very best with condolences to those at the bottom of the heap?

5. In boom areas, U.S. employers in certain field, especially farming and the building industry, are strapped for workers. Tough labor positions have been filled by illegal aliens. Suppose a home-building contractor needs additional labor to meet deadlines for buyers. Would it be morally acceptable for him to employ illegally migrated Hispanics to do construction work when he cannot locate local citizens who want to work? Should the employer take into account the wife and children of an illegal male immigrant worker in making this decision?

6. Is the strength of the ethical behavior of a corporation the critical component in determining the success of the corporation?

7. Ethics is usually viewed as abstract, but measurement would make it concrete and provide an overview of an organization's or business person's ethical attitude. Do you think there is a way to measure objectively the ethical performance of companies and/or business leaders?

Chapter 6

Success and Greatness
Seeking Perspective Through a Trilogy of "Sevens"

Like some Triassic reptile, the theoretical view of ethics lumbers along in the far past of Sunday School and Philosophy I, while the reality of practical business concerns is constantly measuring a wide range of competing claims on time and resources against the unrelenting and objective marketplace.

Laura Nash

Money buys everything except love, personality, freedom, immortality, silence, peace.

Carl Sandburg

Because the world sees wealth, power, and prestige as the indicators of success, we have been conditioned to seek them with all of our might. But our Lord has a different criteria for evaluating success. He calls us away from society's symbols of success and urges us to seek after "His kingdom and His righteousness" (Matt. 6:33). Many who are considered least important by society may find themselves sitting in places of honor at the great banquet feast in the world to come.

Anthony Campolo

I don't care too much for money. Money can't buy me love.

John Lennon and Paul McCartney

Success is not a place at which one arrives but rather . . . the spirit with which one undertakes and continues the journey.

Alex Noble

Perhaps you wonder that we have such inflexible rules in the choosing of men. We will not employ a man who drinks or smokes cigarettes or gambles. You see, we have had several tragic cases in the organization. Young men have fought their way up to prosperity and gone to pieces.

J. C. Penney

The work of God, even though it is unique, remains a model for human work. It affirms that work is good and Godlike in principle. The work of God is creative, orderly, and constructive. It is universal. It benefits people and other 'creatures. It declares the very nature of God and bears his imprint or signature. Human work can do no better than emulate God's work.

Leland Ryken

WHAT ARE THE WORST SINS OF THE AMERICAN WORKPLACE? IS IT possible to succeed in business without losing your faith in God and commitment to his Son Jesus? Is it possible to accumulate a great deal of wealth and wise investments without losing your soul? If you made an earnest attempt to apply Christian moral principles to your workaday business environment, would this attempt automatically curb your career potential? Are the actions you must take to "get ahead" in your career simply not congruent with biblical values and ethics? How does a Christian define "success"? And "greatness"?

Let's be honest here. It's so easy to give pessimistic answers to these questions. For many Christians it is virtually impossible to achieve simultaneously "success" in the business world and "success" in the Christian life. It's an either/or choice. Or is it?

We'll approach answers to these questions in a rather unique way, by looking at a trilogy of "sevens" adapted to the workplace. Along the way we'll spend some time discussing the true nature of success and greatness.

STILL DEADLY AFTER ALL THESE YEARS

Most of us would likely have trouble naming the seven deadly sins. In 1996 a scary Brad Pitt movie, "Seven," used them as a theme. A handful of websites are dedicated to explaining them. One author, William S. Stafford, claims these seven sins remain a powerful misery index for discerning broken relationships, addictions, and other social dysfunctions. They are cited here for any possible relevance to the workplace.

The seven deadly sins are all cited and discussed in the Bible, but the list was drawn up in the Middle Ages by Catholic theologians. What rendered them deadly is the destructive nature of these sins and how they lead to a hodgepodge of related sins which also destroy character.

Anger

Nearly everyone gets angry at work. The characters in the Bible often got angry too. There is such a thing as good anger, sometimes called "righteous indignation," and bad anger. Good anger protects relationships and projects of value, such as the family or justice or personal integrity, and sinful anger aims to intimidate, profane, or destroy other people, other races, society, or God. Anger becomes sinful when it turns to rage, thus putting the negative emotion in control of the man or woman who holds it. Because people spend more time in the workplace than any place outside home, and interact with such diversity of people, there are numerous occasions which invite and provoke our anger.

Envy

Most of us notice how other people in our work environment seem to achieve, seem to earn, or seem to live. Comparisons may be inevitable. Envy is a cheering section for the misfortune of people we know. There may be "general" envy for a class of people or "particular" envy for one person we know. Extreme envy is malicious. It is bitterness of heart. It is strong resentment that others have and enjoy their position and blessings. So strong is this negative emotion that it keeps us from appreciating and cooperating with other people and may drive destructive behavior toward those who are envied.

The remedy against envy? Gratitude. Count your many blessings. Name them one by one.

Gluttony

Theologians of long ago may have placed gluttony on the list as a reminder that overeating and overdrinking can kill anyone. Aristotle talked about the "Golden Mean" and the apostle Paul urged that Christians be known for their moderation in all things. Going to extremes may be an attempt to gain control of one's life while excluding God. Gluttony is seldom the result of people loving food and drink too much, but is a dysfunction that something is wrong in one's spiritual life and/or personality.

Tying gluttony with business ethics seems a formidable challenge. Suffice it to say, there are a few professions in which people are expected to attend frequent occasions for eating and drinking. To cite one: several times each week a church minister may be expected to eat and demonstrate much appreciation for the food served—dinners in homes, church suppers, group meetings with meals, receptions, lunch appointments, etc. In fact, not only is gluttony by a preacher easily forgiven, but it is seemingly urged on him by sisters in the congregation whose self-esteem is tied to the taste of their dishes.

Lust

Lust is usually connected with sex. The contemporary workplace throws men and women together in a working environment which depends on varying degrees of cooperation, trust, and good will. Thus work is the new social center; sexual attraction is inevitable and common. The sheer number of hours spent together opens a door to intimacy at some level.

Lust is not sex. The first stage of temptation is not lust. Lust is single-minded, persistent pursuit of sex (or anything else) that distorts its biological or moral purpose. Lust reduces another person to an object. Lust is a strong craving or desire for another person or thing. It's a "would if I could" attitude. Lust produces depersonalization, loneliness, thoughtlessness, disrespect, addictions, and denial of God. Jesus admonished people to take radical steps to control lust.

Greed

"Show me the money!" an aging pro-football player shouts several times to his young business agent, Jerry Maguire, in a movie that is titled by the same name. Most folks are not quite as blunt and loud as Maguire's insistent client (played by Cuba Gooding Jr.)—but are they less greedy?

Social critics and political pundits labeled the 1980s as the decade of greed. Many investors violated laws and codes of ethics to enhance their wealth. Mergers to multiply profits led to massive layoffs. Many savings and loan institutions failed through corruption and mismanagement. Indeed, the 1960s, 1970s, 1980s, and 1990s have been decades of extreme consumerism—no amount of material possessions seem to be enough for many people.

Greed has also been known as avarice and covetousness. The three terms mean essentially the same thing—idol worship, substituting material goods for God and others, excessive love and desire for tangible things. Greed is as connected with lapses in business and professional ethics as is any deadly sin (with the exception of the last one on our list).

The answer to greed: a complete shift in attitude. Take economic justice seriously and try tithing all your blessings. Focus on values that you'd like to be remembered for after you have died and departed from your family and friends. Consider that they will not likely remember you most for your salary and benefits you pursued so relentlessly. Consider the bumper sticker that says: "Live simply so that others may simply live."

Sloth

To put it bluntly, sloth is laziness. In fact, it may be worse than laziness—despair, inertia, spiritual listlessness, no desire for the good, no desire for God, no commitment to any worthwhile pursuit or value. This may sound like chronic couch potatoism. Sloth is a bargain with nothingness. A going-nowhere-fast syndrome. It may involve all talk and no action. Why is it that the harvest is plenty, the workers are many, but some workers with opportunity, skills, and at least some adrenaline do little or nothing? Answer: sloth.

Pride

Pride is the kingpin of them all. Sin has many tools, the old saying goes, but pride is the handle that fits them all. Pride is the predecessor of destruction, biblical wisdom informs us.

Aren't workers supposed to have pride in themselves and pride in their work? Of course. There is a "forgivable" pride that is best understood as self-appreciation and self-nurturing, a pride that makes positive affirmations about one's worth and efforts. And there is a deadly pride that dethrones God and places self as the most important thing in all the universe. One kind of pride is self-esteem and self-respect; sinful pride is self-worship. It is self-serving, vain, dominating, ambitious, and, at times, manipulative and cruel. Sinful pride destroys relationships—at work, at home, anywhere.

Pride drives a lot of people. It provides a great impetus for competition and money acquisition. Pride leads people to be critical, negative, rude, aloof, arrogant, haughty, inconsiderate, high-blown, puffed-up, stuck-up, or stiff-necked. Pride leads people to insist on their rights, whether in the office or on the highway, even when such insistence becomes ridiculous; it fuels much frivolous litigation. It fuels conflict at work and firings.

Pride itself may be driven by either low self-esteem or inflated self-esteem, by insecurity and the need for more and more conquests, or by insensitivity and blindness to real people and their emotions in the social environment. This "dark side of excellence" reveals itself when self-worth becomes overly linked to demonstrable success and when core values and principles are set aside in pursuit of money or position.

SEVEN CREATIVE TENSIONS

The impact of Christian faith on business affairs and management in the work world is a complex one, to be sure. Laura L. Nash, author of *Believers in Business*, contends that this impact is best understood as a series of sustained tensions that continue when Christian business people seek to be both effective in business and faithful in Christian practice.

Tension One: The Love for God and the Pursuit of Profit

A successful business life requires time and energy and, often, capital. These demands which bring material rewards of successful business conduct are not evil, but they can distract a Christian from his/her primary responsibility. Jesus warned: "No man can serve two masters."

How do you make it in the business world without spending a huge amount of time on worldly, profit-oriented problems and decision-making? How much is too much? Did not Jesus often warn about obsessions with wealth and power? Where do you draw the line?

Tension Two: Love and the Competitive Drive

The Christian is called to love all kinds of people, even one's enemy. And yet in the real world, so much of our success is based on successful competition. This is true in athletics, of course, but in the business world the game is real. In order to compete, many contend that one must develop a sense of detachment from the feelings of others. But how do you love people with whom you compete and are attempting not to get too emotionally involved? Can we honor God in all we do when we are fiercely competitive?

Tension Three: People's Needs and Profit Obligations

This tension impacts corporate owners, boards, and managers who make decisions that impact the lives of others. Do you place the emotional and career needs of your employees or the profit margin of the company higher? Are not the needs of the business above any one individual? How can managers maintain a commitment to the individual respect and dignity of all employees?

Tension Four: Humility and the Ego of Success

Is it possible in the business world for Christians to couple self-confidence with humility? Obviously, self-inflation goes against the grain of Christian ethics. "Hyperinflated self-regard contributes to broken relationships with God and one's neighbors," declares Nash. And yet, self-confidence and self-reliance are important in the business world.

Tension Five: Family and Work

In the Christian tradition, the family has always maintained great significance. What is the connection between family, faith, and work? Is it possible to succeed in business without neglecting your family? The "juggling act" metaphor is so appropriate to this tension.

Tension Six: Charity and Wealth

Personal wealth is a fact of life for successful CEOs. Scripture calls all of us to responsible stewardship and concern for those less fortunate. Are wealth and position morally neutral concerns? How much does a successful business person owe to someone less fortunate?

Tension Seven: Faithful Witness in the Secular City

Christians in business find many opportunities or even pressures to participate in practices that go against their faith. Yet, Christians are called to witness their faith in the secular world as salt and light. How does the Christian business person find black and white in a world of business gray? How active, if at all, can a Christian be in witnessing to his/her faith in the work world?

Does faith make a difference in the successful Christian business person's thinking? Absolutely! Yet this faith does not resolve all the ethical issues. There are many times in which the Christian business person will need to make a basic choice—who am I serving? Nearly two thousand years ago, Jesus confronted His disciples with a crucially important question that still haunts us: "What will a man profit if he gains the whole world and forfeits his soul? Or what will a man give in exchange for his soul?" (Matt. 16:26).

In borrowing the language of the marketplace, Jesus demands that we consider profitability, net gains, or bottom line. May we paraphrase Jesus' words: "Does it make good business policy to devote a half-century of your best time and energy and talent to squeezing all the money and prestige out of this world that you can, only to lose your very soul and your relationship with your God for all eternity? Is that smart? And let's talk values. You have only one soul. Is there anything worth trading for your soul?" We are finite creatures. We can't have it all. These ancient words of Jesus still haunt us, challenging our worldly ambition.

With all other definitions of terms and concepts in this volume, it is most important that we define "success" and "greatness."

SUCCESS

The corporate culture in which you work plays a large role in determining what is expected of employees and how "success" is defined and interpreted. The size of the business organization, the style of decision-making, and how the business is organized also have an impact on how people think of themselves and evaluate their personal success.

Most of us assume that success can be measured by external indicators. This is how our non-Christian peers evaluate our success. Most relate success to power, or status, or authority. Society tends to encourage the use of money as a measure of human value; therefore, most will make some connection between personal wealth and success. Thus the pursuit of money may come to seem more important than the pursuit of life. And the successful business person will plan for growth. Of course, these definitions are all subjective. By these standards, the prosperous farmer that Jesus told about was a highly successful citizen (see Luke 12:13–21).

Undoubtedly, you have heard many sermons and admonitions about not allowing others to define success for you. You may consider yourself a mature and independent thinker. You see yourself as self-motivated and inner-directed. You, like nearly everyone else, want to believe that only you define success for yourself. However, your need for acceptance and affirmation from our colleagues, your need for your peers to think highly of you, your need for them to give you respect that will open new doors of opportunity, all blind you and most others to how much we allow our social and professional environment to define success.

How, then, shall we define success? By last fiscal year's profit margin? By performance reviews? By how much complaints have dropped? By company growth? By how far down the "career track" one has moved?

Certainly without dismissing any of these relevant indicators, Christians are wise to return to the perennial question of both theology and philosophy—What is the chief end of a man or woman? Why did God create human beings? What is the purpose of our human existence? The answer: our chief purpose in human life is to give glory to God and blessing to humanity. The wise author of Ecclesiastes informed his readers and future generations that the "whole" of human life was to "reverence God and keep his commandments" (Eccles. 12:13).

The Christian life on planet Earth, temporary as it may be, is but a reflection of the eternal mind and heart of God the Father. When it is lived well, such a life glorifies the Giver of all life. The Christian life is also an "impact" life—people's lives are impacted, perhaps only in small ways such as salt and light, for good. The Christian life is designed to be a life of joy and fulfillment, even in the midst of pain and suffering. Christians may feel successful when they are experiencing the grace and affirmation of God and the joy of everyday life as it's lived in various roles and various places.

THE RIGHT TO DROP OUT

"Drop out" is an expression which is brief and clear. It also is totally negative. It is almost always applied to people under age twenty-five, and usually to young men and women aged twenty-one or younger.

A young man may drop out of school, draw cash from his savings, go to western Europe with a small group of peers, and tour the countryside on his bicycle, camping out along the way and enjoying the scenery and meeting new people. A young woman may interrupt her university studies, join a medical mission team, and spend a year in Central America, sharing and living out the good news of Jesus Christ. Another young woman may drop out of her professional studies to marry the man she loves and work full-time to finance his studies in medical school. Another youth may drop out of college, much to the surprise of one's parents, and spend a year working full-time at a relatively low-paying job.

Are these "drop-outs" failures? Are there lapses in their moral commitments? Or have they not simply exercised one of their precious freedoms—the right to take a break from parental agenda, a break from societal expectations, a break from ordinary, predictable life and seek adventure? On the other hand, consider the forty-five-year-old male, a college graduate with professional training, who chooses to spend many hours day and night in recreation "with the guys," whether playing card games, bowling, or whatever. Consider the thirty-five-year-old homemaker, content to spend many hours at home watching soap operas and reading romance novels. Would anyone think to apply "drop-out" to this man or woman?

The rhetoric of most business schools is "push hard," "be persistent," "swim with the sharks," "move to the next wrung on the ladder of success." Business magazines toast people who climbed to the top of the corporate ladder. Advertising and commercials feature young people (seldom old people) who exude success. Should not young people be liberated from the pressure of media images? Rather than more junior vice presidents and junior executives, does not our society need more dreamers, more dissenters, more mavericks, and more truly independent thinkers? From this latter group have emerged a few facsimiles of Henry David Thoreau, Mother Teresa, Thomas Jefferson, and Adlai Stevenson, to name a few, and not to mention many great creative artists.

Sometimes finding the right road to success and fulfillment in life is by taking a few detours or side trips from the road others have placed us on. That's not true for everyone, of course. Maybe not true for most. But it is true for some. History is filled with drop-outs and loners and nerds who listened to their own drummer. Most surely, the first century Palestinians who laid down their nets and followed Jesus at his beckoning must have been viewed as "drop-outs" from commercial fishing and even from mainstream society.

But what if they should fail? Failure is their right. It is our right, too. Society attempts to dictate the standards of success; but every individual possesses the right to buy those standards and measure performance accordingly or to rewrite those standards according to personal values. Success and failure should be viewed as individual visions, as they were in colonial and early national days of our nation, not rigid categories.

Failure is not automatically bad, and success is not automatically good. There are such powerful lessons in failure. Sometimes we learn more from our failures than we learn from our successes. And no one is truly a failure, the former great UCLA basketball coach John Wooden once declared, until he or she starts blaming personal mistakes and shortcomings on somebody else.

The good news about job and career failure in our society is that there are plenty of other job opportunities out there for hard-working, creative people with desire and dedication. The good news about moral failure is that God's grace is fulsome and abundant.

GREATNESS

Success and greatness are related, to be sure, but Jesus had more to say about the latter. Success seems to be time-bound, connected more with the present, while true greatness transcends one's own generation. For example, one may be thought successful among his/her peers because of business success, but in the ensuing years no future citizen thinks of him/her as a *great* man or woman. In a Wednesday evening men's class discussing the difference between success and greatness, these comments were offered: "Success is the battle; greatness is the war." "Success is destination; greatness is how you conduct yourself as you travel to your destination." "Success is *what* you are; greatness is *who* you are." "Success is getting your book published; greatness is having that book truly impact readers' lives."

Stephen Covey, in his highly sensible and practical volume *The Seven Habits of Highly Effective People*, challenges readers to consider two kinds of greatness. The first kind is often reduced to a set of rules and techniques for succeeding in the business world. You know the right way to conduct meeting. How to make shrewd business decisions. How to get along with all kinds of employees. How to win through intimidation. How to make favorable first impressions through personal charm. How to remember everyone's name after the first meeting. How to be a tough negotiator.

There's value in all of this, for certain, especially if we avoid the temptation to be dishonest or manipulative. We may develop the "right" style, the "right" words, even the "right" intention, but without moral principle and the trust and good will of others, we won't achieve lasting success or *primary greatness*. Covey calls this focus on technique the "Personality Ethic" and notes it is like cramming certain facts in your mind and trying to impress others that you are a brilliant person. It's like cramming the *Cliffs Notes* on a literary work on midnight before a big exam and trying to impress the professor that you have thoughtfully read and pondered the entire work. You sometimes get by this way. You may make an "A" in some of the courses. You may impress a few people. But if you don't "pay the price," do the hard work, you never achieve true mastery of your field. This approach is just as ridiculous as trying to "cram" on a farm, Covey says—to forget to plant in the spring, play all summer and then cram in the fall to bring in the harvest.

Secondary greatness is based on short-term successes. You win a few games. You impress a few people. You make a little money. You get a little publicity. You learned to get by because you knew how to "play the game." Even if you did not have substance, you at least had style. Like the actress who always asked after every public appearance—"how'd I look?"—you know how to dazzle everyone immediately to get attention.

Many people with secondary greatness (acclaim, status, wealth, position, and/or talent) lack the traits or virtue that make for primary greatness. One indicator in this primary void is their failure in long-term relationships. Many have failed as mates, business associates, parents, and even friends. The traits of secondary greatness alone cannot nourish the roots of primary greatness. If there is no deep virtue at the foundations of one's character—the right stuff—the superficial nature of one's "greatness" or "success" will eventually become evident to those who attempt depth relationship with such a person.

THE MAGNIFICENT SEVEN

The number of ethical dilemmas which the average business and professional person will face in his/her career are myriad. Often there is not time to carefully weigh, analyze, and seek counsel on all options. Decisions so often must be made with haste.

Are there some moral common denominators which will anchor our business lives in something of lasting value and meaning and thus give our business decisions a sense of ethical direction?

The "magnificent seven" represent the distillation of ethical values from moral philosophy throughout the centuries. In their general form they state what most responsible thinkers value, in some way, about life, about others, and about human behavior. Though they are general, they can form a foundation for principled decision-making in any business or career. When wrestling with a difficult ethical decision on the job, the thinking Christian can ask, "Will the action I am about to take in this job situation serve to advance or to impede one or more of these universal principles?" Such sensitivity to moral concerns at work will render our decisions more value-based than simply business-as-usual based.

Dignity of Human Life

Each woman or man has dignity and deserves respect as a human. This principle means that we may not act in ways that harm or injure innocent people. It means that all who labor, no matter how menial their task responsibilities, must be treated with respect. It means that businesses are concerned with the safety and security of their employees and their clients or customers. It means that product-testing is taken seriously.

Autonomy

All persons are intrinsically valuable and have the right to self-determination. Each person has a right to make choices which affect his/her own career or destiny. Each person is a free moral agent. No employee deserves to be treated as a slave.

Honesty

The truth should be told to those who have a right to know it. The ethics of business are foremost about integrity, truth-telling, and honor. Honesty pertains not simply to interpersonal relations at the work site, but also to claims about products and services, sales, reports, records, and advertising, to cite a few general areas.

Loyalty

Promises, contracts, and commitments should be honored. The keeping of pledges and promises, maintaining the public trust, quality service, and reliability of the organization, keeping of confidences and secrets, respecting company property, honoring just laws, policies, and rules are all a part of loyalty.

Fairness

People should be treated justly, fairly, impartially, and equitably in all relationships and transactions. Justice is giving to every person his/her due. Fairness tolerates personality, religious, racial, and gender differences in colleagues, clients, and customers.

Humaneness

Our actions ought to accomplish good, and concomitantly we should avoid doing evil. Obviously, business affairs are conducted for the purposes of personal and corporate profit and self-interest, but not at the expense of others' welfare. While humaneness is a principle with many possible interpretations, the golden rule is an ancient, time-honored standard which points business persons in the right direction.

The Common Good

Actions should accomplish the "greatest good for the greatest number of people." In moral philosophy, this standard is called "utilitarianism." Company policies and actions impact people in various ways, but ethical decision-making serves to benefit the welfare of the largest number of people, while protecting the rights of individuals. The common good is also served by the pursuit of excellence—opening new lines of both horizontal and vertical communication; developing new skills of employees; providing special training and education; pursuing excellence at all levels. No work at any corporate level that is less than best can be meaningful and rewarding—or profitable—in the long run.

These principles are general enough to be "fleshed out" and enacted in most if not all business situations, but abstract enough to be manipulated by rationalization and unchecked self-interest. The ethical business person will continually reflect on the moral dimensions of his/her business life and behavior, remembering always that one's most noble motives and deeds can be tainted with self-interest and seeking the counsel and support of ethical-minded friends and colleagues.

QUESTIONS FOR GROUP DISCUSSION
AND PERSONAL REFLECTION

1. What is the greatest tension you face as a Christian in your current professional life and career?

2. Can you think of other sins you would add to the list of "most deadly sins"?
3. Do any of the following sins exist at your workplace (check the ones you know about personally)?

___gossip	___rudeness	___rage
___addiction	___pornography	___racism
___dishonesty	___drunkenness	___harsh words
___selfish ambition	___illegal activity	___theft
___selfishness	___drug abuse	___gambling
___adultery	___laziness	___cursing and profanity
___prejudice/ disrespect	___harsh strife between workers	___dirty jokes/ filthy talk
___slander	___bribery	___false witness
___hatred	___insubordination to authority	

Are there other sins that you would cite? What can you do about any of these sins in your workplace?

4. What are some healthy ways in which you can reduce the stress in your life that is created by the clash of Christian principles and values, on the one hand, and non-Christians and secular values in the workplace, on the other hand?
5. Have you ever heard someone say: "Watch out for that guy. He's one of those born again Christian-types and you can't trust him!"? or "You'd better watch it when you go into a business deal with one of your own brethren. You might get shafted bad!"?
   Are such warnings and innuendoes fair? If so, what would cause Christians to get such a bad reputation in business dealings? When might it be dangerous to do business with other Christians?
6. How do *you* define "success" and "greatness"?
7. Do you agree with the distinction between primary greatness and secondary greatness? Isn't it possible that a person may possess the character traits of primary greatness (such as integrity, courage, respect for others, etc.) but lack the key communication skills to "get across" this greatness to others?
8. Do you know some "drop-outs" that you highly respect because of what they became or achieved in nontraditional ways?
9. Profession and occupation can turn into obsession. Workaholism (a topic we'll discuss in chapter 18) can transform an important part of life (our way of making a living) into a way of life unto itself. Is it possible that the root cause of workaholism is that it is a spiritual problem? Maybe the workaholic is not secure in his/her relationship with God and others. Maybe she has not internalized the truth that God's love is not conditional. Maybe she has not fully felt that God validated her personal value at the cross of Jesus (Eph. 2:4–9).
10. What does it mean to be "rich toward God" (Luke 12:21)? Is it a sin to build bigger production facilities, bigger office buildings, bigger warehouses, bigger markets, and bigger business networks?

11. The apostle Paul made a strong statement about success and greatness to the Corinthian Christians: "With us therefore worldly standards have ceased to count in our estimate of any man; even if once they counted in our understanding of Christ, they do so now no longer. When anyone is united to Christ, there is a new world; the old order has gone, and a new order has already begun" (2 Cor. 5:16–17, NEB). As a Christian, can you honestly say that "worldly standards have ceased to count" in your estimate of any other person? Have worldly standards ceased to matter when you consider personal success or greatness?

12. How would you describe your personal relationship with money? What is it that money will buy, and what are things money cannot buy?

13. As a Christian, would you accept a job that provided skills and training that you really wanted, but that also required you to regularly miss the Sunday morning worship assembly of Christian brothers and sisters?

14. Are Christians in the business world persecuted today? If so, in what ways?

Case Study

Richard Morrison is a young Christian businessman and residential contractor who builds quality homes in Williamson County, Tennessee. At times he will enter a contract with another purchasing party to build a custom home according to specifications. Richard's homes usually sell 7on the market for $250,000 to $400,000.

Richard entered a contract with a client to build a home for the client and his family. The new residence was contracted for sale in the $300,000 range. A deposit of earnest money was required for the contract to be consummated, and the client agreed to an amount of $60,000.

After the construction was nearly completed, the client came to Richard with a look of great consternation. "I regret this deeply," he confessed, "but my firm is transferring me out of state and I am unable to purchase this house. I beg of you to please return my earnest money or at least a large portion of it so that I can acquire a residence in my new location."

Richard is not legally obligated to return one cent of the earnest money. What should Richard do? As a Christian, does Richard have a moral obligation to return any of the earnest money?

Chapter 7

To Tell the Truth
The Simplicity and Complexity of Basic Honesty

Among the people I know at the top of the nation's major corporations, the personal quality that is regarded most highly is a solid, unwavering sense of integrity. The higher a person moves up in business, the more important it is for his peers and superiors to feel they can depend on his word. They have to know that he's a "straight shooter" in every sense of the word, one who won't cut moral corners to further his own interests.

Donald V. Seibert

The Lord detests lying lips, but he delights in men who are truthful.

Prov. 12:22

Leadership requires followship and following is an act of trust, faith in the course of the leader, and that faith can be generated only if leaders act with integrity. . . . The person or organization that has integrity can be trusted. From trust comes security, the individual's knowledge of how the world around will respond to his actions. There can be no leadership without integrity.

Lawrence Miller

If a promise (even a minor one) is not kept, if ethics are compromised, and if

management behaves inconsistently, then the strategies necessary to survival today simply can't be executed.

Tom Peters

If you're starting out in business you have a grace that you can always keep. If you start with quality and the truth, you'll never have to stop. There will be no reason to. But once you stop telling customers the truth—or don't tell the truth from the beginning—you'll find it's difficult to start later. The value of honesty, like virginity, lies in its irreplaceability. I'm not talking about image, either. I am talking about what's genuine. You become what you say, and what you say becomes you.

Paul Hawken

Integrity is a singular virtue with multiple branches in one's life experiences. If you had $100,000 to invest, I dare say would not trust someone to manage your portfolio whom you know to be cheating on his wife or lying to his employer on a variety of matters.

Rubel Shelly

ONLY human? As if humanness were a blueprint for instinctive, reflexive reactions to situations, like the rest of the animal kingdom. I see "human" as the unique opportunity to use our mind and will to act in ways that elevate us above the animal kingdom. . . . I reserve "that was very human" for something that was magnificent— like courage, altruism, artistry.

Laura Schlessinger

Poker's own brand of ethics is different from the ethical ideals of civilized human relationships. The game calls for distrust of the other fellow. It ignores the claim of friendship. Cunning deception and concealment of one's strength and intentions, not kindness and open-heartedness, are vital in poker. No one thinks any the worse of poker on that account. And no one should think any the worse of the game of business because its standards of right and wrong differ from the prevailing traditions of morality in our society.

Albert Carr

THE STORY IS TOLD OF AN ANCIENT PHILOSOPHER NAMED DIOGENES who went about the streets of Athens with his lantern and a declaration: "I'm looking for an honest man." Pascal once stated that we should not expect to meet more than three or four honest people in one lifetime. When we reflect on the credibility problems of contemporary politicians, sales people, and advertisers, only to name a few, we are tempted to conclude that Diogenes and Pascal were not off target.

Is simple honesty always the practical option in the workplace? Let's consider a couple of real-life cases. In the first, a young Christian college coed has been employed in a clothing store. She has become concerned over pricing policies in the store. Her supervisor informed her of how the system worked. Prices are marked above a retail price that the owner would gladly settle for. Then, when items are placed on sale on a rotating basis (usually 10 to 33 percent off the labeled price), the store gets the retail price they sought all along. The owner is understandably even happier when people buy nonsale items at the inflated price. It's only on the clearance rack where items are priced 50 to 75 percent off regular price that the customer gets a true bargain. The young Christian woman, believing deception to be woven into pricing policies, wrestled with her conscience about continuing her employment at the store.

In another case, the director of a continuing adult-education center advertised an open position on his teaching staff. Among the five or six applicants was a middle-aged, family man. The man had completed an earned doctorate, possessed several reputable publications to his name, and listed excellent references. In the interview the director was impressed by the gentleman, but, with desires he rarely shared with others, preferred a female for the open position. An attractive female with only a few credit hours above the bachelor's degree was among the applicants and the director knew he wanted her on his staff. In convincing himself he was considerate of the man's feelings, he offered his rejection to him in these words: "I've discussed your qualifications with our current staff, and we all agree that you'd make a wonderful choice with whom we'd be happy to work together, but it would not be a good choice for you. The truth is, you are overqualified for this position. A person with your credentials should be teaching in a university graduate school."

Just what does it mean when a store marks merchandise 10 to 30 percent off "regular price"? Don't most customers realize that merchandise or products at nearly any price will bring profit to the owners? Isn't this standard marketing practice or is it crass deceit? And what does "overqualified" mean? After all, the applicant apparently was not "overqualified" before the interview. An employer wouldn't waste time talking with people who were overqualified. In essence, what "you're overqualified" means is "sorry, Bud, but you don't get the job." But has the director been guilty of telling a gross lie or is he simply using a factual reality in a deceptive way so as to spare the applicant's feelings?

Both Christian discipleship and self-respect demand a high degree of honesty about oneself and about others. There must be a candid recognition of one's moral commitments and moral relationships. And as for Christians, a simple, basic integrity is a vital part of the foundation of discipleship. A dishonest Christian is a contradiction in terms. Integrity is absolutely basic to our witness in the world and especially in the workplace. No matter how faithfully we keep the rituals, recite the creed, restore the pattern, or donate to the poor, if we are not honest men and women in the eyes of our business partners and clients, we have nullified the faith and destroyed our witness.

Let's proceed with a definition: *A lie is any intentional effort to deceive.* To deceive other people is to purposely misstate something, to purposely mislead them with some verbal or nonverbal language, or to conceal some truth from them which they have a right to know. Our business and professional world is the arena in which many Christians have the most unrelenting and persistent temptations to lie.

KINDS OF LIES

Not all lies are created equal. There are "little white lies" and there are "big whoppers." Augustine identified eight kinds of lies. The relationship between lying and the truth has always been complex. But can thinking Christians make a distinction between "acceptable" lying and "unacceptable" deception?

At the risk of oversimplifying the phenomenon of deceit, consider three general categories of lies:

1. **Lies to protect others,** as in "I love your new hairdo" or "what a great presentation to our board." These are well-intentioned lies intended to grease the gears of the workplace. Few people want searing honesty when they are guests at a dinner party or viewing a newborn baby for the first time. Of course, lying to protect coworkers and colleagues may seem like a literal job-survival issue, as in "I'm going to have to lie about this or they'll be fired on the spot."

2. **Lies to promote self-interest,** as in "the computer swallowed the budget analysis due today" or "my car wouldn't start and thus I was late to the staff

meeting." All of us fear reprisal, reprimand, disgrace, embarrassment, or penalty. To tell a lie is tempting when seeking to avoid such strongly negative repercussions to what we've done on the job or who we've become. Undiluted greed may motivate much deception, as in the celebrated case of author Clifford Irving, who stood to reap large sums of royalty money from a bogus manuscript which he claimed was an authorized biography of recluse billionaire Howard Hughes.

3. **Lies to cause harm,** as in "trust me on this one" or "my opponent in this campaign has a big skeleton in his closet." Little wonder we do not trust used car salesmen (or sales people in general, for that matter). Surveys show that citizens believe there is less honesty in government than even ten years ago and that government officials cannot be counted on to tell the truth when discussing a volatile issue. (A credibility poll is cited in the discussion section of this chapter.)

What is the value of commitment to truthfulness? First, to be true to ourselves is a matter of emotional and spiritual self-preservation. To be dishonest is to destroy a portion of our wholeness (*integer* is a Latin word meaning whole, complete, solid) and to lower our self-respect. Second, dishonesty is a betrayal of another person, the abuse of the faith and confidence of another person. Third, willful deception undermines the trust which is the fabric of a workplace or professional community (and any community, for that matter). The apostle Paul's admonition for everyone to speak the truth with his/her neighbor was a practical one: "for we are all members one of another" (Eph. 4:25).

Like other Christian virtues, total Christlike integrity is an ideal that might never be reached in perfect measure. A Christlike integrity is not natural, any more than loving one's enemies is a natural response to deep hurt caused by others. We can work at being more honest as the years of maturity pass—a kind of progressive integrity. Total honesty is a path we are on, not a plateau we have reached. For everyone but God, integrity is a not a perfect destination to be reached but a lifelong quest.

Studies and surveys have confirmed what ordinary common sense tells us, i.e., that integrity is the most important trait that enhances the success of business executives. In the fast-paced business environment where decisions often must be made rapidly, where work is often delegated, and where subordinates cannot always be monitored, it is important to be able to trust and believe in colleagues. The trust that exists among colleagues is best inspired by superiors who model honesty and trustworthiness in all transactions. If higher level managers possess a reputation for total honesty, subordinates will take notice among themselves, perhaps saying, "Honesty is crucially important to my supervisor; therefore, I'd better always tell the truth about this unit's performance [or some other matter]." How regrettable it would be for an employee to say, "Oh sure, I could be totally honest in this report, but honesty is not very important to my supervisor, so why should it be to me?"

THE WHOLE TRUTH AND NOTHING BUT THE TRUTH . . . ALWAYS?

How much truth is needed in business and professional relationships and transactions? We may be thankful there is a significant group of business and professional people who are committed to telling the truth in all business transactions and telling it at the right time and in the right manner. This highly ethical group seems to be in the minority. The majority might concede that deception is impossible to avoid totally. Some might resort to deceitful words or nonverbal communication, but only with some regret and second-guessing. Others seem to hold to a "bungee cord" theory of truth—throw in a little cord of truth and then stretch it as far as possible to make advantage bounce their way. Still others may have no compunction about lying at any time, confirming truth in the late Adlai Stevenson's adaptation from two Old Testament scriptures: "A lie is an abomination unto the Lord and a very present help in the time of danger."

To our issue: Is withholding just some of the truth always unethical? Suddenly the issue of simple honesty begins to get complex.

Performance Evaluation

If supervisors are responsible for giving a written and oral performance evaluation and rating, may they alter numerical ratings in order to motivate better performance in the future? Does one colleague tell another colleague that her speech before the entire assembly "totally bombed" because her stage fright was so evident? And what about workplace disciplinary action? Is there not a time for sympathy and kindness that compassionately understates shortcomings and another time for blunt, forthright candor which serves as a clear warning. On the college and university front, statistical evidence substantiates a rising "grade inflation" in the last generation; on some campuses a "C" is no longer average and a majority in any particular class may "earn" an "A" or "B."

Advertising and Public Relations

Does it matter if claims for a product or service are exaggerated? Doesn't everyone expect "puffery," those claims for a product that few people take without the proverbial grain of salt? And what about celebrity endorsement of products. Does it matter that a renowned professional athlete may drive around in a Porsche or Mercedes, but that he endorses a Ford Escort as the best car for the money on the road? Does it matter how often Michael Jordan eats at McDonald's restaurants?

Resumes, References, and Recommendations

Do not the vast majority of resumes contain exaggeration? Are not many awards and achievements cited on a resume either overstated, misstated, or reported out of context? And how well do the "big-name" references on the resume really know the person submitting the resume?

What about those glowing recommendation letters which are awash with hyperbole? A professor may write a glowing letter of recommendation for a graduating senior to be admitted to a prestigious law school, thus reflecting favorably on the professor and the undergraduate department. Another professor or some other professional may write an unabashedly hyper-glowing treatise of praise for a personal friend in hopes of giving an edge in landing a sought-after position. Are there times in which supervisors and professionals must decline a request to write a letter of recommendation? Or might they agree to write such letters as personal favors but attempt vagueness in describing an applicant's strengths and attributes? Should those who read such letters of recommendation employ a personal discount system, such as translating "one of the best" as "pretty good" and "brilliant" as "smarter than most"?

Business Bargaining and Sales Negotiation

Most business people from time to time feel almost compelled, in the interest of themselves or their companies, to engage in some form of deception when dealing with customers, clients, organizations, government officials, or even other departments within their own company. The deception can take several forms: a deliberate lie or misstatement, exaggeration of facts, concealment of facts, or understatement or omission of pertinent facts.

Is anything wrong with such deceit? How much business strategy is conducted like a game wherein rules allow the parties to take advantage of the other's situation, ignorance of facts, or special needs? Imagine yourself as a party to the purchase of a new automobile. You go to a dealership that sells the make and model you are most interested in. You know that you are not going to pay full-sticker price for the car. When you negotiate to purchase this new automobile, you know that your sales person and his/her manager has information about the cost and value of the vehicle that you cannot access directly. The dealer representative may tell you that the offer is one hundred dollars over invoice, but you might wonder if the car has two invoices or if the dealer is receiving a large rebate from the manufacturer upon the sale to enhance dealer profit. On the other hand, you know more about your motivation and your other purchase options—after all, there are lots of dealers and scores of similar models for sale in any urban area—than you reveal to the sales person. Is it morally wrong to bluff? Can you pretend ignorance? What if you attempt to use one dealer's bid to lower the bid of another dealer?

Most of us know that sales representatives will overstate the value of their products and services. We know that negative information about their offerings are unstated or played down as insignificant. Aren't the strength of one's hand and one's bluffing ability major factors in who gets the better end of the deal? Is this deceit and unethical manipulation, or is it all a part of the game? Does business operate by a different set of ethical rules than the rules which maintain healthy organizations such as churches or civic clubs and, most certainly, which maintain intimate relationships?

Investigative Reporting

When is it morally permissible for a business organization, such as a newspaper, to tell lies in order to discover and report the truth?

For decades FBI agents have posed as other characters in order to catch people engaged in egregiously unlawful behavior. Federal agents have masqueraded as drug dealers in order to convict some of the most ruthless peddlers of illegal drugs. In the early 1970s, the *Tennessean* commissioned reporter Jerry Thompson to pose as a rabid racist and join the Ku Klux Klan in order to gather firsthand information for a series of feature stories. Twenty years or so later the same newspaper assigned reporter Jim East to go undercover, posing as a homeless person, to infiltrate Nashville Union Rescue Mission for five weeks. A fake ID card was produced for East, and he used a disguise and told falsehoods to effect his pose. East's assignment was to confirm or deny reports of violence, filthy conditions, overcrowding, and violation of safety standards within the mission. Millions of Americans know of the 1992 ABC *Prime Time Live* telecast accusing Food Lion stores of selling spoiled meat, tainted fish, and rotten produce and of other unsanitary practices of which the general public would not have imagined; information for the program was gathered by reporters posing as grocery workers and by use of hidden cameras.

Lest we stray too deeply into the specific field of media and journalistic ethics, we return to the basic question: may business and professional people deliberately lie in order to accomplish a specific organization purpose? May professionals be imposters if such total deception seemed necessary to protect the people? Would the good accomplished—presumably information gained to assure greater life, liberty, and pursuit of happiness for the general public—justify the use of otherwise unethical means?

SELF-DECEPTION

Is it possible to "lie to oneself"? If the phrase is taken literally it would not seem possible to tell an outright lie to oneself and then simultaneously be deceived and hurt by it; this would involve one person playing the roles of both perpetrator and victim. On the other hand, if we understand "lying to oneself" as a figure of speech that must not be taken too literally, we will observe many strategies by which people show disrespect for themselves and others by evading the whole truth.

Just as outright lying is a character flaw, or vice, so also is intellectual dishonesty. The two differ in that simple honesty is telling the truth to others, while intellectual honesty involves being honest with yourself. Biblical theology informs us that sin has such a deceptive dimension; the human heart is capable of rationalizing almost anything. The sin of pride provides the context in which self-interest can dominate every business decision.

In business and professional life, as with other vitally important relationships, our values and ego are entwined with ways we expend emotion and energy. This ego and emotional investment blurs our objectivity so that we may unconsciously distort reality. We may give up or "hang in," be supportive or nonsupportive, follow the rules or bend the rules, work hard or not work hard in ways different from coworkers, all the while convincing ourselves that we are performing well. Our desire to have good results or move up the corporate ladder obscures realities we would ordinarily know to be true. The result is that we do a "con job" on ourselves and the only person we fool is ourselves. Consider some strategies of intellectual dishonesty:

1. **Rationalization** is reasoning in a biased, though socially approvable, way. It aids in justifying specific decisions and behaviors and aids in softening the disappointment connected with unattainable goals. Even callous brutality can be rationalized as necessary or even praiseworthy; Adolf Hitler saw the extermination of all European Jews as his patriotic duty. Many employees who steal from their employer rationalize that they simply took what they rightfully had coming to them. Other employees may rationalize selling out a coworker, employee, or boss just to impress someone else; the "selling out" may mean gossiping, tattling, or ridiculing someone in the workplace to make themselves look good.

   Rationalizing usually is "rational" enough at least to convince the person who's doing it that he/she is justified. But rationalizing is a sin on top of a sin. First, one does something that is wrong and intended to punish or create trouble for someone else. Then, one lies to oneself, allowing one to persist in hurtful behavior without questioning what he/she is really doing.

2. **Compartmentalization** involves keeping certain areas of our lives free from moral scrutiny and moral reflection. Many a combatant during warfare has simply said, "I'm just a soldier doing my duty." A cabinet member in a corrupt administration could say, "I'm just doing what the president ordered me to do." An employee who is falsifying a claim may say, "I'm just doing what my supervisor instructed me to do." Albert Speer, architect of the Nazi death-camp system, seemingly separated his family and social life from a larger moral perspective by saying, "I'm just doing my job."

3. **Nonreflection** is akin to both compartmentalization and willful ignorance. It means divorcing one's behavior or decision-making from moral consideration. An investment officer who leaks confidential information might say, "I'm not even going to think about what I have just done."

4. **Selective attention** means ignoring the unpleasant and focusing only on immediate matters. A supervisor who may fear the possibility that her favorite colleague is having an intimate affair with a person in another department within the company may turn her attention to paper work and other detail when the evidence of indiscretion is right before her.

5. **Emotional detachment** means numbing our emotions from unpleasant realities. It is plain denial of our real feelings.

6. **Repression** is "selective forgetting," or a defense mechanism by which threatening or painful thoughts and desires are excluded from consciousness. One

becomes an "amnesic" with regard to piercing truth. How easy for a worker to "forget" that an important task delegated days before somehow did not get done!

EMPLOYEE THEFT

We all know that people on the job steal from their employers. Theft is dishonesty in action. It's so commonplace that company losses can be astronomical. By some estimates, U.S. companies lose about $25 billion annually because of employee dishonesty, neglect, and disruption. The American Management Association estimates that as many as 20 percent of businesses that fail do so because of employee crime; bank losses alone cost $250 million each year. Employee drug use can cost companies a total of several billion dollars a year due to absenteeism, lost initiative, diminished productivity, and accidents. Employee violence also costs companies millions each year.

To a point which concluded our first chapter: *preventing* unethical practices is far wiser than dealing with them *after* their occurrence. Though a congressional ban on mandatory polygraph tests in hiring has been in effect since the end of 1988, many companies now resort to pre-employment psychological testing (honesty tests) to identify potentially problematic employees. The honesty tests are legal and more economical and more easily administered than polygraph tests. Some questions have been controversial; some samples: How strong is your conscience? Does everyone steal a little? Do you always tell the truth? Have you ever had thoughts you would not want made public? Applicants are also asked their personal history, if any, with drug use, drunken driving, forgery, vandalism, traffic violations, and other nondesirable behaviors.

Some testing companies attempt to draw a personality profile of the applicant. Once the tests are taken, they are evaluated by the tester and each applicant is given a "risk" rating of high, moderate, or low to be used in the overall assessment of the applicant. Though the tests are useful, some critics of the method have raised valid questions over their efficiency and the unevenness in standards of administering the tests.

Not everyone steals, of course. So, who steals? And why? Would any of us steal, given the right situation?

These questions are not easily answered. Demographic studies of people who steal on the job have established that such employees:

1. have few ties to the organization or the community;
2. are more likely to be new employees, part-time employees, and unmarried employees; and
3. work in low-paying, low-status jobs.

Can we consider "who steals" in behavioral terms? There is no definitive answer, and it may be too simple to say "People steal because they need the money" or "People steal because they are bad people." Various studies give some insight into the phenomenon. Hollinger and Clark (1983), as well as others, offer explanations in several categories:

1. **Economic pressure.** Individuals steal after getting into serious financial difficulty, such as incurring a stifling indebtedness, large unexpected medical bill, or gambling losses.
2. **Demographic theories.** Many thefts appear to be committed by young, inexperienced, and part-time employees. Such people may have less emotional ties to the company and to other employees; they may feel that they have less to lose by loss of their job.
3. **Opportunity.** Everyone steals, given the opportunity. The more opportunities, the more thefts. Sure, this seems pessimistic about human nature, but evidence shows that the single best predictor of theft is the perceived chance of being caught.
4. **Dissatisfaction.** Employees dissatisfied with their jobs, employees who feel they are not treated fairly or paid adequately, are more likely to steal.
5. **Norms.** Informal social norms do not discourage employee theft. For example, if a new employee learns that everyone else in his/her division cheats of his/her expense account, the new employee is likely to do likewise.
6. **Attitudes toward theft.** Some individuals steal because it is exciting, thrilling, and challenging; others because they have actually believe or talk themselves into believing that what they are doing is not really theft.
7. **Power through theft.** Theft is a way to assert power or control and attain status.
8. **Theft as a safety valve.** Through theft, people express their frustrations, let off steam, and retaliate against the organization.
9. **Instability.** Dishonesty at work is a form of pathology and emotionally unstable individuals are more likely than stable employees to steal from the organization.

WHITE-COLLAR CRIME

When managers and top executives act dishonestly on the job, their misdeeds are handled quite differently from the misdeeds of lower-level employees. Some observers do not like the term *white collar,* because few of the misdeeds of upper-level employees are handled through the criminal justice system (just as few street crimes are handled through civil suits or administrative penalties, such as loss of license). Still, nearly everyone knows what is meant by the term.

White-collar crime may be distinguished from other acts of employee dishonesty in three ways:

1. The amount of money involved is much higher for white-collar crime than for virtually all other individual acts of employee theft.
2. The individuals who commit white-collar crimes do not fit the profiles for other employee theft or street crime. White-collar crime is usually committed by employees who are well-educated, affluent, and highly respectable individuals.
3. The motivations for white-collar criminals are not as likely to be the same as motivations for low-level employee dishonesty. Lower-level employees are more

likely to be motivated by revenge against management, lower pay in the organization, and the desire for power or status. Upper management has, presumably, gained those advantages.

What motivates upper management to commit acts of theft and dishonesty? No clear pattern seems to emerge. Cressy (1986) and Cherrington (1986) discussed several motives for white-collar crime in work organizations:

1. **Fear of failure.** Managers and executives are under substantial pressure to produce results; a failure might seem devastating.
2. **Norms.** If managers believe that certain illegal or dishonest acts are in fact acceptable, they engage in them.
3. **Unsharable problems.** Executives may face what seem like insurmountable financial problems which cannot be solved through normal, legal channels. Some managers face catastrophic losses.
4. **Altruism.** Some crimes are committed for the good of the company, the community, or society. A dishonest bid might help a local official land a vital road or bridge to be built in a local community.
5. **Careless expediency**. This attitude allows one to bend the rules to ensure success. The habit of rule-bending may have continued so long that the misdeeds become standard operating procedure.
6. **Simple greed.** This may involve an addiction to money-making and success itself. The scandals involving top Wall Street officials have often been explained in terms of wealthy people seeking even greater riches.

Let's be less pessimistic: Just as there are stunning incidents of theft and other dishonesty in American business life, there are, perhaps, far more cases of courageous honesty and fairness among employees. Of course, an understanding of integrity in its fullest sense is something that may require years of business and professional life. And a reputation for business and personal integrity may require a lifetime to create. Developing integrity has been compared to the process of cleaning up a shattered glass or mirror. One begins by picking up the largest and most obvious pieces of broken glass; next, one notices most of the tiny pieces, slivers, and chips. It may seem that it's nearly impossible to sweep up all the tiny fragments, and an observer may well point to a piece or two that's been missed.

This little analogy also instructs us that integrity may be about little things as much as or more than the really big ones. We can make it obvious that we are telling the truth and keeping our commitments about the really big matters in our lives (the big pieces of broken glass we pick up). Yet, how we react in less-important matters may set the tone for how we handle strategic business situations. There may be small specks on the floor we feel we can never pick up, but most people will appreciate the good clean-up job we have done.

Remember that the "little stuff"—the "little gray areas" in business—provides the context wherein the real spiritual battle lies. How we handle the "little stuff" in business provide a great index to our friends and associates as to how we would handle the truly "big stuff." Tolerance of small deceptions makes us vulnerable to acceptance of larger deception. On the other hand, pleasing God by integrity and trustworthiness in small matters equips us for larger ministry opportunities. "Whoever can be trusted with very little can also be trusted with much," Jesus taught; "and whoever is dishonest with very little will also be dishonest with much" (Luke 16:10).

This raises the question: Who is honest and why? The question is a formidable one, for the simple reason that acts of dishonesty attract far more publicity and attention than acts of simple integrity. We will consider the motivations and methods for courageous integrity in our next chapter.

QUESTIONS FOR GROUP DISCUSSION
AND PERSONAL REFLECTION

1. Honesty is a respected and prized virtue in our society. As children we are taught "honesty is the best policy." Honesty is not simply an honorable guidepost to the conduct of our daily affairs, but every major religion, in one form or another, teaches that honesty is valuable and important. We know that certain kinds of dishonest behavior is subject to legal sanctions in nearly every society.

   When we ask people why honesty is important, however, we get a variety of answers: "It is the best policy, you know" or "I was always taught that" or "The Bible says all liars will find themselves in the lake of fire."

   Have we simply accepted the belief or doctrine that honesty is important without stopping to ask *why* it is important? Why is honesty so important in business life and everyday social life?

2. Should a morally responsible person make distinctions in deception? Are some lies worse than others? Is it appropriate to lie when protecting the feelings people hold about themselves or their families? How about information you have been told in confidence? How about bad news that you think someone is not ready to handle? What about a little exaggeration of a job resume? What about a small amount of unreported income on a tax return?

3. Immanuel Kant (1724-1804) sought moral principles that did not rest on contingencies and that define actions as inherently right or wrong apart from any particular circumstances. To Kant, reason alone can yield a moral law. To always tell the truth, regardless of circumstance, was one of Kant's "categorical imperatives." What do you think? Is it ever morally right to tell a lie? If so, under what circumstances?

4. Think back to a time in which you told a lie, or a half-truth, at work. Why did you tell the lie? What was the consequence of the lie? If you had this situation to relive, would you handle it the same way?

5. Is it possible to lie to oneself? If so, what are some of the most effective strategies people use in self-deception? What would motivate people to lie to themselves?

6. Self-deception is discussed in a negative way in this chapter. However, could self-deception ever be beneficial and supportive of self-respect and self-esteem? Consider how an

athlete gets "pumped up" to play a championship ball game. Consider a person who has an intense case of stage fright and is required to make a speech to a large audience. Might that person get "psyched up" to make the speech by engaging in innocent self-deception about his/her public speaking skills or the desire of the audience to hear the speech?

7. The apostle Paul called his generation "crooked and perverse" (Phil. 2:15). Was his generation much different from ours? The U.S. public believes that the standards of honesty and ethics in general are declining in this society, a view held by all age groups and in each socioeconomic level. The general public does not give high marks to workers and professionals in most of the twenty-four occupations tested in a Gallup poll in terms of honesty and ethical standards. Consider the professions with their individual rankings of high credibility:

Clergymen (64 percent)	Stockbrokers (19 percent)
Druggists, pharmacists (61 percent)	Business executives (18 percent)
Medical doctors (53 percent)	Senators (17 percent)
Dentists (51 percent)	Building contractors (17 percent)
College teachers (47 percent)	Local political officeholders (16 percent)
Engineers (46 percent)	Congressmen (14 percent)
Policemen (42 percent)	Realtors (13 percent)
Bankers (38 percent)	State political officeholders (13 percent)
TV reporters, commentators (33 percent)	Insurance salesmen (13 percent)
Funeral directors (29 percent)	Labor union leaders (12 percent)
Newspaper reporters (26 percent)	Advertising practitioners (8 percent)
Lawyers (24 percent)	Car salesmen (6 percent)

What is your opinion of this poll? Would you rank any of the professions higher? lower? Why do clergymen not have closer to 90 percent or above in credibility rating? Are there any honest car salesmen in our society? Incidentally, this poll was reported in *The Word in Life Study Bible* (Nelson, 1996, p. 2145). Pharmacists also quote a Gallup poll which shows their profession having the highest credibility rating of all jobs and professions for several years in a row. Perhaps we should use such polls only to get a general idea of ranking and not to victimize any business or professional person by a stereotype.

8. You do not have to work for an organization very long, at a management or nonmanagement level, to realize that your interests and desires are often on a collision course with the interests and desires of the organization. If the stakes are important enough to both parties, then a serious conflict of interest has arisen.

When a person is hired, he/she commits to discharging contractual obligations in exchange for salary. Thus the employee performs the specified job assignment and devotes energy within the framework of prescribed hours in exchange for pay. Implicit within any work agreement is the principle that employees will not use the business organization for personal advantage. Of course, one may gain status and ego satisfaction from employment with a firm, but that employment is not intended to provide unauthorized personal gain at the expense of the company.

Below is listed several common unethical practices. (Some of these terms will be defined under "Key Terms" in the appendix.) As you consider each one, on a scale of one to ten, place a number after each one; put down a "10" for the offenses that you consider to be the greatest moral offenses and a "1" for the least moral offense at work. Put a zero for any behavior you think is not unethical in any way. Are any of these practices morally justified?

    a. Passing blame for errors to an innocent coworker

    b. Divulging confidential information

    c. Falsifying time/quality/quantity reports

    d. Claiming credit for someone else's work

    e. Padding an expense account over 10 percent

    f. Pilfering company materials and supplies

    g. Accepting gifts/favors in exchange for preferential treatment

    h. Giving gifts/favors in exchange for preferential treatment

    i. Padding an expense account up to 10 percent

    j. Authorizing a subordinate to violate company rules

    k. Calling in sick to take a day off

    l. Concealing one's errors

    m. Taking longer than necessary to do a job

    n. Using company services for personal use

    o. Doing personal business on company time

    p. Taking extra personal time (lunch hour, breaks, early departure, and so forth)

    q. Not reporting others' violations of company policies and rules

    r. Playing computer solitaire in all the free time that can be possibly arranged

Which of these practices, in your opinion, is more common?

9. Obviously, the topic of business ethics is much broader than the topic of honesty in the workplace. Of course, the issue of integrity at work is at the foundation of many ethical dilemmas, but there are varied concerns and rights of so many different people associated with business.

Do you think that good business ethics requires absolute honesty and candor? In bargaining, negotiation, and determination of prices, it is well-known by all parties that each side is operating with partial information. This issue was raised in the text of the chapter. We used the illustration of purchasing a new automobile: both you and your sales representative know more facts than you are willing to "share up front." The next moves may seem more like a poker game. Is the game-playing of negotiation morally wrong? If not, is there a point at which it could become unethical?

10. Do you consider an exaggeration an out-right lie on your resume to be an immoral act? After all, nearly all managers are aware that most applicants stretch the truth to put themselves in the best possible light on a resume and in an interview. Isn't this part of the game? Wouldn't an interviewer expect you to have cast yourself in the best possible light?

11. Case study: Janet Lambert gets along well with her boss, a congenial, hard-working man whose only vice at work is having a very cluttered desk and office. Once when her boss

was expecting a very important phone call, the call came in at a time when he was out of the office. Janet forgot to tell him about the call and failed to put the phone notice on his desk. After her supervisor expressed much consternation about not receiving the call, she slipped the phone notice under a stack of papers and other debris, thus leading him to believe he had misplaced or failed to see the important slip of paper. Janet never said a word about the incident. Question: Did Janet lie?

12. Do you think "I'm only human" is an acceptable excuse for doing wrong? To some, "I'm only human" suggests that people operate under some animal instinct that allows them no choice but to do the wrong thing. Do you agree? Could it be that "I'm human" is actually a reason for *more* ethical rather than to act out of greed and selfishness? (Note the quotation from "Dr. Laura" at the beginning of this chapter.)

13. From a Christian perspective, do you consider it a sin to do the least you can get away with on a job? Of course, doing less work than we are capable of is easily rationalized in our minds. Do you think that doing the least possible is a way of expressing anger about some work issue? What kind of message does this send to coworkers?

Case Study

Put yourself in the following situation: Dana Brooks works for Premiere Motors, a company which sells late model luxury cars—Cadillacs, Lincolns, BMWs, Saabs, and the like. Dana enjoys her work because she likes to meet people and likes nice cars. Bringing the two together brings Dana much satisfaction.

Dana's problem, as a Christian, is with a fellow sales representative, Philip Hood. Philip openly admits that he'll say anything to make a sale. She has overheard him many times misrepresent facts such as origin of vehicle, company's wholesale investment in vehicle, performance and overall reliability of the vehicle. Philip has "bald-faced" lied about whether cars have ever been wrecked or returned to a paint shop.

Dana has talked to Philip about her ethical concerns, but he simply laughs at her. The sales manager is the owner of the firm, and he is rarely on the lot. Besides, his only concern is about profit. What does Dana do?

Case Study

Nancy Christian is a competent and dedicated registered nurse. She left hospital employment to work for Dr. Jackson Bethero, one of the city's leading surgeons. Dr. Bethero delegates much of the interpersonal communication with patients to Nancy. Having been a dedicated surgeon for twenty years, the doctor now believes he needs to spend more time with his hobbies of hunting and fishing. Nancy believes her boss needs that time for himself.

Nancy's problem: Dr. Bethero instructs her to lie to patients and their families on a frequent basis. She knows that at least once each week that he performs questionable surgery. She knows how he exaggerates the health hazard for a patient opting either to wait or not to have the surgery. All to frequently, Dr. Bethero arrives at a hospital to discharge patients hours after he promised a family he would be present. When families call for the doctor, Nancy feels trained to say, "Sorry, he was called into surgery" or "He was summoned to the emergency room," all the while knowing that he may be home in bed or out in the woods with his four-wheeler stuck in mud or at the boat ramp reeling in his fishing boat.

Nancy covered for him willingly for many months. Now she is finding herself doing this much more than she feels comfortable doing. Does Nancy have moral responsibility?

Case Study

Phil Williams has decided to purchase a new automobile. Actually, he is interested in a late model, used vehicle. When he finds the model he is interested in, he begins to negotiate with the dealer representative. Phil's final offer is still two hundred dollars below what the salesman says the car can be delivered for.

"I'll tell you what," the salesman says, "I can't go any lower on the price, but I can do something for you to save you some serious cash. You bring me a check for this car for the sale price minus three thousand dollars, then bring in the three thousand in cash. On the reverse side of the title transfer I will put down the sale price for three thousand less than you are paying. That will save you the sales tax on three grand. How's that?"

Phil Williams is a Christian. He is an elder in a local congregation. He knows what the salesman is doing is dishonest. He knows, too, that he can save some money by going along. What should Phil do and say in this situation?

Chapter 8

The Right Stuff
Some Reflections on Moral Integrity and Moral Courage

Leadership is a calling. It's a belief in serving something other than yourself, serving a higher cause. . . . The people who are most inspiring to me are people who have an unshakable belief in the rightness of their mission; they become selfless servants of their mission and their cause. That belief is automatically transferred to their followers.

Failure cannot be part of the vocabulary of the extraordinary leader. You must have confidence in yourself, confidence in your team, confidence that no matter how tough the challenge is, we will prevail. That type of attitude can quickly turn around a fearful organization.

H. Norman Schwarzkopf

Why doesn't America work? Because for too long too many people have waited for someone else to do something. Change starts with us.

Can we make America work? Yes. Emphatically yes. The key is to restore a high and morally rooted view of work that once again inculcates in the American character those historic virtues of the work ethic: industry, thrift, respect for property, pride in craft, and concern for community.

Charles Colson and Jack Eckerd

Integrity includes but goes beyond honesty. Honesty is telling the truth—in other words, conforming our words to reality. Integrity is conforming reality to our words—in other words, keeping promises and fulfilling expectations. This requires an integrated character, a oneness, primarily with self but also with life.

Stephen Covey

Integrity has to do with our behavior when no one is watching—no one, that is, except God. When we're out making sales calls, when we're alone in our office, when we're making deliveries, when we're at a convention—when we're all alone, do we still work as if the boss were right there next to us? We should, because our ultimate Boss is!

Doug Sherman and
William Hendricks

Life is not a popularity contest. . . . You just have to focus on living in a way that's honest and true.

Anita Hill

Values are principles and ideas that bring meaning to the seemingly mundane experiences of life. A meaningful life that ultimately brings happiness and pride requires you to respond to temptations as well as challenges with honor, dignity, and courage. Actually, values can make difficult choices or dilemmas appear more clear-cut because they focus on concepts of ethics, virtue, and morality—qualities more resilient against "circumstances" than emotions generally turn out to be. Values ought never be the first thing you drop when you think you got a "better offer," like a rich boyfriend, or a better job with more money, or whatever your needy/greedy heart desires.

Dr. Laura Schlessinger

A man is measured by the expanse of the moral horizon he chooses to inhabit.

Sandor McNab

REAL-LIFE SCENARIO NO. 1: IT WAS THANKSGIVING WEEK, 1996. Ethiopian Airlines Flight 961 was hijacked by three men, who demanded the plane fly to Australia. The pilot informed the hijackers that the aircraft was low on fuel, but the hijackers moronically refused to believe that information. With the plane's remaining fuel being savagely drained, it was only a matter of time until the Boeing 767 ran out of fuel and crash-landed into the ocean off Grande Comore, the largest of the Comoros Islands, a tropical archipelago between Madagascar and Mozambique. Only about fifty of the airline's 175 passengers survived the crash.

Among the casualties was Dr. Ron Farris, age forty-six, whose parents live in Nashville. Farris was one of those rare people whose life stood as an enigmatic counterpoint to the world's values. Years earlier he had relinquished a successful surgical practice in Kansas to serve God and humanity as a medical missionary amidst the poverty and deprivation of Africa. Since 1987, Farris, his wife, and four children (ages seventeen, sixteen, fifteen, and twelve in 1996) had served as a medical missionary family (Mrs. Farris is a nurse) for the Church of the Nazarene in Africa, managing medical clinics and educating about forty thousand people each year. During this time, Farris's pay was eight hundred dollars a month.

Ever since Farris was a young boy, attending Sunday School in churches where his father was minister, he planned to be a missionary doctor. He heard his teachers talk about Africa and decided he wanted to go to the big continent. "Believe it or not, he never wavered. We call that a call from God," declared the elder Farris. "Providence had a hand in it. We watched his life, the way he studied, and saw him prepare for it." William J. Prince, chairman of the board of general superintendents for the Church of the Nazarene, declared, "Ron Farris's heart beat for the people of Africa, and he demonstrated his love for them in a tangible way by dedicating his heart and life to missionary service. His death is a great loss to not only his family, but to the denomination, and to the people of Africa."

Real-life scenario No. 2: How frequently newspaper and broadcast-news reporters and editors find themselves under attack for a perceived general lack of values and ethics, and for practicing "sleaze journalism."

Of course, "sleaze" is fairly popular. All one needs to do is check the magazine racks nearest the check-out lane at grocery stores. The popularity of a *National Enquirer, The Star, Globe,* and even *People* magazine, admittedly a much more respectable publication than the others, is evidence to the reality that the American public enjoys the private affairs and peccadillos of other citizens, especially the rich and the famous. Even weird news about the poor and undistinguished holds fascination. And then there is Geraldo, *Hard Copy*, and Jerry Springer.

Besides not viewing such programs or purchasing such publications, there is little that most of us who oppose such sensationalism masquerading as news features can do in protest. Carol Marin was an exception.

Carol Marin, whose peers contend that she brought a sense of integrity to every journalism assignment she ever assumed, was coanchor at Chicago's NBC affiliate WMAQ-TV in 1997 when she learned the station had hired talk-show host Jerry Springer to do commentary during newscasts. Marin had opposed his being hired as a commentator. She called Springer "the poster child for the worst television has to offer." Those who have seen low-life guests rehearse their grievances and then break out into profanity and fist fights on the show might likely conclude that Marin's critique of Springer is not overstated.

Marin knew, of course, that Springer had a right to his opinions and the right to express them at some point on the airwaves. She also knew the general public has problems differentiating journalistic expertise from entertainment features, Tom Brokaw from Jerry Springer. She knew that entertainment and prurient interest in private affairs which masquerades as news coverage on issues of public concern and interest threaten a society's core values.

When Carol Marin's concerns were not heeded, she did the one thing she felt that her moral values and moral principles compelled her to do—she resigned her position as coanchor in one of the nation's largest television markets. Her resignation drew national attention, keeping the debate over true journalism versus sensationalism alive.

Real-life scenario No. 3: In 1991, Lisa Higley worked as a supervisor of account executives for NCNB (now one of the nation's leading banks) in their mortgage company in Charlotte, North Carolina. She informed her boss that their family would be moving and that she would resign once their house was sold.

Lisa's boss said that her leaving the company would be best because the whole department would be moved to Texas. There had been a rumor about a move to Texas, but her boss had publicly denied the rumor in meetings. While the denial about moving the operation to Texas was communicated, secret plans were being made for the relocation.

Lisa was given a confidential assignment to decide which people in the department to offer positions to and decide who would be terminated. No relocation package would be offered, so the employees would have to relocate from North Carolina to Texas at their own expense.

Lisa felt that she was not treated fairly because she was asked to lie. Lisa felt that the employees should have been given a choice. How do you know if someone will relocate until you ask? How do you decide for someone what they will give up to keep their job? This was the most flagrant offense while she worked there, but many times during her five and a half years she wondered if management lied when it was convenient.

Lisa resigned earlier than planned and stated her reasons. The bottom line was Lisa did not think it was fair for management to ask her to lie.

Real-life scenario No. 4: Ed Todd is a Christian managing consultant whose office is based in Brentwood, Tennessee. He is contracted by the management of business firms to survey the entire organization, conduct interviews, perform analysis, and then recommend to management certain steps to enhance efficiency and increase profits. The bigger the corporation, the greater the opportunity for Ed and his staff of professionals to earn income and enhance their firm's reputation.

Ed has enjoyed his partnership with a variety of corporations. He was surprised, however, when the management from one of the nation's largest breweries asked if he would be willing to consult with the firm. "What are your goals?" Ed asked. The answer: streamlining operations and increasing sales and profits. "And do you have funds for this consultancy?" Ed asked next. The brewery management informed him that the company had earmarked $100,000 for such consultancy for the current year.

Ed thought about their request. Here was an opportunity for his firm to earn some revenue. He also thought about his Christian values and how they should be applied in this situation. After a brief time Ed gave his reply: "I am flattered that you are convinced that I could provide counsel and directions for the greater business success of your company. However, as a Christian, I do not want to use my professional training and experience to enable any company to sell more beer or earn greater profits from the sale of alcoholic beverages. You will need to locate another consultant."

Moral integrity is a vital foundation for the everyday moral life that should be taken with us directly to the workplace and the marketplace. Knowing the right thing to do is one thing. Having the "right stuff" and doing the right thing are something else. Fortunately for the human family, history is dotted with men and women who, over the centuries, dared to dream the impossible dream and fight the unbeatable foe to make the world a better place.

The previous chapter discussed simple honesty. Simple honesty alone is not a sufficient guarantee of integrity. To have integrity means to have wholeness of life. Integrity has a much broader connotation than simply being honest, a major point in Stephen L. Carter's excellent volume, (Integrity), published in 1996. Of course, one must demonstrate a measure of truth-telling in order to have integrity; on the other hand, one can be honest, even brutally honest, without having integrity.

A person may take prideful satisfaction in telling everything he/she knows and would never deliberately mislead. Is this real integrity? Consider a couple of illustrations drawn from Carter's study:

Illustration One: A man who has been married for fifty years confesses to his wife on his deathbed that he was unfaithful thirty-five years earlier. The dishonesty was killing his spirit, he says, so now he has cleared his conscience and is able to die in peace. The man has told the truth that he kept secret for so long. He has unbosomed himself. Is he a man of integrity? Or has he shifted the pain to his wife at a time when there is no emotional risk to himself?

Illustration Two: Having been taught all his life that women are inferior to men in talent and intelligence, a manager gives to women on his staff less-challenging assignments than he gives to men. He does this, he believes, for his own benefit—he does not want the women to fail. When one of the women on his staff does poor work, he does not criticize her as directly because he expects nothing more. He tells others he is acting with integrity, because he is managing his organization according to his deepest convictions. Is he a man of integrity? After all, he has not lied about his prejudice. (Incidentally, in the above illustration we could substitute "blacks" or any other minority group for "women.")

The Pharisees once grudgingly offered a compliment to Jesus: "'Teacher,' they said, 'we know you are a man of integrity and that you teach the way of God in accordance with the truth. You aren't swayed by men, because you pay no attention to who they are'" (Matt. 22:16). The Pharisees' compliment was a prelude to a tricky question they next posed to Jesus about the legitimacy of Roman taxation. "Teaching in accordance with truth," even Jesus' critics saw a person whose words and actions converged with the ring of credibility.

Most of us might be willing to concede the sheer honesty of certain people without being convinced they possess integrity. Before pursuing the basis of integrity, we might travel in time to revisit briefly the moral thought of ancient philosophers and biblical writers.

VIRTUES

Historically, moral philosophy has paid close attention to character traits and activities that are distinctively human and, taken together, constitute the good life for human beings. Qualities which make for excellence philosophers call *virtues*. These may include natural qualities such as speed, strength, or intelligence; acquired qualities such as expertise at public speaking or accomplishment in playing the piano; qualities of temperament such as a good disposition or a sense of humor; spiritual qualities such as faith, piety, or fidelity to vows; or qualities of character such as benevolence, kindness, courage, perseverance, or wisdom.

By a "good person," most people usually mean someone who is morally good, whether or not he/she exhibits any other qualities we admire. Albert Speer had a unique job. He was the official state architect under Hitler in the Nazi regime and eventually was second only to Hitler in power. He possessed both great intelligence and remarkable administrative skills; additionally, he was a sensitive and caring man with his family and friends. Nonetheless, his involvement and leadership in the Nazi war agenda preclude our judging Speer as a man of moral integrity and goodness.

Christians may be especially reluctant to label a man or woman "good," for their conviction is that God is the ultimate judge and the only one who can attain infallible knowledge of the heart and soul. There are books and movies which invite us to appreciate a character's dedication and performance in a category totally separate from the character's moral commitment and allegiance. In the movie *Heat*, for example, which pits a gang leader who pulls off precision bank heists (played by Robert DeNiro) against a skillful detective (played by Al Pacino), a mutual respect develops between the protagonist and antagonist. At a luncheon shop encounter, the DeNiro character morally neutralizes his life of crime and tells the Pacino character, "Like you, I gotta do what I do best." Audiences seem divided in their loyalty to these two characters because each displays both loyalty and physical courage. The essence of moral integrity and moral courage, however, must surely begin with a commitment to a high and mighty cause.

VICES

While "good" traits of character are often called virtues, the "bad" traits are called "vices." A vice is a trait of human character or a habit that is considered to run counter to the welfare of an individual or his/her relationships. Vices, like other habits, may develop unconsciously and deeply entrench themselves in the person's behavioral patterns.

In popular thinking, vices may only be little habits of indulgence—such as occasional drinks of whiskey, smoking, personal wagers, overeating—which seldom present major threats to the social fabric of a community or a business organization. Perhaps we should remember that Jesus himself was accused of being both a drunkard and a glutton (Matt. 11:19) since he came "eating and drinking." Recall that Jesus declared that "nothing outside a man which by going into him can defile him; but the things which come out of a man are what defile him" (Mark 7:15). This radical statement may lead us to the tenable conclusion that motive and intention have more to do with virtue and vice than individual actions.

When one is kindly, lovingly, and generously disposed, when his/her utmost desire is to be a blessing, then one is virtuous, even if the actions seem to obscure such disposition. A vice is essentially the opposite: a disposition toward selfishness, greed, and harm which then cloaks itself in deceit, including self-deceit.

SIN/SINS

That humans are in serious trouble from which they need deliverance by a Force greater than themselves is a fact assumed everywhere in the Bible. The plight of humans is one of sin, not merely one of fate, finiteness, ignorance, or mere mortality.

Biblical writers generally assumed the fact of sin as sufficiently obvious and drew from several words to discuss it.

Moral theologians properly distinguish between "sins," violations of individual commands and expectations that God expects of all morally accountable people, and "Sin" (best noted, perhaps, with a capital S), one's rejection and denial of our true relationship with God and the attempt to organize life on some other basis. Consequently, any definition of sin must involve both humans and God in the wrong relationship to each other. Saints are sinners who have been forgiven by God's grace and, though they still commit and confess "sins," they steadfastly remain faithful to God.

MORAL DEFECTS/WEAKNESSES

Moral defects and weaknesses become evident in the thinking of most of us as we struggle to honor our moral values and live up to our moral convictions. Our spiritual experience may become much like that of the apostle Paul:

> So I find this law at work: When I want to do good, evil is right there with me. For in my inner being I delight in God's law, but I see another law at work in the members of my body, waging war against the law of my mind and making me a prisoner of the law of sin at work within my members. What a wretched man I am! Who will rescue me from this body of death? (Rom. 7:21–24)

There are various ways in which one may display moral weakness:

1. **Lack of discipline.** Most people are conscious of times in which they have failed to exercise discipline or self-control. We may commit ourselves to being chaste in our sexual relationships and then fail. We may commit ourselves to a certain weight reduction diet and then fail. We may tell our supervisor that we can complete a project by the deadline and then fail.

2. **Inner conflict.** When we are pulled strongly in two directions, the self can be divided against itself, thus evoking intense inner conflict. Unless these inherently disturbing feelings of inner turmoil are successfully resolved, we face possible suffering from feelings of shame for who we are and guilt for what we've done. There are both healthy and unhealthy ways of avoiding these negative responses to weakness of will.

3. **Excuses.** An excuse is a personal explanation offered as a justification or as grounds for being pardoned from failure to live up to one's standards. To be human is to be prone to excuse-making, for all of us seek to maintain our self-image and self-respect.

   Excuse-making can be categorized according to two purposes: lessening blameworthiness and justifying the behavior. In the original workplace, Adam and Eve used a blame-lessening strategy when the man said, "The woman which you gave to me, she gave me the fruit, and thus I ate it," and the woman declared, "This serpent beguiled me and I ate it."

A behavior-justifying strategy is intended to convince others that the act was justified. Imagine, for example, that Adam and Eve had answered the Lord: "Yes, God, you're mighty right, we did eat of that forbidden fruit, but what's so wrong about that? You put it there and said it gave knowledge of good and evil. If you hadn't wanted us to eat it, you shouldn't have stuck it right in front of our faces!"

Again, all of us offer excuses for failures, big or small, to live up to our standards or commitments. Perhaps the workplace and the classroom provide the arenas which evoke the most interesting, most creative excuse-making. Some excuses are weak and totally self-serving; other explanations are valid excuses. Assessment of excuses is complicated. Reality is, of course, that just as we can pass private judgment on the excuses we offer to others, so do others pass their own private judgment on the validity of excuses we offer them.

4. **Fanaticism.** A fanatic is characterized by excessive enthusiasm and intense uncritical devotion to some cause or point of view. In social conversation, a fanatic is someone who will not change his/her mind and does not change the subject. Fanaticism is a moral weakness because the fanatic has lost balance and proper perspective in the pursuit of even good objectives.

The most extreme fanatics may pursue goals with methods that harm other people. Terrorists undertake goals with an excess of zeal and personal danger to everyone who is in harm's way. Less extreme fanatics may be found in nearly all organizations of any size, thus we may expect to encounter them at work.

5. **Hypocrisy.** Another defect in moral integrity is to proclaim oneself to the world as being morally committed to a cause but then failing to make an honest effort to live up to that commitment. Words of concern and commitment are usually spoken effortlessly. Action may be costly. It's relatively easy to write a company mission statement or a professional code of ethics—living up to such public declarations is the real challenge!

MORAL INTEGRITY: FOUR STEPS

Moral integrity is about character. Character is more than reputation. It is more than stated beliefs and opinions. Character encompasses core values, deepest convictions, and highest moral commitments that define each person as unique and ultimately shape one's life. Character is what we truly are when no one requires, influences, requests, or demands that we act a certain way; as Dwight Moody once expressed it, "Character is what you are in the dark." We "flesh out" our character in everyday decisions, thoughts, and actions. Integrity is the consistency, the wholeness and harmony, of our proclamations and our deeds.

Drawing from the previous discussion, and also adapting ideas from Stephen Carter, becoming a person of moral integrity will involve four steps.

Take Time To Discern Right from Wrong

Discernment is tough work. It presupposes intelligence and clear, incisive thinking. It also means reflective thinking, perhaps in a retrospect of many years of experience and learning.

Too few of us know what we really believe and value. Rather than giving the time and emotional energy that go with discernment, it is much easier to "go with the flow" and give allegiance to "group think."

Following the crowd can pose its own dangers to truth and justice. The refusal to think independently is the seedbed of mob violence. On the other hand, supporting a dissenting position does not automatically make one morally right. Keep in mind Thoreau's observation that someone's willingness to die for a cause does not make that cause right. Risking one's life does not prove one possesses truth and integrity. Our own beliefs and values can lead us down the wrong path.

Make a Moral Commitment

This means bidding farewell to neutrality. Moral integrity requires honesty about who one is and how earnest and committed one is to moral causes. Decide that there is a cause worth standing up for and fighting for. Re-examine your values. Determine what is good. Focus on the moral issue(s) that concern(s) you most. Consider what should be done about that issue. Be realistic about what can be accomplished; it may be that little more can be done than raising consciousness about the issue.

Take Action

This is where the rubber meets the road. Act concretely and decisively on your moral principles. Keep your moral commitments and the promises you have made. Remember that maintaining moral integrity may entail going against the grain of societal expectations, social rules, and even the laws of the land. Additionally, it may require bold action in the face of danger or significant risk to live up to one's commitments and moral convictions. While cowardice leads one to shrink from strong opposition and danger, courage leads one to confront and deal with obstacles when risk, danger, and/or hardship are inherent within the situation. Synonyms for courage include mettle, spirit, resolution, and tenacity.

Ethicists often distinguish between physical courage and intellectual courage, the latter we may call "courage of one's convictions." *Physical courage* refers to courage in the face of risks to body and life. Examples of physical courage are numerous. One might also think of a thirty-two-year-old English teacher named Shannon Wright, who literally placed herself in harm's way on behalf of her students. Upon hearing gunfire, Ms. Wright selflessly placed her own body between a thirteen-year-old girl and the deadly bullets which took her life in the tragic 1998 Jonesboro, Arkansas, school grounds ambush by two male classmates.

Courage of convictions refers to times when people act courageously because of a strong commitment to abstract principles of justice, fairness, integrity, kindness, or goodness. One might think of the courage of convictions held by Martin Luther when he nailed his protest in the form of Ninety-five Theses to the door of the church at Wittenberg. Or, one might think of Martin Luther King Jr.'s determined commitment to civil rights; whatever one may think about King the person, as a reformer for equal justice and equal rights, this young Southern Baptist minister risked his life almost daily before he was eventually assassinated in Memphis, April 1968.

Actually, the most striking examples of courage manifest long-term patterns of both physical and intellectual courage. One might think of an Old Testament hero, a young man named Daniel, whose steadfast loyalty to Yahweh on foreign soil landed him in a den of lions. A reading of Revelation in the New Testament offered encouragement to early Christian disciples whose confession "Jesus is Lord" rather than "Caesar is Lord" usually carried the penalty of violent death. Finally, to cite one more example, one might think of Winnie and Nelson Mandela, whose faithful devotion to ending apartheid in South Africa entailed perseverance through many years of unjust imprisonment, even months of solitary confinement.

Forthrightness

Allow no one to be uncertain about your commitments. This final step is "deceptively simple," as Carter points out, but is often the most difficult of all—if you are living an authentically moral life of integrity, you must be willing to openly declare that you are acting consistently with what you believe to be right.

Thus, be able to explain why you have done something against the grain of expectation and social rules. Declare it publicly. Say it clearly. If you have violated an ordinance or injunction in pursuit of what is just or right, be willing to pay the price that society levies against you for the violation.

If a person opposes the federal government allowing commercial logging operations in a northwestern rain forest, he might write letters, publish articles, or purchase space in newspapers and magazines to publish a protest. If he secretly cheats in major ways on his income tax forms, could he convince himself and closest friends that he is engaged in a moral act of civil disobedience to protest government laxity on environmental issues? On the other hand, what if the citizen openly announces to the IRS that he would withhold tax money in protest of environmental policy, faces a judge, and serves a jail sentence for tax evasion? Obviously, the former act is selfishness disguised as moral protest; the latter is protest rooted in moral integrity. As Carter points out, "honesty is most laudable when we risk harm to ourselves, but it becomes a good deal less admirable when we instead risk harm to others and there is no gain to anyone other than ourselves."

A PRACTICAL APPLICATION: WHISTLE-BLOWING

The moral decisions we make at work may be the most challenging we will ever make. Many situations may arise at work which require us to balance our moral obligations with a consideration of the rights and interests of others as well as with our own self-interest. Cases arise, as we shall illustrate, which pit loyalty to the business firm against obligations to third parties.

Managers and other employees owe duties of loyalty, service, and obedience to their companies; these duties can frequently supercede even pressing personal needs. However, in both law and ethics, there is a limit to these obligations. Under law, no employee is required to obey unlawful orders from a superior. Nor do loyalty and obedience require us to comply with unethical job demands or orders.

Whistle-blowing provides an illustration of conflict between the interests of others and personal moral responsibility. Whistle-blowing refers to one employee seeking to stop an illegal or immoral behavior of an employer or organization (or perhaps someone within the organization) by alerting top management, or, failing that, by notifying people outside the organization. The whistle-blower may believe that the behavior of an organization or a superior within the organization is unnecessarily harmful for third parties, in violation of human rights, or runs counter to the stated purpose of the business firm. Perhaps the most noted case of whistle-blowing in American history was Roger Boisjoly's decision about blowing the whistle on the *Challenger* space shuttle's mechanical problems.

Several points should be considered in our definition. First, whistle-blowing can be done only by a member of the organization. If a reporter does an investigation and uncovers certain facts and then publicizes them, this is not whistle-blowing. If an outside witness who has nothing to lose observes illegal activity in a company and notifies enforcement authorities and testifies in court, this is not whistle-blowing. Neither the reporter nor the outsider has any obligation or sense of loyalty to the business organization, and neither has reason for "second thoughts" about making the information public; the employee is expected to work as directed and act only in the best interests of the organization. Second, the whistle-blower must have concrete information that is not currently public; there is something new to alert interested third parties. Whistle-blowing is not the same as "sounding the alarm," the latter being an attempt to arouse public concern about an issue involving the business organization. Third, whistle-blowing involves matters of substantial importance. Merely leaking evidence of managerial incompetence or self-serving but otherwise harmless decision-making might not qualify as whistle-blowing. Fourth, whistle-blowing generally circumvents normal channels of communication. And finally, whistle-blowing is done voluntarily rather than in the normal course of job assignments.

Managerial judgment of the moral character of whistle-blowers varies between two extremes. Some regard them as "ethical conscientious objectors" who place public interest and public safety above their own careers; others regard them as untrustworthy and disloyal coworkers who seek notoriety at the expense of jeopardizing the entire work team. Actually, all kinds of people "blow the whistle": morally ideal, seriously disturbed, chronically disgruntled, self-promoting, and mentally disturbed people. In most situations, whistle-blowers are driven by a sense of moral integrity, individual responsibility, and high personal moral ideals.

How does a person with high moral integrity make a decision about whether or not to blow the whistle on superiors acting illegally, unethically, or carelessly? Does a worker risk losing a career or job for just any injustice? We all frequently encounter situations in which human welfare is imperiled—disease and deprivation in underdeveloped nations of the world to the homeless people who approach us on the street asking for money. Even if we respond to some of these causes or situations in a concrete manner, we certainly do not lay aside our career plans or jeopardize our current employment to do so. In view of this, why must we look out for the best interests of our managers, our coworkers, and/or our clients?

In making a decision about whistle-blowing, the issue of self-interest may certainly and validly come into play. A worker's need to save his/her job is a fairly important value, to say the least. Most of us, including moral philosophers, make a distinction between moral reasons and prudential reasons. "Moral" refers to the interests of God and others. "Prudential" (from "prudence") refers to considerations of self-interest. Obviously, moral and prudential considerations can pull us in different directions.

Ideally, one makes a decision based on which considerations, either moral or prudential, are heaviest. For example, morality does not require us to make major sacrifices of job and career to right relatively minor wrongs; on the other hand, in protest of a major social injustice in which one contributed a major role, a person might sacrifice something highly important in order to lead to a change and live with one's conscience. In reality, most workers are probably too biased to make such an objective decision which weighs personal moral values with prudential considerations.

At a more practical level, the following admonition may be taken as a moral rule in business and professional ethics: Whenever an employee encounters a situation with the business organization that he/she is convinced will threaten the health, safety, or life of another person or persons (or that clearly violates laws or corporate policies), and the situation has been missed or neglected by others responsible for dealing with it, the employee then must take clear corrective action—first by going to superiors and, if no satisfaction, then going outside the company to effect change. Maturity, good judgment, and keen insight are required of the dedicated employee in making a decision about whistle-blowing. Upper management, too, has an ethical responsibility to maintain a corporate environment which enables employees to fulfill their sense of moral responsibilities and also allows employee concerns to be voiced and handled respectfully and confidentially.

CONSIDERATIONS FOR MORALLY JUSTIFIABLE
WHISTLE-BLOWING

To summarize our discussion of whistle-blowing, consider the following questions in deciding whether to blow the whistle in a specific situation:

1. **Does the situation contain significant moral importance?** How serious is the moral violation? How immediate is the danger? How specific is the violation? Of course, the whistle should be blown only for a grave moral or legal infraction. And the more general the accusation, such as "this company is not acting in the best interests of its customers," the less necessity and impact of the alert. A drug that is about to be placed on the market which has serious side effects that were not detected by the U.S. Food and Drug Administration and that were covered up by top-level officials might be considered a "clear and present danger." How direct and predictable is the harm?

2. **Has the whistle-blower gathered all the pertinent facts and placed them in proper perspective?** Are the charges well-founded? Are the facts verifiable? Has a standard of "compelling evidence" been met—evidence that any reasonable person in a similar situation would be convinced that the activity in unethical or illegal?

3. **Is the whistle-blower acting from an appropriate moral motive?** Is the whistle blown from a sincere desire to expose unnecessary harm, violation of human rights, or conduct counter to the mission of the organization?

4. **Has the whistle-blower exhausted all internal channels of protest before going public?** Is the decision to "go public" the last resort? Surely loyalty to an organization mandates employees to seek an internal remedy before airing "dirty company laundry" in public. And surely every organization of any size requires that any employee take up any matters of concern with one's immediate supervisor before proceeding further—unless the immediate supervisor is central to the problem.

5. **What is the best way to blow the whistle?** To whom should the significant information be forwarded? How much information should be forwarded? Can the information be revealed anonymously or must it be accompanied with a signature?

6. **What chance for success does whistle-blowing in this instance have?** Sometimes the chances for achieving the needed reform are good; often they are slim to none; most fall between the two extremes. For reasons of prudence, whistle-blowing that has no chance of success may be morally unjustified. If, on the other hand, reasons of conscience motivate the concerned employee, the whistle should still be blown despite a perception that it will not be successful.

A CHARACTER AUDIT

Just claiming to be a Christian while on the job may not be enough to make any real difference in anyone's work life. The sad truth is that one cannot count on someone who claims to be a Christian automatically to be highly ethical at work. With some employees, such a profession can be counterproductive. One occasionally hears: "There's so-and-so. Watch out for him. He's one of those born-again Christian types, you know."

We close this chapter on moral courage in business and professional life with a challenge: Conduct a personality and character audit. You probably recall one of Socrates' best-known declarations: "The unexamined life is not worth living." There is Scriptural support for such an audit. "Examine yourselves to see whether you are in the faith," the apostle Paul commanded; "test yourselves" (2 Cor. 13:5). Of course, we are making a more practical application of the doctrinal test Paul likely envisioned.

Begin your audit by asking a few key questions: Do I attempt in all situations to apply my Christian faith to moral dilemmas at work? Do I relate to all coworkers, whether superiors or subordinates, with the manner and attitude that Jesus related to other people? Do I tend not to question the orders to someone "above" me, especially when that person has authority to influence my life for better or for worse? Do I follow authority blindly? Am I able to see my possible role as a participant in the immorality inflicted on other individuals, businesses, and social institutions? Do I understand the true motivations—whether in self-interest, prudence, or moral principles—for my moral decisions? Have I been clear-headed and incisive, or do I suffer from tunnel vision? Am I courageous enough to be consistent in my moral judgment and action? Do I apply the same standards to myself that I apply to others? How would I work if I had absolutely no supervision, but drew the same or a higher salary? If in practicing my profession I could do whatever I wanted with absolutely no consequence of being observed or reviewed, what would I do?

These are just some of the questions that a personal inventory might include if we are to combat the all-too-natural tendency to make the strongest case for selfish and prudential reasons for business and professional behavior rather than emphasize the moral reasons.

QUESTIONS FOR GROUP DISCUSSION
AND PERSONAL REFLECTION

1. Questions from the first real-life scenario which opened this chapter: Do you believe that Ron Farris was called by God to go to Africa? Does this story illustrate the difference between a calling and a vocation? Did the Farris family demonstrate moral courage? In your opinion, how typical is it for someone to resign from a high-income job and settle for a ministry that requires sacrifice and commitment?

2. Questions from the second real-life scenario: Carol Marin drew a line in the sand, or a line on the news desk, so to speak. Was her action courageous? Given her attractive appearance and long-standing reputation for honor and integrity, does it take moral courage to resign a position when it should be easy to land another similar position? If you had been Marin, would you have been troubled to work in a regular newscast with Jerry Springer at your side?

3. Do you agree with the author's distinction between "Sin" with the capital S and sins?

4. Do you think of excuse-making as lying?
5. Have you ever known someone to act on the "courage of personal convictions" on the job? Have you ever acted with moral courage on your job? Have you ever blown the whistle on some superior on the job for behavior you honestly believed to be unethical and/or illegal?
6. Whistle-blowing presents definite risks and dangers to the whistle-blower. Retaliation for whistle-blowing is common and takes various forms—blacklisting, poor job-performance evaluations, demotion, fast dismissal. Whistle-blowers may suffer career disruption, ostracism, and financial hardship. Given the high emotional and financial price that whistle-blowers must pay, do you think whistle-blowing is morally justified? Is the price of exposing misman-agement and corruption in business and professional life too high to pay in most cases?

There is a deeper philosophical issue. Does any employee, hired by a company and delegated responsibility and assignments for the salary he/she accepted, have any moral right to blow the whistle?

The following text cites some considerations you might make before you would approve someone's blowing the whistle on a large business organization. To cite these considerations does not answer all the questions about taking strong moral action.

   a. It is important to go through internal channels to seek satisfaction before going public, but what if the attempt to use internal means of protest means indefinite delays in getting action on the concern and/or exposes the potential whistle-blower to severe retaliation? Would you advise circumventing means of internal protest?
   b. Can one justify not using internal channels when the entire organization seems mired in the unethical wrong-doing that there is little hope that using internal chan-nels would accomplish anything positive?
   c. The text of this chapter asks the whistle-blower to attend his/her motive—just why is an employee going public with information harmful to the organization? But, really, does it matter what motivates the whistle-blower, so long as the information of serious offense is accurate and the danger to third parties is real? Might not an employee be justified in whistle-blowing if his/her real motivation was revenge for personal mistreatment in the department?
   d. What good can be done when a concerned and distressed employee blows the whistle over a legitimate organizational misdeed but the employee knows that no change will be accomplished? Should the whistle be blown only when there is reasonable chance for success?

CONSIDER HOW YOU MIGHT COUNSEL THE FOLLOWING PEOPLE in real-life work situations in which moral issues of integrity, responsibility, and prac-tical concerns of self-interest come in conflict:

Case Study
The question of self-interest often emerges in work situations. Debi Shelton is a cashier and short-order cook at the "Tank and Tummy Truck Stop" on Interstate 95.

She is asked to write up phony bills so the truckers can submit them to their supervisors and receive larger expense account reimbursements than they really deserve.

Debi does not think that this is right, so she complains to her own supervisor, Cliff. Cliff sympathizes with her concern, but explains that the restaurant is highly dependent on truck drivers' business and making them happy is just one way to ensure it. (Debi has also heard that the management tolerates female prostitutes in the back lot for truckers who park overnight, and she is quite distressed about this possibility. But, as a day-shift employee, she has not seen this firsthand and does not bring the matter up to Cliff.) Cliff just laughs at Debi's suggestion that she should be transferred to work in the establishment's gift shop (Debi knows that even there some souvenirs are marked up 300 percent).

After exasperating conversation, Cliff finally orders Debi to write up the overpriced bills at the truckers' bidding. Obviously, the morally right thing to do would be to refuse and the morally excellent action might be to report the practice to the trucking firm's management. But Debi is a recent divorcee with no formal education beyond high school and stands little chance of a better job in the depressed economy in her community. With children to raise and no other means of financial support, the consequences of job loss for Debi would be substantial.

Debi's part in the wrong-doing seems to be minor. Even the actual impact of the dishonesty on the major trucking firms seems to be pretty minor. "Don't my personal and family needs take precedence over exercising my moral convictions in this situation?" Debi asks herself.

Soon Debi asks you the same question. After all, for years you have been Debi's best friend. Both of you are attempting to live the Christian life. Does your morality require you to make huge sacrifices to right relatively small wrongs? What do you advise Debi?

Case Study

Elissa Wilson works at the shoe department of Castner Knott and has been employed there for three years. As an employee benefit, Castner Knott gives their employees a 25 percent discount on their purchases and their immediate family's purchases. They are very clear about only immediate family being eligible for the discount, and printed on the discount card is the policy for dismissal if the discount is abused.

The first ethical dilemma Elissa faces with this is that friends want to use the discount for their purchases. Although Elissa knew it was morally wrong, deep down she ends up buying things for anyone who asks. She rationalizes that Castner Knott was still making a profit even with a 25 percent discount, "so we were both winning."

Elissa has never really thought a lot about the wrongness of her actions. She knows it is against company policy, but she does not think of it as a sin. Every time Elissa has used the discount for other people, she felt a little bit guilty, but now realizes that "it was wrong to do Castner Knott that way."

What does Elissa say to her friends and family who continue to pressure her to purchase goods at an employee discount? Does moral excellence require her to sit down with management and confess that she has violated the employee purchase discount policy? Or should she simply dismiss the whole matter as "no big deal"?

Case Study

Kerry Lambert is a sales representative for a company which issues a wide variety of insurance policies and retirement plans. He travels throughout the state of Tennessee, usually with his colleague, to make presentations to various groups about the benefits of his company's policies.

Kerry comes to you with a dilemma. His colleague and traveling partner has developed a system of making extra money from their company in ways that Kerry considers unethical. For example, his partner might report expenses for meals which he did not purchase. Quite often his partner has spent the night at a friend's home in the town in which he was working but later collected expenses for a motel room that he did not use. This colleague has also been charging long-distance phone calls to the company for several years. All of this activity is against company policy.

Should Kerry blow the whistle on his colleague, who otherwise is a congenial person and highly capable sales representative? Kerry has already confronted his colleague about the unethical activity, but his only response was to "blow it off" and instruct Kerry not to worry about it. It's obvious, Kerry reasons, that their company should more closely monitor their agents' activities and that it should require meticulous documentation by receipts, but that is not the point. Does collegiality obligate Kerry to say nothing about these violations of policy to their employer? Does loyalty to the company obligate Kerry to report the infractions? What should Kerry do?

Case Study

John Lupini is single, is thirty-five years old, and has a management position in a banking and investment firm which employs about fifty other people. John has advanced in this firm and is highly satisfied with his job.

John has been feeling generally run down and has complained of several small ailments to his physician. When a routine check-up did not reveal anything specific, John's doctor encouraged him to undergo a blood test for AIDS. Well, lo and behold, John tested positive, which means that the antibodies for HIV are present in his body. He is infected by the virus, and it is probable, given his symptoms, that he has AIDS.

John loves his job. He knows his long-range future is uncertain at best. He has a number of days accumulated on his sick leave. He certainly would like to be an honest person and confide with his boss that he has AIDS, but he knows, realistically, that word will be out all over the firm. He knows that some people will be very reluctant to be around him, especially at meal time. He knows that customers will be informed in hushed tones of his condition. John believes he has a legal right to continue working at the firm until a total disability, but he knows that honesty about his condition may lower worker morale. He doesn't enjoy being at the center of controversy. The shame of the AIDS stigma is already heavy upon him.

If you were John's best friend and he came to you for advice about his work situation, what would you tell him?

Case Study

Mary Jo Vaillancourt is an instructor in a kindergarten. She enjoys everything about her job, especially the children she teaches and her salary. Mary Jo is concerned about Emily Compton, the director of the program. Emily has hired her own daughter, barely out of college and unable to land another teaching job in the county, and another relative as teachers on the staff. It seems that Emily's daughter and other friend are the least competent of the teachers on the staff.

Emily can be a bear to get along with. She can criticize easily, but does not take criticism to be any more than a personal affront. Mary Jo wants to keep her job, but the possibility of even more nepotism from Emily for the coming school year seems to be more than she wants to stomach.

Mary Jo knows that there are a number of other applicants that get overlooked for opening positions. Other teachers experience some resentment that is building. What does Mary Jo do, if anything?

Case Study

Dot Norman is a devout Christian. She believes it is important to be honest and fair with everyone. She is hired at Kroger and continues working there for several months. She notices that several of her coworkers think nothing of helping themselves to candy or produce at break or lunch time. One worker will drop a big bag of cookies on the floor, joke about the "accident," and then have a snack at the check out lane for the remainder of the day. She has seen coworkers put small packages of expensive items in their pockets (such as cosmetics, film, razor blades, etc.)

This troubles Dot, but she asks herself if it's "that big of a deal." What should Dot do?

Case Study

Karen Osborne is a secretary for a large legal firm. Karen is asked by her boss to lie to his wife about his whereabouts when his wife inquires by phone or drops by the office. He instructs his secretary to tell her or anyone else who calls that he is in a business conference which will likely last the rest of the day. The secretary is fairly certain that her boss is having an affair with another woman who calls her boss quite frequently and has long conversations during the work day. At times this woman shows up at the office. Karen's boss seems to relate to his visitor most warmly and a little self-consciously. Upon her arrival, he immediately invites her into his office and closes the door. Karen is uncomfortable with her boss's lifestyle and she believes it is morally wrong to lie about herself or anyone. She has tried to broach the subject with her boss, but he brushes her concerns away with humor or distractions. What should Karen do?

Case Study

Gregg Lawrence knows that a fellow worker occasionally snorts cocaine on the job. Should Gregg inform the boss?

Case Study

Joe Whitehouse, an accountant, learns of the illegal activities of a client, including deliberate violations of building codes? What should Joe do?

Case Study

Harry Cotham works for a British-based firm that manufactures and installs giant turbines, which pump natural gas out of the earth. As a consulting engineer he is sent to various spots around the globe during the installation process. In one big unit that was about to be installed for a university, Harry discovered a defect in the structure. He does not know what the impact of this defect might be once the unit is operational. He immediately informed his boss and the owner of the company about the defect. Both men have drug their feet about rectifying the problem. Should Harry inform the purchasing agent of the university about the defect if his own supervisor and the company's owner do not say anything about it?

Case Study

Lynn Caudill knows that her immediate supervisor uses company time and equipment for personal business. In violation of the department rules, Lynn's boss ties up a desk-top publishing computer and program for publishing her own church bulletin and garden-club newsletter. At times her boss even solicits the assistance of another worker in the unit to help her with these personal projects. Lynn wants to get along with her boss. Should she blow the whistle?

Case Study

Bob Moseley works for Bell South. He has access to a company truck and tools. One of Bob's cousins asked him if he could borrow the truck. Bob allowed this. Then the cousin asked Bob to help him move and wire his telephone service and to provide some assistance is setting up a bootleg television cable service. Bob's cousin assured him that he would take responsibility and reimburse Bob for the gas and materials that are used. What should Bob do?

Case Study

Valerie Stroop manages a big department at Nashville Tech. She manages several related jobs and records expenses for each separately. One of Valerie's jobs has overrun expenses due to some last minute changes in her faculty's requests and her failure to keep tight control on departmental spending. One of her other jobs is well under budget. Could not Valerie simply charge the extra expenses to the job that's under budget. The bottom line would be the same, and Valerie would not be held accountable for factors that she did not control well.

Chapter 9

Basic Respect/Basic Rights
Our Debt to One Another at Work

Never esteem anything as of advantage to you that will make you break your word or lose your self-respect.

Marcus Aurelius

Do nothing out of selfish ambition or vain conceit, but in humility each consider others better than yourselves.

Paul the Apostle

Business never was and never will be anything more or less than people serving other people. . . . From the

beginning we have visualized customers as our neighbors, whom it is our neighborly privilege to assist toward buying what they need and want at the lowest fair prices. . . . In other words, we interpret the golden rule as the mandate of service.

J. C. Penney

In everything do to others what you would have them do to you, for this sums up the Law and the Prophets.

Jesus

A CRUCIALLY IMPORTANT PRINCIPLE FOR ETHICAL BUSINESS LIFE IS that all business and professional people develop and maintain respect for other people—for all people actually and not simply those with whom one works. In this chapter we will consider respect for others in the broadest terms and allow Christian workers to make most of their own applications. Before closing, we will suggest some applications and then look at two controversial issues.

Three kinds of respect may be delineated:

1. **Minimal respect.** All individuals, simply because they are human beings like ourselves, deserve a minimal amount of respect. The human being—with his/her capacity for moral reasoning, memory, moral discretion, autonomous decision-making, making and keeping vows, penitence, and so forth—is different from all other animals in God's creation. Because of such uniqueness, each human merits respect.

2. **Character respect.** When we admire or value other individuals for their general character or for specific character virtues, we have accorded them character respect. While minimal respect is totally inclusive, character respect is

highly subjective and exclusive. One, for example, might accord great respect to Mother Teresa for her compassion and lifetime devotion to the poor and dying on the streets of Calcutta, India (character respect), while insisting simply that an apprehended criminal not be beaten by his arresting officers simply because he is a human being (minimal respect).

3. **Divine respect.** The Bible depicts a God who created human beings in his own image and who loves and cares deeply for every woman and man, girl and boy, simply because he gave them life and spirit. This same God who created us also seeks our salvation from the guilt of our wrongdoings and wants us to have fellowship with him. This God does not show partiality toward his created children, regardless of their race, nationality, or ethnic background (Acts 10:34; Titus 2:11–14).

Several scriptures summon us to respect and esteem other people. Paul instructed the Philippians to "Do nothing out of selfish ambition or vain conceit, but in humility consider others better than yourselves. Each of you should look not only to your own interests, but also to the interests of others"(Phil. 2:3–4). To the Romans he commanded, "Accept one another, then, just as Christ accepted you, in order to bring praise to God" (Rom. 15:7). Peter told his readers to "Clothe yourselves with humility toward one another, because, God opposes the proud but gives grace to the humble" (1 Pet. 5:5).

Moral philosophers have long dealt with the issue of how respect is shown to other people; some take respect for persons to be the fundamental moral principle. This kind of respect is not simply a matter of calling people by their proper titles, such as "Your Highness" or "Mister Chairman," nor is it a matter of proper politeness in social situations. Respect for others is a special kind of respect, often called "Kantian respect," after the German philosopher Immanuel Kant (1724–1804), and is captured in a familiar moral principle: *Never use other people merely as a means to your own ends.*

When we respect others we recognize the reality that all adult humans are autonomous beings and free moral agents. Our behavior is the product of our choices, big and small, and our choices emerge from our values, our convictions, our training, the major influences on our lives, and our moral reasoning. That is what makes people free, autonomous individuals. To respect others is to accord the freedom and understanding, perhaps even appreciation, for their choices about convictions, lifestyle, goals, and aspirations.

Respect for others is such a powerful moral concept, a concept we have attempted to state positively. Respect means that we do not erect barriers and throw obstacles in the way of people attempting to exercise their freedom and autonomy. Perhaps the concept of respect for others can also be understood by citing some of the more common violations of minimal respect.

VIOLATIONS OF MINIMAL RESPECT

In our listing we will not discuss the truly major violations of minimal respect, such as cruelty and coercion, physical abuse, murder, and rape.

Sexual Harassment

In the fall of 1991 much of the nation was riveted to a series of televised Senate hearings. Ordinarily, Senate hearings spawn boredom and apathy. This time, however, the principals were Supreme Court nominee (and now Justice) Clarence Thomas and Professor Anita Hill. The subject was neither new nor was the phenomenon uncommon: sexual harassment.

Sexual harassment is any sexually-oriented act or practice involving coercion, intimidation, or unfair sexual conduct. Although sexual harassment takes many forms, the message is always the same: "I have power over you, and you have a lot to lose if you complain."

Sexual harassment generally occurs in an environment where authority relationships are unequal; for example: the workplace, where an employer or supervisor can threaten to fire or demote an employee unless sexual favors are granted and inappropriate touching and comments are freely made; in academia, where close relationships between professors and students are encouraged by some schools and where students seek to influence the process of final grades; in church, where honest attraction can develop between a preacher and a church member, especially in a counseling situation which leads to transference and counter-transference of emotions that are appropriate only in each party's primary relationship.

The topic of sexual harassment is so relevant to the workplace that we will devote a special chapter to it later in this book (chapter 15).

Prejudice

Prejudice is an unfair and unreasonable attitude toward other people based on a categorical judgment about their physical characteristics, such as race, gender, or ethnic origin, or based on their group affiliations such as social class or religion. A prejudiced attitude may be expressed in oral communication and in behavior or in practices, laws, and institutional policy.

Prejudice can be either overt or covert. Overt prejudice is easily discernible to others and even to the prejudiced person. The sexist boss may claim that female employees are inferior. The white racist may claim that all blacks are inferior in intelligence. The anti-Semite may denounce all Jews as shrewd, conniving opportunists. The most dangerous, insidious form of prejudice, however, is covert (hidden, concealed). Covert prejudice is also called "visceral" because it is so deeply rooted in the psyche that it is not recognized or acknowledged; a person with covert prejudice uncritically and unconsciously adopts and acts on prejudiced attitudes toward other people or groups of people.

Stereotyping

Stereotyping is holding a standardized mental picture of all members of a certain group based on superficial characteristics, incomplete information, unmerited value judgments, or preconceived beliefs and attitudes. Stereotyping literally means "to repeat without variation." Negative stereotypes violate basic respect of others by denying them acceptance and standing as a unique man or woman whose emotions, needs, goals, aspirations, and life situations are different from all other men and women.

Racism

Racism is prejudice and unfair discrimination based on race or, as one person expressed it, "racial prejudice plus power." Racism is expressed in the intentional or unconscious use of power to separate, isolate, or discriminate against others. The racist believes that his/her own racial origin and racial traits are superior to those of other races and that, consequently, discrimination is legally and morally justified.

Sexism

Sexism is prejudice and unfair discrimination based on gender; the term is typically applied to males who entertain prejudiced views against females. Sexism is a term which emerged in the 1960s with the women's movement, which also popularized terms such as *male chauvinist* (to which "pig" is often suffixed), *misogyny* (hatred of women), and *patriarchy* (socially sanctioned male dominance). For Bible-believing Christians, the view toward women's role in the workplace and society may be colored by one's view of biblical teaching on the woman's role in the church and in the home.

Ageism

Ageism is prejudice and unfair discrimination based on one's age; the term typically applies to men and women in advanced years. In 1977 the U.S. Congressional Select Committee on Aging heard arguments for and against mandatory retirement; the following year, age was included among the categories of discrimination prohibited by the Civil Rights Act of 1964.

Passive-aggressiveness

Passive-aggressiveness, a seemingly contradictory term, refers to behavior that is widespread in important relationships. It is a method of game-playing and manipulation through silence or neglect or failure to attend/respond to another's needs. Passive-aggressiveness has been called "sugar-coated hostility." Passive-aggressive people use silence as a weapon, refusing to deliver the greatly needed words of assurance, love, and encouragement. They are an hour late, a dollar short, a block away, and armed with excuses to deflect responsibility. Passive-aggressiveness is an attempt by a weak person to demonstrate disrespect for another or to thwart authority rather than to confront interpersonal issues in a healthy and direct manner.

LESSER VIOLATIONS OF MINIMAL RESPECT

Ridicule

To ridicule someone is to treat someone as an object of scorn or mockery. Ridicule implies a deliberate, often malicious, belittling of some person or cause. Mockery implies scorn often ironically expressed as by mimicry or sham deference, as in young-sters mocking a helpless "wino." One may ridicule through malicious humor which camouflages one's spite and mockery of an individual or group.

Put-downs

When Archie Bunker called Edith a "dingbat" and admonished her, "Stifle your-self," audiences laughed. In real life, verbal abuse and put-downs, admittedly among the most familiar indignities of everyday life, are anything but funny. Although some put-downs may seem appropriate responses to someone's arrogance and pomposity, most put-downs reflect malice and contempt toward someone else. Unfortunately, a "sick" workplace is an environment where put-downs and ridicule erupt easily.

Both ridicule and put-downs can warn of physical violence to come, and verbal abuse alone can destroy a relationship. While everyone can lose his/her temper now and then, and even throw mean, acid-laced statements at a loved one or coworker, the verbal abuser has a different style and motivation. The abuser uses words and emotions (such as anger and aloofness) to punish, belittle, and control his/her partner; the abuse and ridicule continue compulsively and constantly with little empathy and rare apolo-gies. Just as with physical abuse, practitioners of ridicule and put-downs express a need for domination and control. And, not surprisingly, most practitioners are men—men who find it easier to give up physical abuse than verbal abuse.

Bigoted Humor

Telling and enjoying jokes is an almost universal experience which seems to make daily burdens lighter and bonds jokester and listener together. Joke-telling is also a popular avenue for conveying covert prejudice. A bigot is someone who is obstinately and intolerantly devoted to his/her own opinions and prejudices about other individ-uals or groups.

Bigoted humor violates a basic respect for other people. Almost every group of people in the American society, with the sole exception of the white American male—women, Indians, the Polish, blacks, Jews, blond-haired women, overweight people, short people, homosexuals, southern white mountaineers, just to name a few—has been the subject of bigoted humor and bigoted stereotyping. Whether we tell or laugh at a bigoted joke, we are usually sharing the prejudiced attitudes expressed in the joke or story.

Off-color Humor

Off-color jokes and stories often contain an element of scorn and ridicule for certain individuals and groups. Since sexuality is such a vital part of life, few would contend that a joke or story containing a sexual theme is automatically "dirty" or "off-color." Consider, however, two points: first, to tell someone a joke or story that the hearer will consider to be "crude" or "off-color" is to show disrespect for the listener; second, sexual or scatological humor may convey derogatory and scornful views toward certain individuals or groups. Humor about the sexual activities or bodies of very old people in health care facilities, for example, may berate all older people.

Rudeness

Rudeness is a major violation of accepted standards of proper behavior, dress, and speech in a given society; it is being in a rough, non-refined state (uncouth). As such, rudeness may seem simply a matter of etiquette and not everyday morality. After all, rudeness may be defined more by the context and culture than by absolute rules; a frank sexual comment that is flattering to one woman may be a devastating offense to another woman. However, rudeness may be much more than a violation of etiquette and entail demonstrating disrespect for others.

The following are some traits of the functionally inconsiderate, and as you read them, consider which behaviors are excusable lapses in ideal etiquette and which of them demonstrates an insensitive disrespect for other people: ignore phone messages; never ask how you are or how your family and work are doing; talk loudly to their friends while you try to concentrate on work or study; spend more than fifteen minutes rehearsing a vacation they've taken or an operation they've had; are always late and never offer an excuse; break appointments at the last minute; say "I'll get right back to you" and never do; offer no apology when they interrupt or inconvenience you; do not know the meaning of phrases "It's on me" or "What's your opinion?" or "What's happening in your life?" or "What can I do to help you?"

Snobbery

Snobbery is an attitude that one is superior to all other people except for the group in which one belongs. A snob tends to rebuff, avoid, or ignore those he/she regards as inferior and may seek to associate only with those he/she considers equal or superior in importance and worth. The snob may project an offensive air of superiority in matters of morality, wisdom, intelligence, and taste, impairing the self-esteem of others in their immediate social environment.

Snobbery becomes a moral issue when one's intention is to cause others to suffer—to feel inferior—because of one's alleged superiority. Snobbery is frequently accompanied by hypocrisy, as when one pretends to be better or more important than one actually is, and by arrogance, in which one makes unwarranted claims of superiority or flaunts authentic superiority in offensive ways.

JOB DISCRIMINATION—A MAJOR VIOLATION OF RESPECT

To practice discrimination in employment is to make adverse decisions against employees or job applicants based on factors totally beyond their control. The discriminatory decisions may be made by an individual manager or may be woven into the corporate culture in policy form. Discrimination is the unequal treatment of equals. It involves false assumptions about the inferiority of certain groups and harms individual members of those groups. It violates elementary social justice by denying a significant portion of the population full and equal participation in the marketplace. From a Christian perspective, job discrimination based on factors that people are born with violates biblical mandates that people be treated with dignity and respect. Few people would defend job discrimination openly today, of course, but its practice was once long-standing and the battle to overcome it continues.

Evidence of historic prejudice and discrimination in all sectors of American public life has been abundant. Quite expectedly, the workplace has been a major arena in which discriminatory policies have been practiced. The seeds of long-standing discrimination have borne the fruit of inequality. Poverty is about three times as more likely among black, Hispanic, and Native American families than white ones. Because minorities are usually the last hired and the first fired, unemployment is highest among racial minorities. Many blacks and women feel that they are clustered in low-prestige, low-paying, dead-end work. Female workers speak of a "glass ceiling," an invisible barrier in many corporations that allows them to rise only so far within the organization; the "glass ceiling" means they are relegated to lower-paying, "pink-collar" job classifications. In the professional world, women are represented in all the major service areas—law, medicine, education, counseling, and so forth. The number of males in the professions, however, far outweighs the number of female professionals; for example, 99 percent of the dental hygienists, but less than 10 percent of the dentists, are female.

Since 1954, when the Supreme Court struck down racial segregation in public schools in its famous *Brown* v. *Board of Education*, both Congress and the Court have made strategic moves to effect racial integration and protection of citizen rights in public organizations. As early as 1961, President John F. Kennedy signed an executive order urging federal contractors to take "affirmative action" to ensure that applicants were treated fairly regardless of race, creed, or national origin. In 1963 the Congress took a swipe at unequal pay for women by passing the Equal Pay Act.

The following year the most important piece of legislation regarding civil rights at work was passed by Congress. The Civil Rights Act of 1964 (amended in 1972 as the Equal Employment Opportunity Act) prohibits all forms of discrimination based on race, color, sex, religion, and national origin. This landmark legislation is a federal umbrella protecting all U.S. citizens, and it applies to all employers, both public and private, with fifteen or more employees. In 1967 the Age Discrimination in Employment Act was passed (later amended in 1978). Other acts and executive orders require the federal government as employer to provide equal opportunities for the handicapped and for veterans. The Equal Opportunity Commission (EEOC) is charged with the important responsibility of enforcing these acts.

In recent years, programs based on this legislation have been formulated to implement and ensure fair and equal treatment of all people in the workplace. Nevertheless, unequal practices persisted. To remedy discriminatory practices, the federal government in the early 1970s instituted an affirmative-action program.

The intention of affirmative action is to identify and remedy unfair discrimination practiced against many people who are qualified for jobs. The program has been controversial since its inception. Several terms are employed in discussing job discrimination:

Preferential hiring: an employment practice designed to give special consideration to people from groups that traditionally have been victimized by racism, sexism, or other forms of discrimination.

Quota hiring: the policy of hiring and employing people in direct proportion to their numbers in society or in the community.

Reverse discrimination: the unfair treatment of a majority member (usually a white male) in employment practices.

Arguments for Affirmative Action

1. **Justice requires that we compensate for the results of past discriminations.** "No one can deny the nation's history of racism and sexism. Prejudice and discrimination have been deeply embedded in the major social, political, and economic institutions of our society. Often the discrimination has been vicious and unrelenting. We must not ignore the sins of our forefathers, even if complete compensatory justice is impossible."

2. **Preferential treatment is the only way to overcome current racism and sexism.** "Bias in the workplace has not completely left us and anyone who thinks that is not the case is whistling 'Dixie' in the most inappropriate places. We know that the unemployment rate among blacks is higher than the rate among whites. There is also a glass ceiling. Racial stereotypes abound. White men have a competitive edge they do not deserve."

3. **Affirmative action is necessary to break the cycle that keeps minorities and women locked into low-paying, low-prestige jobs.** "Women and minorities have been trapped in a socioeconomically subordinate position. We need to break the pattern and heal rifts. Even if racism and sexism were dead in their tracks, something no bright person would concede, with mere nondiscrimination in employment and promotion it would take a century or more for minorities to equalize their position."

4. **Women and minorities need role models in all walks of life.** "The nation needs all kinds of people in all kinds of professions and careers just to let youth know that there are all kinds of possibilities for them if they demonstrate talent and perseverance. A young black who has never seen a black surgeon is less likely to aspire to surgery as a career; a young girl who has never met a woman as a CEO of a major corporation is less likely to imagine herself in the same role. Tokenism in specialized careers may not be very convincing."

Arguments Against Affirmative Action

1. **All job discrimination on the basis of race and sex is inherently unfair.** "Such programs violate the right of white men to be treated as individuals and to have sexual or racial considerations not affect employment or advancement

decisions. Why should white men bear the brunt of social and economic reform."

2. **Affirmative action itself violates the principle of equality.** "All human beings deserve equal treatment. No one should be denied a job because of gender or skin color. To discriminate against anyone on the basis of sex or race, white males included, is inherently unfair."

3. **Reverse discrimination creates resentment and social tensions.** "White males who have been denied jobs and promotions justifiably feel cheated and naturally come to resent minorities and women. And why shouldn't they?"

4. **Reverse discrimination stigmatizes minorities and women.** "Minorities and women may not be respected for their accomplishments, but instead may be objects of suspicion. Their reputations may be tainted by knowledge they were given special advantage at the expense of others. Affirmative action thus injures the very people it is designed to help. The policy of hiring and promoting blacks and women because of their race or sex solicits attention to their lack of qualifications and creates the impression that they could not succeed on their own. Furthermore, affirmative action may actually diminish the respect of society for the many hard-won achievements of women and blacks, thus eroding the legitimacy of what has already been achieved."

5. **Reverse discrimination wastes the best human resources.** "Why have a system wherein the best-qualified people for a job don't get the job? Can society afford to waste its best human resources in such a competitive world? It seems unjust for society to set standards of achievement and then to thwart the expectations of those who have measured up to those standards. If it is a noble ideal to reduce the importance of race, gender, and other factors in American society, then affirmative action and preferential treatment defeat this ideal by heightening our collective consciousness of these differences."

Comparable Worth

On a similar matter, should men and women of similar skills and training and with similar responsibilities be paid essentially the same salary? Some federal judges have said yes. In essence, the *doctrine of comparable worth* holds that women and men should be paid on the same scale, not just for doing the same or equivalent job tasks, but for doing different jobs of equal effort, skill, and responsibility. Advocates of this doctrine note that the higher the percentage of women in an occupation, the less that occupation pays. When women dominate an occupation, a "pink collar" career has been established that pays less than "white collar" careers dominated by men. Opponents of the doctrine of comparable worth contend that many women are more wrapped up in family issues than men and that they freely seek less taxing and more flexible jobs and thus are not entitled to any upward readjustment of their salaries. Others say that such a doctrine is impossible to implement fairly; "How are different jobs evaluated and compared?" they ask.

The issue of workplace justice is indeed an ethical issue, and job discrimination based on race, gender, age, color of skin, and other inconsequential factors is one of the deepest violations of dignity imaginable. Rights figure prominently in arguments both for and against preferential treatment programs. Would it not be fair to concede that, while affirmative action once served a valuable purpose, some of its implementation actually aggravated rather than healed racial tensions? The U.S. population is now composed of approximately 28 percent minorities, and corporate management is now aware that it is unwise not to utilize a workforce that reflects the racial and ethnic mix in the local community. By the turn of the century, it is estimated, women, minorities, and immigrants will compose approximately 80 percent of the new hires in the U.S. labor force.

POLITICAL CORRECTNESS— EVIDENCE OF BASIC RESPECT FOR OTHERS?

The 1990s ushered in a near obsession with political correctness. The "P.C." movement was concerned with both proper behavior toward people who are different from the majority and appropriate language choices when addressing or discussing others.

Look around your office, shop, or factory. Chances are, you'll see some different faces from those you might have found a generation ago. There is more diversity today in U.S. workplaces and schools than ever before. Workplaces once filled with white men now have more women and more minority workers, especially African-Americans, Hispanics, and Asian-Americans. The percentage of whites in the U.S. workforce is declining, while the percentage of minorities is rising. Blacks made up 10.3 percent of the workforce in 1982 and 11.1 percent in 1994; for Asians, it was 2.5 percent and 3.2 percent; Hispanics, 6.1 percent and 9.1 percent; and whites, 81.3 percent and 76.7 percent. Today, there are workers with limited English, workers who wear turbans or yarmulkes, and workers who are openly homosexual. Diversity is fast becoming the norm.

Language is also certainly important. It is not simply the vehicle by which we talk to each other, but a vehicle for thinking about each other. For, as linguists Edward Sapir and Benjamin Lee Whorf suspected as early as the 1940s and postmodernist psychological theory has confirmed, language is not merely the mirror of our society—it is the major force in "constructing" what we perceive as "reality."

The "P.C." movement began with noble intentions. Are those good intentions being served by political correctness as currently practiced or advocated in company policy manuals? Does political correctness demonstrate basic respect for others? We will briefly look at both sides of the debate.

Arguments for Political Correctness

1. **Political correctness is intended to help people speak about others in nonjudgmental and nondiscriminatory ways.** "The practice of political correctness is a forceful statement of justice, equality, and respect. It removes the judgmental connotations of one's words about other people. We know that one

of the big barriers to effective interpersonal communication is judgment that slips into our words and tone of voice."

2. **Political correctness demonstrates sensitivity and courtesy to all kinds of coworkers, thus setting a positive tone for the working environment.** "Political correctness means being sensitive to individual uniqueness in terms of race, physical appearance, nationality, age, and ethnicity. It thus helps level the playing field at work."

3. **Political correctness exhibits inclusiveness and equality.** "The message of political correctness is 'Our differences do not really make a difference. We're all in this thing together.' We all know that actions of upper-level management can create and modify the corporate culture, for good or for ill. Politically correct language choices should enable people in firms to think of others as equals, thus facilitating shared goals and shared values."

4. **Political correctness helps people understand the underlying assumptions and implications of their behavior and language.** "A lot of times we just talk without thinking about the assumptions underlying our words and actions. Political correctness provokes people's thinking about others in constructive, unifying ways."

5. **Political correctness builds trust by demonstrating that the company respects its employees and their dignity.** "The result is that they are more likely to be satisfied and productive workers. When political correctness is used by managers in both oral and written downstream communications, it provides a powerful example of appropriate language and behavior for workers to follow."

Arguments Against Political Correctness

1. **Basic respect and good manners cannot be legislated.** "How we feel and act toward others are matters of the heart—not matters of choosing the right words for company manuals and internal memos."

2. **Total equality in any environment is not necessarily a noble goal.** "Let's face it: people are different and will always be different. A black man will always be a black man and a white man will always be white. There are other ways that demonstrate that superficial differences are insignificant than by punctiliously attending to and monitoring our nouns, pronouns, and titles."

3. **Political correctness becomes burdensome and ridiculous with its excessive verbosity and unnatural word choices.** "It places a burden on people who seek direct, clear, and informal communication with others so that they meet some requirement to speak in neutral, ambiguous terms. Of course, we all know that the brain surgeon could be female and the church secretary could be a male, but who cares if a generic pronoun which could refer to either male or female is a 'he' or a 'she'? Where's the big sin when some females could possibly be included in familiar terms such as 'watchmen,' 'chairmen,' or 'fishermen'? Do we really prefer 'milkperson' over 'milkman' and 'personhole' over

'manhole'? "Does 'differently abled' communicate a person's condition any better than 'physically handicapped'?

4. **Removing moral judgment from language is no virtue.** "The divorce of moral judgment from human language seems to be attempted in all public institutions, but does this make us a better society? Everyone needs guidelines. To substitute 'sexually active' for 'promiscuous' or 'an affair of the heart' and 'intimacy' for fornication and adultery does not make a better society. And what does an "alternative lifestyle" really mean? Christianity is an 'alternative' and 'counter culture' lifestyle, for that matter. The entire 'P.C.' movement is based on taking relativism to an extreme where all traditional morality is assailed and everyone is tolerant of everything, even behavior that everyone once thought to be deviant.

"The issue is not so much about political correctness as it is about moral correctness, and moral correctness is not taught by making every transaction as value-free and morally neutral as possible. Political correctness might actually soften reality to the point of dishonest communication and tolerance of every deviant and immoral action."

5. **Political correctness tends to make victims of everyone who is different from the majority.** "Once judgment is removed from language, a sense of personal responsibility is also removed; therefore, the inappropriate behavior of others may be explained by their victimization by individuals or society as a whole. Do we really want to call a 'panhandler' an 'an urban survivor and unaffiliated applicant for private-sector funding'? Is a fat man simply 'horizontally challenged' and a failure one who is 'incompletely successful' or 'an individual with temporarily unmet objectives'?"

DEMONSTRATING RESPECT AT WORK

A class in business and professional ethics at David Lipscomb University, Nashville, Tennessee, was asked to submit brief, practical suggestions for demonstrating respect at work for colleagues and partners. All but the last six suggestions came from that class:

1. Take criticism in a positive tone because you are all working together for the betterment of the company. Have an open mind.
2. Always be understanding that certain topics are private (salaries, opinions on topics, etc.) and not open for in-depth discussion.
3. Try to help out a coworker whenever possible because, more than likely, you will need his/her help at some point in time.
4. Always be friendly, courteous, and smile.
5. Remember birthdays.
6. Keep mouth closed when brain not in gear.
7. Stick to business—leave personal matters out of the office.
8. Pray for your coworkers.
9. Exercise the golden rule.

10. Complete your work on time so that others will not have extra work to do.
11. Use compliments when appropriate instead of put-downs.
12. Always keep lines of communications open regarding projects, deadlines, schedule changes.
13. Trust your coworkers until they prove you wrong.
14. Be willing to help out coworkers, even if it's "not your job."
15. Listen.
16. Be on time for the workday, meetings, etc.
17. Respect others' personal space and privacy.
18. Realize that the opinions of others that are different from yours are not necessarily wrong or worth less consideration than yours.
19. Try to make your coworker's job easier by doing little favors. If, for example, you have used the copier and then you notice it is almost out of paper, then take time to fill the paper tray for the next person.
20. Knock before entering someone's office.
21. When you're making fifty copies of a four-page document and a coworker has a one-sheet, one-copy job, let her go first. Remember to fill the paper drawer if it's empty, and if it's jammed, fix it. If you don't know how, find someone who does.
22. Don't interrupt a conversation between coworkers or between a colleague and the boss unless it is absolutely necessary. If you do join a conversation, make sure you are not ignoring or excluding someone who was there before you.
23. Food should be eaten or disposed of right away, or your cubicle could become the office compost heap.
24. Don't leave dirty office mugs in the sink or slimy, unidentifiable objects in the garbage disposal. Avoid microwaving smelly leftovers.
25. Blurting your own thoughts while someone is in mid-sentence is rude, inconsiderate, and self-absorbed—three traits that compromise credibility and likability. Always stay focused on whomever is speaking.

(See Corporate Network/Common Sense in the appendices for additional ways to demonstrate respect for others at work through etiquette.)

SPECIAL EXERCISE:
THE ATTITUDE ASSESMENT STIMULUS

Complete the sentence with the first idea that enters your mind, not with what you think you should say. There are no right or wrong answers.

1. My opinion about black people in America is _____
_____.

2. The Jews that I know about _____
_____.

3. When I see a man or woman I consider to be highly overweight _____

_____.

4. White people should _____

_____.

5. An attractive, blonde woman will _____

_____.

6. Black people are best at _____

_____.

7. White people are best at _____

_____.

8. Small town and rural Southerners should be known for their _____

_____.

9. Homosexuals should _____

_____.

10. My parents think (or thought) that people of another race _____

_____.

11. A woman at work will _____

_____.

12. If I have a prejudice toward any group, it would be _____

_____.

QUESTIONS FOR GROUP DISCUSSION
AND PERSONAL REFLECTION

1. What are three kinds of respect for others?
2. What is meant by "Kantian respect"?
3. Is every individual human being worthy of being accorded minimal respect because each is a human? What about psychopaths, for example, who lack any conscience about what is morally right and wrong and may be capable of committing a gruesome murder and then sleep soundly for eight hours the following night? How about the sadistic torturers among the Nazis who performed grisly experiments on Jewish subjects? Is it possible that we might respect some animals more than we would respect certain humans?
4. Is there any kind of biblical insight to help us to understand why people develop and maintain a highly negative, unfair view of other people?
5. Is it possible to eradicate all racial and ethnic prejudice from our minds?
6. How politically correct should our language choices be in order to respect sensitivities about race, ethnicity, handicaps, and gender?
7. Does sexism actually exist in the American workplace? After all, a woman can be elected to Congress or appointed to the Supreme Court. She can even run for president and be elected. She can chair a university department or a corporate board. Her plight is far better than the plight of women living in Middle East nations. So, is the glass ceiling now removed? Do women have equal opportunity in the workplace?

8. In November 1996, an incident involving the Texaco Oil Company became widely publicized, much to the embarrassment of company officials. An audio tape of Texaco officials making racially prejudiced comments to one another in a boardroom meeting was leaked to the press. White officials were overheard calling black employees "black jellybeans" that should be kept at the bottom of the jar. Within days, a suit by fifteen hundred minority employees at Texaco was settled by a $140 million payment.

Do you think that racism is rampant in corporate America, especially at the upper-management levels, or that racial discrimination and racist attitudes are much less common than ever before in our society?

Do you think that black racism is just as bad as white racism? That is, behind closed doors and in the comfort of private, small, and racially homogenous groups that both whites and blacks are likely to speak with equal derision about the other race?

Does privately expressed prejudice qualify as racist behavior?

Is legally enforced affirmative action the only answer to the various forms of discrimination which may exist in the workplace?

9. What are some examples of rudeness in the workplace that you have witnessed personally? What was your reaction?

10. Is the apostle Paul's commandment to do nothing out of vain ambition and to esteem others better than self realistic for aspiring workers, supervisors, and career people in various professions? Is it possible for anyone to obey that command at work?

11. After the passage of the 1964 Civil Rights Act, employers scrutinized their hiring and promotion practices and attempted to eliminate sources of discrimination. Even the best efforts of companies did not always succeed in eliminating sources of discrimination. Programs that intended to bring "simple justice" to the workplace were soon called "affirmative action."

As discussed in the text of this chapter, "affirmative action" refers to programs of hiring and placement which take into account race or gender. The purpose is to correct long-standing imbalances in employment which have put certain groups at a disadvantage, either in the company itself or in society as a whole. Blacks and women were intended to be the main beneficiaries.

Affirmative action raises many questions worth considering. We might begin with a central issue: How does one define "opportunity"?

Are there strong moral arguments either for or against affirmative action? Does affirmative action violate the principle of equality? Do blacks or women have a right to be given preference in hiring or promotion, and do white males have any rights that are violated when preference is given on the basis of race or sex? Should this generation of majority Americans make reparations for wrongs committed against previous generations of American minorities? The compensation argument is based on the idea that justice requires that people who are wronged deserve to be compensated in some way, but what is just compensation for the wrongs of discrimination? Who ought to be compensated? And who ought to do the compensating? Does this current generation owe special treatment to Asians and Spanish-speaking minorities who have most recently come to our borders? Yes, we broached some of these concerns in the text of the chapter, but the issue is too complex to summarize in a few paragraphs. What do you think?

12. Congress acted in 1978 to include age among the categories of discrimination prohibited by the Civil Rights Act. The year before, a Congressional Select Committee on Aging considered arguments for and against mandatory retirement. Arguments for mandatory retirement reflected the following factors: (a) older persons may be less well-suited for some jobs than younger workers; (b) older workers are less flexible and may experience physical and mental decline; (c) mandatory retirement may save face for workers no longer able to function adequately; and (d) it may provide a predictable situation allowing employers and employees to plan ahead. Arguments against mandatory retirement reflect the concern that it is inherently discriminatory: (a) it is contrary to equal employment opportunity; (b) chronological age is a poor indicator of ability to perform a job; (c) a forced policy can cause problems for workers by limiting their work life and salary potential, thus adding to financial hardship; and (d) it can cause loss of skills and experience in the workforce.

   What do you think? Is mandatory retirement a form of job discrimination? What moral issues might arise when considering mandatory retirement? Do you know of certain classifications of workers who need to step down from their job after they reach a certain age?

13. Do you think a manager of a U.S. department store which has hired a number of Hispanics can have an "English only" policy for employees while on the job, even if English is only a second language to these employees? Might this depend on what part of the country the store is located and upon what language most of the customers usually spoke?

Case Study

Lynn Bradford works in real estate. Like other businesses, this is a tough, competitive field to be employed. Lynn knows that in real estate, as in other business, he is not allowed to discriminate on anything or anybody, whether it be on the basis of color, sex, religion, or nationality.

One day Lynn was working with some buyers and attempting to render professional service in assisting their location of a house. One of the buyers demanded, "Show me a neighborhood that doesn't have any niggers living in it." The use of the "N" word offended Lynn. He had been taught in his real-estate class that some people might pose as buyers and make these kind of inflammatory statements in order to test the ethics of the real-estate agent.

As a young man, Lynn faced an ethical dilemma. If he went along with the buyer, he would be guilty of breaking a law against racial discrimination in property sales. But he also knew that if he did not go along with them, he could lose some qualified buyers and a commission. Lynn had his own indebtedness. He has monthly rent and car payments. He needed that commission. What is Lynn's moral responsibility?

Chapter 10

Beyond Maximizing Profits
A Survey of the Stakeholder Model

Business is a major social institution that should bear the same kinds of citizenship costs for society that an individual citizen bears. Business will benefit from a better society just as any citizen will benefit; therefore, business has a responsibility to recognize social problems and actively contribute its talents to help solve them.

Keith Davis

The view has been gaining widespread acceptance that corporate officials and labor leaders have a social responsibility that goes beyond serving the interest of their stockholders or their members. This view shows a fundamental misconception of the character and nature of a free economy. In such an economy, there is one and only one social responsibility of business—to use its resources and engage in activities designed to increase its profits so long as it stays within the rules of the game, which is to say, engages in open and free competition, without deception or fraud. . . . Few trends could so thoroughly undermine the very foundations of our free society as the acceptance by corporate officials of a social responsibility other than to make as much money for their stockholders as possible.

Milton Friedman

If a young man fathers a child, then it is not unreasonable to expect him to support and nurture that child. There is little argument about that proposition. Yet if a corporate executive makes a decision to close an inner-city factory—a move that will make it more difficult for many young men to support their children—he is likely to be applauded as a wizard of corporate restructuring and rewarded with bonuses of millions of dollars. If he can get the same work done in Mexico for one-tenth the labor cost, he's simply a shrewd businessman.

Who will denounce him as irresponsible? In the Candidean world of free-market economics, his pursuit of narrow self-interest ultimately produces public good. Why not see the runaway father's narrow self-interest in the same entrepreneurial light?

David Moberg

A person's character is revealed in his or her dedication to all aspects of quality: the product or service itself, the production and distribution processes and their impact on the environment, the work life of those associated with the product, and the social impact of the product in its usage. If a manager is concerned only about the quality of the product and ignores the quality of the workers' lives or the impact of his business on the environment, he is trying to segment quality. But quality cannot be segmented.

Perry Pascarella

An ethical business firm is defined for our purposes as an enterprise that has earned the respect and trust of its employees, customers, suppliers, investors, and others by striking an acceptable balance between its economic interests and the interests of all parties affected when making decisions and taking actions.

Francis J. Aguilar

DOES BUSINESS HAVE AN OBLIGATION BEYOND THAT OF MAKING money for its owners? A few decades ago this question would never have been raised. The business of business, it was assumed, is profit.

In the 1950s, with the problems of the Great Depression behind the nation, this assumption began to be questioned. Human needs were identified as more than a paycheck and worthwhile products and services. The large corporation, such as General Motors, was recognized as a broadly based, socioeconomic institution. The corporation assumed, or should assume (according to some), a set of both primary responsibilities and secondary responsibilities to groups that may have no direct connection with the company's ownership or operation.

Is there truly an alternative to the model of maximization of profit as the only corporate responsibility? The answer is in what is often called the "stakeholder" model. The concept of a stakeholder is a valuable device for identifying and organizing the multitude of responsibilities that corporations have to different people. Stakeholders are those individuals or groups whose welfare may be seriously impacted by a corporation's decisions or activities. Because these individuals or groups have something to gain or lose in a corporation's decision-making, they thus hold a "stake" (or claim) in corporate management and behavior.

Potentially, there are many stakeholders—management, customers or clients, stockholders, creditors, bondholders (or others with a financial investment), employees (both active and retired), suppliers, community neighbors, governmental agencies, and the general public. This view of business ethics envisions a network of relationships with lines of connection linking stakeholders to one another. There are interconnecting lines with other businesses. The ethical responsibility of each corporation is to serve fairly and in proper balance the interests of all groups associated with the business.

The word "stakeholder" is chosen considerately. Yes, it reminds us of "stockholder," a much more familiar term. The original stakeholders of any public company were indeed the stockholders, the shareholders and investors. The term represents the broadening base of American corporate life; large companies are often multinational in operations, thus impacting wider, more diverse groups of people. The term also suggests the dynamic interaction that goes on between a corporation and all the women and men who either serve it or are served by it. All of us who use major systems of communication or who drive automobiles or depend on public agencies and institutions for goods and services (is anyone excluded?) are stakeholders in U.S. business to some degree.

Granted that managers and other business leaders have ethical responsibilities to their company's stakeholders, what exactly are those ethical responsibilities and how do they relate to one another? Does a business manager have the same moral obligations to one group of stakeholders that he/she does to another group? That is, are the claims and needs of one group just as important as those of any other group? How are conflicts among the needs and interests of various stakeholders to be resolved? Attention to product design and safety which benefit the customers and clients may not be in the best interest of the stockholders who look only at the bottom line. A commitment to affirmative action as a way to improve public relations of the company and to benefit the local community may not be in the best interests of current salaried workers who feel their job security threatened. Is it possible to weigh the relative power and ethical responsibility of the various stakeholders?

These complex issues may not seem interesting to those who only seek simply to know what the Bible teaches about work, but they are real-life issues in the contemporary world which affect millions. As we approach these challenging issues, we will briefly describe five groups of stakeholders. As we proceed, we warn readers in advance that there will be far more questions than there are answers.

OWNER/STOCKHOLDER–SHAREHOLDER

In spite of the growing concern about all the parties who are impacted by business decisions, it is indisputable that the first duty of the company's managers is to maximize profits and dividends for the firm's owners/shareholders. Even the most progressive, the most socially conscious, business executive must seek a profit.

The basic point: the bottom line is still the most important matter. The bottom line is not the only consideration, of course, but the concerns of owners still come first. The reason is obvious—unless management serves its owners and shareholders well enough to receive a fair return on their investment, the business firm will not survive.

Not only must business executives manage money and other resources efficiently in their pursuit of profit, but they must manage all resources honestly and fairly. Herein lies the ethical challenge—to manage both efficiently and honestly. The imperative of both efficiency and integrity gives rise to numerous moral quandaries over management practices.

Why are "smaller" unethical practices treated with more tolerance the higher one goes up the corporate ladder? Is expense-account-padding less offensive among owners and higher executives? Are executive perquisites an ethically sound system for rewarding managers for their special skills? Do executive salaries, which are many times higher than the lowest level of employees in the same firm, constitute an ethical practice? Are all "standard practices" ethical? These are but a few of the questions which arise when we consider the ethical responsibilities of owners, investors, and top-level management.

EMPLOYEE STAKEHOLDERS

To say that a company could not function without its employees is to state the obvious. In this century there have been significant changes in the U.S. corporate life which have impacted the American workforce. Foremost among these changes is the shift from our manufacturing economy to an economy based on communications, knowledge, and information management. Also, reflecting the diversity of the general population, the U.S. workforce is now composed of a higher percentage of females, blacks, Hispanics, Asian-Americans, and other minorities. The white male is no longer the dominating force in American work life; although, it may be contended, he still holds a prime position among the elite professions.

However the workforce may be depicted socially or demographically, the basic needs and concerns of employees remain the same. The most basic concern is employee rights. Whether employees work in offices and board rooms as salaried workers or in factories and fields as hourly laborers, they are convinced of an entitlement to fair wages, fair treatment, a safe work environment, and benefits. Additionally, employees seek and expect trust and respect from their superiors, but such trust and respect are difficult to quantify in concrete measures.

One strong indicator of organizational respect for employees is the style in which management relates to employees. The assumptions about employees and the conduct of managers on the job can do more to enhance or diminish the work environment than any other single factor in labor-management relations. Long a standard in management theory has been the analytic framework of the late Douglas McGregor. By looking at two extremes, called Theory-X and Theory-Y in McGregor's proposition, it is possible to see the range of belief differences that can occur.

Theory-X managers make certain assumptions about workers: most people dislike work and will avoid it if they can; workers must be forced to perform; most people lack ambition and dislike responsibility; most people must be controlled and threatened with punishment; most people are inherently self-centered and resistant to change. Theory-X managers are likely to provide autocratic leadership and closely lead workers by giving orders and directions and following their orders by close monitoring. They expect little more of employees than that they follow orders.

Theory-Y managers also make assumptions about workers: the typical worker does not inherently dislike work; the average person learns to accept and even seeks responsibility; external controls and threats of punishment are not the only means to get people to do an adequate job; the intellectual ability of the worker needs to be respected; individuals accept change when the primary pressures for change are self-imposed. Theory-Y managers are most likely to be democratic; they invite new ideas;

they respect the input and convictions of their subordinates. Theory-Y managers can be virtually nondirective.

Quite obviously, the Theory-Y management style provides the opportunity for employees to participate in the managerial decision-making, which impacts the success of the business organization, and to build self-respect, good morale, and skills that lead to job satisfaction and career advancement. Participative management, employee participation, or Japanese-style management, are names for Theory-Y management assumptions being implemented and covering a wide range of opportunities for employee empowerment. The traditional hierarchical or paternalistic style of management is no longer suited for the work ethic and emotional needs of a generation of better-educated, better-trained, more-independent employees.

Employees as stakeholders have other needs and concerns beyond fair salary and benefits. One is health and safety on the job. Many manufacturing and production jobs involve dangerous risks and health hazards for employees. Some health hazards are not identifiable until years after the production of new materials or products. According to the National Institute of Occupational Safety and Health, an average of thirty-two workers are killed on the job each day of the year in the United States and another fifty-five hundred suffer a disabling injury. Translation of these accidents into dollar amounts has totaled billions in wages and an enormous annual loss to the gross national product. Critics of the Occupational Safety and Health Administration (OSHA), founded in 1970, have accused the agency of being lax in establishing permanent standards and spotty in implementing its mission "to ensure so far as possible every working man and woman in the nation safe and healthful working conditions." Complaints from telephone operators, computer-data-entry secretaries and other keyboard workers, supermarket check-out clerks, to name a few, have complained about failing vision, carpeltunnel syndrome, aching wrists, and other crippling injuries. These may seem like minor complaints, but they are anything but minor to those who suffer from them.

Employees are also greatly interested in respect for their basic rights while on the job. Privacy is widely acknowledged today to be a fundamental right, yet employees are fully aware that their companies possess a great deal of confidential information in personnel files and data banks. As employees, we volunteer a great deal of personal information to our employers, because we know corporations must document their labor force according to gender, age, race, and handicap status. Government collects a great deal of personal information about all of us. Disclosure of this confidential information to unauthorized parties can violate employee rights, as bosses have learned after successful lawsuits filed by former employees. Companies may guard against such lawsuits by refusing to reveal anything about former employees except the dates of their employment. Salary information, disciplinary action, and formal performance reviews may rightly be considered confidential information.

Also, managers may obtain additional private information rather easily. Among the tools available are polygraph machines, pencil and paper tests measuring honesty and personality traits, extensive computer networks for storing and retrieving information simply by inputting a Social Security number, concealed microphones and cameras, and fast and inexpensive drug tests. Computer technology has the potential for recording the frequency and number of telephone calls made by an employee, the number of key strokes on a data processor, the number of errors and corrections made, even the amount of time away from the desk. Any use of such technology is defended by managers on the grounds of the shifting nature of work (more dangerous and complex manufacturing demands close monitoring) and the shifting nature of the workforce (more employee use of illegal drugs, more employee dishonesty, etc.).

Privacy issues can arise on the job itself. Employees may access computer files and confidential personnel information. A supervisor may rummage through a subordinate's desk drawer or locker, even when it is marked "private." Of course, an employer may have legitimate interest at stake in an employee's behavior and possessions on the jobsite, and there is no full consensus among lawyers and ethicists about how to define the right of privacy. We certainly conclude that privacy is *not* an absolute right. Managers must monitor employee work performance as an essential part of conducting business. Maintaining the right balance between the rights of employers and employees in matters of privacy is not an easy task. However, in any questionable invasion of privacy, the burden of proof must fall on the organization to establish the validity of the infringement.

CUSTOMER–CONSUMER STAKEHOLDERS

In March 1997, the Liggett Group Inc., makers of Chesterfield, L&M, and Lark cigarettes, shocked the corporate world by making a confession. The smallest of five major tobacco companies admitted that cigarettes are addictive, that they cause cancer, and that tobacco is actively marketed to minors. The confession reversed a full generation of denials to the contrary by major tobacco officials. Soon, other high-ranking tobacco officials were joining the chorus of confessions, regrets, and pledges of reform. The entire cigarette industry, since the mid-1960s when the surgeon general announced his conclusions that cigarette smoking constituted a health hazard, has provided concrete evidence that customers' and clients' best interests among all stakeholders do not always come first.

Among a business corporation's stakeholders, the customers, clients, and consumers deserve respect and constant attention. The business world among advanced nations is too competitive and customers are too intelligent and informed to continue business with a company unless they are fully satisfied with the value of the products and quality of services. Gone are the days in which a corporation could exploit the ignorance of its customers or the monopoly the company held in the market for maximum profit.

Consumers and customers have a number of concerns. The chief one is product safety. In generations past the United States was largely a rural society. Farm households produced a wide range of homemade or local-market products, ranging from manu-facturing of housing, furniture, and clothing to the production and preservation of food. Indeed, farmers and their families could satisfy most of their own physical needs. When manufactured products were purchased, there was a tacit understanding of the principle of *caveat emptor*—let the buyer be aware. After all, consumers have a free choice about buying a product. They have the obligation of inspecting a product, if only by kicking the tire of a new automobile, before using it. And they certainly know that salespersons will make exaggerated claims about their products. Shrewd consumers reached for the proverbial grain of salt.

Today's lifestyle is radically different. Much time is spent commuting in automo-biles. We travel greater distances in commercial aircraft and fly more frequently. If unable to dine at one of many restaurants, we pop instant meals into microwave ovens for a quick nutrition. We depend on electronic communications systems for business and entertainment. We buy ready-made clothing. We take drugs to cope with physical maladies or alter our emotional states. We also take drugs to help us lose weight. Indeed, there is an increasing interdependence and complexity in today's economy. All of us depend heavily on business organizations in our professions and careers for survival and in our private lives for pleasure and enrichment. Caveat emptor is no longer adequate to meet society's needs for product and services safety.

Of the many ethical issues involved in product safety, none is more controversial than the responsibility of manufacturers to compensate citizens who suffer some physical injury or financial loss as a result of defective products. The mere fact that a product is put into the hands of customers in a defective condition that poses an unreasonable risk is sufficient for holding the manufacturer liable. Strict product liability is the doctrine that the seller of a product has legal responsibility to compen-sate the user of that product for injuries suffered due to a defective aspect of the product, even though the seller has not been negligent in permitting that defect to occur. Strict liability is not absolute liability, for the manufacturer is not responsible for an accident or injury in any conceivable use of a product. The customer has some responsibility for routine maintenance that is prescribed and of following prescribed safety regulations.

Of the 20 million Americans per year who require medical treatment from product-related accidents—110,000 are permanently disabled and 30,000 die—who really is at fault? Put another way, where does one draw the line? What moral rights do customers and consumers as a stakeholder group possess? Is caveat emptor a satis-factory standard in sales and advertising since the whole public-relations industry is prone to puffery? Does a corporation have a moral obligation to ensure that customers receive all the information they need to make informed purchasing decisions? Should industry protect consumers in a paternalistic manner, forcing them to accept products and devices that will protect them (the example of automotive airbags comes to mind)? When a company's product has been discovered to have a defect that is a mild threat to safety, must it spend large sums of money to recall and correct the product? Finally, when a firm's products have injured people, what are its obligations to correct or compensate for the harm to customers?

There are other areas of moral concern for consumers as stakeholders. One is the issue of product quality. Does the product measure up to the claims made about it and to reasonable consumer expectations? Doesn't the customer have the moral right to receive what he/she pays for? What kind of warranty should be given on major purchases, such as an automobile? Express warranties are the claims that sellers explicitly state. Implied warranties include the implicit claim that a particular product is fit for the ordinary use for which it is employed; advertising can result in implied warranties.

Pricing is another customer concern. For sure, prices generally do reflect labor, material, overhead, and other operating expenses. The widespread availability of products at different prices makes it difficult for consumers to compare products even from the same manufacturer. Some price codes can only be understood by managers and sales personnel. Deception is common in retail marketing. Some clothing, as well as other goods, are packaged and labeled at a price higher than any retailer needs or expects to sell it; a "suggested retail price" or "compare at . . . " price listed on a product may be intended only to mislead the customer. Bogus "clearance sales" and "introductory offers" often mislead customers. Also, a customer decision to purchase some products may lead to unpredicted costs for the customer. The woman who purchases new tires for her car at a "great price," for example, may discover the total of her purchase much higher than she expected after she is charged for mounting, tire stems, balancing, alignment, warranty, and old tire disposal.

For many consumers, a higher price for comparable products means higher quality. Is there a moral issue when a higher price does not represent higher quality? Is there a moral issue when psychological factors enter pricing decisions? And what about price-fixing, wherein competitors holding a monopoly in a limited product or service area agree to hold the line on a higher price for the same product or service? What about artificially driving up the price of a product to maximize profits?

Labeling and packaging introduce other concerns. Customers do need a certain amount of information to make rational consumer choices; often this information is not easily attained. Doesn't business have the moral responsibility to provide safe packaging and clear, accurate, and adequate information on its labels? Labeling and packaging are deceptive when the size or shape of a container, a picture, or description, or the deployment of such vague terms as "new and improved" or "economy size" mislead customers in some significant way. All steadfast dieters know that labels can be misleading. For example, what is more misleading than "low-fat" "low in cholesterol" or "no cholesterol." Even more confusing are canned or frozen foods labeled "best-buy," "prime," "choice," "all meat," "home-cooked" or "home-style." Even packages can be shaped to mislead customers on the amount of the product they are purchasing.

And finally, concern over the deception and unfairness in advertising must be a major moral issue. Advertising is all-pervasive in our lives. Pick up a magazine or newspaper, watch a television show, travel city streets and highways, go to a ballgame, even use a public restroom, and you will be bombarded with commercial messages. The frequency of advertisements on television or radio may be obnoxious, and the quality of some ads may be tasteless or even offensive, but the most creative efforts of Madison Avenue possess a strong entertainment value. More than that, the best efforts of Madison Avenue have a persuasive impact on millions of consumers. Approximately 2 percent of the gross national product is currently devoted to advertising. Like it or not, advertising is here to stay.

We have already considered (in chapter 4) the role of advertising in affluent societies in terms of creating a culture of consumerism and widespread demand for a higher standard of living. Now we raise the topic of advertising again in terms of its techniques to influence consumer behavior on a day-by-day basis. A strong case can be made for the contention that advertising invites people to dispense with their ability to think logically. Consider these abuses of advertising:

1. **Concealed facts.** No one expects advertisers to present a balanced perspective to consumers as might a college professor on whether to purchase a product or service. The ethical issue arises when concealment of facts takes advantage of people by misleading them. Sometimes visual ads are staged or "doctored" by additional materials or coloring to make claims for a product more dramatic. Most of us know that the platter of food shown on television looks much brighter and bigger than the one received in the restaurant being advertised. Can anyone imagine a man's head being lathered and kept neatly and equally divided between two shampoos—Denorex, which tingles, and some other tingle-less brand?

2. **Exaggeration.** Standard practice allows advertisers to make bold claims for a product or service which are unsupported by evidence. This is especially true in the skin care, grooming, weight loss, physical conditioning, good health and nutrition categories—an umbrella which covers a lot of products and claims. Obviously, the line between "puffery" and outright deception is difficult to draw.

3. **Ambiguity.** Some words are tools in trade for the media advertiser—"extra," "stronger," "total," "best," "finest," "most," to name a few. "Helps" is another valuable word, as in "helps fight tooth decay," "helps eliminate odors," or "helps fight aging"—almost any claim can follow the word "helps." The danger of misleading through ambiguity is omnipresent and raises an important moral concern: How vague and ambiguous can claims become without intentionally misleading and even harming consumers?

4. **Sex appeal.** Many advertisements appeal to emotions and circumvent the reasoning process, and no psychological appeal is any more potent than sex. Sex can be associated with about any product, from grooming to automobiles. How, for example, is it possible for a new automobile to have "sleek, sexy styling"? One might wonder if a lawn mower or farm tractor might also be given "sleek,

sexy styling"? Some critics contend that strong pitches for products linked with sex appeal is an exploitation of the subconscious motivation. Subliminal advertising is advertising at a level beneath our conscious awareness, a vast area where some psychologists claim lies the greatest reservoir of human motivation.

Forty years have passed since Vance Packard's disturbing revelations in *The Hidden Persuaders* (1957) convinced readers that advertisers deploy these techniques of influence that we are powerless to resist. If anything, subliminal advertising and psychological appeals have increased in recent times. One example among countless others is the connection made between smoking and appearance; studies show that women equate smoking with thinness because models in the ads are strikingly thin (note that Virginia Slims have a long, slim shape). Most use of psychological appeal is subtle, for sure, but how much sex appeal is too much sex appeal?

The Federal Trade Commission (FTC) was established earlier in this century to protect consumers against fraudulent and deceptive advertising. Though criticized, the FTC has protected the American public against the most blatant abuses of media advertising.

LOCAL COMMUNITY STAKEHOLDERS

What is the responsibility of a business organization to the community in which it exists? After all, the organization is nestled into a community from which it draws human resources, public services, and utilities. Not surprisingly, many corporate leaders now talk about the moral imperative of "putting something back." Such investment is also a practical matter, as community involvement is simply good public relations for the company.

How "socially involved" should a company become with its immediate community? Should it take on obligations beyond the bottom line? Should it tackle larger social issues such as public schooling and unemployment? Should it provide relief and services after a natural disaster? Should it support the community arts? What about community athletics? Should it provide special services to the poor and underprivileged?

There is a wide variety of ways in which a company can prove itself to be a good local citizen, from giving money outright to community projects to lending time and talents of its skilled people to vital community projects. The more-involved companies find their own future and stability inextricably bound to the future and stability of the community. Companies which depend on wide community support, such as banking and investment organizations, have much more to gain by community involvement.

GLOBAL COMMUNITY STAKEHOLDERS

Multinational corporations are businesses with operations in more than one nation. Global business is on the rise. When a U.S. consumer purchases a new automobile, he/she may not know the nation of final assembly or the diverse national origin of the car's major parts from the name of the manufacturer or the model. Some companies reach the virtual outer circles of production, sales, and marketing.

The sheer size of these multinational operations creates many ethical concerns, concerns which are compounded by the diversity of cultural norms and values that are part of the context in which business decisions are made.

There are a number of practices common in multinational business that provide opportunities and pressures for unethical conduct. Ronald Green, in *The Ethical Manager* (1994), lists several of these, including:

1. small-scale bribery: payment of small sums of money or other goods to a foreign official or business employee to speed up the routine actions or violate some official duty ("Baksheesh" and "grease" payments are clearly common and openly accepted in many lesser-developed countries);
2. large-scale bribery: major payments made directly or indirectly to government or corporate officials to induce a violation of law or influence policy;
3. gifts: even lavish ones, favors, entertainment, expensive travel, and even call girls;
4. pricing: pricing practices that favor selected customers, deceptive invoices, dumping products at prices well below those in the home country, price-fixing, and bid-rigging;
5. products/technology: the export and sale of products or technologies that are banned for use in the home country but legal in host country;
6. tax evasion practices/financial misdealing: tax havens, evasive forms of transfer pricing, or illegal transfer of currency;
7. violations of employee rights in host country: operating in unsafe working conditions or participating in forms of racial, religious, or sex discrimination normally prohibited in the home country;
8. environmental abuses: exploiting a host nation's reduced vigilance or lax legal standards to pollute the environment or to dispose of toxic wastes;
9. violations of intellectual property rights: product or technology copying in contexts where the protection of patents, trade names, or trademarks is not well enforced;
10. political influence by multinationals, such as tampering with voting or other political processes.

In the wake of a series of major international bribery scandals, the U.S. Congress passed the Foreign Corrupt Practices Act (FCPA) of 1977. The act forbids managers of U.S. corporations to pay bribes, directly or indirectly, to foreign political officials. This act does not prohibit all kinds of bribes, for example, the more modest payments to managers of private companies or payments made under innocuous sounding procedures (e.g., "facilitating" payments).

No "made in the USA" law can shield business managers from the acute moral dilemmas they encounter in conducting the affairs of a multinational corporation. In an ideal economic world, decisions by consumers or governments will be made on the basis of such fair and rational criteria as quality, price, necessity, and service. Unethical practices such as bribery and extortion seriously jeopardize this process. When unethical practices such as bribery and extortion are given free reign, a corporate culture is created wherein power, manipulation, and deviousness become the *modus operandi* for political and corporate decision-making. The ideal business environment would not tolerate moral ambiguity, conflicts of interests, and devious manipulation.

On the other hand, consider the realities of the international scene: lax enforcement of laws in some foreign countries, competitive pressures from other multinational companies, ease of concealing questionable practices, the perception that "every business organization is doing it," and, finally, the conviction that a practice may not be morally wrong because it is firmly rooted in native cultural values and customs. It is not hard to see that both major and minor slippages from high ethical standards are unfortunate aspects of economic and political life on the international scene.

Alas, our survey of stakeholder interests must be concluded. We have surveyed a wide range of practical issues. We have noted the complexity of conflicting moral claims and values. A book-length study would be necessary to treat the stakeholder model in detail. And, realistically, there is no reason to think that the moral maze created by modern corporate life will ever become any easier to traverse than it is currently.

QUESTIONS FOR GROUP DISCUSSION
AND PERSONAL REFLECTION

1. The basic theme of this chapter is that, instead of serving only the interests of stockholders or shareholders, corporations are operated for the benefit of all those who have a stake in the enterprise, including customers and clients, employees, suppliers, and the local community. But on what basis, however, might one argue that corporations have a moral obligation to take stakeholder interests into account in corporate decision-making? This is not to say that customers, employees, the general public, and so forth, are not important to the operation of the corporation. Do corporations have a moral obligation to undertake some actions and restrain from others on the sole basis of an impact on the interests of these groups?

   Some business theorists and ethicists reject the stakeholder model on the ground that the interests of all groups other than owners/stockholders constitute constraints on corporate behavior in pursuit of making profits rather than goals themselves. In other words, the main goal of any business corporation is earning profits. In pursuit of that goal, the corporation must meet certain responsibilities toward groups of people impacted along the way to profits; the objective of business is not to "take care of" groups connected by the business.

   What do you see as the primary responsibility of business organizations? Should a corporation assume any more social responsibilities other than those prescribed by law?

2. Is there a need for laws to protect the interests of stakeholders other than the owners/shareholders? Could we not argue that the owners/stockholders in promoting

their own interests will also automatically promote the interests of the entire organization and those of society as a whole?

3. Does business have a social and moral responsibility for the welfare of its clients and customers? Consider a business that sells a possibly harmful product. There may be no better illustration of this than tobacco.

   Take Kentucky, for example. This state's residents grow more of it, sell more of it, smoke more of it, and vote more on it, and even bought more church houses and paid preachers' salaries with it, than any other state in the union. Tobacco has been a $900 million annual business in Kentucky. The whole culture is dependent on tobacco. Which of the following two lines of thought should tobacco growers in Kentucky (and in Tennessee and Virginia or elsewhere, for that matter) advocate:

   a. "It's proven beyond a reasonable doubt that smoking cigarettes and other uses of tobacco are harmful to one's health. Thanks be to modern medical science for exploring the ways that our lifestyle can be injurious to our physical well being. Perhaps tobacco products should not be labeled as illegal, but we petition the government to label tobacco as a drug and place these products under the regulatory umbrella of the Food and Drug Administration."

   b. "Sure tobacco may not be a product for children, but for centuries it has been a form of pleasure for millions. Tobacco use is an individual choice and there are fifty million Americans nationwide who enjoy a good smoke. The entire culture of the upper South is dependent on this tradition, and further government regulations would just cut deeper into the growers' profits and do little to address the difficulty farmers have in replacing tobacco with other crops that have not proven to be as profitable. Tobacco is available, it's legal, and it's as American as apple pie, hot dogs, and Chevrolet. Let's leave it alone."

4. Do you think American business people and the personalities which promote U.S. products assume moral obligations which extend beyond the U.S. borders? Consider a couple of examples:

   a. In April 1996 a labor activist accused Kathie Lee Gifford of promoting a line of clothing made by thirteen- and fourteen-year-olds working twenty-hour days in factories in Honduras. Though at first she tearfully denied it, later Kathie Lee learned the charge was true. Her story is not the only one. Celebrities make millions lending their names to enterprises they rarely visit in industries they know little about. Michael Jordan shrugs off charges by labor activists that Nike's line of Air Jordan athletic shoes are made under appalling conditions in Indonesian factories. Who is to blame—the celebrity promoting the product or the company which contracts for its production? Or anyone? What are moralists to make of the fact that workers from the sweatshops have criticized U.S. reformers because the cancellation of contracts has put people out of work who desperately need the money?

   b. While smoking is no longer "politically correct" in the United States, and, in fact, is under siege of threatened regulations and lawsuits, U.S. tobacco companies are going global to ensure profits for decades to come. International sales for Philip Morris and

R. J. Reynolds have quadrupled over the past decade, while domestic sales remained flat; the foreign market represents more than half of total sales. Big tobacco is going after the heavy populations of Russia, China, and Eastern Europe. Is this imperialistic exploitation? If tobacco use is a major concern for the health of Americans, should it not also be for the populations of other nations? Does moral responsibility for American business leaders end at our borders? Dare we conclude that American business people possess a social conscience only when they are forced to be ethical by the law?

5. As implied in the previous question, many countries around the world rely heavily on child labor, not having the kinds of protections and restrictions written into law as in nations like the United States. Is it morally responsible for nations such as the United States or other consumerist nations to be partners in trade with them?

6. Other than performing voluntary, isolated acts of charity, such as contributing to a community chest for the poor or sponsoring a Red Cross blood drive, what kinds of service (if any) or philanthropy should a company do for the community in which it does business?

7. Is it morally right for Christian employees to join organizations such as labor unions and to exert pressure, and even strike, against an employer over wages or hours or other provisions of the working agreement?

8. Should companies address social problems in the communities in which they are located and/or market their products and services? The social needs might include hunger, health care, literacy training, skills training, affordable housing, and minority-owned businesses, to cite a small sampling.

9. In the past quarter-century there has been an explosion of discussion on the issue of employee rights. One of those issues is that of employee privacy in the workplace, both a major and a complex issue. We have already made the point that employers have the right to monitor and evaluate workers' performance and employees have a right to privacy and dignity, but such a generalization may not help us resolve individual cases. Give thought to the following practices:

   a. Honesty tests which inquire into personal habits and interests, family life, and sexual attitudes and adjustment.
   b. Polygraph testing.
   c. Gathering all kinds of medical information.
   d. Monitoring the nature and length of employee use of the telephone.
   e. Monitoring the mileage of employee use of company vehicles.
   f. Random drug testing.
   g. Random searches of lockers and desk drawers.
   h. A manager reading a subordinate's electronic mail messages.
   i. A top-level manager requesting (though it cannot be legally mandated) HIV testing for all employees.
   j. Use of hidden cameras in restrooms.

   Which of the above might be justified in typical employment situations? Are there some practices that could not be justified because of less-intrusive methods being available? Are there some practices you know of that you consider morally wrong regardless of the work situation?

10. Do you think a worker has the right to refuse to perform what he/she believes to be hazardous and dangerous work assignments as delegated by the supervisor and still retain a job? How much can a supervisor coerce a worker?

11. The concept of employee rights and privacy is broad, encompassing many specific issues. How far can a business organization go in restricting employee behavior outside of work hours? For example, how would you feel if your company announced it would not hire smokers and that it would dismiss employees who did not cease smoking by three months? How would you feel if your company announced that it would no longer permit employees to date coworkers or clients of the firm? Would there be any justification for either policy? Might one attempt to protect the health of workers in whom the company has a vested interest and the other provide a safeguard against a sexual-harassment suit? In either case, would you feel that your employee rights had been violated?

12. What are rights that you personally want your supervisor to honor and respect with great care?

13. How would you answer the following charges against advertising as practiced in our culture:
    a. Many advertisements are irritating, lack taste, and are offensive.
    b. By appealing to the emotions and manipulating the needs and desires of consumers, advertisements create wants and hinder consumers' ability to make rational choices.
    c. Advertising is wasteful and inefficient. The money spend on advertising does not create new products people can consume; it is used only to persuade people to purchase products already on the market. Advertising automobiles, for example, adds up to one thousand dollars to the cost of a new vehicle—money which could be saved by the consumer or used by the manufacturer to produce a better product.
    d. Advertising creates desires for expensive brands of luxury items appealing to people's yearning for status.

14. Advertising is not intended to produce knowledgeable consumers; therefore, it should not be faulted for every failure to educate the general public. Not every false belief is of such credibility or importance that consumers should be protected from it. Yet there is a certain standard of rational consumer behavior, and advertising is deceptive and unethical when it achieves its goal by preventing consumers from attaining this standard.

    Where do you think the line is crossed? Do you consider advertising slogans to be examples of deception? For example, do we take at face value Avis's claim to "try harder" and Gallo's claim to "release no wine before its time." Is Wheaties really "the breakfast of champions"? Are these serious claims to truth or just suggestive rhetorical devices? Are we getting serious education about medical treatment by hearing from Bayer ads that "all aspirin is not alike"?

15. Do you believe that so long as products are legal (such as liquor, tobacco, and condoms) that manufacturers have a right to advertise them without restriction? How could one

harmonize restrictions on advertising with the freedom of speech guaranteed in the First Amendment?

16. Surely we concur that blatant deception in advertising is unethical. Do you consider manipulation in retailing to be unethical? Manipulation often involves no false or misleading claims, but instead takes advantage of consumer psychology to make a sale. For example, odd-cent pricing may make a price look lower. Rather than list gasoline at $1.35 a gallon, it is advertised as $1.34.9; "three for a dollar" or "buy two, get one free" merchandising is common. Sometimes, instead of raising the price on a product (such as a candy bar), manufacturers will reduce the substance or content and maintain the same price. Do you find this to be objectionable? What about the infamous bait-and-switch technique, in which a customer is lured into a store by an advertisement for a low-priced item and then subjected to a strong sales pitch for a higher-priced version?

17. Should management have the right to read any e-mail messages sent through the company's network? Is all computer data as much company property as the computers themselves?

Chapter 11

Excellence

One does not become excellent at something primarily by focusing on and avoiding what is wrong and bad but by focusing on and pursuing what is right and good. . . . Excellence and praiseworthiness are not the mere nonexistence of wrong and bad things; they are real and independent moral qualities in and of themselves.

Russell W. Gough

A man may make many mistakes, but he is not a failure until he starts blaming others.

Coach John Wooden

A winner is someone who recognizes his God-given talents, works his tail off to develop them into skills, and uses these skills to accomplish his goals.

Larry Bird

By working faithfully eight hours a day, you may eventually get to be a boss and work twelve hours a day.

Robert Frost

Be nice to people on your way up because you'll meet them on your way down.

Wilson Mizner

Ask not what your company can do for you, ask what you can do for your company.

Don Baiocchi

History and hindsight require no vision. You only stumble when you're moving.

Robert Goizueta

What lies behind us and what lies before us are tiny matters compared to what lies within us.

Oliver Wendell Holmes

MANY OF US MAY BE UNCOMFORTABLE WITH THE IDEA OF "excellence" being applied personally to something we do or something we are. The word may have a connotation of superiority. Few of us may feel true superiority about the things we do, and we are "turned off" by people who act superior when they are actually mediocre.

Truth is, however, most of us are capable of attaining excellence in some area of our lives—the highest grade in the class, a skill we have mastered, a character trait we

140

have nurtured, or a work detail we can perform better than anyone else in the organization.

Excellence means standing out in the crowd. Its meaning is derived from two Latin words meaning "to rise high" or "to rise out of." To rise above others—to be "outstanding"— means to put one in plain view of all others. It is a position to be admired and respected.

With the exception of athletic prowess, excellence has nothing to do with being physically stronger, taller, quicker, or more agile. With the exception of beauty pageants, excellence has nothing to do with physical beauty or a shapely figure. And no longer is it a title of honor, such as those worn in England after the sixteenth century (e.g., "Your Excellency"), whose personal virtues were not always evident to the masses. Nor is it simply a title for bishops, governors, and ambassadors.

Instead, the meaning of excellence in most contexts includes not simply outward performance but some inner virtues or qualities which render a man or woman morally strong. This notion of excellence harmonizes with the ethical doctrine of Jesus, who continually instructed us, especially in his Sermon on the Mount, that the inner person was the essence of true righteousness.

Aristotle (384–322 B.C.) wrote forcefully about the need to achieve excellence or virtue, not simply in some field of labor or business but as human beings generally. To develop virtue is to develop moral excellence. This distinguished philosopher of antiquity insisted that only when we develop our truly human capacities sufficiently to achieve this human excellence would we have lives blessed with deep happiness (*eudaimonia*).

Any discussion of excellence seems simplistic. This chapter will, therefore, read differently from the others and readers will be addressed more directly. Living with excellence, rather than simply discussing it, is the challenge. Daring both to overgeneralize and oversimplify the whole issue, several traits of moral excellence in business and professional life are cited here:

Moral Philosophy and Moral Values

The morally excellent person has developed a broad system of moral philosophy and moral values. Many ethicists distinguish between morality in a broad sense and morality in a narrow sense. In a narrow sense, morality is a code that provides rules for the situations we ordinarily face. Business ethics is often taught in terms of moral responses and moral rules for specific situations at work—whether one considers age or gender in hiring, whether to force employees to undergo drug testing, whether one should "blow the whistle," and so forth.

Underneath moral responses to specific situations is a much broader framework or foundation. This broader philosophy contains not simply the individual rules, but also the values, ideals, and aspirations that shape our lives. This philosophy may be carefully considered and systematized; quite often it is developed unconsciously through an evolution of thought and experiences in various roles and relationships. Your moral philosophy incorporates your faith in eternal verities, your understanding of God, your source of moral authority, your understanding of human nature, tradition, and society, and your place in this world. Professionals in various fields will be guided, consciously perhaps, by the rules in professional codes, but also, unconsciously perhaps, by a deeper, broader philosophical foundation.

Inner Virtues of Character

The morally excellent develops deep inner virtues of character. These primary virtues include respect for others, personal integrity, moral courage, commitment to ideals, diligence, persistence, self-confidence, kindness, and compassion, to name some of the most important ones. We have already discussed some of these virtues. None of us lives in a vacuum, and social pressures are all about us, but the business organization may well be the environment in which it is most difficult to maintain these virtues. In biblical theology, these inner virtues are called "fruit of the Spirit" (Gal. 5:22–25).

Responsibility

The morally excellent man or woman assumes full responsibility for his/her decisions and actions. He/she does not attempt to shuffle off blame to others for personal mistakes or short-comings. "The real key to happiness is maintaining responsibility," declares Rabbi Harold S. Kushner. "It's having an ongoing relation with people who depend on you and whom you know you can depend on." Professor Russell Gough writes, "From the standpoint of personal character, we must take responsibility for who and what we presently are as well as who and what we hope to become. And while our personal growth does indeed require help from others, the fact remains that others, including God, can help us if and only if we are willing to be helped."

The mature employee accepts responsibility for his/her behavior, actions, and responses to situations. The consistent use of "I messages" indicates an awareness of personal responsibility. When someone says, "You make me so angry" or "My secretary always gets on my nerves" or "My supervisor just depresses me whenever I'm around her," that person is deflecting responsibility from self and projecting it onto another.

Consider the difference between "You Messages" and "I Messages":

"YOU MESSAGES"	"I MESSAGES"
"You make me angry."	"I am angry."
"You have rejected me."	"I feel left out of things."
"You make me sad."	"I feel sadness."
"You make me happy."	"I feel happy."
"You blame everything on me."	"I don't like being blamed."

No one can make you angry without your permission. And that's true for any other emotional state. You choose to be angry or sad or joyous or happy, jealous or secure, encouraged or discouraged. Sure, another party may be a major contributing factor in our emotional state, but you must own final responsibility.

Can you make the following statement as a silent declaration to yourself: "My actions are mine. Your actions are yours. I am responsible for choosing my responses to you. I am responsible for the way I react to you and the way I see you. And from the way I see you—as either accepting or rejecting, as friendly or hostile, as either friend or foe—emerge as much or more from my personal feelings than from your actions. My feelings, in turn, affect my responses. All of my feelings and all my responses are *my* personal choices. I am responsible for all my actions or reactions. I make the choice."

Teammate

The morally excellent worker considers himself/herself not so much a competitor with others but a teammate with others. Winning is such a big value in the American culture. We treasure trophies, blue ribbons, and inscribed bronze plaques. "Winning isn't everything; it's the only thing," the late Vince Lombardi is often quoted as declaring. Living in a capitalist society underscores the need to win; our system of criminal justice and civil litigation also emphasizes competing to win. Our national preoccupation with professional and collegiate sports supports mightily the notion of competing to win. Throughout American labor history, labor and management have fought each other—sometimes literally and too often bloodily—to determine which side would win.

The unspoken assumption is that competition improves performance. Winning a competition does brings its unique rewards, but it may rarely help a person develop the virtues of moral excellence. Competition may increase unnecessary pressures. It may hamper creativity, especially in areas wherein standards of winning are so subjective. Those who finish first—such as the first to break a "hot" news story (e.g., the bombing in Atlanta's Centennial Park during the 1996 Olympics)—may not finish best. Competition in public-policy debate, academic debate, or the criminal courtroom may put more emphasis on winning by any means than seeing the truth as objectively as possible.

The morally excellent person does not need to prove himself/herself by beating others. He/she may even avoid certain kinds of competition and does not "obsess" over the skills and talents of others when one's personal gifts are just as good or different. Such a person is self-confident and does not worry about being labeled a failure. This person is in competition with self and is totally "free to be me." He/she enjoys teamwork with congenial colleagues who mutually nurture one another's gifts and skills.

Inner Satisfaction

The morally excellent person does not work simply for money, but also works for the inner satisfaction of contributing to a worthwhile cause. The one who works solely for money is likely to feel cheated when it does not increase as he/she had hoped for. The morally excellent worker knows that he/she is a person of worth and is willing to work diligently regardless of the salary. When one's goals include using and developing gifts and talents, interacting meaningfully with other people, developing skills for the future, then that person has discovered the extra payoff besides the paycheck. This kind of excellence will keep one moving—perhaps moving on to a better job!

Commitment to Causes

The morally excellent person is committed to causes that really matter. Organizations must be held together, and that is possible only by a reasonable amount of personal commitment from the members of the organization. Ideally, workers will be able to find employment with an organization in which they need relinquish only minimal personal freedom and preferences and find it easy to subordinate themselves to organizational goals. Such subordination is a measure of one's loyalty to "the team."

Self-respect

The morally excellent person has self-respect. It is so unlikely that you can give respect to others unless you respect yourself. The challenge of respect is first being able to build a positive self-concept and truly respect and esteem yourself, and then you will be able to extend and receive the respect and esteem to and from the other person, party, or work unit.

If you are thinking only in terms of yourself, or in terms of another person, party, or organization (such as a union or management team) to care for you, protect you, or even love you, it is like looking through the wrong end of a telescope. The partnership, protection, and security which satisfy your deepest yearnings are not first a taking but a giving. Instead of asking in a Rodney Dangerfield–style, "Why don't I get more respect?" you might need to ask, "How can I express more understanding and respect?" The respect and understanding we are speaking of grows out of satisfying relationships rather than out of clearly written working contracts.

The old cliche is still true: *A better world begins with you.* So how well are you taking care of yourself? Often, if you enhance your self-esteem, that is all you need to do to be capable of viewing others in a more positive light. Since you rely on others to help you build your self-image, remember that others depend on you to build their self-esteem. Let's list practical suggestions to enable you to be a "self-tending" person and build a reservoir of self-respect and self-esteem from which you can draw in enriching all your relationships:

1. **Take credit for your achievements.** Stop giving "luck" the credit you deserve and need. Believe that it was your planning and preparation, using the gifts, talents, and enabling given to you by God that brought your success and accomplishments. They are yours. Claim them to the glory of God!

2. **Maintain a physical appearance that is personally rewarding and satisfying.** If the way you look concerns or worries you, change it. Lose weight, gain weight, change styles, whatever. Seek attention that reinforces self-validation. Beware of self-deception that projects the message outwardly of "I don't care." Get in touch with how you really feel.

3. **Maintain fiscal responsibility and stability.** Poor money management chips away at one's self-concept and self-respect. Don't overspend to boost ego. Ultimately, that results in self-defeat. Self-tending involves growth in fiscal affairs.

4. **Expect acceptance.** If you look for rejection, you'll find it. Expect to be loved—you'll act to attract. Expect and look for the best.

5. **Accept the "self-ness" of others and their right to it.** Learn to accept responsibility only for your own behavior and reactions. Don't demand, either overtly or in your mind, certain behavior patterns from others. If, for example, the other person does not demonstrate the "appreciation" you expected, then don't expect it. If the other chooses not to express or share appreciation, that's a personal choice that belongs only to the other. It may have nothing to do with you personally. You are involved in self-tending—not self-pity.

6. **Accept and develop your sexuality to the fullest.** Guilt feelings resulting from your honest, God-given sexuality can unnecessarily immobilize and destroy you. Fulfill inner needs through education and the direction of God's wisdom on this personal dimension of your life. Sexual energy is such a major force in our lives. Allow sex to build and refresh you, not tear you down. Never use it as power and control over others or allow others to use it in that manner. Do what is morally right for you—no more, no less. Don't be used by others. Don't use others.

7. **Maintain an honest and open manner.** You'll always have some secrets, but revealing yourself in an honest and open way will contribute to your self-acceptance. Lying and "wearing a mask" can create a toxic relationship with oneself.

8. **Maintain a high-quality lifestyle.** That doesn't demand spending big money. It can mean taking what you have and using it to the best advantage. Keep clean and neat, personally and in your living quarters. Get some new clothes, even if you haven't worn out the old ones—it'll make you feel like a new person. If you have an older car, clean and polish it and keep it in good mechanical condition. Drink from crystal and eat from china occasionally. Splurge a little on yourself. Do all you can with a flair and a quality.

9. **Appreciate being alone.** Do not equate being alone with loneliness. Enjoy your own company. View being alone as a positive experience and self-exploration and enjoyment. Remember that it's better to be alone for the right reason than to be with someone for the wrong reason.

10. **Accept help from others.** Accept compliments. Accept aid and support. You deserve it and, furthermore, others have needs that can only be expressed in giving. Learn to receive. Don't insult others by rejecting their good will.

11. **Build commitment through goals and passion.** Find something you really love doing and you'll never "work" a day the rest of your life. If you cannot maintain positive feelings about your current job, then get another one. Look forward to going to work. Believe in the importance of what you are doing.

12. **Don't live past failures or mistakes.** Certainly, all people make mistakes and many fail—many times. Seek the forgiveness of God and others and then move on with your life. After several early political and social failures, ultimate success placed Abraham Lincoln in the White House. Develop and maintain positive thought patterns about yourself.

13. **Maintain moderation.** In eating, in drinking, in leisure, and in other lifestyle choices, feel good about your habit pattern. Stay in command. Tune the body. Exercise improves your outlook and self-image, all the while relieving stress and challenging you to do more than you think you can.

14. **Deal with the idea of others in a positive manner.** Give positive feedback.

15. **Listen and listen with expectation of hearing something valuable.** Listen for an idea. Listen for self-improvement and development. Listen to remember—be active. Avoid defensiveness. Know that good listeners are better communicators than good talkers. You learn more with open ears than with open mouth.

16. **Tackle a creative project**. Creativity of all kinds builds self-worth. If you've always wanted to write the "great American novel," then go to it. If you have wanted to learn to use a computer, but were reluctant to start, then sign up for a computer class. If you've been out of school for a while, considering returning. Begin a new hobby.

17. **Get to know some important people.** Are there some people you have looked up to with awe and respect? Tell them so. If possible, make their personal acquaintance; if not, write them a letter. You may be surprised how approachable such people are, and it will work wonders for your self-respect. Try this without fear of rejection.

18. **Give careful thought to your moral convictions.** Know what you believe in and speak out appropriately and tactfully for your convictions.

19. **Affiliate yourself with prestigious and worthwhile organizations.** Join at least one worthwhile organization, whether the Rotary Club or Bird-Watchers of America. We discover ourselves in involvement with others. It is difficult to love ourselves until we are accepted by people we esteem.

20. **Most important, give priority to your relationship with God and the development of your spirituality.** Give much consideration to the faith premises which undergird your life. Make your faith your own. Know what you stand for. And know that the basis of your self-worth is not in human achievement, but in what God thinks of you and has already done for you.

21. **Watch out for self-pity.** Self-pity does not generate self-respect. It only keeps alive the unhappy past. Failure is no disgrace. It provides proof that you are human. If one approach doesn't work, it doesn't mean your goal is wrong; it does mean that your plan needs to change. The more times you fail, the greater the chance of success. Deal with your setbacks by talking to informed friends.

22. **View change as a challenge.** Losing your job or getting lost in the shuffle or reorganization isn't an end of a career—it's the beginning of a new one. Dwelling on what "was" only keeps you from seeing what could be. A long-term view of you is what you need. Take an inventory of your skills. Prepare for something better.

23. **Be optimistic.** If you think you can't, you won't. A "can-do" attitude every day helps dreams come true.

24. **Maintain perspective.** Being stuck in a job you don't like is not a life sentence. It may be an opportunity to witness to your faith, your values, and your Lord. Find value and something positive even in the most difficult employment situations. As long as you continue to refine your game plan, your current situation should only be temporary. Build confidence by taking baby steps.

25. **Use humor to deal with change.** Change and stress are Siamese twins. A megadose of stress afflicts you when things aren't going well in your career. Relief that is more effective than drugs may be as close as your nearest joke book or video of a riotously hilarious movie.

26. **Finally, be a constructive non-conformist.** "Be not conformed to the world, but be transformed by the renewing of your mind" (Rom. 12:1). This does not mean to make extreme, negative reactions in all situations, but to take creative, respectful stands for truth and conviction.

Mental and Emotional Health

The morally excellent person maintains good mental and emotional health. Any mention of mental health opens a major, complex subject that is not the main purpose of this book. Mental health cannot be taken for granted. "Mental health exists," declares George E. Vaillant. "Inner happiness, external play, objective vocational success, mature inner defenses, good outward marriage—all correlate highly."

In her book, *Current Concepts of Positive Mental Health,* Marie Johoda lists six general features of mental health:

1. Mentally healthy people are in touch with their own identity and their own feelings.
2. They are oriented toward the future and over time are fruitfully invested in life.
3. Their psyches are well integrated and provide them means of coping with and resisting stress.
4. They possess a sense of independence (autonomy) and recognize what best suits their needs.
5. They accurately perceive reality without distortion and yet possess empathy— the capacity to sense the feelings of others.
6. They are masters of their environment—able to work, to love, to play, and to be efficient in problem-solving.

To this list we might add a seventh characteristic—mentally healthy people have a sense of humor.

Another checklist which may help us assess our own mental health is found in psychiatrist Milton Berger's book, *Working with People Called Patients.* Among the twenty-four characteristics cited are some of particular importance:

1. a capacity to accept and assume responsibility for oneself;
2. a capacity for spontaneity, wholeheartedness and commitment;
3. a sense of curiosity and capacity to accept imperfection and incompleteness;
4. a sense of humor and a capacity for playfulness;
5. a capacity to be open to, rather than deny, the evidence that one's senses perceive;
6. a capacity to be in touch with one's feelings and to take appropriate action in response to what one perceives, acknowledging that there are times when the appropriate "action" is inaction;
7. a minimal tendency to externalize responsibility or blame others for one's behavior;
8. a sufficient degree of tolerance for anxiety to continue functioning in risky and stressful situations and to accept helplessness at times;
9. a capacity to live with frustration and to postpone "present pleasure" for "future profit" at times;
10. a capacity to ask, to give, and to receive simply, without strings or reservations;
11. a capacity for appropriate dependence, independence, and/or interdependence;
12. a capacity for satisfaction and joy in daily living, at work, at home, or in leisure activity;
13. a capacity to live with the ambiguity and paradoxes of life; and
14. a capacity to be open to serendipity, or taking pleasure in unexpected "happenings."

Personal Growth

The morally excellent person is concerned about personality growth. "Are you a happy person?" This may be one of the most important questions in your life. Regardless of how you answer the question, there is no doubt that a happy person will have satisfying work experiences and an unhappy person will find, even in the best of all jobs, many miserable work experiences.

The quest for satisfaction and happiness may be a lifetime adventure, but its outcome is determined more by a series of choices we make rather than by genetics, fate, or luck. Developing this sense of happiness and satisfaction with life is intimately linked with on-going personality growth. The main research in the field of social and behavioral sciences has found, perhaps to no one's surprise, that being neurotic, sick, poor, lonely, and the like contribute to dissatisfaction with life. Statistical analysis of these factors indicates that they account for only about 30 percent, on average, of what matters for satisfaction. There are large numbers of people who are pleased with their lives and their jobs despite hardship and large numbers of people who complain despite having many life advantages.

Happiness and satisfaction are rooted in self-knowledge, self-acceptance, self-love, self-nurturing, a high sense of self-esteem, and a high sense of self-worth. "Happiness is having a sense of self—not a feeling of being perfect, but of being good enough and knowing you are in the process of growth, of being, of achieving levels of joy," declares Leo F. Buscaglia, well-known educator and author; "It's a wonderful contentment and acceptance of who and what you are."

A worker with excellence is constantly maturing. You do not have to be young forever, but you can be immature for all your life. Maturity is a choice. A mature person is characterized by many of the same traits which relate to happiness (mentioned above).

What is maturity? An anonymous answer to that question has appeared several times in Ann Landers's newspaper column:

> Maturity is the ability to control anger and settle differences without violence or destruction.
>
> Maturity is patience. It is the willingness to pass up immediate pleasure in favor of the long-term gain.
>
> Maturity is perseverance, the ability to sweat out a project or a situation in spite of heavy opposition and discouraging setbacks.
>
> Maturity is the capacity to face unpleasantness and frustration, discomfort and defeat, without complaint or collapse.
>
> Maturity is humility. It is being big enough to say, "I was wrong." And, when right, the mature person need not experience the satisfaction of saying, "I told you so."
>
> Maturity is the ability to make a decision and stand by it. The immature spend their lives exploring endless possibilities; then they do nothing.
>
> Maturity means dependability, keeping one's word, coming through in a crisis. The immature are masters of the alibi. They are the confused and the disorganized. Their lives are "mazes of broken promises, former friends, unfinished business and good intentions that somehow never materialize."
>
> Maturity is the art of living in peace with that which we cannot change, the courage to change that which should be changed—and the wisdom to know the difference.

Faith and a Christlike Life

The morally excellent Christian man or woman is constantly deepening faith in God and a commitment to live a Christlike life. Our Christian faith places a certain perspective on every relationship and every experience in life. Our faith is not simply a way of seeing certain things—it's a certain way of seeing *all* things!

The faith that you bring to your occupation or profession is no substitute for education, training, or technical competence. The Christian business person is not spared the need for knowledge of markets, supply and demand, labor-management relations, future trends, laws about occupational safety and health, or technical competence simply because he/she is a Christian.

A Christian maintains the conviction that the gifts and talents that God has given him/her are special blessings to be developed, expanded, and employed in the spirit of service to all humankind. The Christian in the workplace is not motivated by some need to earn salvation—indeed, salvation is a gift of God through his abundant grace. Christians develop and deploy their skills for the purposes of renewing God's creation, finding satisfaction in personal and professional development, meeting the needs of their fellow citizens, and rendering life better for themselves and their families. All of this is part of the stewardship of life to which Jesus called his disciples. In his parable of the talents (Matt. 25:14–30), Jesus instructs us in the responsibility to use to the fullest extent whatever resources God has graciously given us.

As the Christian in the workplace subjects all of his/her competence, skills, talents, and training to the service of humanity, he/she is motivated by gratitude to God. High competence and skill in some occupation or profession provide the worker with a form of power in this world. They open doors of opportunity. They grant access to special doors and special environments. The Christian worker sees this power as the means of expanding a sphere of influence on others.

In the workplace the Christian acts as a redeemed man or woman. He/she is passionately concerned about justice, which, in an ideal sense, is the goal for the use of power, abilities, training, skills, and all other resources. Biblical ethics provide the Christian worker with the ways in which these resources and all relationships are to be conducted. Through Christian faith we learn of the dignity of other women and men, the value of human life, and the inestimable worth of a single individual in the sight of God. Though one is often caught between the world of godly ideals and spiritual sentiments on the one hand and the world of harsh realities and agonizing choices on the other hand, the Christian response to ethical issues at work is qualitatively better than the response of non-Christians.

Most of all, Christians in business and professional life know that career success and immense material prosperity are not the ultimate goals of the human journey upon earth, for they well remember the words of their Lord:

> If anyone would come after me, he must deny himself and take up his cross and follow me. For whoever wants to save his life will lose it, but whoever loses his life for me and for the gospel will save it. What good is it for a man to gain the whole world, yet forfeit his soul? Or what can a man give in exchange for his soul? (Mark 8:34–36)

THE FIVE PERCENT RULE OF THUMB

A friend, Dave Crouch, once informed an adult Sunday school class of "the 5 percent rule of thumb" in business life. Crouch's point: In most business transactions, we expect to receive exactly what the contract calls for. It does not matter if the exchange is over goods or services to be purchased, nor does it matter if the contract is formal (in writing) or informal (a "gentleman's agreement"). As an aside, in "the old days" a man's word was the only contract needed to guarantee that specified goods and services would be delivered; in today's world, a carefully drafted, signed document is necessary, and even then one party may refuse to honor the agreement or contest the interpretation of that document.

Given the greed and selfishness, along with market competitiveness, in the contemporary world, there seem to be a growing number of business and professional people who attempt to give the purchasing party 5 percent less than the agreement specifies. The extra 5 percent increases the immediate profit margin. Watch out for those business people and other workers who attempt to shave off 5 percent in terms of time, quality, goods, and/or services to the purchasing party whenever they think they can get away with it. "Be careful in the business world," Crouch urged, "because you do not always get what you think you are getting."

On the other hand, encouragingly, a minority of business and professional people, as well as workers in general, diligently seek to give the purchasing parties 5 percent *more* than the agreement specifies. This "over and beyond-ness" trait usually translates into quality service, good will, respect, trust, and friendship. Giving 5 percent more than is strictly required is likely to enhance the ultimate bottom line in any business. Some observers see the Chick-Fil-A Company as a business organization that gives "a little bit more" to its employees by making it convenient for them to attend worship services and giving abundant samples of their products to passers-by.

Is giving "a little bit more" a biblical concept? We answer in the affirmative. In his Sermon on the Mount, Jesus admonished his disciples to give even more than what was demanded of them by the enemy—how much more so by customers who make demands or requests (see Matt. 5:40–42)? Scripture also speaks of the law of sowing and reaping—a person reaps in abundance what he/she sows earlier, "therefore as we have opportunity, let us do good to all people, especially to those who belong to the family of believers" (see Gal. 6:7–10).

Perhaps the strongest direct admonition of Jesus regarding generosity in all matters is recorded by Luke:

> Here is a simple rule of thumb for behavior: Ask yourself what you want people to do for you; then grab the initiative and do it for them. . . . Help and give without expecting a return. You'll never—I promise—regret it. Live out this God-created identity the way our Father lives toward us, generously and graciously, even when we're at our worst. . . . Be easy on people; you'll find life a lot easier. Give away your life; you'll find life given back, but not merely given back—given back with bonus and blessing. Giving, not getting, is the way. Generosity begets generosity. (Selections are from chapter 6 as paraphrased by Eugene Peterson in *The Message*.)

Years ago as a young pulpit minister, the author occasionally used as sermon material a simple poem, its authorship unknown, entitled "A Little More." A search in an old college notebook of sermon illustrations uncovered this almost forgotten, simple verse which packs a profound insight:

A LITTLE MORE

We recall the kind old grocer,
When the sugar he would pour,
How he'd tip the scales to balance,
Then he'd add a little more.

And his business, how it prospered,
Folks were always in his store;
For he'd give an honest measure,
Then he'd add a little more.

So, it is with life, my brother,
We would write a better score,
When we've done what is expected,
If we'd add a little more.

QUESTIONS FOR GROUP DISCUSSION
AND PERSONAL REFLECTION

1. What are some examples of immature behavior that you have witnessed at the workplace?
2. Should you ask favors of others at work? Does that make you feel dependent on others, or does it make others feel important? How do you show others at work that you value them as persons or value their opinions? Is this "kissing up"?
3. What is the difference between "I messages" and "you messages," and why is it important to use "I messages"?
4. Can anyone make you feel a certain emotional state, such as anger? Can anyone else make you happy?
5. Do you think there is too much emphasis on winning in our culture?
6. What are some attitudes you can adopt to keep you from feeling personal rejection at work?
7. There is research showing that suppressed hostility, dealing with a nonsupportive boss, and little job mobility as among the most important predictors of heart disease among working women. The same is probably true for many working men. The less clout a person has on the job, the more likely the worker suffers from stress. For women in such jobs—secretaries, clerks, sales clerks, waitresses, nurses, and others—there are no easy answers. When one's work is to help or serve others, it's hard to take control of the work you do.

Suppose that you are in a frustrating job situation. What are some practical ways in which you can make the best of your work and workday—and your health?

8. "The individualism of American life, to our glory and despair, creates anger and encourages its release," writes Carol Tavris in her book *Anger: The Misunderstood Emotion*. "For when everything is possible, limitations are irksome. When the desires of self come first, the needs of others are annoying. When we think we deserve it all, reaping only a portion can enrage."

This quote provides something of an academic explanation of chronic complainers on the job. Do all of us have a right to complain on the job? Is anger a natural response, or is it usually a conditioned one (i.e., self-taught)? How would you deal with a chronic whiner in your workplace?

9. Using the criteria in this chapter, do you feel that you are mentally and emotionally healthy?

10. How can a supervisor build self-respect and self-esteem in his/her employees? Is a supervisor responsible for how subordinates feel about themselves?

11. Do you know anyone in business who demonstrates moral excellence? Can you tell a true personal story about moral excellence in business and professional life?

12. Have you had experiences with people in business who "give a little more" than you expected? Does your own personal work ethic include "giving a little more" to your employer or to your clients or customers?

Chapter 12

"The Way We Do Things Around Here"
A Look at Corporate Culture

The organization itself has an invisible quality—a certain style, a character, a way of doing things—that may be more powerful than the dictates of any one person or any formally documented system. To understand the essence or soul of the organization requires that we travel below the charts, rule books, machines, and buildings into the underground world of corporate cultures.

Ralph Kilmann

Loyalties are affections. As affections they are initially premoral. Once they are chosen and acted upon, of course, they become moral and significant fonts of behavior. . . . We need to be loyal, it seems, because we need to live for more than ourselves and pursue an agenda beyond ourselves. . . . Loyalty to a company, therefore, is a response to being heard, to being valued, to being cared about. Unilateral loyalty doesn't last long or doesn't happen.

John C. Haughey

A GREAT DEAL IS BEING SAID TODAY IN MANAGEMENT AND leadership studies about "corporate culture." Highly successful companies are presented as examples of firms which succeeded because they devoted much energy cultivating a strong corporate culture. In fact, the existence of a strong corporate culture accounts for the success and effectiveness of certain companies and the lack of it accounts for the failure and ineffectiveness of others. The highly popular book *In Search of Excellence: Lessons From America's Best Run Companies,* written by Tom Peters and Robert Waterman and published in 1982, discussed the characteristics and patterns of interaction within the strong corporate cultures of America's best business organizations.

What is meant by "corporate culture"? "Culture" is a vague word, meaning different things to different people. An anthropologist would mean one thing using culture and a biochemist might have another meaning entirely. Traditionally, culture has been understood simply as the unique customs, artifacts, and values of a group of people. Today, it is commonly accepted by management theorists that organizations have cultures as well, the same distinct customs, artifacts, and values that we associate with individual societies of people.

The term is an all-inclusive one and, as such, corporate culture includes a moral dimension. Let's propose this definition: Corporate culture is the constellation of shared values, customs, norms, and beliefs about all people connected with a business organization which provide the environment for corporate decisions and activities. Want a briefer definition? Corporate culture is "the way we do things around here." Whether carefully planned or inadvertently developed, each corporation has distinctive culture. The organization's culture is like a unique corporate finger print, a unique face, and unique personality and character that separate one firm from all others.

Business in general has an ethic of its own. It is not the same ethic that you practice at home, in church, in intimate relationships, or in other affiliations. There are ethical differences in the management of small communities and large cities, between investment firms and used car dealers, between product manufacturers and service providers, between small businesses and large corporations. Business ethics and business values vary widely from company to company. Moral views of business leaders fall across a rather broad spectrum.

The varied dimensions of a corporate culture may be both explicit and implicit. The formal culture of a business firm or agency may be expressed in mission statements and other idealized proclamations of values and purposes. The actual culture of a corporation may be determined more by the informal interactions between all levels of employees. Some values are proclaimed for public relations; real values get transmitted throughout the organization by informal communication and everyday decision-making.

A wise management seeks to learn the real dynamics of its organization: What are the real values of this company? How does business really get done around here? What values are being instilled in employees? How high is company morale? Are the codes of conduct respected and followed? Is corporate responsibility to the larger community taken seriously? Who really holds the power in this corporation? How does management really feel about our customers? How does management feel about codes? How should this memorandum be interpreted? How does one get ahead in this company?

POWER

To study corporate culture is to inquire about power. Basic to the structure of all human institutions is the will to, and exercise of, power. Every aspect of our society—business, politics, education, religion, marriage, etc.— operates to some degree on the basis of power. In fact, as the philosopher Nietzche put it, "Basic to the human personality is the will to power."

Do you remember the Charles Atlas ads, where there was the skinny, helpless kid on the beach being harassed by the punk and then there was Charles Atlas? The girl walks off with the muscled guy. The skinny guy spends a year working out.

Early on, we learn that "real" males are powerful, that a man without power is a wimp. As adolescents we think of physical strength and athletic ability as the most important signs of power. Later, as adults, popular culture leads us to think of our income-earning capacity and our influence over others as signs of power.

A strong male tendency is the will to dominate, to be in control, not only of oneself but of others. There are power charts for formal organizations. But power can be an important consideration even in intimate relationships, such as marriage. Leaders obsessed with the need to control others and all circumstances ("control freaks") might display the following traits:

1. frequently give strong directives to subordinates at all levels;
2. think "boss knows best" at all times;
3. think they alone have all the right answers;
4. reverse decisions others were authorized to make;
5. monopolize information and decision-making so that others need to come to them for help;
6. seek recognition and praise, even for ideas and proposals of others;
7. keep colleagues in the dark about important decisions that affect them;
8. have developed "founderitis syndrome"—unable to let go of their baby.

Key Terms in Defining Power

Power: The capacity to influence or impact another person or group's behavior (not necessarily the exercise of it). We measure power by the amount of influence a person has in his/her relationships with other individuals or groups. People who feel powerless have little or no influence.

Authority: (related to power) The right to act, decide, direct, approve or withhold all the above.

Status: A measure of comparing one person to another; it is based almost entirely on our perceptions of personal or social worth. Status may be dependent on the symbols that identify the comparative position of a person with those of others (e.g., size and furnishings of an office; parking privileges; clothes; job title, etc.).

Dominance: Based on illegitimate power; power which has not been sanctioned or legitimized by others (e.g., all societies recognize the right of parents to have authority over their children until they are legal adults; to try to control another adult is an effort at dominance).

Politics: The exercise of power; the art of compromise; techniques used to accumulate and wield power. Like power itself, politics may be either positive or negative. Politics and power are inevitable realities of any modern organization.

Manipulation: Dishonest game-playing; deceitful and dishonest role playing to receive a certain result; devious action for selfish purpose.

People often resort to intimidation and manipulation when they lack the valued resources (money, position) or the widespread acceptance of others in order to exercise influence legitimately. When a father or husband resorts to abuse (verbal, physical, etc.), he is attempting to show force but lacks moral authority and legitimate power (respect given by a wife or children). Subordinates may be devious and manipulative in order to exercise power against supervisors.

Status and the Source of Power

Certain occupations have high or low status. A scientist is usually at the top, then doctor, minister, lawyer, engineer, teacher, athlete, down to banker, hourly worker, salesperson. Credibility has a bearing. Generally, few professions have above 50 percent credibility rating; bartenders, used car salesmen, taxi drivers, and janitors are among those who consistently receive low-status ranking.

Power is not necessarily evil. There is negative and destructive power, and there is positive and creative power. There is power to accomplish good and power to produce harm and evil.

Power is controlling the circumstances in which you make decisions. Michael Jordan exerted power in his decision to retire from professional basketball and play professional baseball; he exercised power again when he decided to return to the Chicago Bulls. Jesus displayed power when he willingly went to the cross. To choose to step down from a position when you are not forced to step down is to exercise personal power.

In traditional management theory, power has been classified according to its sources:
1. **Legitimate power** is derived from a person's position in an organization, job assignment, or recognized leadership functions. This kind of power is normal, justifiable, and necessary.
2. **Ascribed power** is power given because of birth or accession; e.g., merely by being anointed, crowned, or born into royalty.
3. **Coercive power** is the ability to threaten, punish, or alter another person's self-esteem or job status. Unfortunately, legitimate power can be used coercively. Coercive power can result from perceptions that a peer has damaging or embarrassing information, as well as from the more direct threats that come from higher authority. The use of coercive power often breeds counteraction that hurts the organization.
4. **Reward power** is the ability to approve action, give promotions, or assign more desirable tasks. Reward power is a great tool for management to use in promoting desired change and productivity.
5. **Referent power** is role model power, when a person's attitude, goals, approach to problems or style is voluntarily copied by others who admire it.
6. **Expert power** is derived from knowledge or skill. People respect the person who is bright or well-trained and well-educated and will seek his/her assistance in solving problems. Over the long haul, expert power and referent power seem to be the most important kinds of power.

Gender and Power

Crosscultural/anthropological research shows that men the world over use their power to dominate women. Almost all societies can be classified as patriarchal, where men dominate. Why is this so? Some answers which have been forwarded:

1. **It is in males' rational self-interest to be dominant.** This gives them choice jobs, material possessions, and control of situations.
2. **Men have greater physical size and strength.**
3. **There is a fundamental personality difference** between men and women, resulting in fact that most hands-on parenting is done by mothers rather than fathers.

   Carol Gilligan developed the theory of women's almost innate possession of a caring perspective as opposed to the justice perspective shared by most males. In making moral decisions men emphasize rights, hierarchy, and autonomy, while women emphasize context, caring, and attachment. Women believe that problems are solved in relationship, while men believe in rules, logic, and abstractions. Men feel secure at the top of the heap—the names highest on an organization chart—while women feel secure in the web of comfortable relationships. Women see life as dependent on connections. Men are reluctant to be interwoven in a dependent relationship.
4. **Experience of early female dominance.** Men seek to control because women controlled them early in life. True in the home and in the classroom. Hence, men have an unconscious fear of being controlled.
5. **Distinct roles given by God or culture.** God wants men to achieve and women to give emotional support. Women can meet their achievement needs only vicariously. Women can do emotional work for men. Men can then have time to see women as nice, soft creatures to desire and want them. Men need women to need them, the argument goes: "Oh honey, you are so strong, I just don't know how I could manage without you."

Empowering is the process of developing power in another person; it is an interactive process where no one must give up anything. Empowered people are in a reciprocal relationship of personality and spiritual growth.

There are some cultural assumptions about power. One is that power exists only in limited supply. That is, in any institution or relationship there are so many units of power and they must be divided some way. The husband may have a hundred units and the wife none or some combination. Or the boss might have ninety units of power and delegate ten units to a subordinate. Another cultural assumption is that most men and women in business will attempt to maximize their power and reduce the power of others in the marketplace.

Jesus had much to say about power (see Mark 10:42–45). He warned against the dangers of seeking worldly power, urging his disciples not to "lord it over" others. He taught that the path to greatness is paved with humble service.

A basic distinction: The Christian use of power is power to serve others, to lift up the fallen, to forgive, to encourage, and to foster maturity. The worldly use of power is intended to control others so that they make your life easier, that they do your will, that they bring you personal satisfaction.

NORMS

At the heart of the corporate culture is another set of principles by which nearly everyone in the organization follows in making decisions. Norms are working principles, largely unwritten and promulgated unofficially, which are widely accepted as standards for business conduct and decision-making. Even though norms are not found in mission statements, professional codes, or policy manuals, they are widely accepted as the basis for implementing company policy and procedure.

The concept of norms need not be negative. They may apply and reinforce stated principles and values with which they are in agreement. Unfortunately, however, in some corporate cultures many norms are at variance with established principles and values. When an employee says, "Yeah, I know what the manual says, but let me tell you how business is actually done around here," then norms reflect the "don't do as I say, but do as I do" mentality.

The following are some declared working principles matched with unstated reality norms:

DECLARED WORKING PRINCIPLES	UNSTATED NORMS
Your personal life is your own.	If you are going to work for this automotive company, you'd better own one of the cars we build.
A clean, professional appearance is all we ask.	If you're going to work for this company, better know that Dockers and Haggar pants are not good enough.
We encourage employees to bring up ideas and complaints.	Never knock it unless you have a better idea.
We deliver top-quality products to our customers at a fair price.	Quality is cut if it really affects the bottom line.
In this store the customer is right.	The customer is right only if we can't always convince him that he is totally wrong.
All expenses must be legitimate and fully reported.	It's not padding—it's perks—and I've earned them.
The benefits of our success will be shared by all our employees who have shared in production.	The top-level managers will be justified in getting ten times what workers on assembly lines get.

DECLARED (cont.)	UNSTATED (cont.)
No long-distance calls for personal reasons can be made; emergency calls must be logged in.	If you don't take advantage of the system you can make one or two calls a week no—questions asked.
Log in the times of reporting to and taking leave from the work unit.	Just write in the times that you are supposed to be in the work unit.
All supervisors are expected to receive training in computer.	Supervisors will receive training unless you've been here a long time and expect to retire soon and don't want to be bothered.
There is no gender discrimination in this company.	Women still average 20 percent less than men in comparable positions.
We hope you can meet your quota.	You'd better meet your quota.
We do not tolerate sexual harassment.	Just don't do something so stupid that you give us a court case.
Our new mission statement and code of ethics is important.	We had a meeting, talked about ethics, and signed a paper that said we would follow it.
Take responsibility for your mistakes so that we can all work together as a team to solve them.	Admitting mistakes is poor personal policy and can get you demoted or fired.
The corporate head has an open door if you need to complain.	There are certain things you better not criticize or question if you expect longevity here.
We're not bureaucratic clock watchers around here.	You'd better not be a minute late.
People—our workers and our customers —are most important.	Profits are the most important.

ORGANIZATIONAL INTEGRITY

Elsewhere in this book we have contended that personal integrity is rooted not simply in a reputation for truthfulness in reporting facts but, more importantly, in consistency between words and actions, ideals and choices, values and behavior. An individual with integrity is a person with all aspects of one's life fully integrated; the old saying, "what you see is what you get" applies to such a holistic life. If you have integrity, your peers see you as credible and trustworthy.

The same principle applies to business organizations. If an organization conscientiously attempts to make policies and decisions in accordance with the high ethical standards and moral values that it promulgates publicly, that organization has integrity. With this consistency between the stated values of the firm and the actual day-to-day operations of the organization come trustworthiness and credibility—organizational integrity.

More than ever before, management in the most effective, and successful corporate cultures realizes how important it is not simply to "talk the talk" but to "walk your talk." Highly ethical managers must model the ground rules they expect subordinates to follow. In few respects do the aphorisms "Actions speak louder than words" and "Practice what you preach" apply more forcefully than to business ethics. Employees are most willing, perhaps *only* willing, to adopt corporate values if they see that managers and supervisors above them have adopted and respected the same values and rules. Norms that are not "in sync" with the declared values and principles of the organization should be pinpointed, disclaimed, and rendered unrewarded.

ENHANCING A COMPANY'S ETHICAL CHARACTER

Business ethics is serious business. Seldom does one pick up a newspaper or news magazine without finding another story of corruption, fraud, or malfeasance in political life, public institutions, or private business. We conjecture that less often reported are the inappropriate actions of small-business owners or local professionals who misuse power or position for personal benefit or use poor judgment in making ethical decisions. We all recognize the difference between right and wrong, even in today's complex and competitive society. Or do we?

We might fantasize that citizens learn their business ethics in schools, colleges, and churches. Truth is, however, business ethics are learned at work—perhaps because of their immense importance and prominence in our culture, the overwhelming importance of vocation and career in establishing workers' identities, and the waning influence on moral training by traditional institutions. College students will learn more about ethics in their jobs than in their courses. American corporate life produces not only goods and services, but also women and men and their ethical values.

How does a manager create a highly ethical corporation? One answer: bring together only employees who have the highest ethical standards and then turn them loose. This solution might be correct for a band of angels singing "glory, hallelujah in the highest," but with the frailty of human nature and the unrelenting pressures for successful performance in today's competitive business environment, it would be folly for corporate leaders to neglect concrete action.

Corporate ethics must be managed as an ongoing process. There is no time for ethical relaxation or dropping one's guard. And now to get practical, managers who are serious about elevating the ethical character of the entire business organization might consider the following briefly stated suggestions:

1. Begin with a mission statement for the entire organization. Being a leader implies that someone is taking others to a destination beyond the here and now.
2. Allow everyone in the business to provide input in writing the mission statement and making application to their work environment and responsibilities.
3. Develop a statement of the ethical posture of the company. Put this in writing. State the moral values the managers seek to be served and respected by everyone

connected with the company. Give every employee a copy. Help each employee see that ethical policies are viewed as an extension of values ("common sense right and wrong").

4. Emphasize the mission statement and moral values of the organization at every opportunity. Post the mission statement in conspicuous places.

5. Adhere uncompromisingly to honesty and integrity in all matters, especially official communications.

6. Tolerate absolutely no racial, ethnic, or sexual discrimination at any levels of the company. Maintain and promote the dignity and worth of each individual.

7. Install a procedure for employees who seek to confidentially report incidents of illegal or unethical conduct or raise concerns and issues related to ethics. Take that procedure with ultimate seriousness. Make certain employees have access to top managers to express concerns.

8. Avoid giving potentially misleading signals as to what is acceptable behavior.

9. Have a clear statement for the punishment of individual violations of stated moral rules. Be emphatic that there is strict enforcement of ethical standards and all violators will be punished according to the book, even those whose violations were not intended to produce personal gain.

10. Be diligent and consistent in uncovering and punishing any violations of ethical standards. Do not play favorites in workplace justice and discipline.

11. Alert internal auditors to ethical issues.

12. Employ an outside consultant and auditors to monitor major operations for possible unethical practices or conduct.

13. Remember that quality management translates quality labor-management relationships. Develop collegiality among workers. Emphasize the value of mutual respect. Help workers feel like they are more than just a number. Give them a voice in company affairs. Foster an open and egalitarian work atmosphere. Place a high value on teamwork. Remember that where close and comfortable relations develop, employees are more inclined to broach delicate ethical issues and consider how to deal with them.

14. Provide truly quality products and services. Consider the obvious ethical implications in the firm's relationship between quality management and quality workmanship on the one hand, and good relationship with all constituents, on the other hand.

15. Staff the organization, especially positions of authority, with ethically minded people. Remember that this is the best guarantor of corporate ethical behavior. Business and professional ethics ultimately depend on the moral values and inclinations of the people doing the work of the firm. Even the best ethical programs and classes cannot succeed if the managers involved do not value basic ethical principles. Remember that ethical people are attracted to firms which already place a high value on highly ethical business conduct; thus the process of hiring ethical people happens naturally. Screen out new hires who have low

ethical standards or who place profit and intelligence above morality (some testing and the interview process might be helpful here).

16. Contract with outside parties—consultants, auditors, advertisers, suppliers, distributors, even customers—who are likely to support the company's ethical policies rather than subvert them. Do not depend on unscrupulous third parties.

17. Provide training and indoctrination sessions which continually emphasize ethical values and policies. Through the time devoted to ethical issues, the status of people teaching, and the quality of the program, all employees may learn of the priority of ethics. Give participants ample opportunities to ask questions, challenge assertions, and actively participate. Help all employees to see the ethical dimensions of their individual work assignments (note that some employees believe their jobs do not involve ethical decisions). Remember that moral lectures sound like sermons. Few people like sermons at work. The training method that utilizes lectures is tantamount to one-way monologue; lectures are not geared to deal adequately with all the confusions and apprehensions. Lesson materials should include real and hypothetical case studies for employees to consider and discuss.

18. Provide full explanations of ethical values and policies to new employees in orientation sessions so there is no way they can misunderstand what is acceptable and what is unacceptable in the company.

19. Give ethical pep talks along the course of the business year. Tell inspirational stories about highly ethical managers and workers. Allow a company lore to develop replete with stories of how CEOs and managers acted with concern for honest business dealings.

20. Develop empathy for your employees. Recognize and identify with the ordinary concerns of your subordinates, especially with regard to company policy and practice. Learn the temptations to unethical conduct that others in the company face.

21. Provide ample recognition and rewards (praise, promotion, and perks) for ethical accomplishment. Consider how seldom attention is ever given to rewarding ethical accomplishments—business ethics serves more as a veto than a plus and you are noticed only if you are out of line. Normal people do not develop fondness for a plethora of "thou shalt nots." Like the Ten Commandments in the Bible, many people become negative or feel threatened when they hear the term "business ethics" or "corporate ethics." Give favorable recognition for laudable ethical actions by employees. Advance otherwise qualified men and women who excel in their abilities to motivate ethical behavior among their peers and colleagues.

22. Provide opportunities through continuing education, workshops, conferences, etc., for the personal and professional growth of all employees.

23. Lastly, remember always that the credibility of senior management's ethical values and ethical intentions rests firmly on how it behaves and makes ethical decisions, and, from the workers' viewpoint, on how it treats them as individuals.

Yes, we conclude that promoting ethical behavior in business organizations is quite costly in terms of money, time, and creative energy. We believe it is also much more costly to neglect promoting and enhancing ethical character/organizational integrity within the corporation.

QUESTIONS FOR GROUP DISCUSSION
AND PERSONAL REFLECTION

1. What is a corporate culture? Is there any connection between corporate culture and business ethics?
2. Do you believe that all relationships operate of the basis of power?
3. Do you believe that all people in the business world seek power over others, either in the open market or in the office or boardroom?
4. Do you agree with Carol Gilligan that women have more of a caring perspective than do men and that men have more of a justice perspective than do women?
5. Over the long haul, which of the various kinds of power is the most important power within an organization?
6. Is there a biblical model for exercising power? Is there a biblical model for empowering others?
7. Is it possible to see godly power as available to all men and women in unlimited amounts?
8. Name three values and principles that your business organization officially stands for. Does your company make an honest attempt to follow its declared values and principles? Does it make ethical behavior a high priority?
9. Can you name any unwritten norms that are operative in your business organization?
10. What are some ways in which corporations can encourage their members to take moral responsibilities seriously?
11. Do you think the use of "politics" is ethical in a business environment? There is no doubt that in many organizations the acquisition and use of power can become a kind of political gamesmanship. Employees can gain a type of power by flattering an ego-hungry manager or by providing special services or personal favors. In many firms, politics, as well as the employees' ability, help determine promotions, salary increases, and desirable job assignments. Recognition of what the boss likes and does not like is a key to successful political action. Should the Christian employee play this kind of game in the work environment? Isn't it basically dishonest?
12. What kind of authority do elders and other religious leaders have in the church? Are there "politics" in the church or other Christian organizations? Do religious leaders exercise power? (Before deciding that this question is out of place in this volume, consider the fact that the typical church is a business.)
13. Do you believe that men who are frustrated in their failure to exercise power in their vocation or profession may attempt to exercise power in their family or in the church?

14. Do the rich and powerful in society deserve special power and favor in the church and other Christian organizations (see James 2:1–13)?

15. If you were teaching a workshop on Christian living, social justice, the distinctiveness of the church, or moral living, and the president of the United States and his family walked into your session unexpectedly, would this alter the content of your lesson? (Yes, this is far-fetched!)

16. Do you think that many church conflicts and splits are about power plays rather than the high and lofty principles that opponents talk about during disputes?

17. How can one know when a person is victimized by a lust for power?

18. Do you think spouse abuse, child abuse, even incest, are symptoms of distorted conceptions of power in the family or frustrations about power in the workplace?

19. Do you agree that "when you have to appeal to your authority to get something done, you don't have any authority"?

20. Should the business affairs of the church or other non-profit, charitable institutions be conducted by a higher, more exacting standard of ethics?

21. Do you agree that there is such a thing as "organizational integrity"? Could you name some large firms or corporations that you believe to possess such integrity?

22. If you are employed by a firm or company, do you know of efforts being made to raise the ethical standards and conduct at all levels of that organization?

Chapter 13

Building Trust

Loyalty is not won outright nor is it everlasting. Rather, it is given by the group as long as they think their leader is worthy of it. . . . The best way to gain and hold the loyalty of your personnel is to show interest in them and care for them, by your words and actions, in

everything you do. And this attitude of concern must be sincere.

Fred A. Manske Jr.

Trust only those who stand to lose as much as you when things go wrong.

Bralek's rule for success

IN A WORKING RELATIONSHIP, LITTLE HAPPENS IN THE WAY OF meaningful progress until the parties to the working agreement learn to trust each other. Therefore, forming a climate of trust is one of the most important tasks for all parties in the workforce. Trust sets a moral tone for the corporate culture. It is also vitally linked to organizational morale.

In essence, trust is the glue that holds business together. Consider how complicated the business world would be if we required mechanisms, such as legal contracts to be signed, to carry out the ordinary, day-to-day transactions which are part and parcel of business and professional life. We must rely on the honesty and dependability of almost everyone with whom we do business.

Is trust a vanishing commodity in today's business world? In the old days, a man's word was as good as a written contract. A promise was a promise. If a man did not keep his word, no one would do business with him again. Today, for two business parties to reach an agreement, skilled attorneys are needed to scrutinize a written contract to insure there are no loopholes for the other party to evade its part of the agreement. Even with the presence of a written contract, one party may eventually feel exploited by the other party.

At any level, whether corporate or individual, trust is absolutely essential for a relationship to grow and mature. How do you create a climate of trust which reduces your own and the other party's fears of betrayal and rejection and builds the hopes of acceptance and support? Is it possible for one party to entrust itself—with its needs, concerns, and vital interests—to another party?

WHEN ARE YOU TRUSTING?

What is it like to trust another person? When are you trusting and when are you distrustful? When is your labor or management group behaving in a trustworthy manner and when are you violating someone else's trust? How do you know when you are being trusted?

Trust is a word everyone uses, yet it is a complex concept and difficult to define. Based on the writings of psychologists, trust may be understood as including the following elements:

1. There is risk in a trusting situation. The choice to trust another person can lead to either beneficial or harmful consequences for your needs and goals.
2. You realize that whether the consequences are beneficial or harmful depends upon the future behavior of another person or party.
3. You expect to suffer more if the consequences are harmful than you will gain if they are beneficial.
4. You feel relatively confident that the other person will behave in such a way that the beneficial consequences will result.

Think of how these conditions apply when a mother decides to leave her young child with a teenage baby-sitter. The mother is aware that her choice could lead to a negative consequence, realizes the consequences depend on the behavior of her baby-sitter, expects to suffer more if her trust is violated (her baby is harmed) than she would gain if her trust is fulfilled (she has time for grocery shopping), and has confidence that the baby-sitter will behave in a way that the consequences will be beneficial. (Some recent television documentaries deploying hidden cameras have demonstrated, unfortunately, that some parents should be less trusting and more careful about baby-sitters and nannies they hire.)

No matter how long you may have worked with your current employer, most likely you are working with people and you are constantly beginning or maintaining, testing, and modifying relationships. Ideally, your work relationships should be just as satisfying, if not more satisfying, than your actual work assignments. You may be involved in a number of relationships on various levels, but their presence does not mean that they are healthily maintained in an ideal climate. Just as a plant may survive without quite enough water and light, so can relationships "limp along" in a less than ideal climate. If trust is the first step toward maximizing the effectiveness of our relationships, how might we describe a climate in which trust thrives?

A CLIMATE IN WHICH TRUST THRIVES

Descriptiveness

Trust grows best in a climate that is *descriptive* rather than *evaluative*. Describing is putting sensory data into words. It's easy enough to know what it means to describe;

on the other hand, it's difficult to know how to describe. You see, when you think you are describing, you may in fact be evaluating or judging.

For example, Darrell Trimble is likely to think of his terse comments as descriptive when he leaves the staff meeting and declares, "I just came from the dullest meeting!" Or as June Caldwell leaves the plant cafeteria after eating her fifth taco, she turns to Sarah and says, "I'm going to die!" In reality, both statements are evaluative and not descriptive. Calling a meeting "dull" does not describe what did or did not happen, and saying "I'm going to die" does not accurately describe the feeling of having eaten too much highly seasoned food. If, however, Darrell had said, "I've just come from a two and one-half hour meeting. There were three reports given, each lasting between fifteen to thirty minutes. There was random open discussion and four motions were made, but none of them were passed," he would have described a meeting that might well be evaluated as dull.

"What's wrong with evaluation?" you might ask. The first problem is that evaluation does not inform; instead, it places a judgment on what has been said or done. One must have a lot of information to offer a judgment. Some of the most dogmatic judgments have been offered with only smatterings of evidence. A second problem is that when you make an evaluation in the presence of another person, that person may become defensive, especially if it is contrary to the other person's opinion. Evaluating can put others on the defensive. Descriptiveness in interpersonal communication helps to eliminate a negative climate.

Spontaneity

Trust grows in a climate that is spontaneous rather than manipulative. When two people on the job have a matter to discuss related to their work assignments, the subject to be discussed is called an agenda (the purpose for the communication). If, for example, Walter Spencer, head of product design, calls Jimmy Burchett into his office to discuss a new product, the discussion of that product is the reason for that meeting—it is the agenda.

Occasionally, however, those talking have what is called a *hidden agenda*—a reason or motive for behavior that is undisclosed to other participants. If Walter called in Jimmy to discuss product design, but really wanted to find whether Jimmy was writing his own reports, finding the answer to this question would be Walter's hidden agenda that controls his behavior. At best, the hidden agenda seems like an easy way of dealing with a difficult issue; at worst, it is gross manipulation.

Trust is possible in a work environment where standards are honored, but where workers feel free to be honest and open in all their dealings with coworkers.

Equality

Tolerance grows in climates where the people are seen as equals rather than in climates where one person is perceived as superior to another. How do you feel when people say something that you perceive as meaning that they know more than you, are better people than you, or that they possess superior judgment and wisdom? Most of us would react uncomfortably to such statements.

The work situation can be a complicated one, for certain. Some people believe that their positions make them superior to those around them; a department head may think that his/her designation makes him/her a better person. Whatever the basis for the assumption of superiority, however, projecting it often results in a negative rather than a positive work climate. This is especially true when the other workers involved are not at all convinced of the superiority.

A climate of trust is not possible without this attitude of equality. True, there are people in your company who have more responsibility (along with the training for it) than others, but equality means being on the same level, or seeing others as worthwhile as oneself. This attitude of superiority is just as frequently communicated nonverbally as it is verbally.

Open-mindedness

Conflict can be lessened and trust increased when coworkers can be open-minded about other people, behavior, and policies. Open-mindedness is flexibility in the way a person processes information. Rather than seeing concepts in absolute terms, an open-minded person is willing to tolerate other sides and examine all the evidence or information.

Dogmatism is just the opposite. The dogmatic person has "LINT"—locked-in negative thinking. Such a person clings tenaciously to his/her value system and judges every new policy and new behavior on the basis of how they fit into that value system.

Some values, however, must be locked in. Mindset should not always be viewed as negative. It is a negative factor only when we are incapable of holding an open mind to welcome new facts or ideas. We must all hold some values secured tightly in conscience's place in order to function in a healthy manner.

Open-minded people may be committed to certain attitudes or beliefs that emerge from their value systems, but they are aware of the common ground that exists between what they believe in and what they have rejected. Their personal judgments are held as tentative, subject to revision after further thought and consideration. In discussion with associates with whom they disagree, they seek a middle ground between their positions in order to resolve the controversy.

Dogmatic participants, on the other hand, focus on their differences. They view the controversy in terms of black and white and never see the shades of gray that lie between their two positions. It can be said that tolerance and dogmatism are mutually exclusive.

THE EMOTIONAL BANK ACCOUNT

A positive work climate is one that allows for the building of trust within the business organization. True, trust is a kind of risk—the ability to risk yourself, to put yourself in the hands or at the service of another party. In a sense, trust is a kind of prediction—a prediction that if you "put yourself in the hand of another," the result will be to your advantage.

When there is trust, people can be who they really are. This sounds like a simple statement, to be sure. When any relationship has trust, neither party needs to be defensive about self. Being yourself becomes easier. Pretension is unnecessary.

We all know about a bank account in which we deposit and withdraw money. Stephen Covey invites us to think about "the emotional bank account," a metaphor to describe the amount of trust which has been built up between parties in a relationship. You can make deposits into an emotional bank account held by another person through courtesy, honesty, goodness, kindness, and keeping your commitments. The other person then trusts you more. Keeping a big promise or commitment is a major deposit; breaking one is a major withdrawal.

If your reserves are high, you can even make a major mistake, apologize for it, and the trust level can remain high. On the other hand, if you develop the habits of demonstrating disrespect, rudeness, and promise-breaking, being undependable, being selfish, and being dishonest, then your emotional bank account becomes overdrawn and your trust level is very low.

All vital and meaningful relationships—whether between employer and employee, husband and wife, intimate friend and friend—are built on trust and fidelity. Trust is built by doing the things that people expect you to do. People trust by extending good faith to the motives and actions of other people. If you are an honest and diligent worker, you will be able to move from a position of minimal trust and confidence in those with whom you work to a position of high trust and confidence.

QUESTIONS FOR GROUP DISCUSSION
AND PERSONAL REFLECTION

1. How would you describe trust in a working situation?

2. What are ways that trust is violated in a working situation?

3. Do you see it as a virtue to be open-minded? Does Scripture ever instruct us to be open-minded? Aren't some people too open-minded?

4. Have you ever worked in a dysfunctional or "sick" office or unit? What happened to make it "sick"?

5. Are there trust and good will in your current business organization? Do the various employees respect and appreciate each other? Are transactions both honest and open, free of manipulation and game-playing?

6. A test for business executives and leaders: Employee loyalty provides the most reliable gauge of leadership ability, and it cannot be bought or secured by favors. "Loyalty is not won outright, nor is it everlasting," states Fred A. Manske Jr. "Rather it is given by the group as long as they think their leader is worthy of it."

Take the following test to get an idea on where you stand:

1. Do you try to develop warm, person-to-person relationships with your subordinates?
2. Whenever possible, do you participate in company social events, recreation or other outings?
3. Do you treat all employees equally?
4. Do you confide in people whom you trust?
5. Do you consider it your responsibility to help your workers succeed in their jobs?
6. Do you show appreciation to your steady day-to-day workers?
7. Do you acknowledge and reward your top performers?
8. Do you meet individually with your associates and colleagues?
9. When an employee fails in a task, do you grant time and opportunity for improvement?
10. When you promise an employee something, do you always deliver?

Chapter 14

Organizational Communication with Respect

Communication is the most important skill in life. We spend most of our waking hours communicating. . . . Seek first to undertand . . . then to be understood.

Stephen Covey

Take heed how you hear.

Jesus

A barrier to communication is something that keeps meanings from meeting. Meaning barriers exist between all people, making communication much more diffi-cult than most people seem to realize. It is false to assume that if one can talk he can communicate. Because so much of our education misleads people into thinking that communication is easier than it is, they become discouraged and give up when they run into difficulty. Because they do not understand the nature of the problem, they do not know what to do. The wonder is not that communicating is as difficult as it is, but that is occurs as much as it does.

Reuel Howe

THE WAY WE COMMUNICATE WITH OTHERS IN THE WORKPLACE IS definitely a moral concern. Our style of communication reveals our attitude toward our work partners and colleagues; it tells something about our respect, or lack of same, for others. Of course, even the best-intended among us can experience major communication breakdowns, and thus this chapter will seem to deal more with practical concerns than ethical issues.

In an effective organization, communication flows in various directions: downward, upward, and crosswise. Traditionally, downward communication was emphasized as the only important direction; but there is ample evidence that if this is the only emphasis, serious problems will develop.

Downward communication flows from people at higher levels to those at lower levels in the organizational hierarchy. This is found in organizations with an authoritarian atmosphere. Unfortunately, information often gets lost or distorted as it comes down the chain of command. A feedback system is essential.

Upward communication travels from subordinate to superiors and continues up the organizational hierarchy. Unfortunately, this flow is often hindered by people in the communications link who filter the messages and do not transmit all the information (especially the bad news).

Crosswise communication includes horizontal flow of information, with people on the same or similar organizational levels.

The two basic means of communication are, of course, written and spoken or oral. Each has its advantages. Most information is communicated orally. The advantage of oral communication is obvious: it can provide for speedy interchange with immediate feedback. Listeners can ask questions and clarify points immediately. Written communication can be more precise and more permanent.

One of the great ironies of our contemporary civilization is that, even though the technology of swift and accurate communication has been developed beyond the wildest imagination of previous generations (telephone, cable, internet, etc.), people often find it difficult to communicate face to face in their most basic relationships—at home and at work! There are so many hidden agenda, manipulative game-playing, faulty assumptions, overriding emotions, and shameless incompetence with communication skills that it may be a wonder that we communicate at all. One person caustically remarked that "conversation in the United States is a competitive exercise in which the first person to draw a breath is declared the listener."

POPULAR MISCONCEPTIONS ABOUT COMMUNICATION

The manager or employee who places a high premium on the attitude of sincerity will also place a high premium on communicating appropriately and effectively. One person has stated that "managers are speaking, reading, writing, and listening beings who spend 70 to 80 percent of their time in some form of communication." The ability to communicate skillfully and effectively is a central part of everything a manager does. Management must communicate to gain understanding, to motivate, and to maintain cooperation from employees.

Communication is also important for the laboring force, not simply because workers want and need to establish satisfying relationships with coworkers, but also because all management-labor relations involve our ability to communicate. Quite often labor-management relationships succeed or fail as a direct result of a communication style.

There are a number of popular misconceptions about communication which prevent professionals and business people as well other workers from experiencing effective communication. We'll state five of these:

1. **Communication is a simple and easy process.** Nothing could be further from the truth. Rather than being surprised when people do not communicate well in difficult workplace or other interpersonal situations, we might rather be pleasantly pleased when they do communicate effectively. Some research indicates as much as 70 percent of all business communications fail to achieve their intended purpose.

2. **Communication can be avoided.** "We just don't communicate" is a common complaint of husbands and wives. One often hears it among supervisors and nonsupervisory personnel as they talk about each other. However, communication is inevitable wherever people live and work together. We communicate with our gestures, our facial expressions, our posture, and our tone of voice, just to mention a few ways. We even communicate with silence. "We just don't communicate" may be translated as "I don't like what we communicate" or "I don't like how we communicate."

3. **Communication is the transfer of meaning from one mind to another.** Technically, a transfer of meaning, in the same sense as we might transfer a crate of cargo from a storage facility to a delivery truck, is not possible. Meaning is not transferable in the same sense that tangible objects are transferable. Your meanings are your personal possession, and though nontransferable, you may communicate them to others if you choose. But when you communicate your meanings (or messages), they are always filtered and even distorted by your listeners (or readers).

4. **You can actually read somebody else's mind.** It's often assumed that if you live or work with someone long enough, you can read the other person's mind. It is true that you can know fairly well what the other person is thinking and feeling; however, both people and situations are always changing and assumptions are the most common and deadly pitfall in interpersonal communication.

5. **Meaning is in words or messages.** Actually, words do not mean. Dictionaries cannot and do not provide us with meaning. Meanings are in people as personal, subjective property. You are free to learn meanings, add to them, distort them, or change them. To the extent that you and your working colleagues have similar meanings (based on similar experiences and shared values), you can communicate with them.

WAYS NOT TO COMMUNICATE

When one person communicates with another through the medium of language, something takes place between these two people that is quite unique in nature. Animals communicate, as we know, but it is the human language system and the intellectual-system capacity behind it that has enabled the development of characteristics that differentiate *homo sapiens* from all other creatures.

Someone has said, "80 percent of the people who fail at work do so for one reason: they do not relate well to other people." Much of the "people failure" on the job is because of communication problems. "It is false to assume that if one can talk he can communicate," declared Reœuel Howe. "The wonder is not that communicating is as difficult as it is, but that it occurs as much as it does."

It has been estimated that we use special communication devices or "spoilers" over 90 percent of the time when one or both parties to a conversation has a problem to be dealt with or a need to be fulfilled. Communication barriers are high-risk responses—that is, responses whose impact on communication is frequently (though not inevitably) negative. These roadblocks are likely to be destructive when one or more persons are interacting under stress, either at home or at work.

At first glance, some of these barriers seem quite innocent. After all, who wouldn't want to receive our praise, reassurance, questions, and well-intentioned advice? Again, these are high-risk responses, rather than inevitably destructive elements in all communication. As high-risk, such devices or spoilers are more likely to

1. block conversation,
2. thwart the coworker's problem-solving efficiency,
3. increase the emotional distance between the two parties, or
4. create more tension in the work place.

Our reference to spoilers is drawn from the writings of Thomas Gordon on the subject of effective parenting. Gordon has devised a comprehensive list of spoilers or blockers which he calls the "dirty dozen" (in his *Parent Effectiveness Training*, chapter 3). We will look at several of these communication spoilers which rear their ugly head in the workplace.

Solution Messages

Solution messages are solutions that apply only to *your* problem and *your* values. The hidden message of "You're too dumb to figure it out for yourself," creates resistance and resentment in the other person. Spoilers and blockers include

1. ordering, commanding, and directing, as in "I order you to . . . ";
2. warning and threatening, as in "You'd better not!";
3. moralizing, preaching, and evaluating, as in "You should . . . "; and
4. advising, offering solutions, and coaching, as in "You ought to tell her you are sorry."

Put-Down Messages

Put-down messages are ones that evaluate, criticize, chip away at the other person's self-image, or convey a judgment. The hidden message is "You're no good," and creates a discount of the message and sender or is internalized as proof of inadequacy.

1. judging, criticizing, and blaming, as in "I told you so," or "You brought it on yourself";
2. name calling, stereotyping, and ridiculing, as in "You hard hats are all alike";
3. interpreting, analyzing, and diagnosing, as in "I can read you like a book"; and
4. probing, questioning, and interrogating, as in "Are you sorry that you did it?"

Indirect Messages

Indirect messages have gentle direction to avoid confrontation. The hidden message is "I don't trust you enough to confront you directly. It's too risky to be open and honest with you." This creates distrust and is often misunderstood.

1. kidding, sarcasm, teasing, and diverting comments, as in "You're a big man on staff, aren't you?"; and
2. silence.

All these roadblocks to effective communication are variations on a common theme—judging the other person. Perhaps the greatest barrier to interpersonal communication lies in our very natural tendency to judge—to approve or disapprove of the position or ideas of the other person. This may hit most of us hard because we do not like to think of ourselves as unfairly judgmental. Although the tendency to make premature evaluations is almost universal, it is greatly heightened in situations where deep convictions and emotions are involved. The stronger our feelings, the more likely it is that there will be no mutual element in communication—two ideas, two convictions, two sets of emotions, two judgments will simply fly past each other in psychological space like two ships in the night.

ORIENTATIONS THAT HELP

The following are attitudes and approaches which use words and nonverbal signals to communicate respect for the people with whom we work:
1. reciprocal trust (confidence, warmth, acceptance);
2. cooperative learning (inquiry, exploration, quest);
3. mutual growth (becoming, actualizing, fulfilling);
4. reciprocal openness (spontaneity, candor, honesty);
5. shared problem-solving (defining, producing alternatives, testing);
6. autonomy (freedom, interdependence, equality); and
7. experimentation (play, innovation, provisional try).

A GUIDE TO FEEDBACK

In all relationships—whether at home, work, or school—the feedback which is truly helpful will meet the following standards:

Descriptive rather than evaluative
By describing one's own reaction, it leaves the individual free to use it or not to use it as he/she sees fit. By avoiding evaluative language, it reduces the need for the individual to react defensively.

Specific rather than general
To be told that one is "dominating" will probably not be as helpful as to be told that "just now when we were deciding the issue, you didn't seem to be listening to what others said, and I felt forced to accept your arguments or face attack from you."

Usable rather than impractical
Feedback is directed toward behavior which the receiver can do something about. Frustration is only increased when a person is reminded of some shortcoming over

which he/she has no control (e.g., "I hate it when you start stuttering when we talk about really important company business").

Timely rather than premature or late

Effective feedback is well-timed. Generally, feedback is more useful when it is received at the earliest opportunity after the given behavior or statement is completed. Please take into consideration the person's willingness to hear it, the support available from others, and its propriety.

Clear rather than vague

Messages are checked to insure clear communication. One way of doing this is to have the receiver rephrase the message in immediate feedback that he/she has received to see if it corresponds with what you as the sender had in mind.

Accurate rather than incorrect

When feedback is given in a group for which such is the norm, such as a training group, both giver and receiver have opportunity to check with others in the group to accuracy of the feedback. Is this one person's impression or an impression shared by others?

Additional standards (norms) for giving feedback effectively:
1. speak to data (behavior observed, not motives imputed);
2. speak to one specific datum at a time;
3. check with the actors (everyone present);
4. give feedback at a useful level;
5. give feedback as near the action as possible; and
6. offer rather than impose feedback.

MAGIC RULES FOR RUINING ANY SERIOUS DISCUSSION AT WORK

Here are some rules for disastrous interpersonal communication at work. Yes, of course, we're being a little facetious, but follow two or three of these directions and you are guaranteed a miserable experience at work.
1. Be as personal as possible when explaining the problem. Try to get your coworker, whether subordinate or supervisor, to take total blame for the problem. Put the accusatory tone in your voice.
2. Bring the matter up when you and your coworker are angry. That way you can put all of your emotion into your speech. Don't mince words. Pull out some profanity if necessary to get your point across.
3. Keep a step ahead. Be thinking of what you are going to say next. Don't worry about whether you are listening to your coworker. Be prepared.

4. Don't back down from what you want. Impress your coworker with what you need and what he/she can do without in order for you to have it. Recall past favors so that your coworker can feel indebted to you. Demonstrate how firm and demanding you can be.

5. Bring up old issues and old agenda. Let your coworker know that you have a good memory, even of previous conflicts that had been resolved. Go ahead and let your colleague become defensive.

6. Correct anything your coworker says which is wrong. Let him/her know who the smarter person is. Use often "that's not what I said" or "you never could handle that job assignment." If he/she cites a mistake on your part, cite a bigger mistake that he/she has made.

7. End by saying something that will never be forgotten. If you are a supervisor, remind your subordinate that you have power to make or break the people you supervise. Leave the impression that you are a little put out.

Let's conclude on a more positive note: once we are fair, clear, and precise in language with others, there are three additional qualities, theorists, and researchers in the behavioral sciences claim, that enhance effective communication. One is *genuineness*—being open and honest about one's true feelings, needs, and ideas. The second is *empathy*—the ability to really see and hear another person and understand that person from his/her perspective. The third is *nonpossesive love*—involving accepting, respecting, and supporting another person in a nonpaternalistic and liberating way.

Effective communication is crucially important. It may also be your greatest challenge in the workplace!

QUESTIONS FOR GROUP DISCUSSION
AND PERSONAL REFLECTION

1. The chapter closed with an appeal to communicate with the character traits of genuineness, empathy, and nonpossessive love. Let's be realistic: Are these qualities of any value in today's competitive business world? (Recall that "loving" is not necessarily "liking.")

2. How can one develop empathy and caring for others?

3. Is there any value in kinesics, the study of nonverbal communication?

4. Is there any value to "politically correct" language in interpersonal communication?

5. What do you believe to be your greatest communication challenge?

Chapter 15

The Wrong Stuff
The Sensitive Issue of Sexual Harassment

I must refuse the compliment that I think like a man. Thought has no sex. One either thinks or one does not.

Clara Boothe Luce

There is a basic need for touch. Touch can make a person seem warm and powerful if it is appropriate. It reduces the sense of distance and isolation and creates more trust.

Stanley Jones

There is little doubt that women have been subject to sexual harrassment in the workplace over the years and that they are more empowered today to stop it. But some wonder about the effects of such empowerment on the relationships between men and women in general at work and whether the new awareness of sexual harassment in the workplace has encouraged women to file charges when no harassment has actually occurred.

Scott B. Rae
and Kenman L. Wong

There is a potential tension between the perceived prerogatives for free speech . . . in the workplace and what we might view as

the hostile environment provisions of the harassment law. It's my own view that it becomes a problem when good sense and good judgment fail to carry the day. What one might perceive as one's right to free expression could create an uncomfortable or even legally actionable hostile work environment. . . . Different people have different sensibilities about what is appropriate and what is offensive. . . . I think that smart employers and intelligently run workplaces prevail on their employees to use good common sense to respect the dignity of others.

Bruce Barry

People think if I had told Clarence Thomas to bug off, that would have ended it. But I said no in a variety of ways. It didn't work. I thought: "Maybe it's my perfume." "Maybe I shouldn't laugh at his jokes." . . . You blame yourself. . . . There are no blanket rules. Assess the situation. Sometimes, it works to say, "Please stop." Sometimes that escalates the behavior. . . . I've heard terrible stories from [female] medical residents who say they wear no makeup and travel in groups to keep doctors from harassing them.

Anita Hill

IN 1995 A SMALL, UNDERFUNDED ARMY OFFICE ON THE PENTAGON'S second floor scraped together $150,000 and employed some actors to make a training film on sexual harassment. Several scenarios depicted encounters of military brass intimidating female recruits. By eerie coincidence the video was shot on location at Aberdeen Proving Ground in Maryland. In November 1996 several female U.S. Army trainees stepped forward and reported to authorities and to network news that they had been seriously harassed and that some had been raped by military sergeants at Aberdeen. What seemed at first to be a local scandal involving two rogue sergeants soon turned into an forcewide manhunt for a rape ring that may have been responsible for sexually assaulting thousands of military women.

Once again, the nation faced the issue of sexual harassment. Fifteen years ago it was a topic that many men, and perhaps a lot of women, would laugh about (as in, "I wish someone would sexually harass me"). In the 1990s alone, we've heard about Judge Clarence Thomas and Anita Hill. We've also heard about Tailhook, which revealed a cavalier attitude by the U.S. Navy toward raunchy, lewd behavior by inebriated fighter pilots who assaulted women at a conference and then tried to cover it up. And well into his second term, President Clinton faced the prospect of the entire nation having heard of Paula Jones, knowing her allegations against him for behavior on May 9, 1991, at the Excelsior Hotel in Little Rock while governor of Arkansas; most Americans had also heard of Monica Lewinsky, although they could not be certain if the president had exploited the aura of his awesome power and prestige in order to gain sexual favors from her.

And while Americans learned of U.S. District Judge Susan Webber Wright's dismissal of the Jones suit on April 1, 1998, because it raised "no genuine issuses for trial," many wondered if an outrageous one-time sexual misconduct could be successfully prosecuted even if the plaintiff cannot prove "tangible job detriment" or that a defendant's unwelcome crudeness created "a hostile work environment." We've read the surveys of women in the workplace which show that about 40 percent have been subjected to sexual assault or harassment while at work, however hazily defined this area of law may be. For millions of working women, the reality of sexual harassment is not a laughing matter that can be easily shrugged off. The issue cannot be abandoned.

THE POWER OF TOUCH

For decades now, psychologists have been telling us about the power in human touch. Watch the busy activity of a toddler, and you'll see an obvious truth—children learn about their world through touch. When a child is alarmed, hurt, or frightened, the first thing he/she wants is to be held. As we grow into adulthood, touch does not lose any of its significance. One of the God-given blessings we enjoy as humans is the potential for giving physical affection, providing reassurance and affirmation, and communicating warmth as we truly seek to improve our interpersonal relations. Our associates, colleagues, and friends also have a need to be touched. There is a subconscious longing for affirmation through contact, but both women and men may suppress this longing because many of them feel that "it's not nice to touch" or that touching will imply or lead to "something sexual."

There is such a diversity of physical touching in the business and professional world. On the positive side, touching can facilitate a sense of trust and empathy; from our earliest childhood days we began to learn how much we can trust people by the way they touch us. Much of the public endearment with the late Princess Diana was based on the willingness of a person of royalty to touch "commoners"—young children, the sick, the elderly, people dying of AIDS. These were the people to whom the late Mother Teresa reached out and touched. And, of course, Jesus touched those who were willing to accept his healing hands.

During times of personal crisis, the experience of loving touch is even more powerful. Within the helping professions, the loyalty of clients to a particular counselor, physician, minister, dentist, or attorney, might be explained not solely in terms of expertise but by the professional's caring and empathy—two qualities enhanced by appropriate touch. While in days past the handshake was the common staple of friendship and greeting, the longer people work together their social environment at work becomes more intimate.

On the other hand, there is much inappropriate use of touch and language. As one female management trainer observed, "There were situations with men of higher authority who would touch me on the arm and it was an 'I can affect your career' message, so I felt uncomfortable. My reaction to it was not to linger but to pull away gracefully." Among the taboo touches in the workplace are touches with sexual connotations such as innuendo, flirtation, and propositions. Less obvious negative touching is connected with a power play, inappropriate affection, disruption of another's work, persuasion, and aggression. The taboo touches range from pokes and lingering hugs to caresses and pats on the any part of the body.

In our post–Clarence Thomas era, a greater concern about sex harassment issues has arisen. Is there any other charge that strikes such fear and anxiety into the hearts of individuals in a workplace setting than the charge of sexual harassment? This may be the only charge in which a male employee may be considered guilty until proven innocent. There are legitimate concerns about due process, or the rights of the accused. Even if exonerated, an accused worker may feel that his/her reputation has been ruined, at least within the firm wherein the allegation was made. Some workplaces are rapidly becoming touch-a-phobic. Many management consultants instruct public officials never to touch employees or clients and professors never to touch students. A favorite phrase of some consultants to business and professional people is: "When in doubt, don't touch. Don't assume."

SEXUAL HARASSMENT AS A LEGAL ISSUE

The legal consideration of sexual harassment has been laid at the doorstep of the generation-old Civil Rights Act (1964). Title VII of that act imposes liability on employers for the discriminatory acts of their employees. The federal appeals court system at all levels has ruled that sexual harassment is an objectionable act that violates the Civil Rights Act because it is based on the sex of the individual. It discriminates against women; it is behavior that rests on male attitudes and assumptions that work against women. To the point: sexual harassment is illegal.

Sexual harassment is also expensive. There is no way to know how much the effects of sexual harassment translate into dollars lost by companies in which it occurs. The costs are incurred when employees quit their jobs, new employees are trained, people stay at jobs but perform with low morale and less efficiency, take leaves of absence— not to mention the cost of litigation.

Can men be victims of sexual harassment? The answer is obviously yes. The movie *Disclosure*, based on Michael Crichton's best-selling book and featuring Michael Douglas and Demi Moore, presented a compelling scenario in which a male was harassed and then falsely accused by a female superior in a multinational firm. By far, however, women are the ones who are victimized the most; therefore, most discussions of sexual harassment are couched in the language of female victimization.

In a major 1998 ruling that significantly expanded protection from sexual harassment, the U.S. Supreme Court interpreted federal law to prohibit workers and supervisors from sexually harassing people of the same sex. The much-awaited ruling gave a whole group of people the right to turn to federal courts if they believe they were harassed because of their gender. The ruling was a victory for refinery worker Joe Oscale, who sued his employer and three colleagues after they allegedly sexually harassed and assaulted him on an oil rig off the Louisiana shore. Justice Antonin Scalia, in writing the court's unanimous decision, said a person's gender or sexual orientation did not matter—the critical issue under civil rights law is whether a person is singled out and discriminated against because of his/her gender. Sexual harassment, then, is not about men and women—it's about power and the abuse of power.

We are familiar with the stereotype of construction or street workers who make wolf whistles and lewd comments to the women who walk past them. Truth is, however, that all types of males in all sorts of occupations and professions have been harassers. U.S. Senators have harassed. Governors have harassed. University professors have harassed. Counselors and therapists have harassed. The phenomenon knows no occupational or professional boundaries. There is a certain arrogance and insensitivity in the perpetrator and a certain vulnerability and humility in the victim.

DEFINING SEXUAL HARASSMENT: THREE CATEGORIES

What is sexual harassment? The Equal Employment Opportunity Commission says that it is "unwelcome sexual advances, requests for sexual favors, and other verbal or physical conduct of a sexual nature." One female author defines it as "sexual attention imposed on someone who is not in a position to refuse it." By definition, sexual harassment is unwanted; if a woman "asked for it," it would not be called harassment. Sexual harassment is discriminatory because it forces a woman to work under an adverse employment condition. In the broadest sense it is a health issue, because harassment can impact negatively the victim's physical and psychological well-being. For women who lose their jobs and/or suffer from headaches, depression, ulcers, insomnia, and other disorders, a health issue is definitely at stake.

Writers have employed different terms to describe several different levels of harassing behavior. For example, at the most "innocent" level is "aesthetic appreciation"—admiring comments about the physical or sexual features of the victim or other women (e.g., "Wow, why can't other women look as good as you do today?"). "Active mental groping" is a term from women who talked about men "undressing them with their eyes."

It is easier to place all objectionable behavior into three categories:

1. **Sexual threats.** "You'd better go out with me tonight if you want to keep your job." This offense is sometimes called "quid pro quo" because sexual favors are demanded in exchange for job security or promotion. The immorality of such a threat is obvious—it is offensive and violates the basic rights of the person employed.

2. **Sexual offers.** "If you can stay over in my apartment this weekend I believe I can think of some ways you can advance to management in this company." Sexual offers may harbor an implied threat to the person who refuses. The working relationship is now tainted by an interaction that has nothing to do with legitimate job performance.

3. **Degrading sexual behavior.** This is the broadest and most pervasive category: dirty jokes, racist jokes, sexual innuendos, leering or ogling at a woman; sexist remarks about women's bodies, clothing, or sexual activities; unnecessary touching, patting, brushing against or other undesired physical conduct. Such behavior is both humiliating and degrading to the victim. It is disruptive and disturbing. Harassment produces a hostile working environment for the victim(s), and courts have upheld the doctrine that a person who works in such an environment does not have to prove that she or he has been harmed in any way, either physically or emotionally, in order to establish sexual harassment.

Most sexual harassment occurs when someone with more corporate power victimizes a person with less power. However, not all harassment is done by a supervisor. A business firm may allow a work environment to be so lax that harassment of all kinds, especially of the third category, goes unchecked. The atmosphere may vary from unit to unit within a firm.

The special pain for the victim is that she seems to be trapped in a catch-22 dilemma. No matter how she deals with her harasser, she risks losing her job, her reputation, and her self-esteem. It seems like a no-win situation for the victim. Some are not aware of steps that can be taken.

DEALING WITH HARASSMENT

How can a victim deal with sexual harassment?

1. **Confront** the harasser and clearly inform him that his attention and behavior are unwelcome. This may be more difficult to do than it sounds because most of us want to please others and we do not want to be thought of as a "prude" or some "squeamish Neanderthal." Do not let the harasser trivialize the issue. Put him on notice that you will move to the next level of action if he continues.
2. **Keep a written record** explicitly describing the incidents of harassment, with date, time, place, witnesses, and your response.
3. **Look for witnesses,** other victims, and further evidence.
4. **Use in-company grievance procedures.** Complain to the appropriate supervisor. Stick to the facts. State the allegations as objectively as possible.
5. **Call a legal-service agency,** state discrimination agency, or the Equal Opportunity Employment Commission if you need to take legal action. You should choose your legal help carefully. A lawyer experienced in handling sexual-harassment cases would have explored strategies to redress typical workplace situations.

Most likely, the problem of sexual harassment in American business life will never completely go away. If enough victims take action, however, the enormity of the problem will be substantially reduced.

The sad truth is that, among the women who have taken action, many have expressed regrets that they had waited so long in tolerating this abuse before acting to stop it. For women to ignore the problem of sexual harassment usually means that the problem only gets worse.

QUESTIONS FOR GROUP DISCUSSION
AND PERSONAL REFLECTION

1. Is there any narrative about sexual harassment in the Bible? How about the story of Potiphar's wife who attempted to seduce Joseph, at that time a young Hebrew lad? What are elements in this narrative which might render the incident a case of sexual harassment by modern definition?
2. Is it fair that we usually think of women as victims of sexual harassment? How many men are sexually harassed? What are some ways that you know of in which men were harassed?
3. Is there anything wrong with expressing appreciation and encouragement for how a coworker is dressed or groomed?
4. Human beings are sexual creatures. We cannot leave our sexual concerns and interests in the parking lot. People enjoy talking to members of the opposite sex who are engaging and attractive. Both males and females can appreciate, with the appropriate time and the right company, sexual references, sex-tinted humor, and physical affection with the

opposite sex. Is it necessary that a serious professional work environment be entirely free from sexuality? Is "too much ado" being made over the issue of sexual harassment?

5. Are business firms responsible for maintaining a work environment in which all employees are free from harassment? If so, how can that be done?

6. When does behavior become offensive or objectionable enough to constitute harassment? After all, what one woman views as innocent fun or a friendly compliment may be seen as objectionable and degrading by another woman. A joke that one woman appreciates and laughs at may be offensive and produce a blush from another woman. (Of course the same is true for different men.) Who can decide what is right? In the case of sexual harassment, who determines what is offensive and objectionable?

7. What do you see as the difference between sexual harassment and sex discrimination in the workplace?

8. Do you think that some women have used the charge of sexual harassment in a power play to injure their bosses when they know that harassment was not the issue? Could a seriously disturbed female employee misinterpret her boss's gestures of respect and kindness and twist them into accusations of sexual harassment?

9. Sexual harassment is not easily defined. Consider each of the following scenarios. Which ones definitely constitute sexual harassment? You might indicate by these categories: "definitely not," "possibly harassing," and "definitely harassment." Consider how your categories reveal your personal criteria about defining harassment.

   a. A coworker of the opposite sex frequently invites you to have lunch away from the worksite.

   b. A coworker continually asks you for a date and you refuse to accept the invitation.

   c. A coworker of the opposite sex tells you that you should read the interview in the last issue of *Playboy.*

   d. A male coworker surprises a female coworker by showing her the foldout of the last playmate and declares: "Now I wish my wife were built like her."

   e. A male places his hands on the back or shoulder of a female coworker frequently during conversation about work-related matters.

   f. A male slips off to a quiet spot in the break room and reads through a hard-core pornographic magazine.

   g. A male has four pictures of women in swimsuits from the Sports Illustrated swimsuit issue on the partition wall of his cubicle.

   h. A supervisor tells a female subordinate a terribly racist joke that is offensive to her.

   i. A supervisor believes that a female in his department is "coming on" to him. He tells her he will be at a conference at the Hyatt Regency for two days. He asks her to meet him at his hotel room for a drink at the end of her work day at the office.

   j. A male tells sexually explicit jokes in the presence of a mixed company of coworkers.

   k. With eyes detached from meeting participants, a worker glances up and down another coworker during a department meeting.

   l. A worker makes slightly suggestive comments about the physical appearance of a coworker.

    m. A male worker enjoys the view of a female worker at the copy machine.

    n. A male professor seems to seek out college coeds who are distressed over any one of a wide range of events, from death of a relative to failure of an exam. This professor also consistently puts his hands and arms on and around the distressed coeds.

10. If you were the CEO of a company, what would you consider to be proper due process for the worker in your organization who is accused by another worker of sexual harassment? What steps would you take? Do you agree that the those accused of sexual harassment should be considered innocent until proven guilty?

11. In January 1998 the story of Monica Lewinsky's telephone conversations with another federal employee became the talk of the news and entertainment media. Allegations of oral sex were widely aired. Some newscasters and talk show hosts even warned their viewers that they were dealing with a sensitive subject that was not suitable for children. Any really big news story will be discussed in the workplace.

    Question: Should people be talking in the workplace about the president's sexual preferences? And, if so, how? Should jokes heard from Jay Leno or Dave Letterman on the subject be passed on to coworkers? Workers have varying sensitivities. Does not the issue of private sex lives of public figures have the potential to cause problems in the workplace, especially if some workers prefer not to be part of sex-related discussions? Is it not better to err on the side of caution and respect for people's rights? Could not the consequences of ignoring that sensitivity be painful? (See the quote at beginning of this chapter by Bruce Barry, a professor at the Owen Graduate School of Management at Vanderbilt.)

12. As part of the Clinton-Lewinsky story, it was rumored that the president gave the intern a dress as a gift. While the rumor had been largely dispelled, it did raise an issue in business ethics and protocol: Are there specific things that the head of a department should never give a subordinate or even peers in the workplace should not give? Obviously, some gifts are safe: a desk clock, bookends, a dictionary-thesaurus set, a subscription to a news or business magazine, a compact disc, a photo frame (without your picture in it), tickets to a cultural event, and so forth. And just as obviously, some gifts are not safe— lingerie from Frederick's of Hollywood, to cite one example. In an era in which there is concern about sexual harassment, what are some gifts (whether too expensive, too intimate, too personal) that should be taboo because they send the "wrong" message?

Case Study

Thelma Searcy is one interesting woman. She is a trainer in a staff development unit of a federal department. She is imposing and almost intimidating in appearance, standing 6'2" or 6'3" and weighing nearly 300 pounds. Yet Thelma has a heart of gold, is highly intelligent, and is an effective trainer. It's comical to watch her drive her little Toyota Tercel.

Thelma is a delightful person to talk to, except on one topic. For, you see, this woman is a "connoisseur" of pornography, if there is such a thing. During slack hours around the office she begins to discuss some adult movie she has seen the night before. She's probably viewed hundreds of them, and she has even brought some to the office to loan out to Bonnie. Your coworkers think this is humorous, and at times they will bring up the subject just to get her talking. Her description of the various porno stars, whom she knows by name, and especially of their body parts is always humorous.

Thelma enjoys but does not seem obsessed by pornography. Otherwise, she seems like a morally responsible person; she seems happily married and has a young daughter and son. However, you get uncomfortable with some of the reports and descriptions from Thelma that others find so interesting and entertaining. Once, a group of workers was in your office. The topic of adult movies came up, and Thelma pulled out a catalog of adult films, sex toys, and other paraphernalia, and everyone seemed to enjoy turning through the catalog with gawks and laughs at color pictures of the products and the names of performers and videos. You didn't say anything at the time, but you are gradually more and more offended.

What do you do about Thelma's outside interests? (Incidentally, Thelma's supervisor, another woman, is a good friend of Thelma and is definitely not offended. In fact, she chuckles at this conversation.)

Case Study

Stanley Preachitt is the pulpit minister for the Olive Pit Community Church. He is liked and respected. Little wonder, he puts in many hours of study in his office.

One of Stanley's staff, knowing there was an opening for a cleaning and custodial worker, recommends a good friend of hers named Oma Balderdash. Oma is hired to clean the building.

Stanley is a friendly, outgoing man. He enjoys joking and conversing with all who come in the office and especially with his church staff. He and Oma strike up warm conversations from day one. Oma lives in the rural area of the county, lacks major education, and presents a different face and body image than what Stanley, a married man and father of three, might find alluring. However, Oma is "taken" by Stanley. She seems to have developed a "crush" on him and makes no effort to hide it.

Stanley likes Oma personally and would not want to hurt her feelings for anything, and he knows Oma and his other female staff member are good friends. He enjoys some conversation with Oma, but finds it more and more intolerable for Oma to visit his office under the pretense of cleaning his office. Next, Oma starts standing near and walking behind Stanley when he is in his chair studying. She places her hands and fingers on him and asks, "Do you need your back massaged today?" or "Do you need a stiff neck loosened up a little?" At times, Oma has pulled Stanley a few inches lower so that she can give him a little peck on the cheek. Stanley knows Oma has seen him being affectionate with other women in his church and feels as though he would hurt Oma's feelings if he asked her to cease these outward longings for affection and attention.

Of late, Stanley has begun to anticipate the time Oma would be coming to clean his office, at which time he leaves the office and drives to the local hospital to visit the patients. He knows, however, that a resourceful Oma will find other ways to be around him. Oma's feelings are important to him, but so is his peace of mind. What should Brother Preachitt do?

Chapter 16

Dealing with Difficult People
Sherman Tanks, Bulldozers, and Others

If your life is free from hostile customers and coworkers, indecisive, vacillating bosses, over-agreeable (but do nothing) subordinates or any of those others who deserve to be called Difficult People . . . consider yourself extraordinarily lucky and move on to pleasanter fare.

Robert M. Bramson

Crisis in dialogue occurs when the participants . . . fail really to address each other but turn away defensively, each within himself, for the purpose of self-justification.

Reuel Howe

Man is distinctly more aggressive, cruel, and relentless than any of the other apes.

Benjamin Spock

FORMER PRESIDENT JIMMY CARTER ONCE DESCRIBED HIS OLD mentor, Admiral Hyman Rickover, respectfully, as having absolutely no tact.

> As a matter of fact all the time I worked for him he never said a decent word to me. . . . If he found no fault, he simply looked, turned around and walked away. However, if I made the slightest mistake, in one of the loudest and most obnoxious voices I ever heard, he would turn around and tell the other people in the area what a horrible disgrace I was to the Navy, and that I ought to go back to the oldest and slowest and smallest submarine from which I had come.

Have you ever worked with someone like that? The work world is filled with obnoxious and abrasive people, some of whom are in supervisory positions. And incidentally, not only is working around unhappy people dangerous to your mental health—it may be a threat to your physical security! Latrell Sprewell's physical assault on his NBA Golden State Warriors coach, P. J. Carlesimo, was a celebrated case in 1997 which, though rare, proved that even highly paid employees can attack their supervisors.

Is your company too small to worry? Probably not, say experts who believe no American business is immune to the problem. We've heard stories of killings in post offices, but actually about one thousand people are killed each year on the job. And workplace violence is expensive, costing American companies about $5 billion in medical bills, counseling and legal settlements. As an aside, an estimated twelve thousand people commit suicide at work every year. Studies show that most of the people who seek to kill or injure their bosses or colleagues are males in their mid-30s who own weapons and consider their jobs the most important things in their lives. Violent people often think, "the boss is a jerk."

Let's turn away from the more grim and morbid dimensions and focus on those obnoxious and abrasive people at work, some of whom admittedly may be intelligent innovators and creative producers. These troublesome folks present special problems for bosses, colleagues, and subordinates alike. Management may go to great lengths to tolerate their quirks and idiosyncratic ways. Still, everyone's patience and good will are taxed heavily and organizational morale may be lowered by the difficult people.

Serious conflict can surface when people attempt to cope with a problematic supervisor or coworker. Left unchecked, a small problem involving one or two people can turn into a major problem which involves an entire organization. Just as a private family that has an adult addict may become dysfunctional with all other family members playing codependent roles, an organization can become "sick" or dysfunctional with all the staff "playing games" of manipulation simply to cope with an unhealthy situation. "Corporations have big meetings around dynamic and dangerous situations," once declared James Shannon, former executive director of General Mills Foundation, "but never even recognize small cancers inside the company—meanness, gossip, distrust, hatred—which are destroying the organization."

Robert M. Bramson's *Coping With Difficult People* notes that behavior patterns that seem to be the most disruptive or frustrating are characterized by the following types:

1. **Hostile-aggressives.** These people try to bully and overwhelm others by bombardment, cutting remarks, or tantrums.
2. **Complainers.** Individuals who gripe incessantly, but never make a move to do anything positive about situations they complain about.
3. **Silent and unresponsives.** People who respond to every important plea for help or communication with monosyllabic answers ("Yep" or "no" or a grunt) or simply a puzzled look on their face.
4. **Super-agreeables.** Very agreeable, personable, polite, reasonable, supportive in your presence, but nonsupportive and even contrary acting when they are away from you.
5. **Negativists.** Always giving knee-jerk negative reactions.
6. **Know-it-all experts.** Condescending, pompous individuals who want you to know they know everything that is worth knowing.
7. **Indecisives.** Those who stall major decisions until the decision is made for them by someone else.

Interestingly, Bramson uses a series of original descriptive terms to identify the difficult people in our lives: Sherman tanks, snipers, exploders, triangular complainers, clams, wet blankets, bulldozers, and balloons.

Behavior of difficult people at work may include:
1. moodiness and irritability;
2. low-impulse control;
3. bursts of anger;
4. unwillingness to listen to another person when there needs to be genuine dialogue;
5. making insinuations or taking little verbal jabs;
6. being highly and unfairly judgmental of work colleagues;
7. criticizing brutally with little or no diplomacy;
8. questioning, unfairly analyzing, or ridiculing his/her colleagues' projects or ideas;
9. displaying impatience with others' problems or concerns;
10. communicating condescendingly with others;
11. insensitivity to the feelings of others, while insisting on "openness" and "candor" and "telling the truth";
12. refusing to delegate to others, because no one can measure up to his/her lofty standards;
13. acting arrogantly, pretending to be a privileged person, acting with the mandate to be different and abrasive;
14. intolerance of the mistakes and idiosyncrasies of others, of whom he/she expects a special license to display personal mistakes and idiosyncrasies;
15. displaying cockiness and self-assurance at obnoxious levels;
16. self-centeredness, the world is expected to revolve around him/her; and
17. displaying favoritism to those who further his/her agenda or cater to his/her immense ego needs.

Well, you know the person. You've worked with this emotionally-draining person before. That person may not have all of the above characteristics, but a combination of several of them can be demoralizing. And, in the most extreme of problem supervisors and coworkers there is even more reprehensible and highly unethical behavior: outright lies, power plays for selfish gain, sabotage of others' work or position, "game playing" or manipulation, and theft or destruction of another person's work or property.

Does it help to consider the old psychological axiom that the more extreme behavior is in one direction, the more likely it is that one is avoiding the reality of just the opposite feelings? The abrasively difficult colleague at work who is self-centered, arrogant, contemptuous, and perfectionist may well be a woman or man strives intensely for perfection, omnipotence, and total control of all situations. That person may have a negative self-concept and a low self-esteem.

To correct all of this, the colleague or supervisor turns to overcontrol, overorganization, oversupervision, and distrust of others. If the person pushes toward perfectionist and unrealistic goals that one is never able to achieve, he/she must be constantly angry and guilty with oneself for failure. That anger and guilt get displaced on others. The greater the gap between the ego ideal and the self-concept, the greater the intensity of frustration, anger, and guilt with oneself. The greater the anger and frustration, the more likely an attack on coworkers to narrow the gap between the ideal and perceived reality.

It's true that such a toxic and abrasive person who exhibits Type-A behavior is especially susceptible to coronaries and strokes. And yes, you will have difficulty mustering sympathy for such a person who is "done in" by one's own excessive self-ishness, drive, hostility, and impatience.

Meantime, how does one deal (or not deal) with such a difficult person?

Fairness

Be even more than fair at the outset and assume that each person is always doing the best of which he/she is capable. Though you are not a psychologist, try to recognize the origins of dysfunctional behavior—negative self-concept, low self-esteem, hunger for affection, eagerness for achievement—and don't become angry with someone else's provocative behavior.

Descriptive Words

Remember that relationships grow best in a climate that is *descriptive* rather than *evaluative*. Describing is the process of putting sensory data into words. Describing is easy to define, but can be hard to do; when you think you are describing, you may be evaluating or judging.

What's wrong with evaluating? For one thing, an evaluation does not inform. More important, an evaluation places a judgment on what has been said or done. Judgment creates a negative climate in which it is easy for people to become defensive.

When coping with the difficult person, it is better simply to describe your feelings in reaction to something damaging that he/she has done. Ask the person to put oneself in your place and imagine how the hurtful words or behavior might feel.

Consideration

Tell the difficult coworker or supervisor that you want her or him to succeed, but that in order for you to help that he/she must take the goals and feelings of other workers into account and only on that basis will you go the proverbial second mile to be helpful.

Control

When negative, provocative behavior of this difficult person "pushes your hot button," avoid impulsive attack. Just walk away if you must in order to keep yourself under control. At the appropriate time, let the difficult person know how he/she made you feel and how others must feel, given the hostile, deprecating, and heavy control tactics or antics to which you were subjected. Let that person know you are "royally ticked," if you need to, and note how frequently such behavior occurs.

Countering

If the hostile coworker challenges, defends, argues, or tries to debate your observations, or accuses you of personal antagonism and hostility toward him/her personally, do not counterattack. Just simply re-state your observations. Counter such statements as "It's obvious you've always hated me ever since I came to this unit," not with a strident retort such as "You're mighty right, you worthless piece of humanity," but with a softly spoken "I'm sorry I haven't been able to communicate effectively what my concerns are."

Dialogue

If your relationship with the difficult person is strong enough, you might attempt a "heart-to-heart," confidential and nonthreatening dialogue with him/her. Gently ask, "Why do you seem to defend or attack in situations that are not confrontive?" or "Why do you think your staff believes you are undermining their most-important projects?" or "Why do you seem to turn every bit of constructive criticism into a win-lose argument?" Note that the word "seem" can serve you well—it comes across less judgmental and makes no accusation.

Most important, allow the person to discuss any personal problems or stresses that he/she may be under which influence his/her behavior at work. If there are severe problems and stresses in the person's private life, guide this troubled employee to professional assistance. Admittedly, this kind of dialogue is more difficult for one to pursue with a supervisor.

Patience

Be patient. People's personality traits are well-ingrained. If this difficult colleague makes progress, it will be slow. If you are the supervisor of a troubled person, consider if he/she needs to be placed in another unit or on another project. Set goals for that supervisee. Some of the processes mentioned above may have to be repeated.

Direct Confrontation

Often the difficult supervisor or colleague will not hear you. Perhaps he/she is too stubborn. Too stupid. Too set on thinking of defensive arguments. Too preoccupied with his/her own little world. Then you must have a direct confrontation, in the presence of witnesses, in which you candidly state what behavior traits have been hurtful; and, in the case of someone you supervise, state and place in writing the consequences of noncompliance of requests for specific behavioral changes.

Leave no doubt about your meaning. Clearly state: "This behavior is unsatisfactory (or "inappropriate," "not acceptable," "intolerable," or whatever). Do not assume that the abrasive person knows. State it orally and in writing. Do not be reluctant to place negative behavior traits in a person's performance appraisal and clearly state that they will not be tolerated.

Advice

Be aware that mere advice to the difficult coworker to "take some time off," "take a long, deserved vacation," or "start playing golf or tennis" may be as useless as a rain shower at sea. Many enjoy the "pressure" they have placed themselves under and may make no major personality changes no matter how many holes of golf they play or how many bass they catch.

Intolerance

If the difficult person that you find it almost intolerable to be around is your boss, then face it: you may have to resign to maintain your sanity. Your mental and emotional health are not worth sacrificing simply to stay on the job of your first choice. Quite often the abrasive personality will assiduously resist all efforts at self-improvement and, even after you follow the above suggestions, will cast about for explanations outside the self for his/her problems.

If you supervise such a person you will have more leverage. You can add stipulations in your performance evaluation for his/her continuance. You can insist on professional counsel. If the person has a formidable commitment to high professional standards, perhaps the process of helping this person is worth the time and patience. Otherwise, just sing "I haven't got time for the pain."

A final point: Could it be that the difficult person with whom you must work or take assignments—whether a bulldozer, Sherman tank, cold fish, classless jerk, or whatever—is being used by God to teach you some lessons? Perhaps the difficult person in your workplace is "heavenly sandpaper" to polish and refine your core character traits! Simply ask, "What is God trying to teach me through that so-and-so pain in the neck (or lower) I have to work with?"

We could try a bit of simple wisdom from one of America's best known preachers, Robert Schuller:

DO IT ANYWAY

People are unreasonable, illogical and self-centered.
Love them anyway.
If you do good, people will accuse you of selfish ulterior motives.
Do good anyway.
If you are successful, you will win false friends and true enemies.
Succeed anyway.
Honesty and frankness make you vulnerable.
Be honest and frank anyway.
The good you do today will be forgotten tomorrow.
Do good anyway.
The biggest people with the biggest ideas can be shot down by the smallest minds.

Think big anyway.

People favor underdogs but always follow top dogs.

Fight for some underdogs anyway.

What you spend years building may be destroyed overnight.

Build anyway.

Give the world the best you've got and you'll get kicked in the teeth.

Give the world the best you've got anyway.

QUESTIONS FOR GROUP DISCUSSION AND PERSONAL REFLECTION

1. Do you work with someone who has an offensive, abrasive personality?

2. Describe the worst boss you've ever had. Describe the worst coworker you've known.

3. Do you feel a moral responsibility to help a troubled employee or coworker to learn how to deal with his/her personality problems?

4. How much personality change do you think is possible for an adult to make?

5. What techniques have you attempted in dealing with difficult people at work?

6. Is it possible to understand the troubled and difficult employee from inside that person's skin? Can we truly put ourselves in the mind and emotion of another person?

7. Does your business organization have any kind of employee-assistance program that can provide counseling and support for a troubled employee and/or that employee's family?

8. Could an addiction to drugs or some other unhealthy addiction explain the abrasive behavior of some coworkers?

9. Does a Christian simply set aside the kindness and gentleness of the Christlike spirit when dealing with an overly aggressive, belligerent employee? How long does one tolerate such people?

10. How would you deal with a coworker who has lost control and is pitching an "adult tantrum"? How would you deal with a coworker who presents a strong physical threat to your safety?

11. How can you tell the difference between a chronic complainer and someone who often has legitimate complaints? What is the trade-off gained by a chronic complainer?

Case Study

In your office there are three or four people who do not seem to have enough to do. Their work assignments are valuable to the company and their work is good, but there is something that really "bugs" you about them to the point that your own morale about them and your mutual supervisor is greatly impacted.

These three or four people use a lot of work time to play computer games or send pointless electronic-mail messages to each other. They are good friends with each other and seem to be addicted to these computer games at the workplace. You don't enjoy the games and would only play them at home if you did. Do you suck it up and try to forget it or do you go to whatever level of management is willing to listen to your complaint? (The immediate supervisor seems not to care as long as work assignments are done.)

Case Study

At a recent staff meeting in which there were guests from the national office of Ed Boyd's firm, Jim's boss scathingly criticizes a coworker who had made some serious mistakes. The coworker, Susan, is humiliated. Her body language cannot hide her shame and embarrassment.

Ed feels that his boss was correct in his evaluation about Susan's work but was improper and unkind to criticize her so cruelly in front of the entire staff and outside guests. Ed is not particularly close to Susan as a friend, but he does like and respect her and feels regret for the incident. Does he have any moral responsibility toward Susan after this meeting?

Case Study

Among the people you supervise, Janet Smellingburg presents a challenge that concerns you, but you wonder whether it is worth the hassle of angering her. Janet asks permission to take equipment home in order to have a quieter atmosphere for office work. Weeks pass and Janet has not returned the equipment. The computer equipment she borrowed may not ever be returned if you do not request it and you suspect the entire family is using it for personal tasks.

If someone else at work needs the equipment, it will be easy to request its return. In fact, if it were returned it would likely sit in the office unused. Yet, you get "royally ticked" when you think Janet manipulates you to grant favors. Otherwise, you like Janet and appreciate her excellent job performance. What should you do?

Case Study

Samuel Liveright, a Christian businessman, owns and manages a condominium complex in Destin, Florida. Much of his time during the summer he spends in Nashville where he faithfully attends the Praymore Church of Christ.

The Praymore Church preacher, Brother I. B. Trooth, has dropped several hints about the pleasures he could enjoy on the beach or deep sea fishing. One day he told Samuel about some wealthy church members who were honored to loan out their beach house to preachers for a free vacation. Obviously, Brother Trooth is suggesting that Samuel grant free use of a condo on the beach for the Trooth family vacation.

Samuel knows nothing of how much Brother Trooth is paid, what his family needs are, or how deserving he might be. He just knows that Brother Trooth, whom he tends to like otherwise, wants a vacation that will cost him $750 in unrecoverable rent. What should Samuel do?

Chapter 17

Conflict Resolution
At Work and Elsewhere

The point here, is that, while my emotions are throbbing with these fears, angers, and self-defensive urges, I am in no condition to have an open-minded, honest and loving discussion with you or with anyone else. I will need . . . emotional clearance and ventilation . . . before I will be ready for this discussion.

John Powell

In the creative dispute, the persons involved are aware of the other's full legitimacy. Neither loses sight of the fact that they are seeking . . . to express the truth as they see it. In no way is either person reduced by this. Such a confrontation, within a healthy atmosphere of love

and genuine relatedness, enables each individual to maintain a unique sense of self, to grow authentically through real communication with other persons, and to realize the worth of simplicity and directness in relationships.

Clark Moustakas

Handling conflict . . . [creatively and respectfully] tends to deepen and enrich companionships. Relationships tend to falter because the individuals in them don't know how to handle the differences between them. To ignore the differences is to resign yourselves to a superficial relationship.

George Bolton

TO EXPERIENCE CONFLICT IS TO BE HUMAN. CONFLICT HAS ALWAYS been and always will be a major characteristic of work situations. Conflict is inevitable where you work or hope to work. Because so much of our lives and energies are invested in our work (not to mention our ego investment), it is only natural that there will be a great deal of conflict in job situations. And the more that people must interact and cooperate to achieve company goals, the greater the potential for conflict.

Good work relationships are like a marriage. The marriage can run smoothly or it can move on its rough course to a divorce. When intelligent and competent people come into a workplace, they bring a great deal of energy. That energy can be channeled creatively toward the achievement of worthwhile objectives; on the other hand, that same energy can be dissipated and squandered internally by interpersonal and team conflicts.

Conflict may be defined as the clash of opposing attitudes, ideas, behaviors, goals, and needs. Knowing that conflict is natural does not keep conflict situations from making you anxious, uneasy, and at times extremely uncomfortable. And, as you know, there are times in which conflict can create for you intense emotional pain and agony. As much as you wish that conflict did not exist, you seldom get through even one day without experiencing conflict in one form or another. Such differences in values, desires, needs, and work habits are the stuff of daily living. Perhaps the biggest reality in causing our everyday squabbles and social friction is the fact that we are humans and not gods. As humans, it is impossible to rise completely above selfishness, betrayal, misrepresentations, anger, jealousy, and other factors that strain and even break relationships.

Conflict is at best disruptive. At worst it is destructive. Once it erupts it is difficult to control. Destructive controversy has a tendency to expand. That's the bad news. The good news is that conflict is not necessarily bad or evil. That may come as a surprise to you, and yet it is true. Conflict may be viewed as a "dangerous opportunity." We first must agree that conflict is a natural by-product of those very qualities which give us personality, an acknowledgment that each person has unique ideas, feelings, motives, and ways of working and behaving. Then we must determine whether the conflict being experienced is dysfunctional (produces a negative effect) or is functional (produces a healthy, positive effect). The key to this determination is the effect of conflict on the relationship or the work team.

FUNCTIONAL AND DYSFUNCTIONAL CONFLICT

Conflict is **dysfunctional** when it
1. keeps you from doing your work;
2. threatens the integrity of your relationships;
3. is personally destructive of your physical and emotional well-being;
4. leads to extreme demonstrations or self-interest at the expense of the organization; or
5. diverts time and energy from reaching important goals.

Conflict is **functional** when it
1. increases involvement;
2. promotes the development of methods for coping with internal problems (provides the impetus for growth);
3. helps define the relationship and allows you to maintain your individual identities;
4. provides an outlet for aggression;
5. increases productivity (resulting primarily from increased interaction);

6. is between groups and therefore increases intragroup (within group) cohesion, and as an aftermath of conflict, unity may be reestablished;

7. promotes self-understanding by compelling you to make decisions and test the relative merits of your attitudes, behaviors, needs, and goals in conflict; or

8. sharpens your communication skills, since much conflict results from poor communication.

We will not discuss avoiding conflict or suppressing conflict. We can only focus briefly on managing conflict within interpersonal relations.

ALL CONFLICTS ARE NOT CREATED EQUAL:
TYPES OF CONFLICT

What is it you are facing when you face conflict? All conflicts are not created equal. Some are easier to manage than others. Here we will divide conflict into five groups. (Remember that we are talking about interpersonal conflict and not major labor-management conflict such as might be experienced at the bargaining table.)

Pseudoconflict

Pseudoconflict, or *non-realistic conflict,* is false conflict that appears to be real. Such conflict stems from ignorance, error, tradition, prejudice, poor organizational structure, or displaced hostility. It exists when people believe that two goals cannot be simultaneously achieved; although, in fact they can be. The tendency in a false conflict situation is to put the choice between actions into an either-or framework (e.g., "either this company raises production costs or it must reduce product quality"). Often you are setting up a false set of choices; it may be possible to do both or neither.

Content Conflict

Content conflict relates to message accuracy. You know already that a breakdown in communications and misunderstandings are a big source of hard feelings and difficult times between people. The conflict may be over a fact; conflicts over facts are fairly easy to resolve. The conflict may be over the interpretation of a fact or an inference drawn from a fact or series of facts. You may come to disagree with another person over whether the increase in steel prices will trigger another round of inflation. This rise in steel prices may be documented as a fact; the result of this increase is a matter of opinion based on interpretation of the fact or an inference drawn from the fact. Content conflict may also be over a definition or over a choice among goals, actions, or means of achieving organizational goals.

Role Conflict

Role conflict results when parties have been cast by tradition and/or circumstances into a role of behavior and expectation. Roles determine what people ought to do as a function of their position. If this role is controversial in nature, conflict is likely to become a habit. Conflict arises, not from personal difficulties, but from the adversarial role that is assigned. Bargaining situations between representatives of labor and management provide one of the most obvious examples of role conflict.

Traditionally, labor and management have negotiated from a built-in adversarial position. Conflict is expected from such a relationship. The members of the negotiating team may experience conflict while operating in the assigned roles and laugh and joke together an hour later. When interpersonal conflict is found either within the managing of the team or within the laboring force, it is frequently related to the roles people occupy rather than to their differences in personality.

Value Conflict

Value conflict is based on a difference in views of life, social principles, goals, or standards that are brought into focus on a particular issue. Values are the cluster of attitudes or beliefs a person holds that serve as a guideline for measuring the worth of various aspects of life. People hold social, political, religious, aesthetic, and economic values. Values are both societal and personal. A value is a frame of reference used to determine the relative goodness of an object, situation, or behavior. Because of the deep-seated nature of values and because values define who we are, conflicts over values are quite difficult to resolve.

Values are programmed into us from the very beginning. During the formative years, our parents, peers, teachers, and society in general tell us what is right or wrong, good or bad, pretty or ugly, and we develop our values as we develop our decision-making process. Psychologists call this imprinting, and they suggest that the values imprinted into our system through our teenage years are likely to remain with us for our lifetime. When our values become locked-in and others seem to effect little change in our convictions, psychologists label our condition "mind-set." Mind-set is the stuff of which prejudice is made. When someone refers to another as "hard-headed" or "stubborn" or even "closed-minded," they are acknowledging their locked-in condition—the source of conflict and interpersonal failures.

Personality Conflict

Personality conflict is based on differences of personal habits or traits which become evident during times of interaction at work. We've all talked about "personality clashes." Have you ever found yourself saying, "There are some people you just cannot get along with"? Personality conflict is often an outgrowth of other kinds of conflict which have never been satisfactorily resolved.

Ego Conflict

Ego conflict occurs when people in conflict view "winning" or "losing" the conflict as a measure of their expertise, personal worth, or image. Herein, the content of the conflict takes second place to the people involved. As a result, ego conflict can become the most difficult kind of conflict to manage. Ego conflicts develop when discussion of content or values is characterized by personal or judgmental statements.

When who you are, what you are, how competent you are, who you have power over, and how much you know become the issue in a controversy, then the conflict becomes an ego conflict. The more time (perhaps even years) that you have invested in a particular affiliation, and the more competent you see yourself about a certain issue, the more likely you are to become ego-involved when your statements are questioned. And once your ego becomes involved, your ability to cope rationally is often impaired. Almost before you realize it, emotions become involved in the conflict, words are said that cannot be retrieved, and the original divisive issues get blown out of proportion.

These are the kinds of conflict arranged in order of difficulty to manage. We only have space for considering briefly some broad-based personal styles and specific strategies for managing conflict.

STRATEGIES FOR MANAGING CONFLICT (BOTH GOOD AND BAD)

Workers engage in many behaviors to cope with and manage their conflict. Some are positive and some are negative. We will list some negative factors first.

Denial

Denial is a total failure to acknowledge that any kind of problem exists. Conflicts can be so threatening, so painful, to some people that they deny their existence. The repression of conflict means "pretending" to oneself and others that everything is all right. In every age people have deluded themselves, crying, " 'Peace, peace,' when there is no peace."

Avoidance

Avoidance and *withdrawal* constitute a physical or psychological removal from a conflict situation. It is one of the most common, and certainly one of the easiest ways to deal with conflict. The paradox of avoidance or withdrawal is that people use it to try to keep a healthy relationship. Yet this behavioral pattern undermines a relationship and leads to the bleak, chilly distance which can be called "ice-o-lation." It is essentially an escape reaction.

Physical withdrawal is the easiest to identify. The employee who has been turned down for a transfer several times may ask not to be considered for future transfers, thus physically withdrawing from a frustrating situation. Other ways of physically withdrawing include absenteeism, taking sick leave when not sick, increasing the length of time when away from the job (whenever possible), avoiding social conversation with the person or group with whom one is in conflict.

Psychological withdrawal may be less noticeable but is every bit as common, as in situations where the individual develops a "don't give a royal . . . " attitude. Employees who daydream on the job may be withdrawing psychologically from a frustrating work environment. Since the work situation seems to be beyond the employee's control, he/she will do the least amount of work necessary to keep the job, not caring if it is done efficiently.

Although both kinds of withdrawal are common, they are dysfunctional behaviors. Avoiding conflict is unassertive and uncooperative—the individual does not pursue his/her own interests or those of the other person or party. The cause and nature of the conflict is not addressed. Withdrawal only has value on a temporary basis for purposes of letting the heat of conflict cool down.

Aggression

Aggression is the use of physical or psychological coercion to get one's way. Through aggression people attempt to force others to accept their ideas, policies, or solutions. Direct aggression may involve physical or symbolic attack, or both. The employee who cusses his/her supervisor for not approving a transfer is exhibiting a direct symbolic attack. A frustrated production worker who thinks that his/her supervisor is the "barrier" preventing goal attainment may verbally or physically attack the person or may attempt, by rumors or other means, to get revenge. Aggression takes many forms, including abusive language, antagonistic behavior, theft, disobedience to instructions, absenteeism, and interference with the work of others.

Through aggression a person may "win," but it seldom, if ever, does anything positive for a relationship. Aggression is an emotional, childish reaction to conflict which short circuits mature and logical thought processes. Obviously, aggression never deals with the heart of the issues in conflict—only with who is bigger, can talk the loudest and longest, or knows more dirty tricks.

Surrender

Surrender or *capitulation* means giving in immediately to avoid conflict. In this pattern there is usually no struggle. Under the guise of being cooperative, a person is yielding and unassertive, neglecting his/her own concerns in order to satisfy the concerns of the other person. This person goes through life without getting his/her needs met. Surrender obviously does not deal with issues in the conflict, and it can create resentment and feelings that will eventually erupt and spill over into other work and social situations.

Compromise

Compromise is defined as "consent reached by mutual concessions." Compromise takes into account the needs and fears of both parties. There are times in which it can be extremely important in the settlement of individual differences or differences between management and labor. It is the way legislation gets passed. It is the only way to progress in some situations.

Compromise can lead to highly undesirable results when it is used rigidly or inappropriately. There are times in which compromise will simply not work, as the ancient story illustrating the wisdom of Solomon makes clear. One day, two women came before Solomon, each claiming a child as her own. The two women were housemates, each had an infant child, and one mother had accidentally suffocated her baby. To settle the dispute over who was the rightful mother of the surviving child in this pre-DNA age, Solomon called for a sword and offered to cut the living baby in half. In that situation, the compromise which was acceptable to one of the women was wholly unacceptable to the real mother for it literally meant the death of her child. Since, in compromise, each party settles for something less than its full needs and desires—a mini-lose/mini-lose method—it should be used as a last resort.

Collaborating

Collaborating is a verbal weighing and considering of the pros and cons of the issues in conflict. It is both assertive and cooperative, the opposite of withdrawal. An effort is made to satisfy the legitimate demands of both parties in conflict. Collaboration differs from compromise because in compromise one looks for some intermediate position that partially satisfies both parties. In collaboration, the two people or parties work creatively to find new solutions that will maximize the goals for both.

As a pattern, discussion follows the problem-solving method: defining the problem, analyzing the problem by looking for the key issues, suggesting possible solutions, selecting the solution that best fits the analysis, and taking action to implement the decision. The method is not the easiest, but when two parties have committed themselves to trying it, beneficial results are possible.

Persuasion

Persuasion is the attempt to change either the attitude or behavior of another person or party through the use of logical and emotional arguments. Usually during all conflict situations, some attempts at persuasion will be made. Persuasion is a time-honored means of gaining acceptance for your ideas and proposals, but is always more effective in conflict situations only after the collaboration procedure has been followed.

GUIDELINES FOR RESOLVING CONFLICT

Conflict need not be dysfunctional and certainly should not be devastating. Here are some guidelines that should help you creatively resolve conflict by the collaborating or discussion method:

1. **Do not fear conflict.** Fear of conflict evokes the negative responses of withdrawal and surrender.
2. **Keep dialogue on the specific topic on which the conflict issues occur.** Do not permit the discussion to degenerate into an open shooting match. Ordering, threatening, judging, name-calling, and other verbal roadblocks are conflict-promoting actions

3. **Keep an open mind about views that differ from your own.** (You might want to go back and review what we had to say about an open mind in our discussion near the end of chapter 1.)

4. **Strive to keep confrontation gentle, but also honest and straightforward.** Deal directly with any sensitive problem without placing yourself in a position that will jeopardize the chances of forming a constructive working relationship in the future.

5. **Agree with your adversary in those instances where he/she has legitimate complaints.** If you deny the reality of that person's complaint, he/she will continue to harp on that point and the issue will remain unresolved.

6. **Test the criteria used in making value judgments.** Time spent on debating judgments or evaluations could be saved once criteria are clarified and tested.

7. **Come to the resolution situation with an attitude of cooperation rather than an attitude of competition.** If attitudes are competitive, participants are likely to be ego-involved. Begin by communicating to the other party that you seek to resolve your differences in a mutually satisfying way.

There's one final guideline that is just as important as the other seven: *Conduct yourself in ways that result in positive conflict management.* One inappropriate method is to approach your conflict situation with a win-lose attitude—that is, if one person wins, it must be at the other person's expense. Such an attitude is a negative one and is difficult to deal with. People playing poker may be contrasted with people working a jigsaw puzzle to illustrate the difference between a win-lose approach and win-win approach. In poker, one person is working and conniving at the expense of others; in working a jigsaw puzzle, each person is working in cooperation with others. Always strive for a *win-win* resolution where no one loses and no one gives up or gives in because both (all) parties benefit.

QUESTIONS FOR GROUP DISCUSSION AND PERSONAL REFLECTION

1. Do you agree that a good working relationship is like a marriage?
2. Is conflict always bad? If not, what values are served by conflict? Is there any narrative or statement in Scripture which offers a positive word on interpersonal conflict?
3. Does the Bible give us any guidelines for resolving interpersonal conflict?
4. What are some different kinds of conflict?
5. Do you think that all conflict at work can be understood as a failure to communicate?
6. What is a value? Are conflicts over values difficult to resolve?
7. What style of conflict resolution have you utilized most?
8. Let's try ranking our personal conflict sources. The arguments, disruptions, and hassles in your life that cause you the most discomfort or pain are usually related to which of the following people? (Rank these on the basis of how much pain and time they cost you.

Use "1" for the category causing the most painful conflict and "10" for the category causing the least painful conflict.)

_____Spouse	_____Coworkers
_____Parents	_____Subordinates
_____Children	_____Clients
_____Other relatives	_____Close friends
_____Supervisor	_____Others

9. Issues about which you feel strongly and about which you most often find yourself in conflict with others are related to which of the following topics? (Rank these and add any others that are significant. Use "1" for the category that most often causes conflict.)

_____Money	_____Drugs or alcohol
_____Sexuality	_____Smoking
_____Minority rights	_____Taxes
_____Women's rights	_____Gun Control
_____General politics	_____Race relations
_____Religion	_____Divorce
_____Welfare	_____Legal system
_____Leisure	_____Church business

10. According to your value system, can you differentiate between high-level principles and low-level preferences? Consider the following case studies in terms of how much energy you would recommend giving them.

a. Ken Allen's coworker continually smokes in the work area they share. The smoke causes him discomfort. Ken's coworker is otherwise compatible. Ken should:_____

_____

_____

b. Kelly Long shared a new product design idea with her closest friend at work, Nancy Morrison. Nancy had the nerve to present it to her unit manager and take full credit. Kelly should:_____

_____

_____

c. Tom Wheeler's best friend, Jim Castleman, defaults on a loan for which Tom cosigned. The two friends had taken a large business loan to purchase a store in the mall selling premium cigars. Tom should: _____

_____

_____

d. Sara Camp's subordinates are obviously pilfering office supplies from their unit, but not enough to significantly impinge on company profits. They are otherwise working well. Sara should:_____

_____

_____

  e. Jim McKinney knows his preacher, Barrett Tyler, is taking sermon material from Max Lucado and Charles Swindoll and presenting it word-for-word as his own sermons. Even the personal illustrations are pilfered. The content of the sermons is good, naturally, but Jim has already read his sources and can hardly listen respectfully to his preacher. Jim should:_____

_____

_____

  f. Kyle Bills usually rides with Jim Crowell to see the University of Tennessee football games in Knoxville. On one trip, Jim had invited one of his neighbors. The neighbor seemed friendly enough, but he frequently sprinkled his conversation with words that Kyle believed to be profanity. Once or twice, Jim's friend took the Lord's name in vain. This troubled Kyle. Kyle should:_____

_____

_____

11. To get more personal, complete candidly the following statements:

  a. The greatest source of conflict for me in my job right now is_____

_____

_____

  b. The greatest source of conflict for me in my family right now is_____

_____

_____

  c. There would be less conflict in my life right now if_____

_____

_____

Chapter 18

Working Too Much

This book, being about work, is by its very nature, about violence . . . to the spirit as well as to the body. It is about ulcers as well as accidents, about shouting matches as well as fist fights, about nervous breakdowns as well as kicking the dog around. It is, above all (or beneath all), about daily humiliations. To survive the day is triumph enough for the walking wounded among the great many of us . . . for the many there is a hardly concealed discontent. The blue-collar blues is no more bitterly sung than the white-collar moan.

Studs Terkel, in *Working*

Of more than 1,200 business students in ten nations surveyed by Cooper & Lybrand, 45 percent named "a rewarding life outside work" as their chief goal.

Wall Street Journal

As soon as you're doing what you wanted to be doing, you want to be doing something else.

Lovka's Law of Living

The worst day fishing is better than the best day working.

Bumper sticker

Making a life is more significant than making a living.

William Willimon

When you like your work, every day is a holiday.

Frank Tyger

I'm constantly amazed by the number of people who can't seem to control their own schedules. Over the years, I've had many executives come to me and say with pride, 'Boy, last year I worked so hard that I didn't take any vacation.' It's actually nothing to be proud of. I always feel like responding, 'You dummy. You mean to tell me that you can take responsibility for an $80 million project, and you can't plan two weeks out of the year to go off with your family and have some fun?'

Lee Iacocca

HURRY, HURRY. RUSH, RUSH. WORK HARDER AND HARDER. PUSH, push. Those simple words sum up so many of the work trends among business and professional people. Many young professionals feel swept up in the emotional equivalent of Marine boot camp—but the three months' survival training is stretched into years of stress-filled life in an unrelenting pressurized environment.

One writer, medical doctor Richard A. Swenson, examines the emotional and psychological stresses of contemporary American life and proposes that we understand today's pressures through the loss of "margin." Margin is defined as "the space that once existed between ourselves and our limits." Margin is the source of calm, security, counterculture, remedy, and energy, and the place where nurturing occurs; it is the gap between rest and exhaustion, the leeway between ourselves and our human limits. Margin is a buffer zone that allows for extra rest, sleep, thought, fantasy, or handling the unexpected traffic jams or other delays without fretting. Marginless living speeds up the time frame of our lives. Small problems can become immense overnight. We hit our limits with frightening suddenness. Little wonder that four out of five Americans report a need to reduce stress in their lives.

Is there such a thing as working too much? Can one work too hard? Can one take work too seriously? Is not work supposed to be our friend and not our enemy?

The Puritan ethic would never have considered these questions, but we live in a pressurized society where competition seems unfair and unrelenting and at times unfair. The modern business office seems always to be a place where every employee should be willing to work overtime and where every job assignment was due yesterday. Someone described our age as a time when people stand in front of the microwave cooking their supper and ordering: "Hurry up. Hurry up."

How much time we devote to our work, the attitude we bring toward our work assignments, and the evaluation we make of our work performance are all linked to our ethical responsibilities toward self. We conclude this volume by considering three fairly old concepts that are linked with three fairly new words: workaholism, perfectionism, and burnout.

WORKAHOLISM

Workaholism is like a disease. Its roots are psychiatric rather than physical. It is a form of compulsiveness. The workaholic is driven to stay at work. This person is neither slowed nor deterred from excessive dedication to work by family values, special events, holidays, or vacations. Work is the most important dimension in life.

Workaholics may have convinced themselves that dedication to a company or work-related goal or project is incredibly high. The workaholic may feel worthy of the praise and best wishes of family and colleagues for such zeal. Reality is another matter, however. Sometimes workaholism is a matter of avoidance—not love of work as much as dissatisfaction with and avoidance of other aspects of life, notably, marriage, family, and friends, or lack of same.

We all may know people who seem utterly unredeemable in their personal lives, but who are great achievers for their company and career. Workaholism may be compensation for an unhappy and unrewarding personal life. Some may attempt to play business roles in their marriage and family life, winding up as dismal failures. In all fairness, however, workaholics are as likely to be men and women who genuinely love what they are doing, get excited with the opportunity to do it, and are perfectly willing for other dimensions of their lives to "go down the tubes" accordingly.

Is workaholism an ethical issue? The answer is "yes" when we consider the impact on workaholism on the worker and other people. Of course, the phenomenon of "working too much" depends on the worker and who is doing the judging. If one finds that he/she is working too long and too hard at a job assignment with no real satisfaction and at the expense of more important dimensions of life, then an ethical problem has arisen.

Do not rule out the possibility that, for some people, work is the highest and most important dimension of their lives. To them, they are doing the most important job in the world. Labeling them "workaholics" may be a way of offending them, discounting the value of their contribution to their business or to the community.

The instruction of Jesus—"Judge not so that you are not judged" (Matt. 7:1)— might be heeded here. The general issue is one of priorities, and one person's workaholism may be another's steadfast dedication.

PERFECTIONISM

If workaholism is excess concern about the quantity of work done, perfectionism is excessive concern about the quality of the work done. Our cultural folk wisdom has included such sayings as "If a job is worth doing, it's worth doing well," "Nothing less than your very best is good enough," and even "There's no such thing as good enough." "Quality" has become a key concept in the new management styles which have emerged since the 1970s. Both labor and management, in private industry and public service, are lectured often on the necessity and methods of "quality."

How well does a job need to be done? How much quality should be built into a product or service? If perfection is the ideal, is that ideal attainable? Is not perfection an abstraction or distraction or a plain impossibility?

Perfectionism tends to pervade everything. The perfectionist likely learned this oppressive mindset from the earliest days of parental guidance. She learned to take full responsibility for all the minor chores and details around the house and was taught the virtue of constant motion until she collapses in bed. When she goes to work she brings this same mindset through the office door. She doesn't simply want to do well on her job—everything has to be perfect. The slightest criticism from her manager is enough to send her into a tailspin. If any fault, no matter how small, can be found in her work, she feels an overwhelming sense of failure. As a result of her unreasonable demand to get everything right at work, she makes herself utterly miserable and everybody else too.

Perfectionism regarding your own work tends to be self-destructive. It tends also to be destructive of interpersonal relationships at work. After all, most people who have unrealistic standards for self will extend those unrealistic standards toward the work of other people. Both workaholics and perfectionists tend to be Type-A personalities whose distorted work ethic leads to high coronary risk. High standards in the work-place are important, but we do no speak simply of high standards. Impossible standards neither encourage or lead to success; the end result is frustration and failure.

The answer to both workaholism and perfectionism lies in the issues of priorities and perspective. If you have decided that being perfect is costing you too much, and if you're ready to change, there are some things you can do to alter your life. Being a perfectionist means we want simple answers that work perfectly, right away. There aren't any of those, but try these:

1. **Change** the tapes in your head, the ones that say you have to score 100 percent on everything you do. Most jobs don't demand that level of performance.
2. **Aim** at average in areas where you can do so. You may put off writing a letter to a friend because you think it has to be perfect. Try taking fifteen minutes to dash it off.
3. **Structure** your work time so that you have blocks of time one or two hours in length during which you can concentrate intensely on a project.
4. **Focus** on what's right with people and situations. If you expect circumstances and the persons in them to be perfect, you set yourself up for disappointment. Look for the good.
5. **Learn** to laugh at yourself. We can get caught in the trap of taking ourselves too seriously. Let yourself see the humor in your life.

BURNOUT

Working too hard. Expecting too much of oneself. Expecting too much of work partners and being continually disappointed. Personal life suffering. Home life suffering. Feeling stressed out all the time. All of this leads to yet another problem—despair and total job exhaustion. The current term for this centuries-old phenomenon is "burnout."

Burnout is a kind of stress. The source of burnout may be in the work ethic of the highly ambitious and hard-working. Or the source of burnout may be the over-whelming work load of the job or the sense that the high demands of a job offer little payback in gratification. When you are experiencing burnout, few of your needs are met even at the most basic levels. In its most extreme forms you suffer at four levels: You are physically exhausted, emotionally drained, intellectually muddled, and spiritu-ally empty, in despair.

When there is despair, the ethical issue quickly emerges: What are we working for? What are we hoping for? The answer for the burnout victim is almost always "too much." And what is the reverse of burnout? Is it energy? Enthusiasm for the job or for relationships? Well, it must certainly include all the action taken and experiences reas-sumed in your life that

1. renew and replenish your energy,
2. increase your self-esteem,

3. enhance your appreciation for life and relationships, and
4. result in the end state of overall wellness.

Overall wellness is a state in which your physical, emotional, intellectual, and spiritual needs are continually attended. Of course, a great deal of distraction is beyond our control and will always undermine our total wellness.

Overall wellness can best be viewed as the direction in which we are moving. The ultimate desire is for us to create a balance, a place where our relationships, work, and activities promote enough healthiness which will counteract the forces that are burning us out.

OVERALL WELLNESS: TWELVE CHECKPOINTS

Overall wellness may be described in terms of twelve elements in your personal life, each described as a general ideal. Some of the elements may represent "sore spots" for certain individuals, and, of course, people tend to get defensive about their sore spots; once defensive, they miss everything. The slightest step toward overall wellness will begin to improve the sense of balance in your personal and professional life.

Your Mouth

People who are experiencing burnout tend to increase their alcohol consumption, use more medication, and change their eating habits, usually by overeating or bringing on high-caloric, low-nutrition foods. They will also say things impulsively, in anger, or direct their hostility at the wrong people.

Both of these kinds of burnout symptoms indicate that you have lost control of your mouth—what goes in it, through it, or what comes out of it. A Christian is especially concerned about the use of speech.

Gaining control over your mouth, whether you go on a diet, decrease alcohol or drug consumption, quit smoking, or switch from coffee or those big whopper Cokes to noncaffeinated drinks, generally has the effect of giving you a sense of control over your entire life.

Exercise

Exercise allows your large muscle groups to work on the tension associated with your job that leads to burnout. Physical health, particularly in relation to the cardiovascular system, promotes sleep, and increases energy in general. Exercise is a behavior that takes your mind off your troubles and is an excellent decompression routine (allowing you to unwind between stressful activities). The exercise program you choose should be entirely up to your personal interests and skills.

Humor

Laughter is still the best medicine. Like exercise, laughter is contrary to worry. If you are laughing, you cannot, at that particular moment, be focusing on your problems or failings. The curative power of laughter and humor is well-documented in Norman Cousins's book, *Anatomy of an Illness*. Cousins overcame what was thought to be an incurable illness with a program that included large doses of humor. The apostle Paul, writing from a prison cell, commanded Christians to "rejoice always" (Phil. 4:4).

A Support System

People who are particularly susceptible to burnout often have difficulty asking for and maintaining the emotional support they need. They are often the people that everyone else leans on and depends upon. They have often received a great deal of positive reinforcement for being strong and being the one who listens and helps. They may have also been negatively reinforced whenever they showed their own feelings or let on that they might be depressed or having a hard time.

Yet, all people need support. They need people in their lives who can listen nonjudgmentally, allow them to air their feelings, and encourage them to go on. Those in high stress or constant giving situations especially need other people to positively influence their lives. (Consider the fact that social workers, counselors, ministers, and others in the helping professions have an extremely high rate of burnout.)

Members of your support system can be family, friends, a professional counselor and/or structured, regularly scheduled support group. In your search for overall wellness, you need at least one close confidante with some distance from your problems. No matter how supportive your spouse or supervisor is, he/she is so close to the situation that is burning you out, and possibly feeling the effects of the same stressors, that he/she will not always be able to maintain the perspective you require.

More Nourishing and Less Toxic People in Your Life

In order to develop a lifestyle that can be "burnout protected" and to increase the delights and decrease the irritants in your current lifestyle, you must begin to understand how the different people in your life affect you. You will want to minimize the negative influences and maximize the good and nourishing relationships. In a state of burnout, you are giving enough criticism, put-downs, and negative evaluations of yourself; you really don't need the people you like and interact with regularly to do more of the same.

The nourishing people in your life are those who listen nonjudgmentally and don't have a "red pencil" mentality. They do not look for your flaws and mistakes; instead, they appreciate and comment on what they respect, admire, and celebrate about you. Nourishing people are generally warm. They may nonsensuously touch and hug often and easily.

Toxic people tend to be put-down artists. They seem to take pleasure in your grief and mistakes and will bring these up for reexamination whenever you are feeling down. They love to say or imply "I told you so" and rarely let you forget a mistake. You will need to find ways to spend more time with the nourishing people and less time with the toxic people.

Cutting down time spent with toxic people requires something called "creative neglect." Creative neglect requires some ingenuity, but basically involves unnecessary interactions with toxic people.

Assertiveness

Burnout is promoted when you operate as a doormat, rarely speaking up for your rights or protesting when you are being abused. Feelings of powerlessness and frustration can only increase when you don't assert control in the situations where input and influence are possible. Furthermore, your needs will rarely be met if you don't make them known. Very few people can read minds.

Assertiveness associated with overall wellness is simply the ability and inclination to ask for what you need. Of course, asking will not guarantee that you will get what you ask for, but it certainly improves the odds.

Time Management

Wellness does not come to those who are overwhelmed. Effective time management is essential to burnout protection. You will want to learn how to delegate, plan, prioritize, and say no (giving up the false assumption that you are the only one who can actually do what has to be done).

Getting Rid of Fritters

Fritters are all of those elements in your life that consume time and energy, but give you nothing in return. Fritters are not the obligations and demands that come with the territory of our regular job detail, but mindless unchallenging activities.

You don't have enough time as it is. You can't afford to waste precious free time on things that drain you, bore you, or just do nothing positive for you. The same time can be devoted to one of the other burnout protection elements that clearly improve your condition.

Re-Creation

Re-creation is time you allow yourself to be alone and away from your trouble and obligations. This is time alone when nobody needs you. It is time you can reflect on life or whatever else seems greater and more important than your job. It is time even to be unfocused, to daydream, to plan, or to fantasize about better days to come.

Experiencing the Arts

Experiencing the arts begins to meet your intellectual and spiritual needs. Whether you choose to listen to music, attend the theater, go to art museums, read poetry or other literature, or browse antique stores, experiencing the arts on more regular basis can do the following:

1. remind you of the exquisite beauty in the world around you,
2. expand your horizons, and
3. familiarize you with the universal themes which make us feel less alone and misunderstood.

A Creative Outlet

Having a creative outlet, a hobby, or a means of expressing yourself functions as a burnout protection measure in several ways. It comes with a built-in sense of accomplishment.

A creative outlet provides a therapeutic distraction. It takes your mind off your concerns while replenishing your energy and increasing your sense of control and self-esteem. By learning new skills associated with your creative outlet, you are expanding your world—not shrinking it.

Spiritual Issues

God has given each person a spiritual dimension. All humans quest for meaning beyond the "here and now." Religious faith can be a powerful source of meaning and purpose. Religion helps people make sense of the universe and the mystery of our purpose in living and working. Like any other potential source of meaning, religious faith seems most authentic and valuable when it enables us to become as fully human as possible.

Attending to your spiritual needs does not necessarily mean going to worship and Sunday school every Sunday without fail; although, it can include such activities. Attending to your spiritual needs does mean regaining a perspective on those things which are greater and more universal than your day-to-day existence.

In general, spirituality can include religion, appreciation of philosophy, meditation, contemplation, or anything else that has meaning for you. Faith in any meaningful and appropriate form in which it manifests itself is an excellent burnout protection measure—it gives you a sense of perspective. A warm and supportive fellowship with those who share that "like-precious faith" can certainly enhance one's spiritual life.

Hopefully, we've said enough in this chapter to provoke your thought about your physical and emotional needs. Let's summarize with some brief exhortations: Remember that you are not infinite. You do not have an inexhaustible source of energy. There are only twenty-four hours in your day. You have a responsibility to take care of yourself. You have not been assigned to take care of anyone else, and you cannot expect anyone else to take ultimate responsibility for you. Expect interruptions in the flow of your life—some will be nuisances, a few will be emergencies, but a number may be wonderful! Learn to say "no" to mounting requests. Practice simplicity. Tap into a forward-looking vision. Maintain your most important relationships. Be loyal to your friends. Be faithful to your God.

Finally: Remember that life is a journey, not a race!

QUESTIONS FOR GROUP DISCUSSION
AND PERSONAL REFLECTION

1. Do you consider how hard one works to be a moral issue or a strictly personal issue?
2. Do you respect a workaholic?
3. Are there certain kinds of professions which seem to attract workaholics and perfectionists?
4. As a supervisor, what could you do to help your employees not overdo job responsibilities?
5. Have you seen workaholics in voluntary organizations, such as the church? If so, how do you explain this phenomenon?
6. Human Synergistics International, located in Michigan, Illinois, is a consulting group which has studied the impact of perfectionism in the workplace and problems it creates. They suggest this simple test to determine the extent of your perfectionism. Respond to each item on a scale of "0" to "3", where "0" equals never, "1" equals seldom, "2" equals sometimes, and "3" equals always.
   a. I feel no matter how well I do, it's never enough.
   b. I feel I must control or anticipate the future.
   c. I'm disappointed after success, when I should feel good.
   d. Others would say I'm too hard on myself and others.
   e. I feel guilty when I'm not working.
   f. I suffer from frequent headaches on weekends.
   g. When I relax, I still think about work or things I must do.
   h. I dominate conversations.
   i. I become extremely upset with standing in line, waiting in traffic, poor service, and anything even slightly out of order.
   j. Other people rarely come up to my high standards.

   These researchers suggest that if you scored between "0" and "10," you don't have much of a problem with perfection. If your score was "11" or higher, your perfectionism is probably causing you problems.

   Unfortunately for some folks, it takes looking death straight in the eye (or some trigger event) before they get serious about living healthy. When you're just thankful to be alive, then you're usually serious enough to make major lifestyle changes. Here is a simple test to measure the healthiness of your lifestyle. See how many of the following statements you can honestly say "yes" to:

1. I balance time between work and play and pace myself to prevent tiredness. __Yes__No
2. I get enough sleep every night.__Yes__No
3. I eat two to four servings of fruit and three to five servings of vegetables every day.__Yes__No
4. I choose a diet low in fat, saturated fat, and cholesterol.__Yes__No
5. I maintain meaningful and fulfilling relationships with others.__Yes__No

6. I discuss my problems and concerns with people close to me.__Yes__No
7. I take part in light to moderate physical exercise (walking, golf, gardening) for thirty minutes at least five times a week.__Yes__No
8. I exercise vigorously for twenty or more minutes at least three times a week.__Yes__No
9. I avoid smoking cigarettes and being exposed to the smoke of others.__Yes__No
10. I drink moderately or not at all (no more than two drinks for men and one for women).__Yes__No

Key: Count the number of times you answered "yes."

Eight to ten: Good for you. Your habits say you're responsible for your health. Keep it up.

Five to seven: You're doing some things well, but there's still room for improvement and change.

Four to zero: You're in trouble. Now is the time to get serious and examine your unhealthy lifestyle.

Chapter 19

He Works/She Works
Reflections on Work and Family

The drill is relentless. Up at 5:30 to shower and pack lunches before waking, dressing and feeding the kids; out the door by 6:30 to drop them at day care and school; on to the office, answering voice mail and scheduling meetings along the way. Call it the work-family juggle. It is a tricky act only the most adroit could hope to master—yet expected daily routine for millions of working parents.
Carol Hymowitz

Quality time is just a way of deluding ourselves into shortchanging our children. Children need vast amounts of parental time and attention. It's an illusion to think they're going to be on your timetable, and that you can say "OK, we've got a half hour, let's get on with it."
Ronald Levant

It's hard to change the hard-driving corporate ethic that dictates: "This is war . . . you gotta be here all the time. You can have a flexible workplace policy that allows somebody to leave early, but if that person walks out the door at 3 p.m. and gets a comment, the culture's not there.
Karen Geiger

The emotional magnets beneath home and workplace are in the process of being reversed. Work has become a form of 'home' and home has become 'work.'
Arlie Hochschild

We have not met a dual career family that is free of stress. You work long hours, have family responsibilities, need exercise and personal time, and are part of a community. That means you will have considerable responsibilities in your life. There will be minor hassles, more serious problems, and major crises. This does not mean, though, that you cannot increase your marital and family satisfaction, your enjoyment of your career, and your sense of personal accomplishment.
Steven E. and
Ivonne H. Hobfoll

AS YOU ADVANCE IN THE BUSINESS AND PROFESSIONAL WORLD, there are twin sets of support systems which become increasingly important—one is internal and the other external.

Your internal support system is composed of your inner resources—your convictions, your faith, your attitudes, and your values. We've already explored these resources from different directions along the way in this book. The external support system is composed of your immediate family and your most trusted friends. We'll offer some comments here on issues that emerge at the intersection of your career life and family life.

An undeniable connection exists between your work life and family life. This is not to say that the correlation between work and family is necessarily a positive, healthy one. Plenty of people succeed in their careers but are sad failures at home. There are some great fathers and mothers, husbands and wives, whose jobs seem boring or whose careers are dead in the water. Your goal, most surely, is success and respect in business and professional life and fulfillment and happiness in family and personal relations. Is that ideal possible?

We might proceed by referring again to the traditional model of work. As we all know, for centuries the typical pattern in families entailed the husband and father toiling as the main "breadwinner" and the wife and mother working at the many tasks involved with "homemaking." While both roles were important, the male was considered the head of the household and the one with more important responsibility and greater income. Such a pattern was rooted both in culture as well as in the ideology of the times, including the traditional interpretation of Scripture.

One of the fundamental features of premodern societies, whether historically or in underdeveloped nations today, is the link between work and home, and the functioning of the family as an economically productive unit. The goal of premodern homes in the western world was to achieve a high measure of self-sufficiency, although total sufficiency of farming families was more of a myth than a reality. Americans have always depended on other community citizens to provide goods and services. We might also be surprised to learn of the diversity of occupations women found during even the Colonial period. They kept shops, worked as dressmakers, laundresses, and in such traditionally masculine establishments as gunsmith and blacksmith shops and tanneries; on the other hand, most of the women in these occupations were likely to have been partners with their husbands and then took such establishments over after their husband's death.

Despite the precedent of a few women working in the male's professional world, prior to the early twentieth century most women worked at home or on the family farm. The traditional view in the United States of the work of men and women may seen strangely ironic and may be summed up succinctly: It was the unemployed man who was perceived to be a social problem, likely to have troubled marital relations, and likely to produce delinquent children; for women, it was the employed woman who was perceived by her peers in virtually the same way.

Among the many developments of the twentieth century that have been characterized as "revolutions," the changing pattern of female participation in the labor force is undoubtedly one of the most significant ones. In 1890 married women made up less than 3 percent of the labor force away from home; now they make up nearly half of it. The rise of the industrial movement enticed many men away from the farms or small shops into the big factories or mines. And World War II, with its demands to fill positions of the men who went to the front battle lines, ushered women in the salaried labor force in both factories and offices. (Incidentally, there had been precedent for women laboring in factories in the latter decades of the nineteenth century in the New England Lowell-type mills.) The modernization of the twentieth century, or more specifically capitalization and industrialization as important dimensions of this larger process, has meant the separation of work and home and the emergence of the family as a unit of consumption rather than production.

Since the influx of women into the labor force during World War II and the decades following, the old restrictions of both ideology and opportunity (related, though separable) have been largely lifted. As we progressed into the twentieth century, with these negative attitudes toward female employment beginning to erode, the workplace was slowly transformed. Beginning with the 1950s, we have seen a growth in the rate of workforce participation by married women with children under six almost tripling between 1950 and 1970. Clearly, work was increasingly becoming something which women do not relegate to the years before marriage and after the children are grown. A study in the late 1990s found that more than half of new mothers are going back to work before their infants can walk; the older and more educated the mother, the more likely she is to return to work before her baby reaches a first birthday, with a soaring 77 percent of college-educated women deciding to juggle motherhood and an outside job.

For years, a traditional working couple situation was the pattern for working husbands and wives. A woman's labor outside the home was viewed as a supplement to the husband's income and was done to help hold the family together and provide for some necessities or desired consumer goods. The husband remained the unique provider, and the woman remained ultimately dependent upon him for material benefit and for social status. Her job was considered not as important as her husband's, nor was her salary as large.

Today many women, both married and single, have entered the business and professional world seeking a career of their own. There is even an increase in the "Murphy Brown" syndrome, with a steadily growing number of never-married, older women opting to have a child. Many marriages have become a two-career family, in which both the husband and the wife hold down full-time jobs and develop dreams and ambitions to become upwardly mobile in their chosen fields. In a dual-career marriage, both spouses are career-oriented and seek to move as high in their companies or professions as their talents and skills will permit.

THE IMPACT OF MODERN TRENDS

What is the impact on individuals and on married partners of a workforce in which approximately half of the workers are female and in the business world in which nearly 40 percent of new businesses are started by women? In answering such a weighty question, we'll offer several brief generalizations.

The first one is that the American family is under more pressures to survive than ever before. There are plenty of pressures on men and women in the workplace just to survive on the job. Downsizings have saddled survivors with more work—and work-place paranoia. The rapid pace of technological change, with its many "faxes" and electronic-mailings, has created a constant crisis mentality that everything has to be done now (or should have been done yesterday). Many business and professional people put themselves under almost masochistic allegiance to superhuman demands. According to research by Juliet Schor, economics professor at Harvard and author, the average American is working 163 more hours each year—or a month more of full-time work—than in 1970. At the same time, some 42 percent of employees nationwide have children under eighteen, and 75 percent of married employees have spouses who also work. Husbands and wives may spend the biggest and best part of their waking hours in a pressurized business or professional environment with other men and women who have no connection with their family. Thus, the values, issues, and needs of one's family compete for center stage with the values, issues, and needs of one's business or profession.

Second, questions of gender and economics will remain of major importance. Throughout the 1970s and 1980s the wage gap between men and women steadily narrowed. In the late 1990s, the gap widened slightly. According to the Bureau of Labor Statistics in 1997, the median weekly earning of full-time working women was just under 75 percent of men's median, down from 77 percent four years earlier. In 1979 women's median income had been 62 percent of men's median income. Younger women earn closer to men's median salary (at 90 percent). Heated debates about equity, job discrimination, and the "glass ceiling" will continue to be waged.

Third, working women have stress-hormone levels that rise each morning and stay high until bedtime, potentially making them more susceptible to heart attack and other health problems. Additionally, working mothers have significantly higher levels of stress hormones than working women with no children, according to research studies. Job strain is about the same in all women, but the working mothers reported significantly higher levels of home strain than women without children, regardless of marital status. Compounding matters, elevated levels of stress hormones have been shown to suppress immunity; higher stress has also been linked with increased blood pressure and greater risk for heart disease.

Obviously, men still seem to do a better job compartmentalizing their work and their family lives. When men work, their minds are generally at work and when they are home their minds are generally at home (yes, of course there are exceptions). Many men who think it is crucially important to separate business and professional life from family life refer to the drive to and from work as a time when they "beam up" and "beam down" between the two. Women are much more likely to experience seepage between the compartments of their work and family life. They are more likely to welcome calls from children on the job, more likely than their husbands to stay at home with sick children, more likely to talk about family with colleagues at work. Men may see themselves in the role of assistant at home ("What can I help you with, dear?"), while women see themselves as the domestic CEO, even when they have full-time employment. As long as men had competent domestic managers (their wives), they were free from domestic concerns and could deploy emotional reserves in the pursuit of personal careers.

Fourth, many women find that home life is so frantic and overscheduled that the workplace is now their refuge. It is their chance to get back to an adult pace and to an adult agenda. Generations of men have cherished the bright order of the work day and thus moved away from the dark jumble of emotion and need at home. Perhaps a generation of women have now learned the same lesson and have adopted typically male values. The office—by contrast to crying, sinus-draining pre-schoolers and stacks of dirty laundry and strewn debris—is where women employees get to feel important and competent, relax on breaks, socialize, and get on with their careers. While home was once the refuge from the cold, impersonal world of work, the two may have changed places. Now work is where the heart is.

Finally, the emergence of two-career families may produce a home environment of much marital conflict and personal guilt. There is much more emotional work to manage, especially in dealing with guilt and making up for the assembly line nature of their children's lives. There is the omnipresent temptation to "emotionally downsize life," convincing oneself that mates and children do not need all that much time and attention so long as there is "quality time." Often the solution to the squeeze—that is, to get better at juggling competing demands—does not seem really a solution after all!

CHALLENGES FOR TWO-CAREER FAMILIES

There are challenges to be faced in families wherein both husband and wife pursue personal careers. If that is your situation now, or you expect it to become so in the future, there are a few practical questions for your consideration:

Priorities

What are the priorities of your married life and family? Every business and professional person must decide which dimension of one's life must be given the highest priority. Most Christian professionals would declare that it is important to place family needs above career needs. Sometimes, however, it is easy to deceive ourselves about our real priorities. We may claim our family is our highest priority, but in reality devote more time and energy to a career.

Stephen Covey proposes a little exercise which may help us determine our real priorities. Covey notes that each of us has a center, though we usually do not recognize it as such and we do not recognize the effects of that center on all dimensions of our lives. A person may be spouse-centered, family-centered, money-centered, possession-centered, pleasure-centered, church-centered, self-centered, and so forth. We can identify our center, that central core value around which we organize the rest of life, by looking closely at our life-support factors. What is it that you will not compromise regardless? What is it that gives you security? comfort? a sense of power?

We might approach our center through a hypothetical situation, Covey recommends. Suppose you have plans for an interesting and romantic evening with your spouse; the two of you have reservations at a nice restaurant and tickets for a concert. Most unexpectedly, your boss calls you into the office and asks for your help through the evening for an important meeting the next morning. What will be your response? The *spouse-centered* and *family-centered* person will think first of the needs of the mate and the family, even if he/she reluctantly agrees to cancel plans for the evening in order to honor the boss's request. The *possession-centered* person will think of the possibility of eventual rewards in income or promotion. The *career-centered* person may think first of the opportunity to learn more about the job, to ingratiate oneself to the boss and collect an "IOU," and to make a solid advance in the corporate ladder. If you are self-centered you will focus on what you will personally want most to do without any regard for mate, friends, or boss. Considering the various ways in which we might respond to an unusual request and opportunity might enable us to clarify the organizing principle of our lives. Quite clearly, to simply say that one puts marriage and family ahead of career does not make such prioritizing a reality.

Conflict

In times of conflict, is there consensus over which of the two careers has the greater priority? Decisions will likely need to be made about whose career takes priority over the other. For example, how does a couple deal with major conflicts of schedule when both careers make important demands at the same time? There may be many occasions when one partner or the other must "lose out" on some career-connected opportunity in order to support the other partner. What if one of you gets the opportunity for career advancement which entails relocation to another part of the country? One way to handle this, of course, is that one of you agrees to long-range commuting, a question so important we raise it next. As much as you might like to treat both careers as equally important, there will be times in which one is given priority over the other.

Living Apart

Are you willing to live apart geographically to maintain two professional careers? The issue of long-range commuting should be faced early in a two-career marriage. Separate careers can be pursued in different cities. Long-distance telephoning, air travel, and electronic mail are modern technological blessings which ease the pain of separation.

At the point of deciding if long-range commuting is a viable option, the two of you must consider the impact of any decision on your marital and family relationships. Some couples may find any separation on a day-to-day basis unacceptable. The decision may be complicated by children still at home. Often, your skills of understanding, negotiation, and communication will be tested. Each of you would benefit from good communication and support by your company management in making such a decision.

Children

What is your philosophy about children? Are your career demands so heavy that having children would only be a distraction? Or do you feel that your married life must "have it all"? Children and finances (and the two are related) are the two areas of greatest conflict in a marital relationship. Children are most certainly a distraction, pleasant or otherwise, from career or any other serious undertaking. If you decide you want both children and a two-career relationship, other questions emerge: Should one of the two of you take an extended leave for parenting responsibility? Should you have children early in your career or wait until careers are well on track? What are your standards for child care? Once again, the skills of understanding the other partner, negotiation, and communication are so important. And no matter what decision you make originally, be prepared for revisions and adjustments as your children arrive and mature.

Household Maintenance

How will you handle household maintenance and parenting issues? The question may seem trivial compared to the others raised. Sometimes the seemingly trivial matters can throw a marriage for a loop. If both of you are working for a good salary, you can easily hire someone to perform the mindless tasks around the house and yard. There will be some tasks that you do not want to delegate to hired help. It should be assumed that each partner will assist the other with tasks that consume more time. Weekends and quality time during the week will come at a premium; shared responsibility can maximize that time (for example, you can visit with each other while clearing the table and "doing dishes" together.)

Inequities

Are you prepared for inequities in income and prestige? Unless you are coowners in a business or colleagues in a practice, it stands to reason that one of you will become more successful, better salaried, and/or more important to the firm or in your practice than the other. Are you secure enough in your marriage relationship for your mate to be more successful than you? Do you feel that you must be in competition with your mate? In our culture, many men are not prepared for their wives to earn more than they earn. What if one of you is enjoying flourishing success and prestige in your career and the career of the other is floundering?

Flexibility, Portability

If you are at the beginning of your careers, should you seek a firm or working situation that encourages "flexibility" and "portability"? Increasingly, there are firms which offer jobs that permit flexible scheduling and for work to be carried and completed off site. Sometimes a full-time job can be compressed into a four-day work week. Some workers, mostly mothers, are requesting part-time work for a period of time. There is a trend toward family-friendly workplaces which provide totally flexible hours, even allowing employees to adjust their schedule on a day-to-day basis, having subsidized daycare in the building, allowing working parents to carry mates and children with them on business trips, and extending family leave with or without pay.

In 1997, just over 30 million U.S. households had home offices and the number is growing rapidly. Though men and women work from home in about equal proportions, women are more likely to work entirely at home. If you decide to work at home, a key concern might be whether you are able to clearly resist the lure of the computer and office files in the home and delegate blocks of uninterruptible time off from work.

QUALITY TIME

As a postscript to this chapter, let us propose a definition of quality time and later invite readers to reflect on the concept: Quality time is time spent in whatever activity that brings family members together in some common goal or purpose, and when the time is over both parties feel good about their shared experience. The shared experience may be intense, such as a "heavy" dialogue between mother and daughter, or not so intense, such as a father and son working on a roof or playing golf together.

To conclude, we have raised only a few of the issues in which business and professional life impact a marriage and family. These serious issues involve ego, personal maturity, shared values, and other inner resources. Alas, there seem to be more models of marital failure among dual-career marriages than models of satisfaction and lasting happiness.

Good news! There is a word of encouragement for Christian professionals. Our marital ties are strengthened by our commitment to the Lord God who created marriage for our lifelong partnership and fulfillment and to his Son who blessed a marriage union by his words and by his first miracle. Christian professionals have a greater motivation not simply to maximize their gifts and talents to the glory of God, but also possess the enabling of the Holy Spirit to honor and cherish the most intimate ties which infuse all activities with rich meaning.

QUESTIONS FOR GROUP DISCUSSION
AND PERSONAL REFLECTION

1. One idea presented in this chapter may be novel to the reader—the notion that women may seek out work or a professional career to escape the ordinary, day-to-day mechanics of homemaking. The idea was developed in a book by sociologist Arlie Hochschild, *The Time Bind* (Metropolitan, 1997) and reviewed in *Newsweek*, April 28, 1997, p. 64. Do you

agree with this idea that a woman's work may be more fulfilling and more of a refuge than her marriage and home life? If so, does this reality mean that home life is now less satisfying than in other periods?

2. Do you think it is selfish for married women and mothers to work for any other reason than economic necessity?

3. Do you think the "rules" change when a husband and wife abandon the traditional working-couple situation to become a "two-career" marriage? If so, in what ways?

4. There are several facts well-established by research of the effects of women in the workplace: employed women are happier, healthier, and feel more valued, even at home, than women who are full-time homemakers. Research also shows that men do more and better child care when their wives work outside the home. Therefore, this culture is not turning back the clock on more traditional family roles.

   Have there been any "negatives" to women's mass movement into the salaried work world of men? For example, do you believe that women's advancement in the workplace during the twentieth century has undermined traditional family values? Has it threatened the acceptance of biblical teaching on gender roles and authority relationships that God established from the beginning of human history?

5. Related to the preceding question: Do you think a marriage in which both partners pursue separate careers have a different pattern of authority and decision-making than traditional marriages? Should such marriages be happier and more satisfying?

6. Let's return to the hypothetical situation cited in the text of this chapter. Imagine yourself wrapping up a work day at the office, a day you had planned to end with your mate and friends at a nice restaurant and closed with attendance at a concert featuring some of your favorite performers. Your boss announces to you that he is in a critical situation. An important meeting will be conducted the following morning and he needs help from you throughout the evening to prepare for the meeting. He does not demand that you work late, but tells you clearly that he would be ever so grateful. What do you tell your boss?

7. In a two-career marriage, would it not be possible that both careers have equal priority? That is, is it necessary for one career to be more important than the mate's career?

8. After years of debate, through the leadership of Pat Schroeder, Congress passed the Family and Medical Leave Act, which directs companies to give workers unpaid time off for emergencies. A recent Congress accepted an amendment that added several billion dollars to welfare reform providing day care services for parents forced to take jobs or lose benefits. Do you think we need more legislation to help working families? Is it government's responsibility to make life easier for families?

9. Working women may put in an extra twenty hours a week on household chores, child care, and running errands. For these women it is clear that having children does impose a stress and thus a woman should take steps to control other stresses in her life. What can a working woman do to reduce stress?

10. Do you think that time-management courses, such as those offered nationally by Franklin International Institute Incorporated, can help career professionals to balance the

often-conflicting demands of jobs, marriages, and parenting? Is the effort at balancing, where some activities must be given up, really no answer at all? Do you know of any other training that might be helpful?

11. Many working parents subscribe in good faith to careerists' most treasured rule of parenting: it isn't how much time you spend with your kids—it's how you spend the time. Is the doctrine of "quality time" a myth? In order to have "quality time," would not a parent need to invest a fair amount of pure time without straining to make it count for something special?

    Furthermore, is there any way to measure objectively "quality time"? Is playing "bumble-bee, bumble-bee, coming from the barn" or "patty-cake" designed to be a higher quality activity with children than driving children to soccer practice? Does the family dinner count as quality time if the television is on in the kitchen? Is watching television together in the den quality time? What if the TV is turned down in volume and the family is eating popcorn? All we reliably know, one writer has quipped, is that whenever time with kids is in short supply, calling it "quality time" makes parents feel better. What do you think?

12. For working parents: Considering your own work situation, what changes could you make to give greater priority to the needs of your mate and your children?

13. What sort of help do you think working men and women need from business to maintain their family values?

14. Is it possible that some companies have done so much for married and parenting employees that they have discriminated against the single and the childless? Childfree Network, a national organization based in California, has brought together about five thousand men and women who resent "parents who think they've done something truly special by having a child." Members say that they demand equal treatment and that they speak for countless others cowed into silence by "a culture of breeders."

    Is this valid? One single woman at work asked, "How do you speak out on this issue without sounding like you hate kids?" Still, with the benefits of time away for child birth, early weeks of childhood, parenting benefits at work, and so forth—are there comparable benefits for the child-free employee? Is there discrimination against the single and the childless? What do you think? Yes, this is somewhat ludicrous, but what about benefits for those who would like time away from work to care for a sick cat or dog?

15. What is the most satisfying part of your job that you would not give up no matter what?

16. What advice would you give to others about balancing a professional career with the demands of marriage and a family?

Chapter 20

When Jesus Wears Blue Jeans

The key to bringing the culture and the Church back together; to renewing the workplace and reforming the Church; to choosing Christ as the Lord of life, rather than leaving Him out of the system—may well be a movement of people who are known for their hard work, for the excellence of their effort, for their honesty and unswerving integrity, for their concern for the rights and welfare of people, for their compliance with laws, standards, and policies, for the quality of their goods and services, for the quality of their character, for the discipline and sacrifice of their lifestyle, for putting work in its proper perspective, for their leadership among coworkers—in short, for their Christ-likeness on and off the job. What could such an army of workers accomplish?

Doug Sherman and
William Hendricks

Both individuals and whole churches are sometimes ineffective teachers because their tendency is to begin with words rather than life. Our sincere efforts at teaching are unproductive because they are not rooted in life. We have not earned credibility in the eyes of the people we want to teach. We somehow think words can replace love, kindness, self-control, and goodness. . . . In

families, classrooms, offices, and neighborhoods, people are less inclined to listen to sermons than to look for examples. Without the actions, they will consider the words empty—and have no interest in hearing them. Please make it your personal goal to share the gospel with someone in your workplace this week. In doing so, use words only if you must.

Rubel Shelly

Our jobs do not simply have spiritual significance by bringing us into contact with non-Christians so we can hand out tracts and lead others to Christ. The work itself is a witness, good or bad, depending on its quality. Being skilled, competent, hardworking, and cooperative will have a great impact on our ability to form work relationships that will contain enough mutual respect for an effective verbal witness. If coworkers can't see Jesus in our work, they might not be able to see why they need Jesus in their lives.

Patrick Klingaman

The issue can do longer be evaded, as is becoming clearer everyday that the most urgent problem besetting our church is this: How can we live the Christian life in the modern world?

Dietrich Bonhoeffer

USE YOUR IMAGINATION FOR A MOMENT. SUPPOSE THAT JESUS IS conducting his earthly ministry currently in Middle Tennessee. He successfully applies for a production-line job at the Saturn plant in Spring Hill. He reports to work on the first Monday morning after his hiring wearing jeans and a plaid sport shirt. Of course, it's probably difficult to imagine Jesus wearing anything in public than a flowing white robe and even more difficult to imagine Jesus putting this assembly line job ahead of the kingdom of God. And, of course, Jesus will want to talk about his Father, and he will seek to get the other men and women in the plant to know him and his will. He most certainly will attempt to make disciples.

Now also, in the Saturn plant, is a diverse religiosity. There are quite a few Baptists, Methodists, Presbyterians, and members of the Church of Christ. This is the heart of the Bible Belt, after all. There are also quite a few Roman Catholics, some of whom moved south from the northern industrial states when opportunity knocked. There are a handful of Jews who work in the plant and a handful of adherents to the Islamic faith. There are a few Asians in the plant who regard Buddha highly. Finally, there a sizable group of nonchurched coworkers who, while not hostile to religion, do not care to hear about it or discuss it.

How would Jesus act in this work environment? Would he discuss with coworkers "the way, the truth, and the life"? Might he organize a discussion group that would meet before or after his shift begins each day? Could he read the Scriptures during break time in the break room? Could he ask for an unscheduled break to baptize another supervisor? Could he wear a tee shirt that has a religious message? Would he ask for extra days leave around Christmas? Would he seize every available opportunity to drive home (no pun intended) a religious message, perhaps by making statements such as "Saturn is just one small part of a vast universe which was created by my Father, the Spirit, and me longer ago than you can ever imagine!"

The idea gets stretched to the point of absurdity after a while, of course, but several of these questions are being raised daily by thoughtful women and men in today's workforce. During the last decade or so, hiring practices have reflected the growing cultural and religious diversity in the United States. Gone are the days when the management of any large corporation can assume that the labor force in a local unit shares the same religious faith and practice. The result is: considerable confusion about when and how employees may express their faith while at work. Problems can arise when an employee's religious customs and practices are not understood or appreciated because they appear to conflict with professional obligations or workplace harmony. The rising number of allegations of religious bias filed with the U.S. EEOC bear this out; in 1996 total complaints stood at 1,560, compared to 1,192 in 1991. To place this issue in proper perspective, however, consider that religious discrimination at the workplace makes up about 2 percent of complaints the EEOC receives each year; most other complaints are related to harassment based on gender or race, no religion.

The first amendment to the U.S. Constitution guarantees religious freedom and expression. How much freedom can be allowed in the workplace?

The answer: It all depends. If the workplace is privately owned, the workforce relatively small, and all employees share basically the same faith, religious expressions are usually welcomed by all. A church office might serve as an extreme example of an environment where ministers and support staff share the same spiritual goals and commitment; however, many small "secular" businesses as well as a growing number of "Christian" companies have established a work environment with strong religious consensus as well. In order to maintain the mission of the institution, some employers screen applicants by asking questions which determine the nature of the religious beliefs and commitment. Unlike racial or gender discrimination, religious discrimination is not typically motivated by hatred, prejudice, or some other morally unjustifiable attitude toward members of certain groups.

A major irony emerges: Employees who accuse their employers or supervisors of religious discrimination are often not being treated differently because of their religion. The problem is just the opposite. Such employees are being treated like everyone else when they contend they have the right to be treated differently because of their religion or lack of religious affiliation.

GUIDING PRINCIPLES FOR WORKPLACE RELIGION RIGHTS

If the workplace is a large corporation, or if the employer is the federal government or a state government, the rules are clearly stated. Three principles guide legal religion rights at work:

1. Drawing from the Civil Rights Act of 1964, there can be **no discrimination or preferential treatment based on religious belief.** One's religion cannot be the basis for hiring or promotion. It must not figure in job-performance evaluation.

2. There can be **no religious harassment** of employees. Religious discrimination also involves the violation of a right not to be adversely affected because of private religious practices and beliefs of employers and other employees. Although aggressive proselytizing has occurred in many companies, a worker cannot badger a coworker about faith or religious practice. A supervisor cannot require subordinates to cease reading books about Buddhist philosophy or admonish them to "go to church." A boss cannot "preach" to a worker or require a worker to attend a prayer and Bible study group.

   Employees should be protected from subjection to a hostile work environment and from religious and antireligious scorn and ridicule by supervisors or fellow workers. If Mary Jo often insults Jim about his lack of faith, her conduct must not be tolerated. If a group of coworkers tease Scott because of his Mormon commitment to a chaste and disciplined lifestyle, their conduct must not be allowed. If other workers tease Mahendra about his sex life because they know that he is a conservative Muslim and will be offended by such comments, then the organization must put an end to that harassment. An environment in which employees simply disagree amiably about religion, however, cannot be defined as "hostile."

3. Managers are required to provide **reasonable accommodation of a worker's religion,** including religious holidays and garb. Since Christians are usually not required to work on Christmas and Easter, for example, it is discriminatory to deny similar release time for Jews on Rosh Hashanah or Yom Kippur.

There are two major exceptions to the above principles: Religious organizations do not have to hire someone who is not an adherent of the official faith of the organization. The special appeal of a Christian college, for example, may be rooted in the reality that all professors and staff are members of the same church; a company which produces literature and music recordings for an entire church fellowship would certainly expect the editorial and creative staff to be members of that church. Second, supervisors in the private sector can lead a Bible study and devotional, but federal and state employers cannot command such exercises; in the case of the latter, the separation of church and state is the determining criterion.

In 1972 Congress amended Title VII by adding Section 701 (j), which declares that there is no religious discrimination if "an employer demonstrates that he is unable to reasonably accommodate an employee's or prospective employee's religious observance or practice without undue hardship on the conduct of the employer's business." If Sharif feels a need to wear a special scarf around her head all day for religious reasons, her employer should permit her to do so unless for some good reason, such as her assigned duty of running a power machine, not to do so. If Ruth needs the day off for Yom Kippur, she should be accommodated if her absence does not impose a heavy burden of the organization (maybe she can work the full day on Christmas Eve so that a Christian coworker can be dismissed early). Put simply, an employer is not acting illegally if he/she cannot afford to accommodate some unique tradition or custom of a worker. Not surprisingly, there have been a number of court cases over alleged religious discrimination which raise the question of what constitutes "reasonable accommodation" and "undue hardship."

Is there religious freedom at work? Clearly yes, if everyone adheres to these three principles intended to insure all workers are given what the First Amendment intends in terms of government neutrality and religious freedom and if all workers are treated with respect and fairness. Despite much variety in workplace environments, religious expressions may be permitted to the greatest extent possible. Workers may read their scriptures during breaks. As long as workplace efficiency is not disrupted, a worker may share religious convictions, invite a coworker to evangelistic services or some other religiously oriented activity. A supervisor may invite his/her subordinates to a child's bar mitzvah or wedding, but cannot require them to attend. In both law and ethics, common sense may be the best recourse for individual work places.

SHARING THE GOSPEL AT WORK

May the gospel be shared at work if legal guidelines are honored? Yes, absolutely. But consider that most discussions about sharing the gospel with coworkers center on words—their bluntness or subtlety, their legality, their timing, their context, and the attitude and emotion behind them. Of course, the gospel must eventually be explained in words, else there would have been no need for four narratives on the life and message of Jesus Christ. But Jesus himself apparently spent the first thirty years of his life without being a rabbi or preacher, choosing to toil in the carpentry shop or spend time in the synagogue or marketplace. Surely he modeled kindness, goodness, peace, spiritual hunger, love, and acceptance—the very heart of the kingdom ethic. After years of living the gospel, he added oral proclamation to his mighty and wondrous deeds of kindness.

The workplace may be the biggest mission field you will ever encounter. What a beautiful experience to lead a coworker to Christ who has witnessed your loving heart, kind generosity, and tranquil spirit. Millions of people all around Christians in the workplace long for these deep attributes of the human spirit. They will be moved more by the power of your example than by the eloquence of your words. The apostle Peter applied this principle to Christian wives who might become frustrated by failed attempts to convert pagan husbands by words; these nonbelieving mates might be more easily converted by exemplary behavior than by words, Peter admonished (1 Pet. 3:1–2). Words of truth are best authenticated by preceding deeds of love and kindness, and the typical workplace provides a wide range of opportunity for nonverbal "evangelism."

QUESTIONS FOR GROUP DISCUSSION
AND PERSONAL REFLECTION

1. Consider our opening illustration. If Jesus reported for work at the Saturn plant in Spring Hill, how might he dress? How would he relate to coworkers in the various work units? What do you think he would do on breaks? Would he talk about anything else besides religion? Would he buy a new Saturn automobile? (Interesting, yes, but a little preposterous to ask the last question.)

2. Consider your own workplace. Do you consider your workplace to be a mission field? What can you legally and ethically do to witness to your Christian faith amidst your coworkers?

3. Have you ever been persecuted at work because of your religious faith?

4. Do you feel that a coworker who is an atheist or agnostic deserves to have his/her "religious" views respected?

Case Study

Jane Ralston is a person you respect very much. She is super-devoted to her God and to her church. You, too, consider yourself to be a Christian, but Jane considers you less than fulfilled as a Christian until you have reached *her level* of commitment and emotional expression. Jane believes those levels can be reached by your attending her church. You attended her church one Sunday at great inconvenience to you, all in an effort to appease her. You even said nice things about your visit there, joined heartily in the song service, and complimented her preacher. All this only seemed to encourage her.

Jane is always coming by your office and wanting to sit down and discuss religion with you. You have dropped hints that such evangelistic efforts are not appropriate at work, so she attempts to schedule lunch and after hours meetings with you. Jane backs off for a while, but then she starts back in her efforts both with you and others by dropping off religious literature with sweet personal messages and promises to return and discuss the literature "after you have had a chance to read it."

You respect Jane and her high moral and religious standards. You know she has your best interests at heart. You went to college with her several years earlier, before she located such religious zeal. You even love her. But Jane is getting to be a royal pain.

What do you do about Jane?

Case Study

Tony Consiglio is a manager at a local Penney's department store; Tony learns that a young college student who works for the store part-time has announced himself to be an atheist. This employee is vocal about his atheism. Though he does not ridicule religiously committed coworkers, he is often in heated verbal dispute during work hours with them about the existence of God. It is difficult to determine who begins the heated religious discussions, which occur mostly when customer business is slow. Tony doesn't like this employee because of his atheism; he admits being uncomfortable with any atheist. Could he fire this employee? Should he?

Case Study

Bonnie McNulty is a sweet, attractive, twenty-five-year-old coworker in your office. She has an engaging personality. People like her easily. Especially men, since Bonnie is rather flirtatious. Bonnie lets it be known that she once worked for an escort service and that she has even traded sexual favors for repair service on her automobile.

Bonnie's lifestyle is somewhat offensive to one coworker, Cathy Parkey, but at least she does not have to discuss it with her. What bothers Cathy is that Bonnie is expecting her third child and this is by a third father. Bonnie "makes no bones" about the flippant way in which this child was conceived. She has never been married and does not intend to be married. Cathy has met the father of this child and he strikes Cathy as one ungrateful, insensitive dude, a "loser" all the way. Cathy is definitely not impressed.

The most bothersome thing to Cathy, as a Christian woman, is that the other fourteen women on your office-building floor are giving Bonnie a baby shower. These fourteen women are attending the shower and purchasing gifts for the expected child and the event will be held in the building's conference room after hours. Your immediate supervisor and a few others will be attending. Cathy really does not want to attend the shower, but she respects her workers and feels that nonattendance will be interpreted as both snobbery and self-righteousness.

What should Cathy Parkey do?

Chapter 21

Extraordinary Commitment
Ideals and Ideas for the Christian Professional

The development and increasing strategic importance of the professions probably constitute the most important change that has occurred in the occupational system of modern societies.

Talcott Parsons

I owe the public nothing.

J. P. Morgan

I don't wonder that so many people search blindly for the 'meaning of life.' What they don't seem to understand is that life does not have meaning through mere existence or acquisition or fun. The meaning of life is inherent in the connections we make to others through honor and obligation.

Laura Schlessinger

Guard what has been entrusted to your care.

Paul the Apostle to Timothy

We make a living by what we get. We make a life by what we give.

Winston Churchill,
Arthur Ashe, et al.

It's easy to make a buck, it's a lot harder to make a difference.

Tom Brokaw

All those who want to reach out to their fellow human beings in the context of one of the many helping professions . . . have to keep reminding themselves that they do not own anyone who is in need of care.

Henri Nouwen

If we are strong, our character will speak for itself. If we are weak, words will be of no help.

John F. Kennedy

Confidence in one's personal morality is the only reliable index to what we could expect by trusting someone with civic responsibility. Bank tellers, notaries public, pastors, judges, physicians, university presidents—all have to provide credible evidence of good personal character in order to qualify (i.e., receive certification, ordination, licensure, etc.) for these positions.

Rubel Shelly

MOST COLLEGE STUDENTS WOULD LIKE TO THINK OF THEMSELVES AS being professionals some day. The opposite of being a professional is being "unskilled," "amateur," or "ordinary." Few want to be amateur, at least not "amateurish," and no one wants to be "ordinary." Of course, not everyone who thinks of oneself as a professional is a professional.

An observation at the outset: Decades and centuries ago life was less complex. Adults performed most of the services they needed. When they needed accommodations and shelter, they built their own houses. When they needed food, they gardened. When they needed clothes, they manufactured them. The sick family member was typically treated at home with homemade remedies. Surplus earnings were usually hidden away at home with other family treasures. Someone once commented that if, in 1790, all the banks in the United States had failed, probably 75 percent of the population would never have heard of the failure and even less would have been greatly concerned. We may think it near intolerable to live in a world without plumbers, electricians, communications technicians, automotive repairmen, and many other specialists that people did not think of needing a few generations ago. (Of course, it's hard to imagine a world without bureaucrats and tax collectors, two specialists that any generation would willingly dispense.)

When did professionalism begin in history? Obviously, there is no official beginning point as to when professionals arrived on the scene. We could argue that whenever special training was required for someone's work to be acceptable, a profession was established. Prior to the early medieval era, the generic term "profession" (*pro fateri*, to confess, own, acknowledge) was understood exclusively in a religious sense; early disciples "professed the gospel" (1 Tim. 6:12) and "professed godliness" (1 Tim. 2:10). Both church leaders and ordinary members professed their allegiance to Christ and the gospel. In the broader sense, anyone who made a public declaration of faith and service to God was a professional. All along, even during biblical times there were lawyers, judges, physicians, and rabbis, who were professionals in a more specialized sense. The medieval Catholic Church used *profession* for the vows of chastity, poverty, and obedience made by those entering cloistered religious life, thus creating a religious professional elite.

The Judeo-Christian tradition from the biblical era through the Reformation enriched the concept of profession with the high moral principle of service to others in a calling that brought honor and glory to God. In the centuries after the Reformation, the professions tended to remain exclusive and small. This elite group possessed high status because they were usually attached to the king and his court. Professionals generally led the "good life"—the life of the leisurely gentleman, the life of a special class shielded from the arduous work of the masses. For centuries professionals were associated with royalty, nobility, and upper-middle classes. In modern times the standards of technical education, competence, and increasing specialization of the professions were measurably enhanced, a process which continues.

We have all been beneficiaries of the division of labor and vocational specialization. This process has laid the groundwork for modern professionalism. Even for the most intelligent women and men, there is not enough time to master every form of expertise and service. All of us need professionals at nearly every point in our lives; and even professionals need other professionals, even professionals within their own "profession" (e.g., doctors need other doctors; a lawyer may need another lawyer; a minister needs other ministers). And through professionalism in its noblest sense, we are able to attain greater skill and a higher quality of service. By producing a higher level of goods and services, the standard of living is raised for all of us.

WHO IS A PROFESSIONAL?

What is required to be a professional? (And who is a Christian professional?)

Special Training

A professional is someone who has pursued special training and education. The professional does not stop with simply knowing the fundamental principles on which a practice is based, but has received specialized training and supervised practice in advancing personal knowledge and developing skills. The surgeon, for example, will have completed basic training in biology, chemistry, health, and anatomy, but will also have studied intensely the science of human illness, treatment, medicine, and surgical techniques.

Obviously, the nature and length of the preparation and training period will vary with the character of different professions. In some fields, such as medicine and law, the requirements are clearly defined. In the professions of teaching, counseling, and ministry, the requirements will vary with the employing institution and personal views.

Certification

A professional is someone who has received clearly defined certification and/or membership within an affiliation of one's peers. Professionals are concerned about excluding from the practice of their profession all amateurs, incompetent practitioners, charlatans, and "quacks." Many professionals must certify with a board of licensing. In nearly all cases, continuing special education is required. All the major professions have developed a code of ethics, and a professional is expected to know and adhere to one's professional code.

Service of Human Need

A professional is someone who is motivated foremost by the desire to employ one's training and gifts in the service of human need and desires. Ideal as this sounds, the professional is not motivated primarily by the desire to make money, but by the desire to enhance the strength of community by promoting good health, advancing knowledge, facilitating understanding, resolving problems, enacting good legislation, and providing other services.

One's profession is, of course, a means of putting food on the table and providing many lifestyle and leisure options, and the professional need make no excuse for reasonable compensation which enables him/her a comfortable lifestyle and the resources for purchasing professional materials or attending professional meetings. The first priority of the professional, however, is rendering a service to the public, or at least to a special community of which one is involved. Even though professionals do not always live up to the ideal, the professional is rightfully expected to render the best personal service possible, quite independent from the dollar amount of reward.

Sound Judgment

A professional is someone who is expected to exercise sound judgment. Much of the professional's work is the exercise of dependable, reasonable judgment. Bankers, lawyers, accountants, physicians, social workers, educators, and engineers are just a few of the professionals whose stock in trade is a body of specialized knowledge and, ideally, a wealth of experience. Both knowledge and experience must be exercised in the best interests of the client.

Good judgment is not the exclusive domain of professionals. Even the most unskilled workers must, at times, exercise good judgment in handling raw materials and discharging other job tasks. Unskilled workers and other nonprofessionals, however, are generally not reimbursed for their judgment.

Young professionals may have only their specialized training to draw from in rendering counsel and judgment. Consequently, young professionals may make major mistakes. A young college professor fresh out of graduate school, for example, may attempt to maintain unreasonably high standards for earning an "A" in his class. A young banker may make a mistake in failing to authorize the cashing of a check, though she is following general bank policy. A young minister may quote too many Scriptures and use too little common sense in a marital counseling session. Illustrations of poor judgment in the professional world are legion.

A key element in the professional-client relationship, as in all relationships, is trust. Not only are professionals paid for using their specialized knowledge and unique experience to make judgment calls for the benefit of others, but part of the value of their professional services resides in the confidence placed in the professional's judgment. Knowing that judgment calls vary from professional to professional, most of us seek counsel from the person we trust or from someone recommended strongly to us by a third party we trust a great deal. How humbling to contemplate the reality that it may take years of interaction between a professional and a client to build strong trust—it may take only one bit of devastatingly bad judgment to destroy strong trust!

Only veteran professionals may truly know the cost and difficulties of truly effective judgment and counsel. Quite often the professional makes decisions in the most complex situations:

1. There may be uncertainty over which values are at stake (for example, providing counsel in a family's decision-making about passive euthanasia or committal of a loved relative to institutional care or an individual's decision about abortion).
2. There may be uncertainty about the relevant facts.

3. There may be uncertainty about the actual consequences of the various alternative courses of action under consideration.

4. There may be serious limitations in knowledge and practical wisdom about the problem or issue, a reality emerging from the first three limitations. Compounding the entire situation may be an urgency for the professional and/or client to take immediate action, an action which will be eventually reviewed and evaluated by other parties.

It may take half a lifetime, or longer, to build a vast reservoir of professional experience to reliably guide the professional in exercising judgment. Even judgment that is subsequently recognized as poor judgment can contribute to the expertise of the professional. "Good judgment comes from experience," as the old saying goes, "and experience comes from poor judgment." And finally, it may take several years before the judgment of a professional is validated as sound, wise judgment or is exposed as unsound, foolish judgment. Let's add patience to the long list of virtues that a professional needs.

Suppose that you as a professional have exercised poor judgment in dealing with a client. Learn from it. Move on. It's not the end of the world (well, perhaps in a few cases it could be). Never waste your pains. Never waste your mistakes.

Care and Consultation

A professional is someone whose relationship with customers and clients is based on caring, consultation. Unlike the technician who works with machines or equipment, the professional typically works directly with people. Of course, in the sense of training, technicians may think of themselves as professionals, too. Many professionals, such as surgeons and dentists, perform technical work; thus, the line between professionals and technicians is blurred.

Again, in an ideal sense, the professional cares about his/her client. The clinical psychologist cares about her counselee. The surgeon cares about his patient. The attorney cares about the organization she represents in a court of law. Even the veterinarian cares about the animals that he treats. Though the professional cares deeply, he/she does not become emotionally involved to the degree that objectivity and independence are sacrificed. Furthermore, the success of the professional-client relationship may depend on the degree of cooperation and mutual support existing between the two parties.

The professional may serve one's client in the most important and most confidential areas of one's life. The true value of a professional's service may not be measured in terms of the remuneration requested. It's also true that the best counsel and other services rendered by a professional may not be appreciated by the client. The marriage counselor who tells a couple exactly what steps that each one needs to take in order to mend their estrangement may run up against an impassable wall of denial; one or both parties in the marriage who prefer estrangement and denial over reality may then unmercifully criticize the counselor as hopelessly incompetent.

An important part of professional training is preparation for client rejection and strong client criticism.

The Christian Professional

A Christian professional is someone with extraordinary dedication to one's profession and to the whole needs of clients and whose practice is viewed as a specific ministry to others. A professional does not have to be a Christian to possess this kind of dedication, of course, but he/she does have the driving motivation of God's grace to energize one's career. Most of us expect even higher professional standards from a Christian professional than from non-Christians, and we have reason for such expectation and disappointment when a professing Christian acts unethically.

The Christian professional may well see himself/herself as the eyes, ears, feet, hands, and heart of Jesus Christ in the contemporary world. This undoubtedly is how medical missionaries consciously view their role in the mission field; other Christian professionals may be equally justified in thinking of their counsel and services to needy individuals as "being Christ" to them.

To summarize, we may now define a professional in the restricted contemporary sense as

1. an intelligent and broadly educated person;
2. possessing special training and highly developed skills and knowledge;
3. working under the discipline of an ethical code developed and enforced by a body of peers;
4. commissioned to satisfy complex needs;
5. making sound judgment and offering competent counsel;
6. participating in a caring, but honest and somewhat detached relationship;
7. entailing potentially dangerous consequences. Additionally, the Christian professional is motivated by one's love for God and is influenced in both judgment and counsel by the words and example of the Lord Jesus Christ.

Do you see the strong ethical dimension in the life of a professional? Quite clearly, ethical choice is a built-in feature of the professional life. Without ethics no one is fully professional, no matter how many problems one solves or clients one sees.

DANGERS OF PROFESSIONALISM

Is the world a better place because there are so many professionals? Surely no one would contend that automatically it is, else why would there be so many lawyer jokes? Seriously, we all know our lives are enriched by the wide number of ethical-minded, competent professionals.

There is a serious danger about professionalism, however. Because professionals are specialists, they may develop "blind spots" in their vision and condone actions that are harmful to the larger community. How easy it is for specialists to see life through the prism of their own deep, but narrow training and practice. With specialization comes one's special interests. Since humans act on the basis of self-interest, the interest of a specialist may be especially narrow and acute.

Is it not easy for professionals to act by their own set of rules? Cannot professionals develop their own sense of ethics? Can they not develop their own rationale for deeds which run counter to standards held by other professionals or nonprofessionals? When professionals organize and promote their own causes, is it not easy to neglect seeing life from perspective of the "common man"? Is it possible that because professionals have undertaken self-sacrifice and hard work in preparing for practice that they all too often believe they deserve special status, special privileges, and much higher income?

At its worst, someone has said, a profession may become a "conspiracy against the public," and at its best it can promote humane values and human welfare, thus raising the quality of life for everyone.

AREAS OF MAJOR ETHICAL CHALLENGE

Because they interact with other people in some of the most significant and, at times, confidential areas of their lives, professionals face ethical challenges that are varied and complex. Each profession is unique in its privileges and responsibilities. Keep in mind the distinctions between morality, law, and professional ethics. Some misdeeds fall into all three categories, others within only one or two. A lie about a golf score falls into the first category, even though the law and one's professional peers would be unconcerned about the falsehood. It is considered unethical for some professionals to advertise their services; although, one might contend such a breach is neither immoral or illegal.

In classifying the specific instances of ethical challenge common to both business and service professionals, one would discover that the majority might be classed under broad categories.

Conflict of Interest

A large area of gray surrounds conflict-of-interest situations in business and professional life. Perhaps no other area of business and professional ethics is so elusive or so subject to intense dispute; thus, we spend more time discussing this category of ethical challenge.

A conflict of interest may be defined as "a situation in which a person, such as a public official or other professional, has a private or personal interest sufficient to appear to influence the objective exercise of his/her official duties." In essence, two or more interests are legitimately present and are competing or conflicting.

This definition may seem too broad since it could be extended to most business and professional relationships. A general rule: *Professionals are expected to be objective, independent, and essentially disinterested when rendering their judgment and counsel to clients.* When a person in a business or professional role, a professional who must exercise a judgment upon which others appropriately rely with confidence, is subject to influences, loyalties, and temptations that would cause those who rely on that person to receive a less-qualified judgment than they have a right to expect, a conflict of interests has arisen.

Important distinctions need to be made:

1. **The conflict in a conflict of interest is not merely a conflict between conflicting interests.** The conflict occurs when a personal interest comes into conflict with an obligation to serve the interests of another. One's official duty is a duty one has because he/she has an office or position and must act in an official capacity. The personal element makes the conflict stronger; one has a personal interest when he/she stands to gain a benefit or advantage from the transaction.

2. **There is a difference between "having an interest" and "taking an interest."** "Having an interest" suggests a pre-existing state of affairs. A professional may "take an interest" in someone else's interest regarding one issue or concern. For example, an elderly single woman may ask her nephew, because he is an attorney, to help her plan her will and estate. The woman loves and trusts this nephew. The nephew thus takes an interest in his aunt's estate planning and may stand to gain in some way, but we must not conclude his legal assistance is necessarily unduly biased or otherwise illegal.

3. **There is a difference between personal and impersonal conflict of interest.** A personal interest may conflict with the interests of another, as we noted. A conflict can also arise when a professional is requested to act in the interests of two different persons or organizations. For example, an attorney may be asked to act in the interests of two different parties whose interests conflict. A public accountant may be asked to audit two competing companies; or the accountant may be asked to simultaneously act as employee for one company while serving as a public auditor insuring the accuracy of financial information reported by that company. In these ethical situations, the professional may face dilemma but not stand to gain personally from ensuing judgment.

4. **There is a difference between individual or organizational conflict of interest.** Organizations can encounter conflicts of interest that are solely organizational in nature and not simply an instance of individuals facing a conflict of interest. An organization such as an advertising firm, for example, which attempts to work for two competing businesses in the same market faces organizational conflict of interest. The advertising agency would be easily tempted to commit the greater resources of time and creativity to the business client which stands to reap greater profits and thus purchase more advertising services. Thus, the difference between personal and impersonal conflict of interests applies to organizations as well as to individuals.

The conflict of interest concept is complex, and it covers a number of moral categories wherein lines of distinction become blurred. It may require skill and good judgment to realize that you are in a conflict of interest situation. Always remember that private and personal interests can color and distort your professional objectivity.

How do you determine if you are in a real, potential, or apparent conflict of interest? Begin by asking: "Will the situation that I am in likely interfere or appear to interfere with my independent judgment that I am expected to demonstrate as a professional?"

Another method of determination has been called the "trust test": "Would significant others in my life (my clients, my employer, my friends, my professional colleagues, or the general public) trust my judgment and counsel if they knew fully of the situation I am in?" Remember that professional relationships are built on trust, and trust that is damaged not only impacts professionals and their clients, but distrust injures the entire professional field.

What do you do when you perceive a real, potential, or apparent conflict of interest? Here are four strong recommendations:

1. Make an "up front" declaration, revealing your private interest in a case or issue to the relevant parties. Let others know the factors that you feel might influence your independent judgment in a situation. You will enhance your integrity with these parties.

2. Take leave or officially remove yourself from any decision-making process in a matter in which you have a private interest. Make it clear to relevant parties that you are stepping aside completely.

3. Maintain healthy and supportive professional relationships with colleagues who zealously share your commitment to high ethical standards. Confidentially seek their advice in the "grayness" of uncertainty—times when there are compelling moral reasons to decide in diametrically opposing ways. Seek their support when the ethical path is clear but the temptation to be self-serving is strong.

4. While discharging professional responsibilities, refuse any gift, favor, or hospitality that would influence or appear to influence your action.

Incidentally, the remaining categories may also be viewed as conflicts of interest.

Abuse of Privilege

A professional quite often possesses a great deal of power and influence through his/her position with a company or other organization. The professional may possess important information and there is certain truth in the old cliche "information is power." There is an omnipresent temptation to misuse one's position for personal aggrandizement or enrichment of oneself or one's friends and family.

Political life is filled with examples of professional politicians who use their position of power and influence to enrich their own coffers, get jobs and contracts for cronies, grant favors for family and friends, and open doors for select individuals which ordinarily would not be open to them. Extortion also constitutes a misuse of position. The business or professional extortionist demands a payment from another party as a condition for making a decision favorable to that party. An extortionist may hint at deciding to take all business elsewhere unless the other party grants a special favor.

Perhaps most abuses of position and privilege may seem subtle and petty in nature. Professionals may recommend to clients other business and professional people for related services. For example, a bank loan officer arranging a home-improvement loan for a young couple may inquire if the couple has committed to a general contractor. If the couple states that they have not hired a contractor and the loan officer subsequently recommends a contractor who just happens to be the officer's brother-in-law. This influence is subtle and perhaps ethically questionable; it need not, however, be viewed as unethical unless the officer requires the couple to commit to the brother-in-law's firm as a condition for the loan.

Breach of Trust in Professional-Client Relationships

Professionals are often privy to highly private and sensitive information that is important to clients; violation of confidentiality is a major violation of trust.

For several professionals, trust and confidentiality in professional-client relationships is crucial to the effectiveness of professional service. Attorneys, counselors, therapists, accountants, corporate CEOs and directors, and physicians, among other professionals, especially require trust and confidentiality and must not divulge information acquired in confidence to advance personal interests—even if the interests of the client are not affected. There is a practical reason for maintaining confidence—counselees and other clients will not retain a professional who does not demonstrate minimal respect to keep client confidence. In some cases, violation of confidence, except in extreme cases where loss of human life is threatened, is a violation of law.

Violation of confidence by a professional is not, regrettably, such a rare and unusual occurrence, and the reasons for it may relate to carelessness or ego defense as much to personal financial gain. For example, a minister may share some confidential information that he gained from a third party in a counseling situation because, perhaps unconsciously, he thinks sharing confidential information makes him appear to be especially insightful or "in the know" and thus an important person.

The effectiveness of a professional with individual clients is rooted in certain key traits, as noted earlier: a caring relationship, respect for others, trust in one's judgment, honoring of client confidence and client feelings, and complete professionalism. A professional's violation of a client's confidence not only greatly impairs those key traits and harms the professional-client relationship—it may be devastating to the client. Professionals do well to make practical application of Paul's instruction centuries ago about trust and the gospel to a young evangelist: "Guard what has been entrusted to your care" (1 Tim. 6:20).

Fraudulent Behavior

Fraudulent behavior is action which is deceitful, manipulative, or intentional perversion of truth in order to get another party to part with something of value or surrender a legal right; a "fraud" is an imposter, one who is not what he/she pretends to be.

Fraudulent behavior is usually more blatantly in violation of law and ethical standards than typical incidents of conflict of interest. Physicians and other medical personnel who made false claims of service to patients or who required services they knew were not needed in order to maximize profits under the U.S. government's Medicare program provide a clear example of fraudulent behavior. Fraudulence may involve outright deceit, false claims, deliberate default on goods or services, destruction of materials, and/or undermining standard business and professional practices. Bribes and kickbacks may be included in this list of fraudulent behavior.

Unprofessional Conduct

Unprofessional conduct covers a wide range of behavior or traits which do not conform to high ethical standards or which represent a violation of trust that clients and the general public expect a professional to maintain. In a sense, this is a "catch-all" category which might include all kinds of unethical professional behavior that may not fit as easily in other categories.

Unprofessional conduct is the opposite of professionalism, which is ethical behavior that meets the highest aims and greatest qualities that mark a profession (or professionals in general). All illegal professional behavior is unprofessional conduct, of course, though we generally use the term to refer to unethical professional conduct which is not illegal and not subject to the harshest sanctions.

All adults who, for years, have sought the services of a wide range of professionals have surely been impacted by unprofessional conduct. Examples of such conduct may seem endless: A surgeon may delay making hospital rounds at the scheduled time, asking that his nurse report that he is in emergency surgery, while he stays home an extra three hours to watch his favorite football team in action. A minister may cancel a long-scheduled meeting with a congregation because he simply does not want to meet his commitment, but he uses his wife's "illness" as an excuse or a "providential hindrance" for his unwillingness to honor that commitment. A male university professor may ask a date from a coed in his class that he finds attractive (at some universities dating is forbidden among instructors and students while the student is enrolled in the instructor's class). An editor may conduct a private free-lance operation and solicit clients who ordinarily seek to contract with the firm for which she works. A banker may divulge to his best friend some financial information about a bank customer that this close friend is curious about. A chief executive might cancel some important appointments, having his secretary make last minute calls and report that her boss was unexpectedly called away, while he joins old cronies to go deer hunting for the day. A writer may conduct negotiation for publication of a manuscript with one firm, all the while conducting negotiations with other firms; each firm commits staff time to her manuscript without knowing she is dealing with other firms. A politician may deliver a speech that is totally plagiarized from another source. A therapist may continue recommending that a client continue making counseling appointments because her case load is low and not because she can offer any further stimulus for positive change. In a private meeting with a group of university students, one professor might attack the instructional competence and personality skills of another professor in a misguided desire to win the group's appreciation. A surgeon may recommend an operation that is totally covered by insurance but is not likely to help the patient.

The ethical sensitivity and conscience of the professional are crucially important in determining the level of professional conduct. So much of the behavior that is neither clearly forbidden by the professional code nor illegal by the criminal code falls into varying shades of gray. Impressions and appearances become almost as important for the same professionals, especially those in careers of moral persuasion, as do realities. The admonition of the apostle Paul might be heeded with great value, "Abstain from all appearance of evil" (1 Thess. 5:22, KJV)

There is great power in a written code of ethics, especially when it is posted and frequently communicated to all concerned parties. But nothing can compare to the power of a role model. What we *do* is clearly more important than what we say we *should* do.

SUCCEEDING IN THE BUSINESS AND PROFESSIONAL WORLD

Let's get practical before closing this chapter: In their work *The Ethical Executive*, Donald Seibert and William Proctor cite ten qualities a person would need to succeed as a business executive. They are briefly cited and adapted for our purposes here because all of these qualities are generally helpful in succeeding as a professional in various service fields as well.

1. **Willingness to continue your formal education.** In today's economy a college degree has become almost a prerequisite for entry into the world of business management; an appropriate graduate degree can give you short-term advantage. As for professions, college education and further graduate education are usually required.

2. **Willingness to continue your informal education.** Demonstrate that you have an active mind and wide range of interests by extra reading and attending workshops, seminars, and other forms of continuing education. Successful people share one thing in common—a high vocabulary. They are also effective in group communication.

3. **Willingness to operate at maximum capacity with minimum compulsiveness.** Test the limits of just what constitutes "working hard" and "your best." Those above you are evaluating your level of dedication to maintaining a high level of productivity. "With minimum compulsiveness" means performing without becoming a rigid perfectionist.

4. **Willingness to be sociable.** You do not have to be the "life of the party" or an aggressive extrovert—just develop a genuine communicativeness with others. Be able to engage in serious conversation. Listen. Be sincere and pleasant.

5. **Willingness to compete for first place.** Seek to be first in a fast field of excellent talent without the "killer instinct" or beating up on others. Strive to do your best.

6. **Willingness to take risks on your own creativity.** Do not be timid in presenting your unique ideas to your superiors. "Nothing ventured, nothing gained" applies to all businesses and professions.

7. **Willingness to be self-confident.** Much failure is rooted in reluctance to develop self-confidence. Focus on potential successes and strengths rather than on failures and weaknesses. Speak up and let your views be known, even if you occasionally get shot down.

8. **Willingness to communicate openly with your superiors.** Promote yourself if you intend to make it as an executive. Call your superiors' attention to your achievements. Take the initiative to keep the lines of communication open with your boss.

9. **Willingness to laugh during business hours.** While a business and professional career involves serious business, the one who takes life and business too seriously is at a disadvantage. Develop a great sense of humor, the ability to laugh appropriately even in grim situations.

10. **Willingness to settle on a comprehensive value system.** Develop a broad set of values that encompasses more than just the profit motive. A commitment to integrity may be the most important trait in the chances for business success and advancement. (This point has been has already been underscored numerous times in this book.)

QUESTIONS FOR GROUP DISCUSSION AND PERSONAL REFLECTION

1. Do you agree that there should be specific criteria for determining who is a "professional"?
2. What is the distinction between between a profession and a business?
3. What is the relationship between morals, laws, and professional ethics?
4. Should money and personal wealth constitute a major factor in determining the profession one enters? How profit-oriented do you think professionals should be?
5. On what basis does a professional determine what to charge clients for service?
6. Is there any justification for the practice of some professionals overcharging the wealthy and undercharging the poor for their services? If so, on what basis is it justified? Are there any dangers? Does it make the professional something of a judge or legislator, collecting "taxes" from the wealthy and dispensing "welfare" to the poor?
7. Should professionals offer services free of charge to any client or group of people? If so, to whom?
8. This chapter noted briefly some major temptations faced by professionals to act unethically. Can you cite additional illustrations of each of these major temptations?
9. Since 1890 hundreds of business and professional groups in the United States have adopted codes of ethics. Some of the codes are vague and generalized in their phraseology.

Others are more or less perfunctory and do not seem to be taken seriously by the entire membership of the profession. (You might want to review what was said about professional codes in chapter 1.) What are the values of professional codes of ethics to members of a profession? To the general public?

10. In your opinion, which is the profession that presents the greatest ethical challenges to men and women in that profession?

11. What are some instances of unprofessional conduct that you have personally experienced?

12. The Jim Carrey character in the movie *Liar, Liar* is a young, divorced attorney who pursues his professional career at the expense of spending quality time with his son. At a birthday party in which the father is absent due to a distraction with a female boss, the son makes a wish that his father could never tell a lie for a twenty-four-hour period. Early in the story the attorney has reached the conclusion there is no way he can win without lying in a divorce proceeding if he represents a client with a weak case.

   Is it possible to be a highly effective professional without occasionally telling lies? Could a practicing attorney maintain his/her success without lying?

13. Professionals are expected to be fair, independent, and objective in discharging responsibilities. It is important to avoid apparent and potential as well as actual conflicts of interest. An apparent conflict of interest is a situation in which a reasonable, outside observer might think that a professional's independent judgment is likely to be compromised.

   Which of the following practices would you consider to be flagrant violations of professional ethics:

   a. "Moonlighting"—Outside employment which may or may not be in direct competition with one's employer. Consider that the moonlighter might take on so many extra assignments that there is much less time and energy to devote to the full-time, regular employing organization.

   b. Use of company property for private advantage—This could range from taking home office supplies for private use to a major equipment or materials theft; it might include personal use of software which is licensed to the employer for organizational use. When would a supervisor's permission eliminate any of this conflict?

   c. Accepting gifts and other benefits—This could range from major bribery to accepting small gifts.

   d. "Self-dealing"—One uses an official position to secure a contract for a private company that you, a relative, or a friend owns.

   e. "Influence-peddling"—One solicits benefits in exchange for using personal influence to advance unfairly the interests of another party.

   f. Post-employment—A professional retires or resigns from a private or public position, having received training and expertise, and opens a new business in the same service area in direct competition with the former employer.

14. Case study from twentieth century history: Professionals are called and dedicated to high ideals. Yet, how does one explain the fact that some professionals have been among the worst criminals in history? Other professionals have entered exploitative relationships with people.

   The most extreme illustration of this fact is the participation of political, legal, medical, and management professionals during the Nazi regime under Adolph Hitler.

The Holocaust is surely the most ethically challenging judgment that could be made on professionals. Political professionals acting under Hitler planned the death camps. Management professionals organized operations for both death and labor camps. "Human resources" experts selected who was fit to work, the others allowed to die. Physicians performed all manner of ghastly experiments on Jewish subjects for the sole purpose of satisfying morbid curiosity. The sheer magnitude of a genocidal policy that exterminated six million Jewish people depended not simply upon Nazi thugs, though there were thugs aplenty, but upon professionals devoted to the Nazi cause.

Given the education, calling, and public commitment of professionals to serving the public interest, should we be shocked when professionals are found guilty of terrible crimes and sins? What explanation might be proposed for understanding the role of professionals in the Nazi regime?

15. Is there anything wrong with a professional having private or personal interests, such as a strong interest in a salary increase or in his/her son making the tennis team at the local high school? If not, when is there a conflict between private interest and official interest?

16. Is there any chance of you personally being in a real or apparent conflict of interest situation in your current position (or the career you plan to enter)? What steps would you take to prevent such conflicts?

17. What do you think would lead one professional to attack another? What, for example, would drive one preacher to attack another preacher in a national publication without having talked with the person whose motives and doctrinal positions he attacks?

18. Would you consider one professional's attack on the competence (or lack thereof) of another professional in the same career to be unprofessional conduct?

19. Do you agree with the text about the dangers of professionalism? Is there anything wrong with professionals organizing to protect their own mutual interests? Can you cite examples of the dangers of professionalism?

20. Do you believe that maintaining a high level of skill and competence in one's career is a matter of professional ethics?

21. Were there characters in biblical times that you would call "professionals"?

22. If an attorney, minister, or therapist gains information as to the identity or whereabouts of criminals who are sought by the police, what is the professional's duty? Do members of the different professional groups have the same duties?

23. When you consult with a professional for personal services or advice (e.g., a minister, a physician, or therapist), is it more important to you that the professional possess a high level of skill and competence within the field, and thus have the respect of professional colleagues, or is it more important for the professional to have a loving, caring, and genuine attitude toward you as a person?

24. Read Paul's charge to Timothy, the young evangelist he loved, in 1 Timothy 6:11–21. Paul was giving both spiritual and ethical advice that an evangelist of the gospel of Christ needed. How much of the advice can be applied to Christian professionals in other callings besides Christian ministry?

25. Does the term "professional Christian" make any sense? Before God, are not all Christians "amateur"? Can anyone be a specialist before God? And what about "professional minister in the church?" Isn't the heart of ministry a service to God and others and not a professional subject to credentials, salary, peer review, social status, and recognition?

26. In the appendix there is a decalogue for homemakers. It was entered almost inadvertently. A friend of the author, Stacy Clayton, was typing this manuscript. After reading some of the dialogues of professionals, she decided to enter a simple one of her own. An early temptation was to delete it, but it remained in a draft of this manuscript and was chosen by some students as one of their favorites.

Question: Do you consider the homemaker to be a professional? To say "I am a homemaker" in answer to the question "What do you do?" usually terminates any conversation about work. Most of us feel like a homemaker's role has been determined for many generations. Is that a fair conclusion? Is a homemaker's work so routine and mundane, and skills required so elementary, that we would not conclude the homemaker is a professional? The homemaker, almost always female, is often caricatured as a woman with low skills, low glamour, low awareness, and little contribution to actual family income. We remember that Jesus commended Mary's spiritual curiosity and seemed to condemn Martha's household busyness (Luke 10:38–41).

On the other hand, consider homemaking as a creative work of several arts which range far beyond routine household duties. In its broadest sense, homemaking nurtures the family at the very heart of what constitutes a family—its most intimate relationships, its values, its strengths, its traditions, its unique character. The homemaker is more than a cook and maid; she serves also as nurse, educator, negotiator, time-management expert, psychologist, and minister, to name a few roles. The Christian homemaker knows that physical acts can have emotional and spiritual significance. The Christian homemaker also has the opportunity to model Christ's unconditional love. Put another way, the Christian homemaker has a wonderful opportunity to create a total living environment where people matter more than material possessions.

Again: Do you consider the homemaker to be simply a worker? an artist? a professional?

Important Note To The Reader

The number of case studies presenting ethical dilemmas for professionals is so numerous and could constitute a large separate volume itself. Case studies prepared for the conclusion of this chapter are thus deleted. However, in the appendix there is a collection of decalogues written by professionals for others in the same fields of service. Some are intended to be facetious and some only half-serious; most are totally serious. Obviously, no effort was made to include all professions.

Appendices

Glossary of Key Terms

Affirmative action—Programs of hiring or placement which take into account race or gender for the purpose of eliminating the sources of job discrimination.

Asset—Something of value owned by a person or corporation, including the right to collect sums of money in the future or the expectation of business from a given community in the future.

Bribe—Remuneration for the performance of an act that's inconsistent with the work contract or the nature of the work one has been hired to perform.

Calling—The summons of God to live one's whole life for his glory; vocation. The work done at an occupation or in a career may be viewed as a way of fulfilling a calling.

Capital—Purchasing power (money) which is not converted, and not likely to be converted soon, to goods or services.

Capitalism—Ideally, an economic system in which the major portion of production and distribution of goods and services is in private hands, operating under a profit or market system. A capitalist system is in contrast with socialism, an economic system characterized by public ownership of property and a planned economy. The key features of capitalism: existence of business companies; a profit motive as the reason for the company's existence; open competition among business firms in the free market; private property and private control over basic economic assets and productive resources.

Career—An occupation for which people train and in which people expect to earn their living for most of their working years. A career is part of one's calling, but must not be equated with calling or vocation.

Caveat emptor—A principle in commerce; without a warranty the buyer takes the risk of quality upon himself/herself; "let the buyer beware."

CEO—Chief executive officer of a corporation or other business.

Collegiality—A relationship of colleagues who share almost equally in authority and responsibility. In a work place, collegiality might involve a basic respect for colleagues, mutual appreciation for each other's work, a sense of connectedness by shared mission and common commitment, and a spirit of cooperation toward achieving common goals.

Contract—A legally binding promise, made by two or more parties, to do or refrain from doing a certain thing, often for the purchase of goods or services in exchange for something of value.

Corporate culture—A general constellation and mindset of shared beliefs, values, mores, customs, behavioral norms, and standard ways of conducting business that are unique to each corporation. Corporate culture may be both explicit and implicit, and its nature is determined more by the beliefs and decisions of high-level managers than by any other party within the corporation. Corporate culture may be a factor that makes one company work while another one languishes.

Corporation—An organization owned by its stockholders, interested individuals or other organizations who contribute capital to the corporation in return for shares (partial ownership) in the corporation. Corporations are legal persons with rights and obligations; they can own property and enter into contracts; they can sue and be sued in civil court, and they can be tried in criminal court. Stockholders' control over a corporation is usually indirect.

Kickback—A percentage payment to a party who is in a position to influence or control a source of income.

Laissez-faire—An economic doctrine, especially popular in parts of Europe and the United States in the nineteenth century, which called for little or no governmental control or interference in a capitalistic economy.

Loyalty—A faithfulness and allegiance to any of the following: one's calling, one's employer, one's company or corporation, one's colleagues, or one's clients. One's loyalty leads to faithfully discharging responsibilities toward these parties.

Moonlighting—The act of an employee taking on employment for more than one employer during the same general period of time (such as a night job when one has a day job), sometimes explicitly prohibited by certain employment contracts.

Nepotism—The practice of showing favoritism in employment practices and employee relations to relatives and close friends. Nepotism raises serious moral concerns regarding both managerial responsibilities and of fairness to other employees or job applicants.

Norm—A working principle that in some way is accepted by all or most of an organization as a standard for decision-making, but may not be written or promulgated officially.

Profession—Professions are occupations assumed by a limited number of people and require advanced education and specialized training, sophisticated skills, and commitment to service to some vital public good. Usually, professionals develop relationships with clients based on caring, consultation, and consent. Because of the specialized nature of professional services and the wide variety of possible services and courses of action, as well as fees charged for same, moral dilemmas arise frequently for professionals.

Proprietary data or trade secrets—Special private information that can affect a firm's competitive standing in the free market. A trade secret is any formula, device, pattern, or special information which is peculiar to one business firm thus giving it advantage over competitors who do not know or use it.

Protestant work ethic—A philosophy about vocation and work which emerged from the theological writings of the great Protestant reformers, such as Martin Luther and John Calvin. Key elements of the "Protestant Work Ethic" include these notions: (1) All work, not simply the ministry of "holy men," is dignified; even the menial becomes holy; (2) all persons are held accountable for integrity in their work under the eye of the Lord of the universe; (3) all work thus becomes serious, therefore one must work with diligence and care from dawn to dusk; (4) the virtuous worker demonstrates frugality and simplicity in lifestyle, because nothing should be wasted on sins of the flesh; (5) there is meaning and purpose to work, even work that seems like menial operations; (6) the laborer should give liberally to charity; and (7) the inevitable fruit of one's labor will be material prosperity, for indeed "God helps those who help themselves."

Responsibility—A position of trust which involves accountability, answerability, sometimes liability, but also rewardability. Typically it includes authority, benefits, and superior-subordinates relationships.

Rights—A right is an entitlement to act or have others act in a certain way. Rights and duties are connected: if you have a right to do something, all others have a correlative duty to act in a certain way. Legal rights are guaranteed by law. Moral rights are derived from special relationships, roles, or circumstances in which we find ourselves. Human rights do not depend upon special relationships, roles, or circumstances (e.g., the unalienable rights to life, liberty, and pursuit of happiness); human rights are universal and they are equal rights and they are non-transferable.

Stockholders—Individuals or corporations who have loaned money to a corporation by purchasing shares of stock (thus a partial interest) in the corporation in exercising the theory and practice of capitalism.

Takeover—The purchase by one business of another, with the purchasing business becoming the owner of the other and responsible for continuing or discontinuing its former activities; when this occurs through stock purchases against the wishes of the business being acquired, it is called a "hostile takeover."

Trade secret—Information learned by an employee in the service of an employer, thus considered the property of the employer and unable to be used by the employee except at the direction of or with the permission of the employer; typically the subject of a contract between employer and employee.

Vocation—The work in which a person is regularly employed, often with a sense of compelling inclination or divine calling.

Work—In a general sense, any form of expending energy to produce something of value, regardless of whether one is paid for it. In a narrower and more common usage, work is an activity for which the laborer receives compensation, financial or otherwise, and that most frequently occurs outside the family and home.

Work ethic—A collection of expectations which define what employers and employees expect of each other and perform for each other.

"Wrongful discharge"—The termination by an employer of an employee's contract without just cause, often alleged in lawsuits whether the contract is in writing or its elements are able to be known by a series of oral agreements and/or patterns of continued behavior.

Appendix B

Decalogues for Professionals

TEN COMMANDMENTS FOR A TEACHER

1. Thou shalt treat each student fairly, remembering that fair doesn't mean equal like in math but that each student receives what he or she needs.
2. Thou shalt weigh all of your words carefully because it is impossible to measure their impact. A positive word from a teacher might bring tremendous change to the life of a student. Negative words can do more damage than we can imagine.
3. Thou shalt work in partnership with parents to prepare each student for life's journey with the knowledge that we can't always clear the path for the child but we can prepare the child for the path.
4. Thou shalt respect each student and treat him or her the way you would want your own child treated.
5. Thou shalt find joy in wrestling alligators while wading hip deep in mud because teaching is often just like that.
6. Thou shalt teach secure in the knowledge that years from now it will be of no consequence what material success you may or may not have had but you may be considered successful because you made a difference in the life of a child.
7. Thou shalt have high expectations for all of your students. Children often achieve little because little is required of them. Require their best!
8. Thou shalt teach expecting success but knowing that some of life's best lessons come from our failures. Students need to be taught to gain from their failures as well as their successes.
9. Thou shalt always give your very best. The profession demands it and is worthy of it.
10. Thou shalt remember that teachers make a nation. Students of every race and creed sit in our classrooms and we teach them our interpretation of what it is to be an American.

Contributed by Debbi Lanham, fourth-grade teacher
Walnut Grove Elementary School, Franklin, Tennessee

TEN COMMANDMENTS FOR BANKING AND INVESTMENT

1. Thou shalt always act in the best interest of the client *and* the bank. The banker is experienced with the products and services he provides and most times has a greater understanding of the financial benefit they might have on the client and the risks associated with the products. The banker can easily be in a position to "sell" a product to a customer that is not appropriate for various reasons, and the banker profit in the transaction. The banker may also often find himself in a position of leverage in a client relationship and be tempted to take undue advantage of that leverage for gain. The ethical banker will always seek a win/win situation whenever possible.

2. Thou shalt not commit fraud. The banker, as any business person, is often in situations where misrepresenting the truth might be advantageous. The banker should always totally disclose all information that is relevant to a transaction, not misrepresenting the truth or hiding things in "fine print."

3. Thou shalt not betray the trust relationship between the bank(er) and client. In the ordinary course of business, the banker has considerable knowledge of his clients' dealings, both financially and otherwise. It is strictly forbidden to disclose that knowledge to someone outside of those who "need to know," outside the company, or to use any of the information for leverage or personal gain.

4. Thou shalt always *right* any *wrongs*. Bankers, just like anybody else, make mistakes. When mistakes are made, it is essential that banker disclose the mistake and take action to correct the error and make whole anybody who may have been harmed, either financially or otherwise.

5. Thou shalt provide timely advice and work to protect the client's best interest. Most bankers who are in the business of lending money have had a customer ask the bank to become a party to a transaction (usually a loan) where the client themselves are taking extreme risks. The idea of risk is, of course, a relative term, and what might be considered risky for some may not be for others. It may be appropriate for some clients to take risks and not appropriate for other clients. The banking officer certainly does not want the client to suffer financial damage above what he or she is able to recover. While this is a judgment call, the banker should make an unpopular decision to discourage the client in a high-risk situation, even if it costs a banker-client relationship.

6. Thou shalt be extremely careful when accepting gifts or favors from clients or potential clients. Usually these gifts are not significant in nature and only a show of respect or appreciation. However, sometimes these gifts can become extremely expensive and enticing, especially where a client is seeking special treatment or privileges. The banker should always use caution in these matters and not allow the client to "buy" influence with these gifts.

7. Thou shalt always act to protect the interest of the shareholders. Bankers must always remember their primary responsibility is to protect the interest of the

shareholders (owners of the company) and maximize the return on their investment, both short and long term.

8. Thou shalt not be too rigid beyond the sense of reasonableness and fairness. All loans carry a degree of risk; however, the bank's lending policy and the training of their lending personnel is designed to manage that risk within acceptable levels. The lending officer should always do what is right for the bank, not necessarily what is popular for the customer.

9. Thou shalt respect your competitor. Because of a common calling and mutual interest in the financial health of the community, bankers have every reason to respect their competitor.

10. Thou shalt always treat fellow associates with the same courtesy and respect as you would a client or prospective client. Banking and investment professionals share a calling of public service to fellow citizens. Professional training and wise judgement are required of executives in finance management. These achievements earn for your associates a high measure of your personal respect and fair treatment.

Contributed by Kent Cleaver, senior vice president
First Union National Bank

TEN COMMANDMENTS FOR HOMEMAKERS

1. Thou shalt acknowledge that one's home and children belong first to God and second to you.
2. Thou shalt make home a haven, a place where its residents can escape the outside storm and not enter a storm.
3. Thou shalt keep negative criticism outside the doors of the home.
4. Thou shalt acknowledge and respect God's presence in the home daily.
5. Thou shalt strive for a reasonable amount of orderliness and cleanliness in the home.
6. Thou shalt remember that the responsibility of teaching all things to children lies first within the home.
7. Thou shalt discipline one's mind and body to be fit, not only to feel good while doing manual work but to enhance the appeal of "being home" for all family members.
8. Thou shalt avoid laziness, idle talk, and excessive spending.
9. Thou shalt put thy spouse before thy children.
10. Thou shalt create a home atmosphere where the very young and the very old feel equally loved and welcomed.

Contributed by Stacy Clayton, homemaker
Franklin, Tennessee

TEN COMMANDMENTS FOR CHRISTIAN COUNSELORS

1. Remember that the primary responsibility of counselors is to respect the integrity and promote the welfare of clients. Thou must also respect the values and beliefs of the clients and take care not impose one's own values on clients.
2. Thou shalt not try to become a "savior" but rather just a people helper. Respect the rights and diversity of each client. A counselor should recognize the limits of testing and testing equipment.
3. Thou shalt not think thou can "cure" thy clients. A counselor must aim for positive client growth and development and avoid fostering dependent counseling relationships. A counselor is not a "control freak" but a facilitator of healthy change.
4. Thou shalt keep thy God and thy family before thy profession. It is God you worship and serve and family you love and for whom you provide. Thou shalt not mix thy personal life with thy professional life.
5. Thou shalt not exploit the trust and the dependency of clients. Most of all, counselors do not have any type of sexual intimacies with clients and do not counsel persons with whom they have had a sexual relationship.
6. Thou shalt make every effort to avoid dual relationships with clients that could impair thy professional judgment or increase the risk of harm to clients. When the dual relationship (such as social, business, or familial) cannot be avoided, the counselor must take appropriate professional precautions such as informed consent, consultation, supervision, and documentation to ensure that judgment is not impaired and no exploitation occurs.
7. Thou shalt not abandon clients in counseling if their needs persist, but provide appropriate arrangements for continuation of treatment, when necessary, following termination. If counselors determine an inability to be of professional assistance to clients, they must avoid entering or immediately terminate a counseling relationship. Relationships must be terminated when it is reasonably clear that the client is no longer benefiting from the services.
8. Thou shalt allow the Bible to inform and guide thy general principles and values. Thou must not, however, expect the Bible to provide a scripture which deals with each mental and personality disorder.
9. Thou shalt keep the confidentiality of the counselor/client relationship. Thou must take steps to avoid unwarranted disclosures of confidential information. Disclosure is required to prevent harm to the client or others or when legal requirements demand the confidential information be revealed. Counselors make every effort to ensure that privacy and confidentiality of clients are maintained by subordinates, associates, clerical assistants, and any others under his or her supervision.
10. Thou shalt realize the situations when thou needest to seek the advice of another counselor. Thou must maintain positive professional relationships with other counselors and draw from their wisdom and encouragement.

Contributed by Deena Trimble, counselor and teacher, and the author

TEN COMMANDMENTS FOR COUNSELORS
(on the lighter side)

1. Thou shalt not try to change a light bulb until it is ready to be changed.
2. Thou shalt refer borderline personality disorder and suicide clients to thy competition.
3. Thou shalt not write the psychological report before doing the testing.
4. Thou shalt read Ann Landers and "Dear Abby" daily to keep abreast of the latest advice. It is wise also to listen to "Doctor Laura" Schlessinger for more complicated counseling situations.
5. Thou shalt not represent thyself as competent to counsel unless thou hast raised teenagers.
6. Thou shalt not break confidentiality with thy client unless he or she threatens to sue you.
7. Thou shalt confront thy colleagues who are stealing money from the coffee machine.
8. Thou shalt keep dual relationships to a minimum—no more than one at a time.
9. Thou shalt not continue to conduct research on thy little brother without thy mother's consent.
10. Thou shalt not listen to thy own advice.

Contributed by Deena Trimble

TEN COMMANDMENTS FOR LEGISLATORS

1. Thou shall not steal ideas from another political party and claim them as thine own.
2. Thou shall keep thy promises despite the political consequences.
3. Thou shall support real issues, ones that affect the daily lives of at least 20 percent of the people.
4. Thou shall be beholden to the interests of all citizens, not just those who elected you.
5. Thou shall follow the dictates of thy conscience, not blindly following socially accepted standards of moral relativism.
6. Thou shall not bear false witness, even if it means losing a few votes.
7. Thou shall not make for yourself idols in the form of high-powered, deep-pocketed lobbyists.
8. Thou shall not lust after another politician's pork.
9. Thou shall disclose all information that concerns the public interest, even if you know the public doesn't want to hear it.
10. Thou shall not covet thy colleague's seniority, popularity, political skills, or ability to secure extracurricular companionship.

Contributed by Josh Brown,
aid to Tennessee Governor Don Sundquist

TEN COMMANDMENTS FOR LIBRARIANS

1. Revere and respect the power and beauty of the written word; always remember that books are the cornerstones of our civilization and they possess the power to transform lives.
2. Dedicate yourself in a service profession to the highest levels of service to all your patrons at all times.
3. Consider it a noble responsibility to preserve the knowledge you access and store for future generations, whether the form be print, media, electronic, or other.
4. Always uphold the principles of intellectual freedom, resisting efforts to censor or bias the thinking of individuals. Inherent in this principle is also the protection of the rights of users to privacy and confidentiality.
5. Recognize and respect intellectual property rights.
6. As you face the new millennium, it is essential to be flexible and open to change, realizing that your traditional roles as information gatekeepers are changing to information navigators, and you are building ramps to the superhighways.
7. Do not advance your private interests or opinions or bias at the expense of users, colleagues, or employers.
8. As professionals, continue to strive for excellence, to enhance your own knowledge and skills, to encourage professional development, and to foster the aspirations of potential members of your profession.
9. Recognize that your influence is broader than your physical walls, just as the influence of books cannot be contained between their covers; as a part of the community of the book, you are an advocate always for the importance of reading.
10. Remember that in any great society, the freedom to read is not merely a privilege—it is a necessity. In our great society, an alarming number are disenfranchised citizens because they cannot read; thus the challenge to conquer illiteracy is especially yours to answer.

Contributed by Carolyn T. Wilson, collection development librarian
David Lipscomb University, Nashville, Tennessee

TEN COMMANDMENTS FOR TRAINERS
AND ADULT EDUCATORS

1. Thou shalt overprepare thy subject matter and teach from the overflow of thy knowledge and experience.
2. Thou shalt not underprepare thy presentation and attempt to overcome thy inadequacy with fillers and flamboyance.
3. Thou shalt use various media for learning—thereby acknowledging that students have different learning styles and no one style/medium is effective for all learners.
4. Thou shalt feel responsible for making learning fun and interesting—not boring, pedantic, or punishing.
5. Thou shalt have unbounding enthusiasm for thy subject matter and its value and application. Without this, surrender thy role to another who has this essential attribute.
6. Thou shalt always assume the attitude of learner—even though thy formal designation may be teacher, lecturer, trainer, instructor—so that thou may always be learning from others, especially thy students.
7. Thou shalt not humiliate, degrade, demean, nor diminish anyone who appears not to understand the content of your instruction or question your presentation thereof—either overtly or subtly. Use their lack of understanding or question to challenge thyself to more effectively convey thy material and question thine own understanding.
8. Thou shalt not assume the posture of always being right—of having the right answer to any question about thy subject matter.
9. Thou shalt humbly approach assessing student learning of the subject matter—fully acknowledging that recitation of content does not imply understanding nor value of application.
10. Thou shalt not take advantage of thy role as an instructor and assume the role of authority figure or replace thy students' own thinking and reasoning with thine own beliefs and values.

Contributed by Nan Macleod, senior consultant in Human Resources
Bell Helicopter, Ft. Worth, Texas

TEN COMMANDMENTS FOR CERTIFIED
PUBLIC ACCOUNTANTS

1. Thou shalt always place service above self. Always keep your attention on the client first and foremost without worrying about your personal fees. If you are concerned foremost with your client's bottom line, your own "bottom line" will take care of itself.
2. Thou shalt do more than what is expected of you. Always think proactively in relation to the client. Do trouble-shooting before a potential problem gets out of hand.
3. Thou shalt stretch yourself a little more than you think you can in regard to a client's challenge—energize yourself, work smart, come early, stay late, be persistent.
4. Thou shalt be diligent to communicate directly and effectively with your client. Communicate at the level of understanding of each client.
5. Thou shalt take special care to maintain independence and avoid conflict of interest. Take steps which enable you to make decisions for your client without allowing personal emotions to sway or distort your best professional judgment.
6. Thou shalt always be fair to all sides of the financial equation.
7. Thou shalt give due diligence to any questionable transactions that you stumble upon. Investigate questionable transactions thoroughly in order to reach a reasonable resolution based on fairness and legality.
8. Thou shalt guard client confidentiality zealously. Remember that financial matters are considered more personal information than even health records (in many cases C.P.A.s know more about their clients than do the clients' physicians).
9. Thou shalt attempt always to provide a fair and justifiable material advantage to each client.
10. Rememberest that thou art human. If you or a client discover that you have made an error, then admit the error immediately and emphatically—your client will respect you even more by admitting your mistake.

Contributed by Melody Smiley, C.P.A.
Franklin, Tennessee

TEN COMMANDMENTS FOR ADVERTISERS, MARKETERS, AND SALESPEOPLE

1. Thou shalt always make thy client's best interest to be thy own self interest. Do not sell or promote anything you do not believe is good for the client.
2. Thou shalt always be truthful in advertising and discussing a product or service. Never, never make false or deceptive claims about your product or your competitors' products and services. Rely more on logic than on emotion to sell your product.
3. Thou shalt never use exploitative advertising in regards to marketing children's products.
4. Thou shalt never advertise or have a price promotion on one product and not have the product stocked in order to induce the purchase of a higher priced or alternative product.
5. Thou shalt never use celebrity endorsers who are not sold on the product or service.
6. Thou shalt carefully consider the products to be advertised and under no circumstances advertise or promote cigarettes and alcohol to children.
7. Thou shalt use discretion in using sex or sex appeal to advertise or sell a product or service.
8. Thou shalt not create false needs in a client or exploit people to sell a product.
9. Thou shalt never exert unwanted pressure on a customer to sell a product or service.
10. Thou shalt never allow the making of personal income to be thy only incentive to sell. Remember that fortune-driven salespeople may do anything to sell any product even it is unneeded, harmful, or deadly. Again, your customer's best interest is your best interest.

Contributed by the author

TEN COMMANDMENTS FOR PREACHERS
(with tongue half in cheek)

1. Thou shalt never attempt to baptize a full size adult in less than two feet of water.

2. Check every button, snap, and zipper before delivering thy sermon, always remembering that it is only the truth that you want to reveal.

3. Thou must never be late for a funeral or wedding and always make certain that thou hast gotten all names straight before each funeral or wedding.

4. Rememberest that no souls are saved in a sermon that stretches beyond thirty minutes. Indeed, the mind cannot absorb what the seat cannot endure.

5. Remember thou that the gospel is good news. Any sermon that begins with sin and grief and ends with sin and grief is not good news for anyone.

6. Be interesting and energetic. A bland preacher produces a bland listening audience, and of such is the despicable condition of the bland leading the bland.

7. Remember thou that in a conflict between the preacher and the elders, the majority of the church members will side with the elders every time. A corollary: never surprise the chairman of your elders' meeting.

8. Rememberest thou that there is no job security in preaching and your position is only as secure as your last elders' meeting.

9. Be thou warm to all people, attempting to hit the happy medium between being a lecherous, overly-affectionate predator and an aloof, cold fish. Remember also that there are huggers and non-huggers; if thou art a hugger, hug all the women and even a few men, and not just hug the young, highly attractive women.

10. When you want to do something original or innovative, but fear criticism, go ahead and do it without asking. Rememberest it is easier to get forgiveness than permission.

(A spare commandment: Remember thou that it is no disgrace to be fired from your pulpit position. Perhaps you were doing your job with great courage, commitment, and integrity, and its the entire church which needs to be fired!)

Contributed by the author

TEN SERIOUS COMMANDMENTS FOR PREACHERS

1. Always be motivated first and foremost by your love for God and your love for people.
2. Always be honest intellectually and be true to your most deeply held convictions; always be faithful to your calling.
3. Pursue study, education, and training—whether formal or private—as a lifetime experience. Always give priority to the content of your message.
4. Develop and maintain a sense of humor.
5. Consider that perhaps the most effective preachers have done work other than preaching.
6. Develop an emotional life support system—you will always live your life in a fish bowl.
7. Always remember that there are very difficult, emotionally distressed people in every congregation.
8. Know that there will be critics and criticism at every church you serve. Be prepared for conflict in every church you serve.
9. Always be as honest and original in your sermon preparation as possible. Thou must not plagiarize the words of another preacher.
10. Remember that a high degree of success in the local church is related to people skills.

Contributed by the author

TEN COMMANDMENTS FOR RETAILERS
(half fun here)

1. Thou shall have no other goal before you, other than selling everything you have without marking anything down. This includes placing merchandise in the customer's basket when they are not looking.

2. Thou shall not bow down to any customer. Saluting, kissing their hand or feet, or any other form of bribing them to come back is recommended.

3. Thou shall not misuse the name of the word "Sale." For the all-mighty consumer knows when they see a sale and when they don't.

4. Remember the time between Thanksgiving and Christmas and keep it important. It is the life blood of your profit.

5. Honor the Master Card, Visa Card, American Express, Discover Card, Bravo Card, Federal Express Card, and any other card that may come out including the ones that have the silly looking picture of the card holder on the card.

6. Thou shall not murder you competitors, only hurt them *bad!*

7. Thou shall be loyal to your customers, putting only the Lord, your spouse, and your kids before them. Okay, only the Lord and your spouse.

8. Thou shall not steal any ideas from your competitors. Borrowing is acceptable.

9. Thou shall not give false promises to your customers. A promise you make is a promise you keep. They will remind you.

10. Thou shall not covet your competitor's home, cars, etc. Customers and sales are *game!*

Contributed by Barry Maxwell, owner
TeamPlay USA, Franklin, Tennessee

TEN COMMANDMENTS FOR LAWYERS

1. Though you may be on a career track headed for great success, thou must always remember to put Christ and your family ahead of your professional career.
2. Thou shalt search for the truth, accept nothing less, argue nothing but the truth.
3. Remember that God is the ultimate Judge—conduct yourself accordingly.
4. Know that what you do unto others in the profession will be done unto you—and then some!
5. Thou shalt not consider yourself to be above your client or the jury, lest you shall surely be humbled and humiliated.
6. Thou shalt represent your client competently and zealously within the bounds of the law, always maintaining confidences and avoiding even the appearance of professional impropriety.
7. As you walk into the courtroom, thou shalt take care of three responsibilities: (a) you know the facts; (b) you know the law; (c) if you are male, you know your fly is closed.
8. Thou shalt be slow to speak, quick to listen.
9. Thou shalt volunteer time and expertise to those who are in need, thus fulfilling a duty to make legal counsel available to all.
10. Thou shalt work in time, attitude, character, and commitment only as you are working unto the Lord.

(An eleventh command: No matter what you are confronted with in the courtroom, be calm, cool, and collected. If you cannot be calm, cool, and collected, yell like crazy.)

Contributed by Daniel Clayton, partner
Kinnard and Clayton Law Firm, Nashville, Tennessee

TEN COMMANDMENTS FOR COACHES

1. Thou shalt be consistent and fair with all players. This does not mean, however, that all players are treated the same.
2. Thou shalt give diligence to being an effective communicator and thus be able to communicate clearly to players, coaches, administrators, press, and others.
3. Thou shalt work hard to be a motivator who encourages players and inspires them to perform at a higher level than they realize they can.
4. Thou shalt be a capable teacher, able to take his/her knowledge and give it to those playing or coaching for him.
5. Thou shalt be a fair disciplinarian who creates an atmosphere of diligence. The coach should demand that his team play hard and be fundamentally sound.
6. Thou shalt be a coach with purpose who has a clear direction and has set goals for his team to attain, as well as personal goals.
7. Thou shalt be an innovator in all areas of the program, able to create new ways to attack problems.
8. Thou shalt be caring and sensitive, developing real relationships with players. Thou shalt be concerned with their growth as people off the playing floor.
9. Thou shalt be a student of the game, always striving to increase his/her knowledge of the game and team.
10. Thou shalt prioritize from a Christlike perspective. Put God first, family second, and your personal agenda third. Remember that to players "it's just a game" and to coaches "it's just a job."

Contributed by Kyle Bills, high school teacher and former head basketball coach
Montgomery Bell Academy, Nashville, Tennessee

TEN COMMANDMENTS FOR GENERAL DENTISTS

1. Thou shalt acknowledge every person's perceived need *before* you begin telling them what you think they need. You'll help more patients that way.
2. Thou shalt know how to plan a perfect day, but expect something to go less than perfect. Learn how to find the joy in all the day's imperfections.
3. Thou shalt know your business, but let someone else run the mundane affairs. Focusing on dentistry is the only way to give patients your best care.
4. Thou shalt choose a great staff and treat them well. Listen to them at regular staff meetings.
5. Thou shalt write a philosophy and vision and stick to them; modify whenever necessary.
6. Thou shalt phone your patients after lengthy procedures, or anytime, to chat and get their input. You owe it to them and yourself, too.
7. Thou shalt be careful about what old fillings you are "watching" at check-ups. Your patients deserve the option of fixing problems before they happen.
8. Thou shalt trim your own dies. Only you can prevent remakes.
9. Thou shalt not rush. Take some time to get to know your patients. Let them get to know you, too.
10. Thou shalt take time off. Your patients never benefit from a burned-out dentist.

Contributed by Kellye N. Rice, D.M.D.
Brentwood, Tennessee

TEN SERIOUS COMMANDMENTS FOR FUNERAL SERVICES

1. Thou shalt always remember that thou art in funeral service first and in funeral business second. Thou shalt remember that all you have to offer that differs from the next fellow is your service.
2. Thou shalt treat each family and person equally, regardless of social or financial status.
3. Thou shalt consider each and every family request regardless of the complexity or perceived unimportance.
4. Thou shalt not tell a family "no" or "that's not possible" until every effort has been made and every possibility has been exhausted. Thou shalt always go the extra mile for your families.
5. Thou shalt remember that the family chose you.
6. Thou shalt show respect to each and every remains remembering that they are defenseless against abuse and disrespect. Let your conversation and actions illustrate your compassion and concern.
7. Thou shalt never speak in a degrading way about any family or remains that are in your care.
8. Thou shalt not forget you do this because you want to and always remember how blessed you are to be able to do what you do.
9. Thou shalt remember that the family is in this with you.
10. Thou shalt not forget the feeling a warm hug of gratitude brings.

Contributed by Bill McDonald, owner and manager
McDonald Funeral Home, Centerville, Tennessee

TEN* COMMANDMENTS FOR FUNERAL SERVICES
(tongue in cheek)

1. Thou shalt always remember the number of the truck-driving schools you could have attended.
2. Thou shalt not require sleep.
3. Thou shalt not forget the name of the deceased or the next of kin.
4. Thou shalt remember to give the minister the correct time of the funeral service.
5. Thou shalt always keep track of where your feet are, especially when they are in your mouth.
6. Thou shalt not roll the body out until the minister has delivered his message.
7. Thou shalt not drive past the cemetery with the procession.
8. Thou shalt know where the cemetery is before you leave the funeral home.
9. Thou shalt not forget which hospital called.
10. Thou shalt not forget to take your cot to the hospital.
11. Thou shalt not fall in a grave while the family is present.
12. Thou shalt not seal the end of your tie in the casket when you close it during the funeral service.
13. Thou shalt seat the ex-wives on different sides of the chapel.
14. Thou shalt not forget that you don't have to be crazy to work in a funeral home, but it might help.

Contributed by Bill McDonald, owner and manager
McDonald Funeral Home, Centerville, Tennessee

*Actually, fourteen.

TEN COMMANDMENTS FOR UNIVERSITY PROFESSORS

1. Thou shalt set no other priorities before thy students' needs.
2. Thou shalt not make unto thee a graven image of a perfect student.
3. Thou shalt call out the names of thy absent students in vain.
4. Remember thy class days and do not let thy absentmindedness keep thee from them.
5. Honor thy students' fathers and mothers, for they pay their sons' and daughters' tuition, as well as thy salary that thy days may be long upon the campus.
6. Thou shalt not kill class time.
7. Thou shalt not commit disgressions.
8. Thou shalt not steal the students' time they have paid for by dismissing them early—even though they will beg thee to do so.
9. Thou shalt not write tricky true-false questions against thy students.
10. Thou shalt not covet thy students' youth, nor their good looks, nor their idealism, nor anything that belongs, rightfully, to thy students and to their generation.

Contributed by James W. Thomas, Ph. D.
Pepperdine University, Malibu, California

TEN COMMANDMENTS FOR UNIVERSITY STUDENTS

1. Thou shalt put no other classes before mine.
2. Thou shalt not make unto thee any graven images like MTV, Nintendo, or AOL; for I am a jealous professor.
3. Thou shalt not have thy name called out in vain; for thereby thy professor will assume thee clueless if thou answerest not.
4. Remember thy class days and keep them wholly; cut classes thou shalt not.
5. Honor thy father and thy mother by writing, phoning, and e-mailing them— and not merely to ask for more money.
6. Thou shalt not kill time.
7. Thou shalt not commit plagiarism.
8. Thou shalt not steal answers.
9. Thy answers shall not be found false and witless compared to thy classmates'.
10. Thou shalt not covet thy classmates' A's and A-'s or any of their grades that are highter than thine own.

Contributed by James W. Thomas, Ph.D.
Pepperdine University, Malibu, California

TEN COMMANDMENTS FOR DOCTORS

1. Thou shalt value life as a creation of God.
2. Thou shalt not patronize ("just tolerate") older patients.
3. Thou shalt always listen with concern, knowing that much of your work is simply listening and giving counsel and support.
4. Thou shalt keep current with all medical discoveries, insights, and technology so as to render the best care possible.
5. Thou shalt seek primarily to better people's bodies, not necessarily bettering your own wallet.
6. Thou shalt be fair and honest in billing, charging, and reporting on financial matters.
7. Thou shalt keep thyself alert at the office.
8. Thou shalt render full care to all people even at cost to yourself.
9. To be a doctor, you shalt care for people's body and total well-being.
10. Thou shalt not sneeze while holding a scalpel.

Contributed by the author and Michelle Culbreth, student
David Lipscomb University, Nashville, Tennessee

TEN COMMANDMENTS FOR BUILDERS

1. Build your house upon rock, not sand (although geotechnical assistance is advised.)
2. Even rocks can be unstable.
3. Expect the best, prepare for the worst.
4. Always seek perfection, never expect it.
5. Remember, the perfect house has never been built . . . and never will be.
6. If it is not in writing, it was not said.
7. Architects draw houses—they do not build them.
8. Remember the drywall and keep it unholely.
9. Covet vacant building lots.
10. Just because it's legal does not mean it is ethical.

Contributed by Richard Morrison, contractor and builder
Franklin, Tennessee

TEN COMMANDMENTS FOR VETERINARIANS

1. Thou shalt hold no other animals before the one you're working on.
2. Thou shalt hold the animal's tongue when placing your hand in the mouth of an animal.
3. Thou shalt hold your own tongue when placing yourself in the mouth of a new situation.
4. Thou shalt not allow excessive pain and suffering.
5. Thou shalt not put yourself in a position of pain and suffering.
6. Remember your day off and make sure you take it.
7. Thou shalt honor your clients and their animals so that you may practice long in the land.
8. Thou shalt not kill, only humanely euthanize when requested.
9. Thou shalt not bear false diagnosis.
10. Thou shalt not covet thy client's payment before services rendered.

Contributed by Monty McInturff, D.V.M.
Franklin, Tennessee

TEN COMMANDMENTS FOR ENGINEERS

1. Thou shall not sweat it.
2. Never draw more in the morning than you can erase in the afternoon.
3. Never break a law of physics unless absolutely necessary and then only by committee vote.
4. Never take more than one data point.
5. Do not confuse possible with reasonable.
6. If you do not know where you are going, you will end up someplace else.
7. Keep your words soft and sweet; you may have to eat them.
8. Walk quickly and carry a piece of paper.
9. If there are no rumors, start one.
10. When all else fails, casually browse through the reading material.

An extra command: Never spit into your waste can.

Contributed by Phil Williams, P.E.
DuPont Engineering (retired)
Franklin, Tennessee

TEN COMMANDMENTS FOR
JOURNALISTS AND EDITORIALISTS

1. Always remember that your rights to free expression are protected by the First Amendment of the U.S. Constitution. And just as you liberally apply the First Amendment rights to your own profession, allow your colleagues and critics to apply these same rights equally to their own expression.

2. Remember that the primary purpose of gathering and disseminating news and expressing responsible opinion is to serve the general welfare. Your role in maintaining good citizenship is informing the general public, challenging citizens to think for themselves, and facilitating their sound judgment on issues of the time. Your profession is a sacred trust that must not be compromised by selfish motives or unworthy purposes.

3. Maintain your independence. Be vigilant to protect the media from those who would exploit and abuse media for self-serving purposes. Make clear that your reports and your opinions cannot be bought or compromised.

4. Consider and judge all people of whom you speak or write with respect, and speak and write with decency and fairness. Errors in fact or judgment should be corrected promptly. Pledges of confidentiality must be honored at all costs.

5. Maintain your objectivity at all times. Avoid even the appearance of impropriety or any conflict of interest.

6. Respect the privacy of both public and private citizens and break it only when the clearest and most obvious need to know emerges. A "need to know" is established when the information you access is essential for responsible citizenship and not simply for sleazy gossip.

7. Dedicate yourself to total truth and complete accuracy, for thereby you build good faith with readers and viewers. Editorials and commentary should also be held to the same standards of accuracy regarding facts used to weave opinions.

8. Do not become so enamored by your own analysis and opinions that you transform your best critics and dissenters into your worst enemies.

9. Seek to preserve the best and avoid the worst in the English language. Keep your own language, grammar, and spelling skills polished. Remember that your computer's "spell-check" is not the final authority in "proofing" your work.

10. Maintain your own reputation for personal integrity and fairness, your news and views for truth and accuracy, and your attitudes and word choices for decency and civility.

contributed by the author

TEN COMMANDMENTS FOR
COMPUTER SYSTEMS ANALYSTS

1. Thou shalt spend more time with thy family than with thy job.
2. Thou shalt not create harmful viruses for other computers.
3. Thou shalt be patient with the computer ignorant.
4. Thou shalt never stop learning about new technology and trends.
5. Thou shalt help others to learn about computing.
6. Thou shalt treat other on-line users with respect.
7. Thou shalt never overprice software.
8. Thou shalt make computers available to children free of charge.
9. Thou shalt never take a job simply for money.
10. Thou shalt never lose sight of thy priorities.

Contributed by Clay Chambers, student
David Lipscomb University, Nashville, Tennessee

Ethical Business Decision-Making

A BIBLICAL BASIS FOR DECISION-MAKING
IN THE BUSINESS WORLD

According to Alexander Hill in *Just Business: Christian Ethics for the Marketplace,* the basis for making value judgments in the business and professional world is deeply rooted in the concept of God. Three divine concepts have direct bearing on ethical decision-making: (1) God's holiness, (2) God's justice, and (3) God's love. A business act is judged to be ethical if it reflects God's character. A society operating in opposition of God's character is one of mistrust, greed, thievery, laziness, human abuse, and bribery.

Three factors that encourage humans to do better are (1) Man is made in "image of God"; (2) God has established social institutions such as government, the legal system, family, and business to promote good and protect the weak from the strong; and (3) Men are called to be Christian, the salt of the earth and the light of the world.

Christian ethics recognizes that the majority of humans are morally deficient and that it will be difficult for the minority to challenge the majority. Nonetheless, it should be noted that people are basically decent and law abiding.

Holiness embraces four components: zeal for God, purity, accountability, and humility. Potential abuses of holiness include: Legalism, reducing holiness to rule keeping, judgmentalism, inflating one's own opinions by unfairly criticizing others, and withdrawal from society.

Justice provides order to human relationships by laying out reciprocal sets of rights and duties for those living in the context of community—business partners, employees, neighbors, and family members. There are four relevant aspects of justice: procedural rights, including due process and equal protection; substantive rights, universal rights that procedural rights seek to protect; merit, which justifies unequal distribution in many areas of life; and contractual justice, which prohibits causing harm to others. When the rights of others are violated, one is expected to make reasonable restitution or pay damages. Although justice is a cornerstone of Christian ethics, serious problems arise when it is isolated from holiness and love.

Love's primary contribution to the holiness-justice-love mix is its emphasis on relationships. There are three prominent aspects of love: empathy, which encourages corporate executives to demonstrate heart-felt concern for the less fortunate and to take genuine interest in associates and their work and personal life; mercy, which takes action on behalf of others by forgiving, redeeming, and healing; self-sacrifice, a willingness to give away the very rights that justice bestows. Potential abuses of love include a narrow focus and becoming a doormat, thus diminishing human dignity.

A balanced view of biblical ethics requires holiness, justice, and love to be respected equally.

Without holiness, love degenerates into permissiveness. Likewise, love without justice lapses into favoritism. And holiness without justice drifts toward a privatized form of religion (Alexander Hill, *Just Business: Christian Ethics for the Marketplace*, Downers Grove, IL: InterVarsity Press, 1997).

EXAMINING THE ETHICS OF A BUSINESS DECISION

Laura Nash, an established author in business ethics, offers the following set of questions for considering the ethics of a business decision:

1. Have you defined the problem accurately?
2. How would you define the problem if you stood on the other side of the fence?
3. How did this situation occur in the first place?
4. To whom and to what do you give your loyalty as a person and as a member of the corporation?
5. What is your intention in making this decision?
6. How does this intention compare with the probable results?
7. Whom could your decision or action injure?
8. Can you discuss the problem with the affected parties before you make your decision?
9. Are you confident that your position will be as valid over a long period of time as it seems now?
10. Could you disclose, without qualm, your decision or action to your boss, your CEO, the board of directors, your family, society as a whole?
11. What is the symbolic potential of your action if understood? If misunderstood?
12. Under what conditions would you allow exceptions to your stand?

All of the questions above are very good in examining ethical decisions; however, it might be wise to use one very basic, simple rule a wise father has always said to me: "If you have to stop and think about whether something is right or wrong, it is probably wrong, so don't do it" (Laura L. Nash, "Ethics Without the Sermon," *Harvard Business Review*, Nov.-Dec. 1981, 81.

The Corporate Network and Common Sense

Today's business environment is a complex arena. There are all kinds of people in all kinds of relationships with other people in the organization. Not only must ethical decisions be made—and that alone is a formidable challenge—but each employee needs the ability to get along with all other people in the organization (another equally formidable task, perhaps)!

A major key to creating successful organizational relationships is understanding both how to treat others fairly and what others expect from us. These responsibilities are determined by our position relative to others in the company.

Everyone in a business organization is part of a network. The following is a list of succinctly stated suggestions and recommendations for building a solid network of business relationships. Some of the suggestions are just plain business sense. Many are rooted in our moral responsibility to respect other people. They are drawn and adapted from Elena Jankowic, *Behave Yourself: The Working Guide to Business Etiquette* (Englewood Cliffs, N. J.: Prentice-Hall, 1986), and the work is highly recommended.

SENIOR MANAGEMENT

Senior management provides the leadership of any corporation. Their decisions give direction and shape the reputation of the company. Employees owe them respect. Demonstrate this respect by the following:

1. DO imitate their style. Watch how they dress, how they move, how they conduct meetings. They are the models for the company, and they expect others to conform to their style.
2. DO show tact and diplomacy. Never insult senior management or make disparaging comments about them behind their backs. Do not snicker at something they say publicly.
3. DO respect their time. Time is money, and the higher up the corporate ladder the more their time is worth. Don't constantly buttonhole a superior without having something worthwhile to discuss.
4. DO keep them informed. Use your discretion in knowing how and how often to do this. A memo at end of the day might be wise.

5. DO respect the hierarchy. The chain of command is there for a reason and applies to everyone. Do not attempt to leapfrog in a hierarchy.

6. DO accept criticism without taking it personally. Be focused on your work assignment. Management has little time or regard for a person who sulks and reacts sourly to constructive criticism.

7. DO try to see things from management's perspective. Look beyond your small part in the whole operation and encourage others to do the same. See the big picture.

PEERS

Peer relationships are crucially important to making your employment a happy experience. They provide an opportunity for making lasting friendships. On the other hand, peer relationships are the most competitive ones in the workplace. With peers we learn the true meaning of teamwork. To make colleagues and allies and not enemies out of your peers, practice the following:

1. DO learn from your peers. Those who climb the ladder most rapidly are those who are able to learn from the mistakes and triumphs of themselves and others.

2. DO share and communicate with your colleagues. Be discreet but don't unnecessarily shut yourself off from others or become highly secretive. A confident executive is inclusive, not exclusive. Of course, do not disseminate confidential information.

3. DO support and assist your peers. You are building good will and demonstrating respect. However, do not perform another person's work assignments.

4. DON'T take advantage of a colleague's weakness. Help the coworker to find a solution to his/her problem.

5. DO respect the privacy of fellow-workers. If a coworker is seeking another job or having marital difficulties or health problems, discuss these matters privately with him/her.

SUBORDINATES

If all goes well with your career you will find that you are responsible for the supervision of more and more employees. There are lots of books and articles on effective supervision. The bottom line is that an effective manager works to establish a basis of trust and mutual respect. How is that ethical task carried out? Here are a few basic rules which apply to all situations:

1. DO remember the simple courtesies in your dealings with subordinates. The most important words you can use with them are "please" and "thank you."

2. DO set the standard. If, for example, you value punctuality, then be punctual. Subordinates generally will not rise any higher in their moral behavior at work than the example you set for them.

3. DON'T use abusive language or profanity when speaking to staff or in their presence. This is an infectious practice and others will feel free to follow your example. Be professional in your discussion about others.

4. DO keep direct subordinates informed of relevant information. Let them know why things are performed the way that they are and keep them informed of policies and programs.

5. DO acknowledge your subordinates' contribution to the company and to particular projects. Give them public credit for a job well done. Never underestimate the power of attribution and acknowledgment.

6. DON'T reprimand staff in the presence of others. If you have personal criticism, share it privately with the appropriate person. In a sense, the responsibility for any failure is ultimately yours, as supervisor. Also, stick with the facts and not the name-calling (say "Your report was, unfortunately, late" instead of "you lazy . . .").

7. DO allow subordinates flexibility in setting their own pace and work habits. Do not interrupt continuously with "rush jobs."

8. DO delegate as much as possible. Don't keep all the interesting work simply for yourself or a few favorites. A subordinate who shines will reflect on you. Otherwise, you will get the reputation of being a hard-working supervisor with foolish work habits.

9. DO look for opportunities to promote from within. Your staff will work harder knowing that they have a chance to be promoted.

10. DO remember the golden rule when supervising. Do not initiate a system that you yourself would not want to work under. Give people credit for attempting to do a good job, though, of course, there are exceptions.

11. DON'T play favorites. Policies apply to all.

12. DON'T get unduly personal with subordinates. Maintain some professional distance. Restrict criticism to matters related to work.

13. DO bring in food on your expense account if you ask office staff to work late. Remember, little things mean a lot.

14. DO insist on a degree of formality when visitors are present in your department. Ask your staff to address you formally if you feel it is more professional in the presence of visitors.

15. DO take employees to lunch on their birthdays. You might also remember the anniversary of their first day at work with your company. Again, little things mean a lot.

16. DON'T ever refer to women as "girls." This is not simply a matter of political correctness, but of simple tact. It's not professional to call your secretary "honey," "dear," "my girl," or to refer to adult women as "girls." Yes, in the "old days" that could be done.

17. DON'T discriminate against minorities in hiring. That's the law in most employment situations. And it's a moral issue as well as legal issue.

SECRETARIES

A capable secretary can be the greatest blessing that a supervisor or executive has. Treat the secretary right:

1. DO make the job description clear right from the start. Explain your expectations in clear, concise terms, and ask for a response. There are so many gray areas that need to be settled on the front end (e.g., making coffee or running your little personal errands).
2. DO let your secretary know where you can be reached during working hours and when you expect to return. This is common courtesy. Plus, an emergency could arise.
3 DON'T ask her or him to cover for you if you are leaving early, taking a long lunch hour, and spending some time down at the bar. Take responsibility for your actions.
4. DO introduce her to guests whenever possible. This is courtesy. Use a formal name.
5. DO treat her as a professional. She's not your slave. Do not expect her to do personal favors for you, such as mend your socks or pick up your dry cleaning or a birthday card for your spouse, except in the rarest of circumstances.
6. DON'T forget that she is an individual. Ask her opinion when appropriate. Seek her advice when it's helpful. Pay compliments.
7. DO maintain your patience if you are a male secretary. Most secretaries are female and that's changing some.
8. DO remember Secretaries' Week. Flowers and a lunch are appreciated by almost all secretaries. All the while remember that it is much more important to treat a secretary as a professional than occasionally to give flowers or a lunch date.

CLIENTS

Your relationship with your clients and customers is crucially important to your success, especially if you provide goods and services for others. Begin with an attitude that is concerned with *quality*. However brief your contact with clients might be, your every interaction with them must reinforce their confidence in your integrity and competence.

1. DO be responsible. Act as your clients' advocate within your company, making certain that their needs are met.
2. DO be punctual. Place a value on their time.
3. DO use tact and diplomacy. Deal with irate clients calmly and professionally. Don't be defensive. Remember, without clients there would be no profit.
4. DO keep customers informed. If there are delays or shortages which affect the order, let the customer know immediately.

5. DO respect the rights of customers to run their own businesses. Be tactful if you have suggestions for them. Small businesses usually appreciate suggestions.

6. DO remember to be friendly without getting too intimate. It's tempting to be too friendly and intimate with clients because you are trying so hard to please. Stay professional with slight formality.

7. DO keep a card index of customers. Keep any relevant data on the cards and refresh your memory by referencing these cards.

8. DO keep abreast of customer accounts. Give customers the benefit of a doubt.

9. DO review your client list from time to time. If someone has stopped ordering, check on the reasons why. Consider if your attitude has in some way impacted your business relationship with a former client.

10. DO remember that *all* clients are important, whether you deal with them once a day or once a year. They all deserve courtesy and attention.

11. DO encourage feedback from customers about your products and service. They will appreciate your concern and it's the only way you can improve your product or service.

12. DO remember to say "thank you."

Eight Rules for Office Workers
CIRCA 1872

1. Office employees each day will fill lamps, clean chimneys, and trim wicks. Wash windows once a week.
2. Each clerk will bring in a bucket of water and a scuttle of coal for the day's business.
3. Make your pens carefully. You may whittle nibs to your individual taste.
4. Men employees will be given an evening off for courting purposes, two evenings a week if they regularly go to church.
5. After thirteen hours of labor in the office, the employee should spend remaining time reading the Bible and other good books.
6. Every employee should lay aside for each pay day a goodly sum of his earnings for his benefit during his declining years so that he will not become a burden on society.
7. Any employee who smokes Spanish cigars, uses liquor in any form, or frequents pool and public halls, or gets shaved in a barber shop will give good reason to suspect his worth, intentions, integrity, and honesty.
8. The employee who has performed his labor faithfully and without fault for five years will be given an increase of five cents per day in his pay, providing profits from business permit it.

Appendix F

Essential Ethics Succinctly Stated

Some classic works on ethics run thousands of pages. To some business students they are about as exciting as watching paint dry. Who reads them? Well, maybe the professors of ethics.

Keep in mind that your character is the total of all the little habits you practice in life's daily routine. The woman or man who has the potential for being a hero in some public crisis is the one who has disciplined her or his life in thousands of minor challenges.

Is it possible to state in a brief and highly understandable form some basic ethics for the workplace? Well, let's try. We'll divide this wisdom into two basic categories: (1) Business lessons too simple not to know, and (2) Essential ethics and practical advice encapsulated in a few simple words.

BUSINESS LESSONS TOO SIMPLE NOT TO KNOW

1. Don't promise what you can't deliver.
2. Don't tell off-color jokes.
3. Resignation letters should only be one or two lines. Don't take parting shots.
4. If you tell a racist joke, be prepared to be fired.
5. Share the credit for successful projects and make sure everyone's supervisor knows of everyone's contribution.
6. Don't get drunk at the company holiday party.
7. Treat your time as if someone is paying for it; someone is.
8. Don't try to fake your relationship with senior managers.
9. Read *In Search of Excellence;* the companies are dated, but the principles are not.
10. Don't open any envelope or read any memo marked confidential unless it is addressed to you.
11. If you don't know the answer, simply say that you don't know.
12. Make sure you can trust someone before you speak your mind.
13. Don't take sick days unless you are.
14. Assume no one can or will keep a secret.

15. Spend your department's budget as if it were your own.
16. Being good is important; being trusted is essential.
17. Always remember, "What goes around comes around."

ESSENTIAL ETHICS AND PRACTICAL ADVICE
IN A FEW SIMPLE WORDS

Although, please consider that some of these declarations may seem a little facetious:

No one can make you feel inferior without your permission.

Too bad that ignorance isn't painful.

Never underestimate the power of human stupidity.

All I want is a little bit more than I'll ever get.

I prefer to be ignorant rather than misinformed.

Never tell your family or even your friends that you're up for a job until you get it.
That way you'll eliminate a whole lot of unnecessary pressure.

It's not whether you win or lose it's how you look playing the game.

I've done so much for so long with so little that now I can do anything with
nothing.

An ounce of image is worth a pound of performance.

If it's a job worth doing, it's a job worth doing for money.

The future isn't what it used to be.

If u c rd ths u c get a gd jb mr pa but if u tlk lk ths u r n rl trubl.

An optimist believes that we work for the best company in the world. A pessimist
is afraid it's true.

When in charge, ponder. When in doubt, mumble. When in trouble, delegate.

There are two sides to every question. And if you want to be popular, take both.

Age and treachery will always overcome youth and skill.

Just when you thought you were winning the rat race, along come faster rats.

All arguments have two sides but some have no ends.

There is nothing better than the encouragement of a good friend.

When all is said and done, it is best to leave it that way.

If you are all wrapped up in yourself, you are overdressed.

Make the least of the worst and the most of the best.

Laugh at yourself first, before everyone else can.

What we love to do, we find time to do.

When all think alike, no one thinks very much.

Think like a person of action, act like a person of thought.

Something you get for nothing is usually worth it.

An ignorant man is one who has talked more than he has listened.

The squeaking wheel doesn't always get grease; sometimes its replaced.

Silent gratitude isn't very much use to anyone.

Folks who never do any more than they get paid for, never get paid for any more than they do.

No job has a future—the future is with the person who holds that job.

Tact is the ability *not* to say what you really think.

When you are right, you can afford to be courteous. When you are wrong, you've got to be.

There is a big difference between free speech and cheap talk.

Keep frowning—you'll get credit for thinking.

The best time to praise a man is when he isn't there.

The quickest way to get people interested in a project is to tell them it is none of their business.

Variety is the spice of life—but monotony provides the groceries.

The man who watches the clock generally remains one of the hands.

God helps those who help themselves, and the government helps those who don't.

It's not the hours you put in, it's what you put into the hours.

Always do right. This will gratify some people and astonish the rest.

When you make two people happy, one of them is apt to be you.

Tact is the art of convincing people that they know more than you do.

Failure is an event, never a person.

The nice thing about teamwork is that you have others on your side.

Do not mistake activity for achievement.

For every problem there is one solution which is simple, neat, and wrong.

Never contend with a man who has nothing to lose.

Do not speak for other people; speak for yourself.

Tact is rubbing out another's mistake instead of rubbing it in.

Law of inertia: Given enough time, what you put off doing today will eventually get done by itself.

Instinct is the nose of the mind.

You're never as good as everyone tells you when you win, and you're never as bad as they say when you lose.

Nothing in fine print is ever good news.

Sacred cows make the best hamburger (Mark Twain).

Don't worry about temptation—as you grow older, it starts avoiding you *(Old Farmer's Almanac)*.

Christ turned water into wine, but He can't turn your whining into anything worthwhile.

We should be careful to get out of an experience only the wisdom that is in it—and stop there; lest we be like the cat that sits down on a hot stove-lid. She will never sit down on a hot stove-lid again, and that is well, but also she will never sit down on a cold one anymore (Mark Twain).

There is hardly anybody who is good for everything, and there is scarcely anybody who is absolutely good for nothing (Lord Chesterfield).

Look at a day when you are supremely satisfied at the end. It's not a day when you
lounge around doing nothing. It's when you've had everything to do, and you've
done it (Margaret Thatcher).
Don't be afraid of going slowly, be afraid of standing still (proverb).
Gossip is hearing something you like about someone you don't (Earl Wilson).

MAKE A DIFFERENCE

Make few promises, but keep all the ones you do make.
Live within your means, and pay your bills on time.
Do more than your share on any project.
Be grateful for your job, and smile when you are doing it.
Get to work early, keep your eyes off the clock, and do your best.
Never cheat your company or your customers.
Be faithful to your spouse, and say only positive things about him or her.
Know what is going on in the lives of your children.
Be especially kind to anyone who appears sad or angry.
Face your own problems with prayer—not pills or booze.
Give people the benefit of the doubt as long as possible.
Use words like "please," "thank you," and "excuse me" often and naturally.
Use the name of God to bless people but never to curse them.
Be generous with praise and stingy with criticism.
Do as many good deeds as you can anonymously.
Apologize when you have been wrong.
Appreciate the beauty that surrounds you in nature.

And finally, in his book *The Dilbert Principle*, Scott Adams offers a few of
"Dilbert's Laws of Work":
Don't be irreplaceable. If you can't be replaced, you can't be promoted.
When you don't know what to do, walk fast and look worried.
Everything can be filed under "miscellaneous."
If you are good, you will be assigned all the work. If you are really good, you will
get out of it.
If it wasn't for the last moment, nothing would get done.
Keep you boss's boss off you boss's back.
Eat one live toad the first thing in the morning, and nothing worse will happen to
you the rest of the day.

A Letter from Jordan Consultants

Jordan Management Consultants
Jerusalem, 26544

Jesus, Son of Joseph
Woodcrafters Carpentry Shop
Nazareth, 25922

Dear Sir,

Thank you for submitting the resumes of the twelve men you have picked for managerial positions in your new organization. All of them have now taken our battery of tests, and we have not only run the results through our computer, but also arranged personal interviews for each of them with our psychologist and vocational aptitude consultant. The profiles of all tests are included and you will want to study each of them carefully.

As part of our service, we make some general comments for your guidance, much as an auditor will include some general statements. This is given as a result of staff consultation and comes without any additional fee. It is the staff opinion that most of your nominees are lacking in background, education, and vocational aptitude for the type of enterprise you are undertaking. They do not have the team concept. We would recommend that you continue your search for persons of experience in managerial ability and proven capability.

Simon Peter is emotionally unstable and given to fits of temper. Andrew has absolutely no qualities of leadership. The two brothers, James and John, the sons of Zebedee, place personal interest above company loyalty. Thomas demonstrates a questioning attitude that would tend to undermine morals. We feel that it is our duty to tell you that Matthew has been blacklisted by the Greater Jerusalem Better Business Bureau. James, the son of Alphaeus and Thaddaeus, definitely have radical leanings and they both registered a high score on the manic-depressive scale. Simon the Zealot tends to be violent.

One of the candidates, however, shows great potential. He is a man of ability and resourcefulness, meets people well, has a keen business mind, and had contacts in high

places. He is highly motivated, ambitious and responsible. We recommend Judas
Iscariot as your controller and right-hand man. All of the other profiles are self-
explanatory.

We wish you every success in your new venture.

Sincerely yours,
Jordan Management Consultants

Office Prayer

Lord Jesus, as I enter this workplace, I speak your Peace, Your Grace, and Your Perfect Order into the atmosphere of this office. I acknowledge your Lordship over all that will be spoken, thought, decided, and accomplished within these walls. Lord Jesus, I thank you for the gifts you have deposited in me. I do not take them lightly, but commit to using them responsibly and well. Give me a fresh supply of truth and beauty on which to draw as I do my job. Anoint my creativity, my ideas, and my energy, so that even my smallest task may bring You honor. Lord, when I am confused, guide me When I am weary, energize me Lord, when I am burned out, infuse me with the Light of your Holy Spirit. May the work that I do and the way that I do it bring Hope, Life, and courage to all that I come in contact with today. And, Oh Lord, even in this day's most stressful moments . . . may I rest in you. In Your strong and powerful name I pray, Amen.

The Bible and White-Collar Crime

Can you find examples of white collar crime or other modern-sounding business behavior in the narratives of the Bible? This was a question the author posed to a class in the Adult Studies Program at David Lipscomb University. The challenge was a formidable one, but it did solicit some interesting responses (to which the author has added a few of his own):

Fraud—Zacchaeus, the short of stature, wealthy tax collector who scaled a tree to see Jesus, may have extorted an unfair amount of tax money from fellow Jews. After consulting with an expert in kingdom ethics, Jesus, Zacchaeus not only willingly offered to make generous restitution, but also donated half of his possessions to poor people. In light of congressional hearings in the fall of 1997 on the Internal Revenue Service, the ancient story of Zacchaeus' insensitivity to fair assessment and collection has a contemporary ring to it (Luke 19:1–10).

Another example of fraud involved Jacob conspiring with his mother in pretending to be his brother Esau in order to gain the special blessing from his blind father Isaac. Long-term relationships were sacrificed for the sake of short-term gain (Gen. 27:1–45).

False reporting—Ananias and Sapphira, a husband-and-wife team in collaboration to enhance their reputation with the young Jerusalem church, lied about the proceeds of a real-estate sale to the apostles. Though they were not required to donate all the proceeds to the church, it was important that they told the truth in sales reporting. Each met an untimely demise on the same day but at different hours (Acts 5:1–10).

Confrontation rather than whistle-blowing—The prophet Nathan confronted Israel's king about his sin with Bathsheba rather than to publicize this information which would embarrass his commander-in-chief (2 Sam. 12:1–14).

Insider information—The archrival Philistines used insider information supplied by Delilah that the judge and military hero Samson possessed strength in the length of his hair (Judges 16). Also, because Judas was one of the twelve apostles, he had insider information as to the location and identity of Jesus at all times—information he shared with the chief priests, which led to the arrest and execution of Jesus. Judas essentially placed his own financial gain above the common good of the cause and the group or company (Matt. 26:14–16).

Breach of contract—Jacob believed that he had fulfilled the obligations of the work contract in order to win the right to marry Rachel. The other party, Laban, used deceit to present the less-attractive daughter (Leah) to Jacob and extorted an additional seven years of labor for marital rights to Rachel (Gen. 29:15–30).

Bribery and kickbacks—The unethical manager in the story Jesus told (Luke 16:1–8) stole money from his employer, a creditor who had loaned vast sums of money, by secretly reducing their debt in order to win those clients' business and friendship.

Unfair labor negotiations—Pharaoh's vacillation on whether the Hebrew slave labor force could be released to travel with Moses is an example of bad faith in labor-management relations (Exod. 7–10).

Greed—There are many examples of greediness by biblical characters. One would certainly include the story of the wealthy farmer whose barns were inadequate to hold a bounteous harvest (Luke 12:13–21); the wealthy young ruler whose emotional connection to his material goods precluded his acceptance of an invitation to follow Jesus (Matt. 19:16–29); the morally bankrupt king Ahab, whose intense coveting of Naboth's family vineyard led to Naboth's execution and the illegal confiscation of the property (the execution was arranged by Ahab's conniving wife having suborned false witnesses for a capital offense; see 1 Kings 21:1–29).

Workplace Humor

ABC'S OF THE WORK WORLD

Time for another lesson in the ABCs of our careers and our lives. Consider these brief definitions from Jim Pawlak as they appeared in the *Detroit Free Press* in the fall of 1997 as you evaluate where you are and where you want to be.

Advertisement: What you do and how you do it. Remember, we are all walking billboards for our skills.

Baby steps: Short-term, easily accomplished objectives designed to build confidence when implementing a new plan.

Circles: The round-and-round of your career path when you don't have a plan.

Doubt: The fear of failure that creeps in when your belief wavers.

Epic: The saga of a work life of forty-plus years. Too many could be titled: "Woulda, Coulda, Shoulda."

Faith: Unflagging belief in yourself, your talents, and your plans.

Golf: A sport that imitates life. No matter how much you practice hitting the ball, you're bound to have some bad rounds. That's par for the game of life, too.

Head-on: Dealing with problems directly. Dodging problems only makes them more difficult to solve down the road.

Intertwined: The bonded relationship of our work and personal lives. What happens in one carries over to the other.

Jellyfish: Spineless people who don't take responsibility for their careers and lives. They always let things happen and then complain about it.

Keys: What you need to open the doors to one's future. Some keys you must have on your life's key ring are education, commitment, planning, follow through, and a network of supporters.

Learning: Connecting what you do know with what you don't know.

Masterminds: A group of people who share your dreams and provide ongoing advice, constructive criticism, and support.

No: The word that you don't know the meaning of when you're committed to achievement.

Open-minded: 1. Accepting of change. 2. Accepting of ideas other that your own.

Perspiration: The result of applying your skills to achieve intense, daily effort. make sure you apply the effort to the most important tasks first.

Quicksand: The sinking ooze you're mired in when you have no plan for your career and your life.

Rat race: The daily race you run when working a job you don't like. It's the only race you can win by quitting.

Static: Words of discouragement. They must be tuned out if you are to generate ideas and turn them into reality.

Think: To formulate in your mind. Thinking is the pilot light of creativity and ideas.

Underachieve: What most people tend to do when they accept labels put on them by others.

Vroom: The sound of adrenaline when career and life plans are hitting on all eight cylinders. You'll know it when you feel the rush.

Why?: The question to ask when someone says: "We've always done it that way."

Why not?: The question to ask when told: "You'll never be able to do that."

X-factor: The intangible factor that separates winners from whiners.

Yo-yo: The ups and downs of life. You control the string, so you can make your life do tricks; just make sure that you don't make your life's yo-yo sleep too long.

Zero: Your real net gain when you don't do your best.

SOME ENLIGHTENING DEFINITIONS
(A FEW WITH RELEVANCE TO BUSINESS
AND PROFESSIONAL LIFE)

Adolescence: The period when a teenager feels he will never be as dumb as his/her parents.

Americans: People with more timesaving devices yet less time that anybody else in the world.

Banker: A pawnbroker with a manicure.

Budget: A systematic way of going into debt.

Coach: One who is always willing to lay down your life for his job.

Dentist: A magician who puts metal in your mouth and pulls coins from your pocket.

Dermatologist: One who makes rash judgments.

Diplomacy: The art of saying "nice doggie" until you can find a rock.

Disarmament: The agreement between nations to scuttle all weapons that are obsolete.

Efficiency expert: The person smart enough to tell you how to run a business but too smart to start his own.

Experience: The name we give our mistakes.

Honeymoon: A vacation a man takes before beginning work under new boss.

Hunch: An idea that you're afraid is wrong.

Incentive: The possibility of getting more money that you earn.

Lame duck: A politician whose goose is cooked.

Life insurance: A policy that keeps you poor so you can die rich.

Pacifist: A guy who fights everybody but the enemy.

Planning: The art of putting off until tomorrow what you have no intention of doing today.

Professor: One who talks in someone else's sleep.

Rich man: One who is not afraid to ask the clerk for something cheaper.

PERFORMANCE EVALUATION STATEMENTS:

"Works well when under constant supervision and cornered like a rat in a trap."

"He would be out of his depth in a parking lot puddle."

"This young lady has delusions of adequacy."

"I would not allow this employee to breed."

"His men would follow him anywhere, but only out of morbid curiosity."

"Since my last report, this employee has reached rock bottom and shows signs of starting to dig."

"This employee should go far—and the sooner he starts, the better."

"This employee is depriving a village somewhere of an idiot."

"OFFICE HOURS"

Open most days about 9:00 or 10:00.
Occasionally as early as 7:00.
But some days as late as 12:00 or 1:00.
We close about 5:30 or 6:00,
Occasionally about 4:00 or 5:00, but
some days as late as 11:00 or 12:00.
Some days or afternoons, we
aren't here at all, and lately
I've been here just about all
the time, except when I'm
someplace else, but I should
be here, too.

EMPLOYMENT APPLICATIONS

From actual resumes:

"I am extremely loyal to my present firm, so please don't let them know of my immediate availability."

"I intentionally omitted my salary history. I've made money and lost money. I've been rich and I've been poor. I prefer being rich."

"Note: Please don't misconstrue my fourteen jobs as 'job-hopping'. I have never quit a job."

"Marital Status: Often. Children: Various."

"Here are my qualifications for you to overlook."

REASONS FOR LEAVING LAST JOB

"Responsibility makes me nervous."

"They insisted that all employees get to work by 8:45 every morning. Couldn't work under those conditions."

"Was met with a string of broken promises and lies, as well as cockroaches."

"I was working for my mom until she decided to move."

"The company made me a scapegoat—just like my three previous employers."

Bibliography

The following books were consulted in the writing of this volume:

Aguilar, Francis J. *Managing Corporate Ethics: Learning from America's Ethical Companies How to Supercharge Business Performance.* New York: Oxford University Press, 1994. A readable small volume which discusses the impact of ethical leadership and initiatives in various U.S. companies.

Arterburn, Stephen. *Winning at Work Without Losing at Love.* Nashville: Thomas Nelson Publishers, 1994. Several listings and light reading from a personal perspective.

Banks, Robert and Stevens, R. Paul, editors. *The Complete Book of Everyday Christianity.* Downers Grove, Ill.: InterVarsity Press, 1997. Contains encyclopedic articles on work, unemployment, unions, business ethics, workplace, calling/vocation, career, professions, etc.

Barna, George. *Leaders on Leadership.* Ventura, Calif.: Regal Books, 1997. Mostly about spiritual and church leadership.

Blanchard, Kenneth and Norman Vincent Peale. *The Power of Ethical Management.* New York: William Morrow, 1988. Brief, readable.

Blazer, Dan G. *You Were Born to Work: So Let's Approach It God's Way.* Nashville, Tenn.: Twentieth Century Christian, 1992.

Boatright, John R. *Ethics and the Conduct of Business.* Englewood Cliffs, N.J.: Prentice-Hall, Inc., 1993. Standard college text.

Bolton, Robert. *People Skills.* New York: Simon and Schuster, Touchstone Edition, 1986. Excellent on assertiveness, communication skills, and conflict resolution.

Bramson, Robert M. *Coping with Difficult People . . . In Business and in Life.* New York: Ballantine Books, 1981.

Burkett, Larry. *Business by the Book: The Complete Guide of Biblical Principles for Business Men and Women.* Nashville, Tenn.: Thomas Nelson, 1990.

Carter, Stephen L. *Integrity.* New York: Basic Books, 1996.

Cotham, Perry C. *Harsh Realities/Agonizing Choices: Making Moral Decisions in a Morally Complex World.* Joplin, Mo.: College Press, 1996. This is absolutely "must" reading for any literate person.

Cotham, Perry C. and Douglas Davis. *TRUST at Work.* Brentwood, Tenn.: Davis Associates, 1987.

Covey, Stephen R. *The Seven Habits of Highly Effective People.* New York: Simon and Schuster, 1989. A best-seller filled with practical advice for ordering one's life and priorities; contains numerous applications to one's profession and career.

Dayton, Edward R. *Succeeding in Business without Losing Your Faith.* Grand Rapids, Mich.: Baker Book House, 1992.

Devine, George. *Responses to 101 Questions on Business Ethics.* New York: Paulist Press, 1996.

Ferrell, O. C. and Gareth Gardiner. *In Pursuit of Ethics: Tough Choices in the World of Work.* Springfield, Ill.: Smith and Collins, Publishers, 1991.

Gordon, Thomas. *P. E. T.: Parent Effectiveness Training.* New York: Peter H. Wyden, Inc., 1970. Contains excellent advice on communication with people one cares for.

Gough, Russell W. *Character Is Destiny: The Value of Personal Ethics in Everyday Life.* Rocklin, Calif.: Prima Publishing, 1998. Classical moral philosophy with readable, practical applications to contemporary life.

Hardy, Lee. *The Fabric of this World.* Grand Rapids, Mich.: William B. Eerdmans Publishing Company, 1990. Excellent discussion on the concept of calling and vocation in biblical literature and Reformation thought.

Henderson, Verne E. *What's Ethical in Business?* New York: McGraw-Hill, Inc., 1992. Standard college text.

Hill, Alexander. *Just Business: Christian Ethics for the Marketplace.* Downers Grove, Ill.: InterVarsity Press, 1997. Strongly rooted in biblical theology; see appendices for a synopsis of Hill's approach.

Hodgson, Kent. *A Rock and a Hard Place: How to Make Ethical Decisions When the Choices Are Tough.* New York: American Management Association, 1992.

Hobfoll, Stevan, and Ivonne H. Hobfoll. *Work Won't Love You Back: The Dual Career Couple's Guide.* New York: W. H. Freeman and Co., 1994. Highly practical volume.

Hybels, Bill. *Christians in the Marketplace.* Wheaton, Ill.: Victor Books, 1973. Personal approach, highly readable.

Iannone, A. Pablo. *Contemporary Moral Controversies in Business.* New York: Oxford University Press, 1989.

Jankowic, Elena. *Behave Yourself: The Working Guide to Business Etiquette.* Englewood Cliffs, N.J.: Prentice-Hall, 1986. Much practical information, especially showing respect to others at work.

Jones, Laurie Beth. *Jesus CEO: Using Ancient Wisdom for Visionary Leadership.* New York: Hyperion, 1995. A lightweight, New Age slant on business leadership which has sold quite well.

Klingaman, Patrick. *Thank God It's Monday: Making Business Your Ministry.* Wheaton, Ill.: Victor Books, 1996. Actually, a quite good book; deeply rooted in Scripture with much useful information in readable format.

Krueger, David W. *Emotional Business: The Meaning and Mastery of Work, Money, and Success.* San Marcos, Calif.: Avant Books, 1992.

Manning, George, and Kent Curtis. *Ethics at Work: Fire in a Dark World*. Cincinnati, Ohio:Vista-Systems (Southwestern Publishing Company), 1988.

Mount, Eric. *Professional Ethics in Context*. Louisville, Ky.: John Knox Press, 1990.

Murphy, Kevin R. *Honesty in the Workplace*. Pacific Grove, Calif.: Brooks/Cole Publishing Company, 1993.

Nash, Laura L. *Believers in Business*. Nashville, Tenn.: Thomas Nelson, 1994.

Nash, Ronald H. *Poverty and Wealth*. Westchester, Ill.: Crossway Books, 1986.

Rae, Scott B. and Kenman L. Wong. *Beyond Integrity: A Judeo-Christian Approach to Business Ethics*. Grand Rapids, Mich.: Zondervan Publishing House, 1996. An impressive compilation of articles and essays.

Rogers, Mike C. and Claude V. King. *The Kingdom Agenda: Experiencing God in Your Workplace*. Murfreesboro, Tenn.: Saratoga Press, 1996. A very spiritual and biblically based workbook that would be ideal for groups.

Seibert, Donald V. and William Proctor. *The Ethical Executive*. New York: Simon and Schuster (Cornerstone Library), 1984. Practical information drawn from insights and experience of a J. C. Penney executive.

Schlessinger, Laura. *How Could You Do That?!: The Abdication of Character, Courage, and Conscience*. Very little about business specifically, but very sound in ethical foundations, especially on responsibility.

Shaw, William H. and Vincent Barry. *Moral Issues in Business,* 7th ed. Belmont, Calif.: Wadsworth Publishing Company, 1998. Standard, but very thorough, college text.

Sider, Ronald J. *Rich Christians in an Age of Hunger*. Downers Grove, Ill.: Inter-Varsity Press, 1984. A classic in modern evangelical literature.

Stott, John. *Decisive Issues Facing Christians Today*. Grand Rapids, Mich.: Baker Book House, 1984.

Toms, Michael, editor. *The Soul of Business*. Carlsbad, CA: Hay House, Inc., 1997. Interviews by Toms with ten business leaders on how to bring creativity, passion, and spirit into the workplace.

Tuleja, Tad. *Beyond the Bottom Line*. New York: Facts on File Publications, 1985.

Wogaman, J. Philip. *Economics and Ethics: A Christian Inquiry*. Philadelphia: Fortress Press, 1986.

Notes

ADDITIONAL BIBLIOGRAPHICAL CITATIONS

The many quotations in this book, especially at the beginning of the various chapters and in the appendices, have been collected by the author from a wide variety of sources over the years. Some of these quotations are found sprinkled in the above cited works.

Chapter 1—Verne Henderson's five basic assumptions which undergird business ethics are drawn from *What's Ethical in Business?*, pp. 50–54. On the first assumption, Henderson draws from Powers and Vogel, two pioneers in the business ethics field.

Chapter 3—the quotation from John Stott is drawn from chapter 9, "Work and Unemployment," in *Decisive Issues Facing Christians Today*, p. 173.

Chapter 4—statistics measuring wealth and poverty in the United States are drawn from a cover story, by David J. Lynch, "Widening Income Gap Divides USA," *USA TODAY*, September 23, 1996, pp. 1–3. The Ron Sider quote from *Rich Christians in an Age of Hunger* is found on pp. 45–46.

Chapter 6—the distinction that Steven Covey explains between primary greatness and secondary greatness is found in his popular *Seven Habits of Highly Effective People,* pp. 21–23.

Chapter 7—the three general categories of lies are cited in *Time*, October 5, 1992. The Hollinger and Clark explanations of why employees steal as well as distinctions of white-collar crime from other acts of employee dishonesty are reported in Murphy, *Honesty in the Workplace,* pp. 35–54.

Chapter 8—Stephen Carter's discussion of the difference between simple honesty and moral integrity is presented in *(Integrity),* chapter 1, "The Rules about the Rules," pp. 3–14. His statement about honesty being laudable when we risk harm to ourselves is found on p. 54.

Chapter 9—the statistics which profile the diversity in the U.S. workforce today are drawn from the ASTD Training Data Book, American Society for Training and Development, 1996; Howard N. Fullerton Jr., *Employment Outlook 1994–2005, Monthly Labor Review*, November, 1995.

Chapter 10—the listing of practices common in multinational business that provide opportunities and pressures for unethical conduct is found in Green, *The Ethical Manager*, pp. 291–92.

Chapter 11—on excellence, is certainly a different chapter from the others in terms of subject matter and depth. Most of the brief quotes in this chapter were drawn from newspaper articles which were collected and filed by the author over the last ten years. The quotation on responsibility from Russell Gough is taken from *Character is Destiny,* p. 11. .

Chapter 14—the discussion of communication spoilers is drawn from Thomas Gordon, *Parent Effectiveness Training,* pp. 39–45.

Chapter 16—for the opening illustration involving Jimmy Carter and for several of the suggestions in dealing with difficult people at work, I am endebted to an article by Harry Levinson, "The Abrasive Personality at the Office," *Psychology Today* (May, 1978), pp. 78–84.

Chapter 18—the author and work quoted, namely, Richard H. Swenson, *Margin: Restoring Emotional, Physical, Financial, and Time Reserves to Overloaded Lives* (Navpress) is reviewed by Eric T. Miller and Christina E. McGill in *Portfolio Manager's Weekly,* April 9, 1997, pp. 6–10.

Chapter 19—Research as well as quotes are drawn from a cover story, "The Myth of Quality Time," *Newsweek,* May 12, 1997, pp. 62–71, and a special section, "Work and Family," in the *Wall Street Journal,* March 31, 1997. See also the cover story in *USA Weekend,* Cokie and Steve Roberts, "When Working Mothers Make Laws," May 9–11, 1997, pp. 4–6. See also the cover story "Refusing to Locate" by Stephanie Armour, *USA Today,* September 30, 1997, pp. 1–2 and a Census Bureau report, *Nashville Banner,* November 26, 1997. Covey's little exercise on determining one's priorities is found in *Seven Habits,* pp. 126–27.

Chapter 21—the ten qualities for succeeding in the business and professional world which were adapted from Siebert, *The Ethical Executive,* are located in chapter 2, pp. 8–34.   .